# Identity, Belonging and Migration

STUDIES IN SOCIAL AND POLITICAL THOUGHT 17

STUDIES IN SOCIAL AND POLITICAL THOUGHT
Editor: Gerard Delanty, *University of Sussex*

This series publishes peer-reviewed scholarly books on all aspects of social and
political thought. It will be of interest to scholars and advanced students
working in the areas of social theory and sociology, the history of ideas,
philosophy, political and legal theory, anthropological and cultural theory.
Works of individual scholarship will have preference for inclusion in the series,
but appropriate co- or multi-authored works and edited volumes of outstanding
quality or exceptional merit will also be included. The series will also consider
English translations of major works in other languages.

Challenging and intellectually innovative books are particularly welcome on
the history of social and political theory; modernity and the social and human
sciences; major historical or contemporary thinkers; the philosophy of the social
sciences; theoretical issues on the transformation of contemporary society;
social change and European societies.

It is not series policy to publish textbooks, research reports, empirical case
studies, conference proceedings or books of an essayist or polemical nature.

Recent titles in the series:

*Social Theory and Later Modernities: The Turkish Experience*
Ibrahim Kaya

*Sociological Beginnings: The First Conference of the German Society for Sociology*
Christopher Adair-Toteff

*Multiple Modernities, Civil Society and Islam: The Case of Iran and Turkey*
Masoud Kamali

*Varieties of World-Making: Beyond Globalization*
edited by Nathalie Karagiannis and Peter Wagner

*Cosmopolitanism and Europe*
edited by Chris Rumford

*European Solidarity*
edited by Nathalie Karagiannis

# Identity, Belonging and Migration

EDITED BY GERARD DELANTY,
RUTH WODAK AND PAUL JONES

LIVERPOOL UNIVERSITY PRESS

First published 2008 by
Liverpool University Press
4 Cambridge Street
Liverpool L69 7ZU

British Library Cataloguing-in-Publication data
A British Library CIP record is available

ISBN 978-1-84631-118-5 cased


Typeset by XL Publishing Services, Tiverton
Printed and bound in the European Union by
Biddles Ltd, King's Lynn

# Contents

# Acknowledgements

The interview and focus group material – and some other primary material – discussed in Chapters 8, 9, 11 and 12 is drawn from an EU 5th Framework project entitled 'The European Dilemma: Institutional Patterns and Politics of "Racial" Discrimination'. We are very grateful to the participants in the project and to colleagues working on the project for their willingness to provide the contributors to this volume with this data.

# List of Figures

# Notes on Contributors

**Çağla E. Aykac** is a PhD candidate in Sociology at the Ecole des Hautes Etudes en Sciences Sociales (EHESS), Paris. Her current research focuses on 'scandalous public figures of Islam' in Europe, with other research interests including public Islam in Europe, the negotiation process between Turkey and the EU, and anti-discrimination practices from both EU institutional and grassroots perspectives. She is co-editor and contributor to a forthcoming book (IB Tauris Academic Series, 2008) on rethinking Europe through Islam.

**Brigitte Beauzamy** is a research fellow at the Interdisciplinary Centre for Comparative Research in the Social Sciences, Paris. Her published research addresses the role of creativity and direct action in the context of transnational social movements, and the politics of gender and ethnic discriminations and exclusions.

**Irène Bellier** is a researcher at the CNRS (National Centre for Scientific Research), Paris. Her research interests include language policy and identity in Europe, institutional analysis, and migration and belonging, and recent published contributions to this area include the edited collection (with T. Wilson) (2000) *An Anthropology of the European Union: Building, Imagining and Experiencing the New Europe* (Berg Press).

**Tom R. Burns** is Emeritus Professor of Sociology at Uppsala University. His research spans a number of fields including power and institutions; sustainable development; migration, structural discrimination and racism; and socio-economic policy analysis. He has published widely in these areas.

**Gerard Delanty** is Professor of Sociology and Social & Political Thought, University of Sussex. His recent publications include (with Chris Rumford) *Rethinking Europe: Social Theory and the Implications of Europeanization* (Routledge, 2005). He has edited the *Handbook of Contemporary Social Theory* (Routledge, 2006), *Europe and Asia Beyond East and West* (Routledge, 2006) and (with Krishan Kumar) *the Handbook of Nations and Nationalism* (Sage, 2006).

**Marc de Leeuw** is an affiliated researcher at the University of Humanistic Studies (Utrecht). He is currently finishing a research project on the French philosopher Paul Ricoeur. Besides this he is preparing a manuscript, together with Sonja van Wichelen, on the changing notions of liberalism and tolerance in contemporary Dutch society.

**Helena Flam** migrated from Poland to Sweden in 1969, where she gained her Fil.Kand. She earned her PhD at Columbia University. She has been Professor of Sociology at the University of Leipzig since 1993. Her texts focus on organizations, social movements, East European states and emotions. She is a co-initiator of the ESA's Network on Emotions. Together with the Leipzig research team she published *Migranten in Deutschland: Statistiken – Fakten – Diskurse* (UVK, 2007).

**David I. Hanauer** employs theoretical, qualitative and quantitative methods in his research and focuses on authentic first- and second-language literacy in different social settings. His research has investigated the multimodal aspects of scientific communication and representation, genre-specific aspects of poetry reading in L1 and L2, cognitive aspects of literary education, fable reading, academic literacy across disciplines and migrant literacy. His research has been published widely in applied linguistics journals. His most recent book is *Scientific Discourse: Multiliteracy in the Classroom.*

**Paul Jones** is a Lecturer in the School of Sociology and Social Policy at the University of Liverpool. His research addresses the politicization of collective identities, and has a particular focus on the relationship between states, discourses of belonging, and major architectural projects. These issues are taken up in his forthcoming book entitled *The Sociology of Architecture: Constructing Identities* (Liverpool University Press).

**Masoud Kamali** is Professor of Ethnic Relations at Uppsala University. He has recently led a major research project funded by the Swedish government entitled *Power, Integration, and Structural Discrimination* and has published widely in the areas of racism, anti-racism and structural discrimination, and multiple modernities. His most recent book (2007) is *Multiple Modernities: The Case of Iran and Turkey* (Liverpool University Press).

**Michał Krzyżanowski** is a Research Fellow at the Department of Linguistics and English Language, Lancaster University. His research focuses on Critical Discourse Analysis (CDA) and specifically on the application of the CDA's 'Discourse-Historical' approach to the study of the discursive construction of social, political and institutional change; multilingualism, language ideologies and policies in Europe; and the role of language in/of the media and European public sphere. Michał has published widely in these areas; recent books include (with F. Oberhuber) (2007) *(Un)Doing Europe: Discourses and Practices of Negotiating the EU Constitution* (P.I.E. Peter Lang) and (with R. Wodak) *Qualitative Discourse Analysis in the Social Sciences* (Palgrave Macmillan).

**Alana Lentin** is a political sociologist and social theorist with a critical focus on race, racism and anti-racism. Her major publications include *Racism and Anti-Racism in Europe* (2004), *Race and State* (2006), and *Racism: A Beginner's Guide* (2008). Her articles can be found in journals such as the *European Journal of Social Theory*, *Patterns of Prejudice*, and *Ethnic and Racial Studies*. She is a Lecturer in Sociology at the University of Sussex.

**Luisa Martín Rojo** is Associate Professor at the Autonomous University of Madrid. Her research draws on socio-linguistic methods, such as discourse analysis, to assess linguistic diversity and the construction of hierarchies of language and language competence. Recent research projects have focused on multilingualism and the question of 'integration' in Madrid schools, and Luisa has also acted as an expert for The European Monitoring Centre on Racism, Xenophobia and Anti-Semitism (Vienna, Austria) and with the City of Madrid.

**Lena Sawyer** is a cultural anthropologist working as an assistant professor in the Department of Social Work at Mid Sweden University. Her research has focused on Swedish society and issues of racism and identity. Her PhD dissertation focused on the relationship between racism, identity, and diaspora among Afro-Swedes. She has also published on the topics of education and discrimination, gender and African diasporas, and the importance of an intersectional perspective in social work research. She is currently working on a project on normalization processes in Swedish social work.

**Bo Stråth** is Academy of Finland Distinguished Professor in Nordic, European and World History at the Helsinki University. His research focuses on the issue of modernity of Europe in a comparative context. The research projects deal with questions of a European political economy and economy as a polity, a social Europe, memory politics, and the conceptualization of public sphere and culture. His research at the University of Helsinki aims at connecting the regional Nordic and European levels of analysis with a global perspective.

**Sonja van Wichelen** is a Postdoctoral Fellow at the Center for Cultural Sociology at Yale University (New Haven). She has conducted research on public debates around Islam and gender in contemporary Indonesia. Her current research focuses on 'transnational adoption' and examines adoption practices in the United States and the Netherlands. Together with Marc de Leeuw she is also preparing a manuscript which explores changing discourses of liberalism and tolerance in contemporary Dutch society.

**Ruth Wodak** is Distinguished Professor of Discourse Studies at Lancaster University. Besides various other prizes, she was awarded the Wittgenstein Prize for Elite Researchers in 1996. Her research interests focus on discourse studies; gender studies; language and/in politics; prejudice and discrimination; and on ethnographic methods of linguistic field work. She has held visiting professorships in Uppsala, Stanford University, the University of Minnesota, the University of East Anglia, and Georgetown University, and in 2008 she was awarded the Kerstin Hesselgren Chair of the Swedish Parliament (at University Örebrö). Recent book publications include *Ist Österreich ein 'deutsches' Land?* (with R. de Cillia, 2006); *Qualitative Discourse Analysis in the Social Sciences* (with M. Krzyżanowski, 2008); and *The Discursive Construction of History: Remembering the Wehrmacht's War of Annihilation* (with H. Heer, W. Manoschek, A. Pollak, 2008).

# Introduction: Migration, Discrimination and Belonging in Europe

## Gerard Delanty, Paul Jones and Ruth Wodak

The emergence of new kinds of racism in European societies – referred to variously as 'Euro-racism', 'symbolic racism', 'cultural racism' or, in France, as *racisme différentiel* – has been widely discussed (see for example Holmes 2000; Macmaster 2001). While these accounts differ, there is widespread agreement that racism in Europe is on the increase and that one of its characteristic features is hostility to migrants, refugees and asylum-seekers who are positioned in exclusionary discourse as the new 'Others'. In this respect European racism is characterized by a hostility that is not exclusively defined by the traditional terms of 'colour' and 'race', as was typical of 'biological' racism in the industrial and colonial period (Fekete 2001).

Accordingly, in many European countries the extreme right has refined its electoral programmes under the rubric of nationalist-populist slogans and has adopted more subtle (or coded) forms of racism. The move away from overt neo-fascist discourse has in fact allowed these parties to expand their electoral support as populist-nationalist parties concerned with a defence of ethno-nationalist 'culture' (Rydgren 2003, 2005; Delanty and O'Mahony 2002; Wodak and Pelinka 2002; Pelinka and Wodak 2002). But this has led to an increase in racist and anti-Semitic discourse, not its decline, since contemporary racism often takes more pervasive, diffuse forms, frequently – and paradoxically – to the point of being expressed in the denial of racism (Van Dijk 1985). Indeed, there is considerable evidence of a normalization of 'othering' (racism, xenophobia, anti-Semitism) in mainstream political discourse and there is much to indicate that this is also occurring on all levels of discourse, ranging from the media, political parties and institutions to everyday life (*Race and Class* 2001; Wodak 2006; Van Dijk 2005; Wodak and van Dijk 2000).

The distinctive feature of this 'othering' is a confluence of racism and

1

xenophobia. The 'new' racism differs from the older kinds in that it is not expressed in overtly racist terms or in the terms of neo-fascist discourse, for instance by some notion of biological or racial superiority, white supremacism or skin colour. Instead, the repertoires of justification that are typically employed use social characteristics (for example, protecting jobs, concern about welfare benefits) or cultural incompatibilities or differences (migrants lack 'cultural competences', 'they do not want to integrate', they are not 'tolerant'). The new racism exploits established xenophobic frames (fear of the other), ethnocentrism, masculinities and 'ordinary' prejudices in subtle ways and often, too, in ways that are unconscious or routinized. For these reasons the new racism has been termed 'xeno-racism', a mixture of racism and xenophobia. While being racist in substance, it is xenophobic in form: its outward defensive mode of expression disguises a stronger opposition to migrants and the continuation of racism in a new guise and widened to exclude different groups of people (Sivanandan 2001; Fekete 2001). The new racism has also incorporated a 'quasi'-anti-racism into it, thus domesticating and diffusing critique. In ways that have been documented on the level of political discourse, but are not yet fully understood in wider socio-cognitive processes, liberal values are inverted. Thus, multiculturalism becomes a defence of the 'national' culture and 'tolerance' and thus becomes an argument to keep communities separate (this is why migrant communities frequently reject the term 'tolerance' and propose 'acceptance, recognition and respect' instead).

Moreover, where the border lies between xeno-racism and the more overt and explicit neo-fascist racism is frequently blurred in political discourse. This is related to the tradition of 'coded' anti-Semitism which evolved after the Shoah: post-1945, explicit utterances against Jews and Roma were tabooed. Instead, a coded discourse emerged which, nevertheless, was and is comprehensible through its pragmatic and semantic traces to wider audiences (Reisigl and Wodak 2001). The degree of coding differs due to the level of tolerance to exclusion in the various European countries. The same is true nowadays in relationship to exclusionary discourses against other minorities. In everyday discourse people tend to be more susceptible to xeno-racism than to the more explicit messages of neo-fascist racism (Essed 1991).

This volume aims to provide some understanding of the many socio-political, historical, discursive and socio-cognitive processes involved in such expressions of *everyday* racism, which are not evident from the more overt expressions of racism, by investigating the narratives of everyday life. Research presented in this volume gives considerable evidence that the kind of exclusionary discourses that are most commonly experienced are precisely those of this 'everyday racism' (Essed 1991). Encounters with the extreme right or with more overt expressions of racist hostility were less common although the riots in the suburbs of Paris in 2005, in Bradford 2002, in Amsterdam 2004 or in Mölleswerde 1990/91 made it obvious that violence is also used as a means by dominated and exploited migrants and minorities as well as by the neo-right. Of course, these riots and conflicts have to be analysed in their respective historical and political contexts if we are to understand both differences and similarities across Europe.

## Discourse and Racism

Following Philomena Essed's important study (1991), we define everyday exclusion/racism/xenophobia/anti-Semitism in terms of symbolic violence frequently expressed indirectly in the coded expressions in everyday-life situations. Such interactions reveal the absence of recognition as opposed to overt discrimination. Migrants often spoke of their racialization by members of the host society as a process that occurs through language as much as in any real sense of injustice. In this respect one mechanism is 'the gaze': the way in which migrants are literally looked at (see chapter 11 in this volume, by Flam and Beauzamy). Language competence is perceived as one of the most relevant gate-keeping devices, with many migrants reporting hostilities when they speak their 'own' language, or that when doing so they are viewed as not competent enough in the language of the majority. Nevertheless, even if they have a command of the language *and* hold the citizenship of the host-country, some migrants report that they are still not accepted or viewed as equal (see chapter 2 by Jones and Krzyżanowski).

In order to capture the multidimensional nature of social exclusion and institutional discrimination we have introduced the concept of 'syncretic racism', which encompasses everyday racism, xeno-racism and other concepts of racism (such as racialization and otherism). By syncretic racism we mean the construction of 'differences' on many levels, which serve ideological, political and/or practical discrimination on all levels of society. Old and new stereotypes form a mixed bag of exclusionary practices, used whenever seen to be politically expedient – such as in gaining votes. We use the term 'syncretic racism' by analogy with the term 'syncretic anti-Semitism', which grasps forms of anti-Semitic discourses and actions after the Second World War more adequately than the traditional concepts of Christian, racial or economic anti-Semitism; see Mitten 1992; Wodak 2004).

The suggestions made in this introduction and throughout this volume are that (i) a new European kind of racism has come into existence and (ii) it is based on a tradition of xenophobic syncretic racism. It is a racism in which the discourse of racism has become dereferentialized, that is, removed from any direct relation with a specific constructed racial subject (Jews, blacks, gypsies), and has become a floating discourse (an 'empty signifier' in the term of Ernesto Laclau and Chantal Mouffe) in which xenophobic attitudes are combined with racist stereotypes. This is not to claim that the discursive object has disappeared: migrants who are 'racially' distinguishable (for instance, black refugees) are more likely to experience greater hostility than other categories of migrants.

What this draws attention to is the discursive – as well as material – nature of racism that is bound up in language and proliferates in our societies in many subtle ways. Differences between various social groups take on a negative character. It is not the fact of differences or the fact of inequalities that produces discrimination or racism, but the generalization of such differences into negative categories and their attribution to whole groups. Each individual experience with a 'foreigner', 'Jew' etc. is viewed as typical of the whole group (while, interestingly, positive experiences with migrants, Jews, others, are classified as exceptions). Indeed, the discursive construction of 'us' and 'them' is thus the foundation of prejudiced and racist perceptions and discourses. This discursive construction starts with the labelling of the social actors, proceeds to the generalization of negative attributions and then elaborates arguments to justify the exclusion of many and inclusion of some. This discursive procedure is systematic for all countries investigated (see chapter 3 by Wodak in this volume). The discursive realizations can be more or less intensified or mitigated, more or less implicit or explicit, due to historical conventions, public levels of tolerance, political correctness, context and public sphere.

## The Institutional Logic of Racial Discrimination

Closely related to everyday racism is what is often called 'institutional racism', which can also be seen as an expression of a structural racism, as opposed to individual racism. In Britain, the term gained widespread usage following the publication of an important government report into the murder of black teenager Stephen Lawrence. The Macpherson Report criticized the Metropolitan Police Service for an endemic institutional racism, which was defined as:

> The collective failure of an organization to provide an appropriate and professional service to people because of their colour, culture or ethnic origin which can be seen or detected in processes; attitudes and behaviour

which amount to discrimination through unwitting prejudice, ignorance, thoughtlessness and racist stereotyping which disadvantages minority ethnic people.

Institutional racism is distinguished from the prejudice, stereotyping and bigotry or the racial bias of individuals by the existence of systemic, pervasive and habitual policies and practices that have the effect of systematically disadvantaging certain racialized groups. In institutional discrimination, then, the problem is not necessarily racist actions or motivations of individuals working in these institutions, but the institutional arrangements themselves. Institutions can behave in ways that are overtly racist (as in racist police officers targeting black people) or inherently racist in the sense of adopting policies that while not specifically directed at excluding racialized groups, nevertheless result in their exclusion (see chapter 8 by Burns and chapter 9 by Flam in this volume). The definition used here does entail some degree of agency; it is not a question of unconscious actions to the extent that it becomes an over-generalized condition of structural inequality. The notion of institutional racism appears to imply the failure of institutions, and those who move in them, to prevent racial discrimination. Mostly, this structural/ institutional racism works through granting or not granting 'access' to relevant domains of our societies.

Although appropriate in the context in which it arose, the term 'institutional racism' may be inappropriate in other contexts. For instance, it cannot without difficulty be generalized to an entire society, but refers to particular – and specific – social institutions. For this reason we prefer the term 'institutional discrimination' to refer to those situations in which migrants and other groups are discriminated by institutional arrangements but where there is not obvious victimization or stigmatization and where there is clear evidence of institutional failure. The term thus refers to the way in which social disadvantages and racial inequality are reinforced by the design of social institutions and individual agency is included. While institutional discrimination can amount to institutional racism, it refers to more general practices of exclusion. The notion of a social practice is important in this context; institutions and institutional logic can be conceived in terms of habituated social practices rather than a hard design or set of given structures (see DiMaggio and Powell 1983). Institutions are reproduced by social action through social actors. Social structures are not separate from social agency, as Giddens and Bourdieu have outlined in terms of notions of 'structuration' and the 'habitus' respectively (Giddens 1986; Bourdieu 1989). This suggests that, on the one hand, racism and discrimination can be integral to institutional processes and, on the other, that they are not separate from individual agency. At the same time, inequality and discrimination are causally distinct. The absence of discrimination, whether overt or institutional, will not necessarily lead to a reduction in inequality.

Notwithstanding these qualifications, institutional discrimination is a striking feature of some of the key social institutions in European societies. Some claim that the key institutions of modern societies are underpinned by a logic of closure in which structural discrimination is built into their design (see Wimmer 2002). Undoubtedly, it is true that in almost every society, the nation-state itself tended to exclude those at the periphery. However, in recent times there has been a major undermining of the dominant hegemonic designs as a result of a gradual move towards postnational membership, especially in European countries. More and more claims can be made by reference to the rights of individuals (Soysal 1994; Joppke 2005). The Europeanization of the public sphere has given migrants more opportunities to mobilize and to bring counter-claims to challenge exclusionary and discriminatory practices. The result of this is that institutional discrimination has become a major site of public discourse and contestation. The evidence gathered in the research presented throughout this book illustrates widespread institutional discrimination and institutional racism along with some of the traditional expressions of racist bigotry. Another important finding is that such practices are resisted and contested in a range of legal, cultural and public contexts.

## The Liberal Tradition

A feature of the contemporary West that has not been fully recognized, especially in the countries of the European Union, is the demise of a political culture based on liberal values. Only the consequences remain. This liberal culture has been the basis of the nation-state since the latter part of the nineteenth century and has defined what we might simply call the modern idea of peoplehood, that is a broadly civic conception of the people as coinciding with a nation. The essential unity of the liberal project – which presupposed an underlying notion of peoplehood – has now given way to a variety of different political streams. With these come new ideas of peoplehood, presenting new challenges for European societies. Liberal values – equality, tolerance, secularism – need to be rethought in a way that is more congruent with the current situation of not just conflicting values but also different conceptions of peoplehood (Benhabib 2004; Smith 2003). Continued adherence to a rigid liberalism may lead to illiberalism and xenophobic anxieties. Somehow a new political ethos will have to be created out of the disparate and often-colliding political currents of the present post-liberal age, if Europe is to resist what these post-liberal anxieties may lead to. Europe today is presented with a dilemma, which can be roughly summed up as a choice of remaining within what we might call a post-liberalism of uncertainty or embracing a more cosmopolitan view of itself (Beck and Grande 2006). From the middle of the nineteenth century European societies moved in the direction of a broadly liberal self-understanding which to varying degrees provided a workable basis for political modernity as it unfolded through the dynamics of nation-state formation and progressive democratization through civil society. The main features of the liberal political ethos are worth noting since its consequences are still with us.

First, liberalism has been characterized by a strong belief in the virtue of tolerance. This has been particularly the case with the Anglo-Saxon tradition since Locke, but it is a feature more generally of European liberalism. The concern with tolerance was principally advocated in the context of religious liberty. In this sense many modern liberties arose from the early modern struggles in Europe for freedom of worship. In some political traditions, most notably those influenced by French Revolutionary republicanism, the principle of tolerance has been reconciled with the principle of secularism, the separation of church and state. In this context, the main tension was the line between church and state, but for many traditions there was no basic conflict. Religion was privatized and in some political traditions (Britain, most Scandinavian countries) it was 'established', that is brought under the political control of the state. In general, the constitutional conservatism that forms much of the liberal heritage has been inspired by an understanding of the virtue of tolerance, in particular with respect to faith. Depending on where they were located in the continuum of secular republicanism and constitutional conservatism, all western and most central European countries shared this aspect of the liberal philosophy. This is true too of political Catholicism since the 1870s. Indeed, the modern age properly begins with the recognition of the liberty of free worship (see chapter 4 by Delanty for more on this context).

Second, related to the principle of tolerance was the assumption of a separation of private and public. In the republican tradition this was stricter, as previously noted, and assumed a more expansive role for the domain of the state, which in effect included much of the public realm. In this tradition, religion belonged to the private domain. However, many countries, of which the Netherlands is the best example, are based on a mix of republicanism, liberalism and constitutional conservatism. In the Dutch case the private sphere is a larger domain of individual liberties and includes much of what in the Jacobin tradition is the sphere of the state. In a particular tradition, which may be called economic liberalism and which has been associated with Thomas Hobbes and Adam Smith, this extends to the pursuit of wealth. What is at issue here is the space of the state in people's lives, and what autonomy is given to the public sphere, as a realm beyond the private sphere and beyond the jurisdiction of the state.

Third, liberalism was closely allied to the idea of national unity in that it was based on the assumption of the essential unity of the people who constitute the political community of the state. In this respect modern nationalism and liberalism developed alongside each other. Underlying both is the basic belief in the principle of self-determination, the idea that a people should rule itself and that every people conscious of itself as a nation should have a state. So the liberal idea of freedom from external coercion was linked to a notion of the autonomy of the political subject. Inevitably this was encapsulated in territorial views of autonomy and peoplehood. The nation-state gave rise to a notion of peoplehood defined in at least four ways: politically 'the people' was a sovereign body which exercised its power through democracy; through national citizenship peoplehood was defined legally in terms of a relation to the state established by rights and duties; a cultural definition of peoplehood arose as a result of ethnic homogenization and which was the basis of national identity for most nations; and finally, through the welfare state, 'the people' was socially engineered.

We have drawn attention to these aspects of the liberal heritage in order to highlight some features of a conception of peoplehood that has been with us for some time and which is losing some of its relevance. Before commenting on this further, a final point of clarification needs to be made. The thesis posed here is not that the liberal political tradition of the modern national state has been in part inherently exclusionary. In the view of many, the nation-state, which was the principal institutional form in which liberal values developed, was a hegemonic order which has finally given way to a transnational order and new kinds of governance (Wimmer 2002). The search for political order is not the same as the establishment of a hegemonic order. Undoubtedly, as John Lie has demonstrated, peoplehood and nationhood have been closely linked, but this does not mean that systematic exclusion is necessarily the basis of all kinds of modern peoplehood (Lie 2004). Liberalism and the nation-state, while certainly tending towards hegemony, did not succeed in over-coming the fundamental tension at the heart of modernity between freedom or liberty and power or discipline (Wagner 2004). It has been a fact of political modernity that no political order has fully captured the social space, which has remained radically open, as Claude Lefort (1986) has also argued.

8

This tension between openness and closure is one of the features of modernity (Delanty 1998). The liberal project certainly established closure on what had been an openness created as a result of the first major transformation of modernity, but did not eradicate openness, not least because of the right and left projects of liberal modernity. The general movement away from the nation-state today – and which could be seen as a new moment of openness – must also be located in the context of modernity and its social transformations. But, of course, it is evident that the openness brought about by the demise of communism, the transnationalization of the state, the enlargement of the European Union, the many faces of globalization, is also marked by new and different kinds of closure, of which the alleged 'war on terrorism' is a striking example.

## The Legacy of the Liberal Idea of 'Tolerance'

Hence, one of the major problems facing Europe is the legacy of the liberal idea of tolerance. As noted earlier, tolerance, which lies at the core of modern political culture, was shaped by the need for the modern state to accept the principle of free worship. While many states, mostly those based on Protestantism, incorporated into their constitutions an official national faith – countries as different as Greece, Norway and Britain for example – the principle was not intended for widespread application, as the experience of the Jews illustrates. Tolerance in these cases was confined to the main Christian churches and was not extended to minorities – especially to non-Christian minorities.

Indeed, the Norwegian case is interesting in that Norway established a national church relatively late and in order to curb the rising tide of political Catholicism. Undoubtedly, too, national churches were useful too in defining the values of the state as Christian. There is a curious revival of this idea today with the idea that Europe is Christian, although little attention is given to the meaning of the term 'Christianity' and to what its relation to Europe might be. When the Netherlands attempted to use the institutionalized system of tolerance known as 'pillarization' as a basis for multiculturalism in the wake of large-scale migration into the country in the 1970s, it was already too late: ethnic diversity did not quite fit into the established pattern of pillarization, which was eventually abandoned, and moreover formal tolerance of diversity did not translate into actual recognition.

The year 1989 marked a huge change. In Austria, for example, bordering several formerly communist countries (Hungary, CSSR, Yugoslavia), first waves of migrants were welcomed as long as the old Communist systems still prevailed (1956, 1968, 1981 and so forth). These tolerant and supportive attitudes changed at once when the Iron Curtain fell. Indeed, one could observe the genesis of exclusionary practices in public and private discourses (Matouschek *et al.* 1995; Wodak and Matouschek 1993). On the one hand, patronizing stances were adopted, telling the East what was expected from them; on the other hand, many politicians from the mainstream immediately stated that 'the boat was full', thus recontextualizing slogans used during the Second World War to justify the closing of borders to refugees from states occupied by the Nazis. Such patronizing discourses have also been recontextualized most recently, with EU enlargement (see Krzyżanowski and Oberhuber 2007).

Thus, in several countries the question has been posed as to where the limits of tolerance lie: Does tolerance have to translate into solidarity with others or does it breed indifference? Does tolerance amount to accepting others who are different and possibly intolerant? In France one hears of an interesting reversal of the liberal discourse: the liberal belief in respecting the other as different requires keeping the cultures separate in order to protect them. Another example of late-liberal anxiety is the discourse of 'liberal xenophobia' that appears to have gained some popularity in the Netherlands in recent years. According to this, liberal values are antithetical to migrants who must be excluded in order to protect the liberalism of the majority, who must also be protected from becoming intolerant. There is an important argument to be developed about recognition as opposed to tolerance (Delanty and Wodak 2005).

It is therefore not surprising that in Europe today the veil and the headscarf have become the symbolic battleground of European democracy. The French public is polarized over whether the headscarf is a religious symbol and therefore cannot be tolerated on the precincts of the school, the traditional territory of the republican state (Kastoryano 2002). Although a French concern, this tells us a great deal about the political subjectivity of Europe, which is experiencing great difficulty in moving beyond a formal multiculturalism to a politics of recognition. The veil and the headscarf, symbols of cultural closure, have paradoxically become the battleground of a closed democracy restricted by a narrow notion of secularism. Perhaps in one respect Joseph Weiler is right when he argues for a revival of the principle of tolerance as an alternative to secularism, but it is hard to see how this return to constitutional conservatism will enhance the prospects of a more inclusive multiculturalism (Weiler 2003).

Of course, we are not suggesting Europe is ceasing to be liberal, but that liberalism has paradoxically given a basis to a new kind of exclusionary thinking that is a mixture of racism and xenophobia. Most racists are liberals today and thus deny their racism through an inverted liberalism. In this respect racism today is different from the past in that we have racism but apparently no racists. The same is true for anti-Semitism (see Marin 2000, who discusses anti-Semitism without anti-Semites and without Jews in Europe). A striking example of this is anti-Semitism in Poland, a country where Jews are almost nonexistent and where apparently anti-Semites also do not exist, or so the discourse goes. This form of racism then differs in another sense: the racialized subject category has now been extended to groups of poor white migrants from other European countries, with discourses of 'otherism' having emerged to explain this extension (see Kamali's 'Conclusion' in this volume). Does this amount to a specifically European racism? To an extent it does. This European racism is a mixture of liberal values and xenophobia, with the inversion of liberal values resulting in a normalization of racism in discourse. The new racism has also incorporated anti-racism into itself, thus domesticating and diffusing critique; multiculturalism becomes a defence of the 'national' culture and tolerance becomes an argument to keep communities separate.

### The Construction of Fear

'Euro-racism' or 'xeno-racism' finds powerful resonances in everyday life and for this reason it can be considered part of what Philomena Essed has termed 'everyday racism' (Essed 1991). Fears, insecurities and anxieties enter into it, giving it form and relevance. But there is often no objective substance to these anxieties, which is what makes them anxieties. Anxiety is a fear that is objectless. It is a fear that cannot easily be given substance. Renata Salecl has pointed out that for Freud, in his work, *Inhibitions, Symptoms and Anxiety*, anxiety has to do with expectations of a danger that does not manifest itself. Anxiety thus seems to be without an object and in this respect it is different from fear, which is based on an external threat to the self (Salecl 2004: 19). It was a central aspect of Freud's theory that anxiety is coped with by fantasy, a story that makes sense and one that helps the subject to prevent the emergence of anxiety. It could thus be argued that there is a connection between anxiety and fear of the other as expressed in racist discourses today. In other words there is more anxiety than fear in the sense that the objectivity of the fear is often groundless and has to be sustained by fantasy (see also Horkheimer and Adorno, who explain the continuous occurrence of anti-Semitism in a similar way).

However, as noted earlier these post-liberal anxieties are not hegemonic discourses that are somehow inherent to modernity, as many claim (see for example Wimmer 2002). There has been an irreversible logic towards on the one side individual rights and on the other a transnationalization of rights (Soysal, 1994; Joppke, 2005). Claims of a new age of exclusion are unjustified. Europeanization is itself characterized by moments of openness and closure. As expressions of anxieties they rarely reach the level of official ideological positions, and are generally marginalized by the main political parties.

The rise in organized xenophobia and racism, as represented by the extreme right, is in part a defensive reaction to globalization, as Manuel Castells has argued (Castells 1997). Globalization and the transnationalization of the state unleash new kinds of anxieties about securities, social status and identity. These anxieties can also be seen as responding to the breakdown of the traditional solidarities of local democracy and class. In this sense they form part of the second wave of post-industrial social movements that have been a feature of the past fifteen years. Such movements fill the space created by the rise of Third Way political parties, that is the tendency for the right and left to move towards a midway position between social democracy and market liberalism. This has opened up opportunities for new political parties, which appeal to the anxieties produced by perceived loss of status in many occupational areas as well as changes in the nature of authority and masculinities. Such anxieties coupled with loss of national status produce powerful sentiments for the extreme right and lead to a re-nationalization of political discourse.

In general it appears that the smaller European countries, with liberal political cultures, are having the most difficulty in adjusting to the altered climate after 1989 and following 11 September 2001. The extreme right now have a foothold in Denmark, Sweden, Belgium, Austria, Norway and the Netherlands. Protected from large-scale migration and transnational processes, capitalism and democracy in these countries had developed within protected national models which were based on a clearly defined sense of peoplehood. As a result of globalization and Europeanization such social models along with their cultural assumptions have been challenged.

However, despite the obvious increase in extreme political parties and populist parties of various kinds, the significance of post-liberal nationalism goes beyond these movements. Post-liberal nationalism is neither a hegemonic expression of the nation-state nor purely a defensive reaction to globalization that can be explained by devious cadres such as those of Jean-Marie Le Pen and Jörg Haider. It is the product of a transnationalization of the state and the crisis of liberalism (see Holmes 2006). It makes its gains on the basis of post-liberal anxieties, such as the fear of too much tolerance, the uncertain limits of the state, and fears and uncertainties about who constitutes the political community and where the limits of its membership lie. It is undoubtedly the case that such anxieties were largely responsible for the defeat of the proposed European Constitution in the referenda in France and the Netherlands in May 2005. The huge public debate in these countries was dominated by social anxieties that found in the proposed European Constitution a focus for fears about immigration (see Stråth 2006 and chapter 1 in this volume).

Central to these anxieties were social securities associated with the nation-state. The left, especially in France, was divided on the constitutional question because of the fear of a loss of securities allegedly guaranteed by the welfare state and a significant element within the right mobilized the population around the defence of securities associated with national sovereignty. In both cases it was the nation-state that was the guarantee of a certain social and cultural model of society that was perceived to be under threat by globalization and Europeanization. The absence of a European social model and the fear of market liberalization unleashed social anxieties to the extent that pro-European middle-class voters preferred the security of the nation-state to the uncertainties of a perceived new political order.

Racism and xenophobia are partially sustained by the decline of nation-based solidarities, resulting in anxieties that are easily translated into xenophobia as well as more direct expressions of racism. Islamophobia is one such current in recent expressions of xenophobia where racism is also present in a direct form. The significance of such forms of xenophobia and racism is a certain normalization of political communication around social issues. The danger then is not always the extreme right, which succeeds in amplifying such anxieties into more overt expressions of racism. This recalls a remark Adorno made in one of his most important essays, published in 1959, 'What Does Coming to Terms with the Past Mean?': Adorno attacked the political complacency of Adenauer's Germany on the question of German guilt and the neutralization of atonement. He reminded the German public that 'National Socialism lives' but in a different form. He considered 'the continued existence of National Socialism *within* democracy potentially more threatening than the continued existence of fascist tendencies *against* democracy' (Adorno 1986: 115). In the present context this danger is evident in the normalization of xenophobia resulting from anxieties that have their origin in the post-liberal ethos of contemporary European political culture.

The prevalence of such anxieties suggests that liberalism is not enough to oppose xenophobia and racism. As we argue here, racism has been 'democratized' inasmuch as it has been rendered less direct and more diffuse. This may mean that some of the worst features of explicit racism have been eroded in some societies, but this has paradoxically led precisely to the proliferation of a 'cultural racism', which is more difficult to overcome since it is to be found in many discursive spaces.

## Perspectives

It is important that these discursive spaces are captured for what can be termed a cosmopolitan peoplehood. Unlike liberal conceptions of political community – which do not go beyond the view that we are all different and require only tolerance of difference – cosmopolitan peoplehood is based on a politics of recognition which entails a positive recognition of difference. Cosmopolitanism is not merely about plurality – the mere fact of multiplicity – but about the positive embracing of difference and the search for an alternative political order. In this respect it differs from the liberal emphasis on tolerance and the tendency found in much of communitarian multi-culturalism to relinquish common ground in an exaggeration of cultural differences. This is not to suggest that liberalism is redundant but that it alone does not offer a viable political basis to address illiberalism. What is missing from liberalism are two key elements: solidarities and recognition.

There are two kinds of cosmopolitan recognition that need to be addressed separately: internal and external recognition (see Beck and Grande 2006). External recognition is easier than the former. It is easier to recognize others who are far away than those within. Internal cosmopolitanism requires a form of recognition that entails self-transformation. As a concept, cosmopolitanism indicates a condition of self-problematization, incompleteness and the awareness that certainty can never be established once and for all. The suggestion then is that Europe needs to develop such a cosmopolitan imagination in order to transcend the limits of existing national loyalties.

Central to such a project of cosmopolitan peoplehood is the creation of forms of citizenship capable of articulating solidarities that go beyond the traditional limits of peoplehood as defined by nation. The result of the absence of such solidarities is an increase in anxieties about citizenship. It is thus possible to speak of a post-liberal citizenship of anxieties today. Whether or not the European project is undermining traditional national forms of solidarity is an open question, but it is evident that it is not enhancing solidarities and forms of recognition beyond gender, class and nation. The constitutional debate in France and the Netherlands in 2005 provided ample evidence of the predominance of discourses fuelled by anxieties of belonging. It would be unduly pessimistic to conclude that more cosmopolitan discourses do not exist given the existence of global civil society and wide-ranging expressions of popular global solidarities (Calhoun 2004; Kurasawa 2004). However, such sentiments and movements have had little impact on questions of peoplehood within Europe, where anxieties resulting from national identities seem to prevail.

## Outline of the Book

This volume addresses these questions across fourteen substantive chapters, as well as in this Introduction and a Conclusion. These chapters are divided into three parts: Part I sets up 'Theoretical Perspectives on Belonging' in the European context and contains four chapters. Chapter 1, by Bo Stråth, outlines a framework within which to understand the processes that have led to narratives of national and European belonging, and the exclusionary tensions upon which they are predicated. Next, Paul R. Jones and Michał Krzyżanowski's chapter 2 addresses similar themes in seeking to discourage the uncritical application of the concept of identity, which they argue is not always helpful when assessing the relationship of migrants to collectives. In chapter 3 Ruth Wodak applies a critical discourse analysis to right-wing political discourse to reveal some of the more general discursive techniques that construct and maintain distinctions between 'us' and 'them'. Next, Gerard Delanty's chapter 4 argues that contemporary discussions of migration, exclusion and belonging must be understood in the context of broader tensions around religion, secularism and transformations in the liberal conception of the social order.

The next four contributions constitute Part II of the book, which is organized around six chapters focused on 'Institutional Forms of Discrimination'. This section addresses the exclusionary discourses and practices of states and their institutions. Initially Alana Lentin's chapter 5 frames this question by assessing the implications of the (ostensible) adoption of various anti-racist stances by European states in the post World War II context; Lentin draws out a range of issues associated with the paradox of anti-racist states that are maintained and legitimated by nationalist discourse. In chapter 6, Çağla E. Aykaç is also interested in such questions in her development of a critical policy analysis of the European Union. Irène Bellier's chapter 7 addresses the concept of human rights in the context of so-called 'multicultural societies', using the Roma as an illustrative case study. Tom R. Burns' chapter 8 draws on a wide range of material to interrogate the concepts of structural and institutional discrimination, which he argues are particularly pertinent concepts when attempting to understand the nature of the discrimination faced by many migrants. Helena Flam's chapter 9 has similar concerns, albeit focused more directly on the discriminatory processes operative in European labour markets. In chapter 10 David Ian Hanaeur uses the controversial cultural component of UK 'citizenship criteria' – the so-called 'Britishness test' – to draw out general themes of migration, territoriality and national identity relative to the nation-state.

Part III, 'Cases of Belonging and Exclusion', is constituted by four thematic discussions. The first of these chapters, chapter 11, sees Helena Flam and Brigitte Beauzamy assessing the relevance of the concept of symbolic violence, now perhaps primarily associated with Pierre Bourdieu, for understanding the 'everyday' forms of discrimination faced by migrants in Europe. Chapter 12, by Lena Sawyer (with Paul R. Jones), looks at the various forms of resistance mobilized by migrants experiencing prejudice, discrimination and racism; of particular interest here are the multiple and complex relationships between illegitimate power and resistance. Illustrating some more general themes, chapter 13 by Marc de Leeuw and Sonja van Wichelen is a discussion of Islamophobia in the Netherlands understood within context of multiculturalism. The final chapter in this section is by Luisa Martín Rojo, who adopts a discursive analytical approach to reveal the language-based assumption that creates hierarchies in education systems. Martín Rojo uses a case study of Madrid schools to support this general argument. Finally, Masoud Kamali's conclusion situates discussions of discrimination, belonging and migration in the context of the structural discrimination he suggests is inherent in ostensibly 'post-colonial' European nation-states.

## References

Adorno, T. W. (1986) 'What Does Coming to Terms with the Past Mean?', *Bitburg in Moral and Political Perspective*. Bloomington, IN: Indiana University Press.

Balibar, E., and I. Wallerstein (1991) *Race, Nation, Class*. London: Verso.

Beck, U., and E. Grande (2006) *Cosmopolitan Europe*. Cambridge: Polity Press.

Benhabib, S. (2004) *The Claims of Culture: Equality and Diversity in the Global Era*. Princeton, NJ: Princeton University Press.

Bourdieu, P. (1989) 'Social Space and Symbolic Power', *Sociological Theory* 7: 14–25.

Brubaker, R. (2002) 'Ethnicity without Groups', *Archives européennes de sociologie*, 43(2): 163–89.

Calhoun, C. (2003) '"Belonging" in the Cosmopolitan Imaginary', *Ethnicities* 3(4): 531–53.

Castells, M. (1997) *The Power of Identity*. Oxford: Blackwell.

Delanty, G. (1998) *Social Theory in a Changing World*. Cambridge: Polity Press.

Delanty, G., and K. Kumar (eds) (2006) *Handbook of Nations and Nationalism*. London: Sage.

Delanty, G., and P. O'Mahony (2002) *Nationalism and Social Theory*. London: Sage.

Delanty, G., and R. Wodak (2005) 'Immigrant Focus Groups: The Perspective of Immigrants (Introduction)', Paper Presented at the Expert Workshop 'The European Dilemma', The European Commission, Brussels, 27 January 2005.

DiMaggio, P., and W. Powell (1983) 'The Iron Cage Revisited: Institutional Isomorphism and Collective Rationality in Organizational Fields', *American Sociological Review* 48, 147–60.

Essed, P. (1991) *Understanding Everyday Racism*. Newbury Park, CA: Sage.

Fekete, L. (2001) 'The Emergence of Xeno-Racism', *Race and Class* 43(2): 23–40.

Giddens, A. (1986) *The Constitution of Society: Outline of the Theory of Structuration*. Cambridge: Polity Press.

Holmes, D. (2000) *Integral Europe: Fast-Capitalism, Multiculturalism, Neofascism*. Princeton, NJ: Princeton University Press.

— (2006) 'Nationalism in Europe', *Handbook of Nations and Nationalism*, ed. by G. Delanty and K. Kumar. London: Sage.

Joppke, C. (2005) *Selecting by Origin: Ethnic Migration in the Liberal State*. Cambridge, MA: Harvard University Press.

Kastoryano, R. (2002) *Negotiating Identity: States and Immigration in France and Germany*. Princeton, NJ: Princeton University Press.

Krzyżanowski, M., and F. Oberhuber (2007). *(Un)Doing Europe: Discourses and Practices of Negotiating the EU Constitution*. Brussels: PIE Peter Lang.

Kurasawa, F. (2004) 'Cosmopolitanism from Below: Alternative Globalization and the Creation of a Solidarity without Bounds', *Archives européennes de sociologie* 45(2): 233–55.

Lefort, C. (1986) *The Political Forms of Modern Society*. Cambridge: Polity Press.

Lentin, A. (2004a) *Race and Anti-Racism in Europe*. London: Pluto Press.

Lentin, A. (2004b) 'Racial States, Anti-Racist Responses: Picking Holes in "Culture" and "Human Rights"', *European Journal of Social Theory* 7(4): 427–43.

Lie, J. (2004) *Modern Peoplehood*. Cambridge, MA.: Harvard University Press.

Macmaster, N. (2001) *Racism in Europe*. London: Palgrave.

Macpherson W. (1999) *The Stephen Lawrence Inquiry*. London: The Stationery Office.

Marin, B. (2000) *Antisemitismus*. Frankfurt: Campus.

Matouschek, B., R. Wodak and F. Januschek (1995) *Notwendige Maßnahmen gegen Fremde?* Vienna: Passagen Verlag.

Mitten, R. (1992) *The Politics of Antisemitic Prejudice: The Waldheim Phenomenon in Austria*. Boulder, CO: Westview Press.

Pelinka, A., and R. Wodak (eds) (2002) *'Dreck am Stecken'. Politik der Ausgrenzung*. Vienna: Czernin.

*Race and Class* (2001) Special Issue: *The Three Faces of British Racism* 43(2).

Reisigl, M., and R. Wodak (2001) *Discourse and Discrimination*. London: Routledge.

Rydgren, J. (2003) 'Mesolevel Causes of Racism and Xenophobia.' *Europe Journal of Social Theory* 6.

— (ed.) (2005) *Moments of Exclusion*. New York: Nova.

Salecl, R. (2004) *On Anxiety*. London: Routledge.

Sivanandan, A. (2001) 'Poverty is the New Black', *Race & Class* 43(2): 1–5.

Smith, R. (2003) *Stories of Peoplehood: The Politics of Memory and Political Membership*. Cambridge: Cambridge University Press.

Soysal, Y. (1994) *The Limits of Citizenship*. Chicago, IL: University of Chicago Press.

Stråth, B. (2006) 'Future of Europe', *Journal of Language and Politics* 5/3.

Van Dijk, T. (1985) *Prejudice in Discourse*. London: Sage.

— (2005) *Racism and Discourse in Spain and Latin America*. Amsterdam: John Benjamins.

Wagner, P. (2004) *The Sociology of Modernity: Liberty and Discipline*. London: Routledge.

Weiler, J. (2003) *Un' Europa cristiana*. Milan: Rizzoli.

Wimmer, A. (2002) *Nationalist Exclusion and Ethnic Conflict: Shadows of Modernity*. Cambridge: Cambridge University Press.

Wodak, R. (2004) 'Discourses of Silence', in L. Thiesmeyer (ed.), *Discourse and Silencing*, Amsterdam: Benjamins, pp. 179–209.

— (2006) 'Mediation between Discourse and Society: Assessing Cognitive Approaches in CDA', *Discourse Studies*, 8(1): 179–90.

Wodak, R., and B. Matouschek (1993) 'We Are Dealing with People Whose Origins One Can Clearly Tell Just by Looking: Critical Discourse Analysis and the Study of Neo-Racism in Contemporary Austria', *Discourse & Society* 4(2): 225–48.

Wodak, R., and A. Pelinka (eds) (2002) *The Haider Phenomenon in Austria*. New Brunswick, NJ: Transaction Publishers.

Wodak, R., and T. van Dijk (2000) *Racism at the Top: Parliamentary Discourses on Ethnic Issues in Six European States*. Klagenfurt: Drava.

# Part I

# Theoretical Perspectives on Belonging

# 1   Belonging and European Identity

*Bo Stråth*

## Some Points of Departure: The Concepts of Individual and Collective

Do human beings need belonging? Or is human self-realization basically an individual issue? The theoretical dimension of these questions has a bearing on questions of discursive power, symbolic representation and linguistic transformation. The question of how identities, solidarity and community are constructed under 'we'/'they' demarcations is crucial. The key problem is also one of everyday mythology and the symbolic terms in which it is conceptualized. The use of a vocabulary of 'construction' and 'invention' in this context does not mean that ties of solidarity and community are created entirely independently, but rather that they *emerge* in a complex interaction marked by historical and cultural conditions. Interests and identifications are not decreed once and for all by specific material/socio-economic positions, but rather evolve in a confrontation with other interests and patterns of identification in processes of problem resolution and search for social compromises. Concepts such as interest and identity are not essential but discursive categories, and as such undergo continuous transformation through processes of social bargaining.

The 'Hamlet Question' – of belonging or not belonging – can be illustrated by the construction of 'the New Man' in two opposite versions (Stråth 2000c: 95–6). Visions of work were the foundation of the chiliastic ideas of the New Man in Soviet Russia. With socialism as a basis, the emergence of a new type of man was anticipated: solidaristic instead of egoistic, collective-minded instead of individually oriented. The icon of this New Man was a male and muscular manufacturing worker with a powerful faith in future progress. The answer to the two questions above is obvious in this version: yes, indeed, human beings do need belonging, and certainly in the most rigid form where feelings of belonging are expressed through the image of a class consciousness. Human self-realization can only occur via a collective such as class.

The other extreme in answering the two questions is today's flexibility language, which can be seen as the (neo)liberal counterpart to the Soviet model New Man, a figure as strong but also as utopian as the older one. The 'Flexible Man' is an all-rounder, highly adaptable to new challenges, creative and innovative. He is independent and emancipated from all restraining social bounds. From the self-realization of the Flexible Man is postulated the emergence of a new and better society; although the tension between adaptability and creativity is not addressed. Thus a critical question arises as to how creative and innovative the remote-controlled Flexible Man really is. Does not his ability to roll with changes make him an achievement-oriented rather than socially stable character with little political loyalty? The individual glorification in this version of the New Man means that the individual is cut from all social ties. 'Self is strong' is the motto. In this vein the influential American psychologist Abraham Maslow describes human development as a progressive process from total dependence on other human beings towards an ever higher degree of independence; this is what emancipation is about. The self-realizing human being is according to Maslow governed from within and free from influences from the cultural and social environment (Maslow 1970). Maslow's vision expresses the American dream of the successful individual who goes his or her own way and can look back over the course of his or her life with the sentiment expressed in Frank Sinatra's hit: I Did it My Way. Maslow's utopian theory about human self-realization has quite rightly been criticized for setting out from the assumption of a perfect being released from its social environment. Nevertheless the utopia is still alive, as the neo-liberal version of the flexible New Man demonstrates.

In sharp contrast to both versions of the New Man utopia stands the argument of philosopher Charles Taylor, who argues that human beings are not only social but also reflecting and self-interpreting beings. A human striving for self-realization has as its point of departure a self-understanding of being a part of a social field (Taylor 1985). The fact that, according to Taylor's convincing argument, human beings are 'self-interpreting animals' who organize their social life by giving meaning to actions and institutions means that the social *relations* and their cultural expressions are at the heart of every social configuration. Social relations mean something different from atomistic and self-imposing individuals. Taylor's emphasis on self-reflection and interpretation means also a demarcation to identities ('consciousness') as more or less automatically emerging from social positions. Taylor's approach is a good point of departure for a discussion of the relations between the individual and its social environment and for the question of belonging.

## Europe and the Nation

During the two centuries following the French Revolution the fiction of the nation constituted the most important social configuration and outcome of social self-reflection and interpretation. National institutions such as in the realms of education, religion and media informed our modes of self-interpretation and consequently individual as well as collective actions, which, in turn, left their imprints on the institutions. However, the fact that many societies in Europe have long been based on the concept of a national cultural-linguistic and/or religious commonality, or the idea of some strong interpretative bond as the cornerstone of the modern polity, should not lead to the conclusion that they are given for ever (Wagner 2001). Strong interpretative bonds change in the long run. The values on which societies based their presumed cultural homogeneity – mainly from a religious to a cultural-linguistic basis – are transformed (see Delanty's argument in Chapter 4 of this volume). Images of a European community and polity over recent decades have transformed although not replaced images of the nation. What remains strong is the affirmation of a social context, an affirmation that is far away from Maslow's individualist ideal.

The national division constitutes the specificity of the European cultural dimension. The idea that a certain commonality of cultural orientations is a prerequisite for the building and maintenance of social and political institutions has informed much of European history but has also led to a long history of divisiveness and conflict. The construction of the nation-states exemplifies this. Ideas of a homogeneous and cohesive European civilization or culture in explicit or implicit opposition to other civilization blocks must against this backdrop be problematized and critically investigated. The conceptualization should deal with a European cultural model based upon diversity. The crucial question to investigate is how diversity and commonality may be reconciled; the internal and external boundaries of the European culture must be seen as open and perpetually negotiated. Precisely the experience of divisiveness, including sustained violence and warfare, is a good point of departure for a self-critical re-appropriation of European history with a shift towards cultural dialogue, rather than cultural homogeneity, as the basis underpinning an emergent European society.

In a time bearing the stamp of thoughts that human beings are superhuman, as such thoughts are formulated by Maslow, for instance, and the supreme rulers of their background and environment in the shaping of their own lives, there is no need for new theories about self-realization. Instead new visions about social responsibility and solidarity are required, visions which do not repeat the dream of the old utopias about holistic community but instead emphasize the connection between the individual and the society. This is the normative point of departure of this chapter. The question to discuss below is what Europe might mean in that respect.

## A Methodological Remark

Nations and other kinds of belonging are constructed socially. In processes of social construction the discursive character takes on essential proportions. In other words, essentialization is the goal of social construction. The nineteenth-century constructors of the European nations, for instance, built their creations on ideas of 'natural' units with deep roots in history, language and religion. They did not, of course, see their constructions exactly as constructions but as formations which came to their 'natural' expressions. Nowhere has this methodology been better demonstrated than in the Enlightenment obsession with classification and ordering of human beings. The abstract construct becomes real and concrete in such processes. Therefore is it important that a constructivist approach to social analysis has a critical deconstructive component, which reveals attempts of essentialization and emphasizes the discursive character of social construction. At the same time we cannot avoid our deconstructions becoming elements of new constructions, which, in turn, must be critically deconstructed, when the academic and political debate tends to forget about the discursive character of social construction and essentialize it. The development of the identity discourse is a case in point. The concept of identity invaded the social sciences in the 1970s – before then it was a concept associated mainly within psychoanalysis – and emerged in a situation of general disorientation when the certainties of the industrial society evaporated and the demand emerged for new interpretative frameworks. The identity discourse went hand in hand with the linguistic turn, which shifted the ontological perspective from socio-economic structures to language itself. But the academic debate on identity gradually shifted the view on the concept from being a discursive category towards essentialization (for a development of this claim see Chapter 2 by Jones and Krzyżanowski). This development shows that deconstruction is (re)construction and demystification is (re)mystification, in a process that, *pace* Weber, does not have any final point of total disenchantment.

## Belonging and Boundarying

There are not only images of Europe as the alternative to the fiction of the nation, as the idea of strong homogeneous nation-states is also undermined from below and within. There is in a city such as Paris, London, Berlin or Rome – indeed, in all big cities – a Warsaw, a Belgrade, a Baghdad, a Beirut, a Tehran, an Abidjan, a Shanghai, a São Paolo, a Singapore... Border lines are perpetually dissolved and recreated. The fixed borders created by blood and iron in the European nineteenth-century processes of nation-building and ethnic separation still contain the foundation myths that once underpinned them, but everyday life in modern cityscapes tells another story. The dynamics of capitalist spatialization have transformed the urban settings into prisms of a world without borders and, yet, at the same time full of borders.

Through the concept of hyperspace in the age of electronic communication this development can be taken one step further. Fredric Jameson argued in the 1980s that the latest mutation in space, the postmodern hyperspace, had finally succeeded in transcending the capacities of the individual human body to locate itself, to organize its immediate surrounding, perceptually, and cognitively to map its position in a mappable external world (Jameson 1984: 83–4, cited in Burgin 1996: 24–5):

> This alarming disjunction point between the body and its built environment ... can itself stand as the symbol and analogue of that even sharper dilemma which is the incapacity of our minds, at least at present, to map the great global multinational and decentred communicational network in which we find ourselves caught as individual subjects.

One response to this incapacity of our minds seems to be the creation of new borders where the old ones evaporate in hyperspace. Exuberant nationalistic rhetoric in exile communities in the West, and the planning of bomb attacks in New York, Madrid, Bali or Amman from a distant café in London or an apartment in Hamburg, can be seen as attempts to infuse new certainty where the old has disappeared. The attack on a whole civilization in the name of another is planned from rocky caves in Afghanistan, and so on. Modernity is not only constant transgression of time and space but also the defining of place as location of emotions and feelings of belonging.

It is not only the borders between here and there, inside and outside, that used to be stronger and more stable than they appear today, but also the separation between past and present. Modern media of reproduction such as photography, film, recorded music and the internet – as well as the explosion of a voracious museum culture – make the past become part of the present in ways simply unimaginable in earlier centuries. As a result, temporal boundaries have weakened just as the experiential dimension of space has shrunk as a result of modern means of transportation and communication (Huyssen 2003). The discourse of history used to be there to guarantee the relative stability of the past in its pastness. Traditions, invented or constructed and always based on selections and exclusions, gave shape to cultural and social life. Urban space replete with monuments and museums, public buildings and spaces represented the visible traces of the historical past in the present. The main concern of the nation-states of the nineteenth century was to mobilize and monumentalize national and universal pasts in order to give legitimacy and meaning to the present and to outline the future culturally, politically, socially. This model no longer works. The endless contemporary debates about history and memory, identity and consciousness are underpinned by a fundamental disturbance not just of the relationship between history as objective and scientific, and memory as subjective and personal, but of history itself and its promises. At stake in the current history/memory debate is not only a disturbance of our notions of the past, but a fundamental crisis in our imagination of alternative futures. The German historian Reinhart Koselleck (2004) has formulated this agonizing development as an ever-narrowing scope between the space of experiences and the horizons of expectation. The information is so overwhelming that we have difficulty ordering it into a cohesive interpretation of our experiences, which, in turn, makes it difficult to design new horizons of expectation. This narrowing scope we experience as the acceleration of time. It goes without saying that such a development gives new preconditions for the question of belonging.

## Belonging and the Concept of Homeland

Homeland is a value-loaded as well as historically contested concept connoting belonging and identity, and is thus a concept replete with poetic and imaginative force. Through this poetical force homeland has connected dreams of a utopian past with images of a better future. In this sense there is a fundamentalist and totalizing core with sharp demarcation between Us and the Other when the poetic imagination is translated into political projects.

The contributions in a recent book on the topic analyse the representations of homeland from multiple perspectives (Robin and Stråth 2003). One section of the book deals with the concept of homeland in Israel and Palestine. To begin with, most of the contributors in this section agree that defining homeland is an imaginative project in which culture, folklore, music and art play significant roles. The homelands of this highly contested region do not enjoy the luxury of certainty. Their malleable shapes and multiple forms are linked intimately to political and sociological acts of exclusion and inclusion, as well as the positionality of narrators. Women and men, peasants and urban dwellers, jostle constantly as they compete for their version of homeland. Another underlying theme of this section concerns the relevance of national frameworks for the homeland project. Here some contributors accept national entities as the most functional framework for defining belonging, while others seek more inclusive, transcendental communities and common notions of belonging.

Ron Robin calls attention to the exclusivist millenarian nature of Jewish and Muslim religious movements as benign socio-religious movements which share a common base of compassion for the masses. Followers are militantly intolerant of hybridity, or any other inclusive political, social or religious alternative arrangement. In increasingly popular movements, these millenarian strains tend to be apocalyptical. Seeking to hasten the coming of the Day of Judgment, believers actively and often violently disrupt discourses that compete with the rigid framework of the true believer. Thus, the millenarian apocalyptical views of popular religious movements legitimize rigid, intolerant and often violent narratives of exclusion and inclusion. Neither multicultural tolerance, nor ecumenical notions of fairness and justice characterize the millenarian homeland, which is forged from divine justice and retribution for all non-believers. Thus, for all its weaknesses, the nation-state provides a relatively benign option for a workable homeland. The underlying tensions between diaspora–homeland, exclusiveness–inclusiveness, the mobilization of religion as a driving force, the cultural construction of territorial community, as well as recourse to universal values as a strategy of reconciliation have played a part in the negotiation of other contested homelands.

Mariangela Veikou's analysis of a Greek dilemma suggests that diasporized communities face a series of sometimes insurmountable obstacles in their attempts to lay claim to a homeland (Veikou 2003). In her analysis of Greek-Albanian migrants to the Greek motherland, Veikou describes the manner in which neither government decree nor cultural constructions have been able to overcome the overpowering cartographical visions of belonging. Her study exposes the limitations of strategies employed by immigrants from Albania's Greek enclaves to establish their 'Greek' identity in Greece. Despite the fact that their enclaves are recognized as part of historical Greece, these Greek-Albanians remain outsiders. Their physical return to the homeland has not fundamentally changed their status as newcomers, perhaps even foreigners.

27

The Greek-Albanians claim culture, language and religion, rather than geographical origin, as the most significant markers of belonging to the Greek homeland. Nevertheless, they remain Greek 'people of the diaspora'; as immigrants they receive favourable treatment, but as Greeks they are second-class citizens, the beneficiaries of temporary and limited rights only. As a migrant group and a diasporic community, the Greek-Albanians are for all practical purposes 'nationally homeless', citizens of two liminal homelands. Marked in Albania as Greeks, and often dismissed as Albanians in Greece, the Greek-Albanians seek to transcend the notion of birthright in a bounded territory by drawing on tradition of ancestral origin. Referring to a common Greek past has, however, proven to be a limited help to the legitimization of their presence in Greece. Transcending cartographical conventions of belonging, and reconciling the worldviews of diaspora with the culture of the homeland, is complicated by cultural preconceptions distinctly tied to a specific locale. The host society refuses to overlook the Albanian origins of the newcomers. Their claim to the right of return is perfunctorily accepted, but routinely thwarted by both law and lore. Thus, Greek-Albanians learn to 'perform': they adopt the dress code and other routine mannerisms of the dominant society. They also learn to forget, as integration demands the effacement of specific cultural manifestations and the unquestioning acceptance of the mores of the metropolis. Based on the reflections of her informants, Veikou argues that the construction of homeland should not be tethered to 'assumptions about the past'; homeland is not a landscape of historic memory, but rather an ambiguous framework in a state of constant reinvention.

Similarly, Senadin Musabegovic describes Sarajevo's besieged citizens as refugees, even though strictly speaking they were not uprooted from their homes (Musabegovic 2003). Here he argues that the status of refugee is not necessarily geographical dislocation. As in the case of Sarajevo one may be expelled, purged and cleansed from the homeland through denial of rights and challenges to the humanity of the refugee. 'A refugee in Sarajevo is not a refugee because he has been expelled from Paradise; he is a refugee because he seeks refuge from death,' he explains. It would appear, then, that a fixation on nationalism, rather than community, is the source of all evil in the Balkans. Nationalism appears in his essay as the greatest and most lethal challenge to workable and functioning, multicultural homelands such as the pre-national, multicultural Bosnian example.

While Bosnia is, in part, a tragedy born out of the imposition of division and differences, South Africa offers an example of how such divisions, once naturalized and embedded into daily life, become impervious to change. Cape Town – 'where the mountain meets the shadow' – is the common homeland of Heidi Grunebaum, a third-generation offspring of Holocaust refugees, and Yazir Henri, a 'coloured' progeny of a 'white'/'black' liaison. They analyse the manner in which racial categories of belonging and marginality have remained immune to change despite the significant superficial political transformation of South African society (Henri and Grunebaum 2003). Cape Town, often the most representative symbol of South Africa, is a tale of two cities. Its commodified version is that of the gigantic flat-topped mountain overlooking golden beaches: this is the homeland of its privileged, mostly white, citizens. The other Cape Town is the unprotected, windswept flats situated behind the mountains and populated by Cape Town's dispossessed people of colour. Post-Apartheid South Africa has not witnessed any meaningful shift in this colour-coded landscape. Grunebaum and Henri identify the famous Truth and Reconciliation Commission (TRC) as an important contributing factor to the lack of change in the Cape landscape in particular, and the South African homeland in general. The TRC did not expose the historic role of oppression and dispossession embedded in the South African landscape. Instead, they argue, the TRC contributed to the very ossification of boundaries of colour and identity. Despite the ostensible objective of revealing the systematic brutality of apartheid, the TRC has led to the sanitization of systems of oppression in South Africa.

Cape Town, as the epitome of the South African homeland, has remained a rigidly divided colour-coded topography, of gated communities on the one hand and sprawling shanty towns on the other. Racial boundaries remain intact; they have merely been presented in 'new conceptual categories such as class, language and culture' (Henri and Grunebaum 2003: 3). But for all practical purposes race and colour continue to limit the horizons of an inclusive South African homeland. 'The spatial boundaries of Capetown remain distinct, obliterating even the memory of how these spaces were manipulated into existence' (Henri and Grunebaum 2003: 3). White supremacy remains intact, because through mechanisms such as the TRC, it has been made invisible. Contrary to the findings of the TRC, 'race violence was not only a physical act, but daily doses of oppression embedded in language and economic praxis' (Henri and Grunebaum 2003: 6). The attempt to 'imagine away' the legacy of Apartheid has, according to Henri and Grunebaum, led to its normalization.

Similarly, John D. Brewer's analysis of history and remembering in Ulster examines the symbiotic relationship between religion, ethnicity and colonialism in another well-known case of a contested homeland (Brewer 2003). His historical and contemporary political analysis of Ulster highlights the manner in which theology produced an ideological construction of Irish society comprising mutually exclusive groups engaged in a uncompromising zero-sum game. Brewer claims that religion has eclipsed all other modes of differentiation in Ulster, and that therefore any future solution for Northern Ireland demands its presentation in religious terms. Ignoring or effacing religion will not solve the conflict over this contested homeland. In Ulster, where the planter class was mostly of Scots Presbyterian origin, theology was not merely a rationalization of political ambitions. While English planters in other parts of Ireland employed the scriptures as a 'convenient rationalization', for the Scots Presbyterian planter community in Ulster, the biblically inspired view of themselves as Israelites entering the promised land 'was fundamental both to their theology and politics, and has remained so ever since' (Brewer: 2003: 287).

It is the continuous salience of religious difference – the ability of religion to eclipse all other forms of identity – that has left the conflict simmering in Ulster. Religion has perpetuated endogamy, residential and cultural segregation and other sectarian divisions. All of politics has been seen in scriptural terms. For most Ulster Scots, the scriptural covenant between God and his chosen people has precluded any form of compromise in the contested Ulster homeland. The language of Ulster loyalists has been replete with biblical allegories and prophecies. The unrelenting stance of Ulster loyalists is impermeable to change precisely because it is viewed in biblical terms. Any compromise is seen as a breach of the covenant with the Lord. Hence, the Old Testament covenant between the Lord and his chosen people has become a template for all contemporary politics. Interpreting the present-day conflict in biblical terms has been at the root of Protestant resistance. Brewer describes the manner in which Catholicism is seen as Paganism in the eyes of Protestant leaders. Opposing Catholicism has been the 'Protestant's sacred duty'. Anti-Irishness and anti-Catholicism transform the fight over a contested Ulster into 'the Lord's Battle', a biblical contest between absolute good and incarnate evil.

It is Brewer's contention, therefore, that compromise and a solution to the problem of a contested Ulster can only lie in promoting different scriptural interpretations rather than denying or ignoring the role of biblical hermeneutics. Ignoring religion or trivializing its presence will not produce alternative meaningful solutions for this contested homeland. However, there are historical arguments for a different view than the one Brewer expresses, historical cases of demarcation between religion and politics. The kind of historical demarcation that occurred in France or Italy does not seem very realistic. However, the Scandinavian model of transferring religious issues to the private sphere might be a model (Stråth 2007).

The concept of homeland does not seem very promising as a twenty-first-century alternative to the concept of the nation-state and the fiction of national identities. Historically the concept has connoted as much sharp and hostile demarcation as the excesses in the name of nation. To the examples above could be added the German *Heimat,* which in the 1930s was appropriated by the right-extremist *völkische* movements that paved the way for Hitler (Petri 2003). The exceptional case that confirms the rule is the Swedish *hembygd* as a pragmatic mix of nostalgic longing and issue-oriented politics (Stråth 2003; Trägårdh 1993). When applied to our multicultural urban environments today homeland connotes nostalgia and diasporic longings for a remote distance and a remote past. There is a need for an alternative conceptualization that emphasizes the continuities and overlappings with other migrant communities, and develops ties to the larger polity in which migrants live, a conceptualization that emphasizes solidarity in the cityscapes of diversity.

Is 'multicultural' then the concept of belonging that we are looking for? 'Multicultural' emphasizes diversity but not solidarity across cultural border lines. 'Multicultural' belongs instead to a neoliberal vocabulary, forming part of an argument that everybody takes care of himself or herself (Máiz and Requejo 2005; Cooper 2004; Brooks 2002; Barry 2001; Bauböck and Rundell 1998). Everybody is allowed to exercise his or her own cultural practices, rites and customs, but there are no social ties beyond the border of each (sub)culture. This perspective fits hand in glove with the language of globalization, and the concept of multiculturalism also emerged in close connection to the fiction of a global market.

In this context, we might ask what the notion of a European identity might represent, as an alternative kind of belonging, less rigid and exclusive than national identifications and the homeland concept, but more solidaristic and inclusive overall than the concept of the multicultural. Can European identity transgress ethnic and religious demarcations and open up a more inclusive and civic understanding of belonging? Can Europe provide the individual with ties of commonality and solidarity?

## Beyond a European Identity: Towards a Social Europe

So, more precisely, when and how did the idea of a European identity emerge? What is the history of the concept? And how is it connected to historically developed images of Europe and to institution-building in Europe since the 1950s? An intensified European integration has gone hand in hand with a growing academic and political search for the roots of Europeanness in history, religion, science and culture (Goddard *et al.* 1994). The meanings of Europe are discourses of power on how to define and classify Europe, on the

31

frontiers of Europe and on similarities and differences. In many versions the emphasis is on Europe as a distinctive cultural entity united by shared values, culture and identity. References are being made to Europe's heritage of classical Graeco-Roman civilization, Christianity and the ideas of Enlightenment – science, reason, progress and democracy – as the core elements of this claimed European legacy. There are subtexts of racial and cultural chauvinism, particularly when confronted with Islam. Europe acquires distinction and salience when pitted against the Other. When the differences within Europe are emphasized, it is often in the form of unity in diversity. Religious differences (Catholic, Protestant, Orthodox Christianity) and linguistic differences (Romance, Germanic and Slavic languages) are seen as correlated (Catholic-Romance, Protestant-Germanic, Orthodox-Slavic), and essentially underlying the major historical and contemporary ethnic cleavages and conflicts in Europe.

The identity of Europe was designed and decided upon at the Copenhagen EC Summit in December 1973 (European Commission 1973). The framework of the meeting was to bring global order to an unexpected crisis: the Bretton Woods Agreement following the Second World War, based on the dollar, had collapsed in 1971 after years of growing tension between the Western European states and their American ally. The Vietnam War underpinned the tension and overstrained the dollar. Friction had increased considerably in the machinery of economic growth and high levels of employment, mass consumption and mass production mutually reinforcing one another, based on the long post-war reconstruction boom, and investments feeding the boom. Finally, in the autumn of 1973, a dramatic increase in the price of oil took the Western world by surprise, provoking a mood of crisis. The notion of a European identity in the 1970s grew from this context into an instrument for consolidating Europe's place in an international order. An attempt was made to establish a European tripartite order of corporatist bargaining, to replace the collapsing national arrangements. In 1977 the MacDougall Report to the European Commission suggested a European Keynesian strategy to bridge the economic crisis and the collapse of key industries, a kind of Eurocorporatist order. A serious attempt was made in 1977–1978 to translate the national tripartite bargaining structures, which had functioned so well during the economic growth of the 1950s and 1960s, to a European level in politics of de-industrialization in industries such as shipbuilding and steel. The idea of a European identity underpinned these efforts. However, during negotiations about capacity reduction and layoffs of labour, loyalties among employers, trade unions and governments followed national rather than transnational labour and capital solidarity lines (Stråth

1987). The proposals in the MacDougall Report were never realized.

The concept of a European identity is of limited value today. Like the classification of human beings according to ethnicity and 'race' it has reached its limits. It should be seen as a historical concept which played a crucial role during a difficult phase of European integration between the 1970s and the 1990s. The twenty-first century requires a new conceptual topography, less Eurocentric and narcissistic, and more global – although in another sense the globalization rhetoric is nothing but a narrative of Americanization, and only repeats the old European version of a 'white man's burden' and civilization mission. In the development of new semantic fields the historically constructed divides through the Baltic (Russia) and the Mediterranean (Ottoman Empire, Islamic world) must be transgressed in internal as well as external terms, within European migrant communities as well as vis-à-vis the peoples which once were seen as East of Europe. I am not suggesting the construction of a new divide through the Atlantic, but that we urgently need more critical distance emphasizing the differences between Europe, in a new mediating role, and the USA. Conceptualization of social theories is, after the collapse of Marxist theory, almost hegemonically American. The debates between libertarians and communitarians – the neoliberal rhetoric – with a unilateral focus on the market concept, and the arguments for rational choice and methodological individualism, are all much more inscribed in a specific American history than in European ones. The same goes for the debate on human rights, democracy and ethnicity and for theories of modernity and 'development'. They have nevertheless imposed themselves also as the point of departure, given more or less by nature, for the European theoretical reflection on society. On this point a conceptualization must be developed that is much more reflective of specific European historical experiences in all their variety. Max Weber, for instance, with his intellectual capacity to see Germany and Europe in a context of global cultures, could be a point of departure in such theoretical reconstruction. Another point of departure could be that aspect of the Enlightenment heritage which emphasizes qualities such as tolerance and intellectual openness for dissident opinions. An urgent task in a European reconceptualization would be to reintegrate the individual in a social context. Here the concept of a European social responsibility could fill a dangerous gap between a growing nationalism in the wake of nation-state legitimacy deficits, and the market-oriented emphasis on the individual deprived of social connections, as Peter Wagner (2000) has argued.

Other important elements in a reconceptualization would be to see 'culture' not as an entity with cohesion and fixed borders, but, as Gerard Delanty and others have argued, as a floppy concept, describing something in flux with no clear borders and with internal opposition and contradictions, discursively shaped in contentious social bargaining processes (Delanty 1995; 1999). It is important not to essentialize Europe but to emphasize the openness of the concept much more than does a 'European identity'. In the same vein, Gerold Gerber (2000) analyses Malta. His point of departure is that the EU is a paradoxical project, as on the one hand the project of European identity is supposed to overcome nationalism and to ensure solidarity among the members, and on the other hand, as in any construction of collective identity, a definition of the Other(s) is required. The inclusion of European 'insiders' implies the exclusion, by whatever criteria, of non-European or not-yet-European 'outsiders'. Thus, humanistic ideals such as equality, freedom and pluralism have come into conflict with the need to exclude. All this has been seen and discussed, of course, and a solution does not seem to be in sight. However, Gerber emphasizes the need to accept ambivalences and paradoxes as a fundamental condition of social life, rather than seeing them as a nuisance to be ordered away. In so doing he refers to Max Weber and Zygmunt Bauman (1991), and he takes note of Neil Smelser's (1998) defence of ambivalence against rational choice. His case study of Malta suggests that politicians and intellectuals, far from being avant-garde, may actually be behind actors in everyday life when it comes to coping with paradox. While political and economic exigencies are likely to force Maltese officials into a choice between Europe and the Arab world, Maltese people may happily embrace the option of being both European and non-European in daily life. As long as the social sciences comply with intellectual and political efforts to construct coherence and order by classifying the social world into categories, they will face the challenges of logocentrism. Yet, a critique of Western metaphysics should not mean the end of science and reason altogether. Starting with Malta, Gerber proposes to develop a social science which takes more seriously 'ordinary' actors – that is, all of us – and their practical solutions to flux and paradox. Politicians, intellectuals and scientists may be inspired by such expertise in how to deal with ambivalence without being afraid.

Self-images and images of the Other are not static entities, but are elements in a continuous process. Anja Hänsch (2000) demonstrates this in a study of Arab emigrants' encounters with Europe. During emigration, the encounter with the Other leads to both a reflection on the self-image and a reflection on the previous image of the Other. These types of reflection start all over again with the return of the emigrants to their home country, where the culture of origin is confronted after the experiences of Europe have left their traces on the emigrants. Emigration functions as a catalyst for the creation and for the questioning of images and self-images. Situations of emigration can be

34

described in terms of liminality or *rites de passage* (Turner 1987; van Gennep 1981). Separation is followed by margin/*limen* and incorporation. The migrant is in a situation of betwixt and between, in a liminal or transitional stage between cultures and countries. This situation leads to a questioning of both culture of origin and the newly encountered culture. Given the great number of immigrants in Europe it seems reasonable to argue that they should be incorporated in concepts expressing community and belonging; 'European identity' is no doubt problematic in this respect. The liminal position does not only refer to migrants, however. Arpád Szakolczai (1998), elaborating on Foucault, has argued that modern Western culture is a continuous liminality, a moment of transition lasting for centuries and rooted in the collapse of the Middle Ages. The transient becomes a permanent state. Thus the migrant situation brings with it a double risk of getting lost, namely the risk of falling in between two cultures, and the risk of falling into the abysses of modernity where anti-structure and uprootedness become part of everyday life.

All these examples indicate the direction in which a new conceptualization of culture and feelings of belonging could be elaborated – a conception that is more historically informed and that allows for ambivalence and transition. The concept of European identity has tended to move in the direction of essentialism, and does not mediate these elements very well. A key question in this regard is to what extent, in what forms and in what context do non-European cultures define themselves in terms of what they discern as European particularities. And, vice versa, to what extent does Europe define itself in terms of what are seen as particularities of other cultures, Islam, for instance?

It is important to advance a much more reflective, hermeneutic and open-ended account of Europe than that currently permitted by the identity discourse. Following Rémi Brague we might say that Europe is not so much based on a substantive self or particular origin but consists of a form of transmission (Brague 2002). Europe began, in what is today seen as outside itself, with an Asian foundation myth ('Europa and the Bull') and an Asian religion. Europe has emerged through the formation of an occidental distinction, which involves the invention of an Other which thereby entails an alienation from its Asian origins. The history of Europe was marked by a progressive alienation from its origin, which it could thereafter only know as Other. The crusades were an important step in this process. While this occidental distinction might have had the positive effect of enabling critical distance from its own core, the dark side of the process is that it has created the image of the Other as hostile and barbaric (Boon and Delanty 2007).

The weakness of the identity concept is that it connotes demarcation from rather than solidarity with the Other. This is at least how the concept has developed during its trajectory from a discursive to an essential category. It is a highly ideological concept in its argumentation for sameness. Literally taken, 'identity' can be understood as 'you are poor and I am rich, but we are nevertheless the same'. The pretension of sameness blurs social difference and the question of power. There is a need for a conceptualization of Europe that emphasizes its social dimension as opposed to a view of Europe as a market, a demos or an ethnos. A social Europe would rather connote republican civic virtues of social responsibility, and from such a Europe the question of belonging could be addressed from new points of departure. A socially integrative Europe should provide space for the crowds of the multi-ethnic, multi-linguistic and multi-religious cityscapes. That would be a civic Europe where belonging stands for social inclusion under conditions of cultural diversity.

## References

Barry, B. M. (2001) *Culture and Equality: An Egalitarian Critique of Multiculturalism.* Cambridge, MA: Harvard University Press.

Bauböck, R., and J. Rundell (eds) (1998) *Blurred Boundaries:. Migration, Ethnicity, Citizenship.* Burlington, VT: Ashgate.

Bauman, Z. (1991) *Modernity and Ambivalence.* Cambridge: Polity Press.

Boon, V., and G. Delanty (2007) 'Europe as a Historical Projection: Reinventing Europe and its Histories', in H.-Å. Persson and B. Stråth (eds), *Europe as Time and Space.* Brussels: PIE Peter Lang.

Brague, R. (2002) *Eccentric Culture: A Theory of Western Civilization.* South Bend, IN: St Augustine's Press.

Brewer, J. D. (2003) 'Contesting Ulster', in Robin and Stråth (2003).

Brooks, S. (ed.) (2002) *The Challenge of Cultural Pluralism.* London: Praeger.

Burgin, V. (1996) *In/Different Spaces: Place and Memory in Visual Culture.* Berkeley, CA: University of California Press.

Cooper, D. (2004) *Challenging Diversity: Rethinking Equality and the Value of Difference.* Cambridge: Cambridge University Press.

Delanty, G. (1995) *Inventing Europe: Idea, Identity, Reality.* London: Macmillan.

— (1999) 'Social Integration and Europeanization', *Yearbook of European Studies* 12: 221–38.

European Commission (1973) 'Declaration on European Identity', in *General Report of the European Commission.* Brussels: European Commission.

Gerbert, G. (2000) 'Doing Christianity and Europe: An Inquiry into Memory, Boundary and Truth Practices in Malta', in B. Stråth (2000a).

Goddard, V. A., J. R. Llobern and C. Shore (eds) (1994) *The Anthropology of Europe: Identification and Boundaries in Conflict.* Oxford: Berg.

Hänsch, A. (2000) 'Emigration and Modernity: On the Twofold Liminality in Arab and Franco-Arab Literature', in A. Höfert and A. Salvatore (eds), *Between Europe and Islam: Shaping Modernity in a Transcultural Space.* Brussels: PIE Peter Lang.

Henri, Y., and H. Grunebaum (2003) 'Where the Mountain Meets Its Shadow: A Conversation on Memory, Identity, and Fragmented Belonging in Present-Day South Africa', in Robin and Stråth (2003).

Huyssen, A. (2003) *Present Pasts: Urban Palimpsests and the Politics of Memory*. Stanford, CA: Stanford University Press.

Jameson, F. (1984) 'Postmodernism, or the Cultural Logic of Late Capitalism', *New Left Review* 146 (July–August).

Koselleck, R. (2004), '"Space of Experience" and "Horizon of Expectation": Two Historical Categories', in R. Koselleck, *Futures Past. On the Semantics of Historical Time*. New York: Columbia University Press. German Original (1979) *Vergangene Zukunft. Zur Semantikgeschichtlicher Zeiten*. Frankfurt am Main: Suhrkamp.

Máiz, R., and F. Requejo (eds) (2005) *Democracy, Nationalism and Multiculturalism*. London and New York: Frank Cass.

Maslow, A. H. (1970) *Motivation and Personality*. New York: Harper & Row.

Musabegovic, S. (2003) 'The Circle and the Present', in Robin and Stråth (2003).

Passerini, L. (ed.) (1998) *Identità culturale Europea. Idee, sentimenti, relazioni*. Florence: La Nuova Italia.

Petri, R. (2003) 'The Meanings of *Heimat*', in Robin and Stråth (2003).

Robin, R., and B. Stråth (eds) (2003) *Homelands: Poetic Power and the Politics of Space*. Brussels: PIE Peter Lang.

Smelser, N. J. (1998) 'The Rational and the Ambivalent in the Social Sciences', *American Sociological Review* 63: 1–16.

Stråth, B. (1987) *The Politics of Industrialisation*. London: Croom Helm.

— (ed.) (2000a) *Europe and the Other and Europe as the Other*. Brussels: PIE Peter Lang.

— (ed.) (2000b) *After Full Employment: European Discourses on Work and Flexibility*. Brussels: PIE Peter Lang.

— (2000c) 'The Concept of Work in the Construction of Community', in B. Stråth (2000b).

— (2003) '*Hembygd* as a Pragmatic Concept: The Alternative Case', in Robin and Stråth (2003).

— (2007) 'Der Volksbegriff in der Organisation der Religionsausübung Schwedens' in L. Hölscher (ed.), *Baupläne der sichtbaren Kirche: Sprachliche Konzepte religiöser Vergemeinschaftung in Europa*. Göttingen: Wallstein.

Szakolczai, A. (1998) *Max Weber and Michel Foucault: Parallel Life-Works*. London: Routledge.

Taylor, C. (1985) *Human Agency and Language*, Cambridge: Cambridge University Press.

Trägårdh, L. C. (1993) 'The Concept of the People and the Construction of Popular Political Culture in Germany and Sweden: 1848–1933', dissertation, University of Michigan, Ann Arbor, MI.

Turner, V. ([1967] 1987) *The Forest of Symbols*. New York: Cornell University Press.

Van Gennep, A. ([1909] 1981) *Les rites de passage: Etude systématique des rites*. Paris: Editions A. et J. Picard.

Veikou, M. (2003) 'Ambiguous Insiders and the Description of "Homeland": Belonging in Immigrants' Ethnic Identity Narratives', in Robin and Stråth (2003).

Wagner, P. (2000) 'The Exit from Organised Modernity: "Flexibility" in Social Thought and in Historical Perspective', in B. Stråth (2000b).

— (2001) *Theorizing Modernity: Inescapability and Attainability in Social Theory*. London: Sage.

# 2 Identity, Belonging and Migration: Beyond Constructing 'Others'

## Paul Jones and Michał Krzyżanowski

Due to the lack of theoretical rigour and precision that so often accompanies its use, the concept of 'identity' is not necessarily the best way in which to conceptualize an individual's relation to a collective. In fact, the casual application of this highly elastic yet undifferentiated concept to empirical research on migration has meant that the potential of 'identity' to operate as an overarching explanatory framework is highly problematic, often serving to hide more than it reveals. We would like to suggest that the notion of 'belonging' is central not only to the sustained critique of the concept of identity, but also for developing a coherent and context-sensitive theoretical model that supports empirical social scientific research in this area. However, and even given these concerns, we are not calling for the abandonment of the concept of identity, but rather for a 'conceptual unpacking', which would allow the multiple, highly complex processes associated with identity construction to be revealed rather than – as is often the case – concealed.

Of course, 'belonging' is not a novel response to the analytical shortcomings of the concept of identity; it has a long history in both political and social theory. But the re-emergence of the term in the social scientific literature (for example, Probyn 1996; Fortier 2000; Sicakkan and Lithman 2005) can be explained by the fact that the concept provides social scientists the potential to capture something of the complexity and multiplicity in a way that arguably 'identity' does not. In part due to the (relative) flexibility of its framework, 'belonging' allows the fluid, constructed nature of many of the processes associated with identity to be analysed and understood in a more rigorous way. Our general argument here is that individuals frequently translate such highly idiosyncratic belongings into the more readily understood proxy of collective identities. Accordingly, in this discussion we are interested in the point at which individual belongings and collective identities meet, which is also the stage at which identities are contested and negotiated. This framework allows us to look at how various patterns of belonging are constructed dynamically, which helps situate 'where' an individual positions herself in relation to collectives of both her 'original' community and the society to which she has migrated. So, in this chapter we put forward a critique of the imprecise application of the concept of identity with particular reference to migration, a research area where fuzzy application of the term is particularly common. Against this backdrop it is important to consider: How are belongings constructed for and by agents in multiple, contested ways? What are the barriers that exist to formal and informal group memberships? Why are migrants inherently a 'special case' in this regard?

## An Identity Crisis or a Question of Belonging?

Brubaker and Cooper have argued that '[r]ather than stirring all self-understandings based on race, religion ethnicity, and so on into the great conceptual melting pot of "identity," we would do better to use a more differentiated analytical language' (2000: 20). Indeed, it seems that the concept of identity is in something of a crisis; although 'identity' is still used a great deal in a wide range of academic writing, there is increasingly an acknowledgement that its unqualified use, sometimes even lacking coherent definition, is highly problematic. Although an in-depth discussion of the development of the term is outside the limits of this contribution, it is clear that the contemporary popularity of the term can be linked to the 'cultural turn' in social theory, with 'identity' perceived by many as a way to mediate, or to recast, central problems in the social sciences, such as the agency/structure debate for example.[1] Unsurprisingly given this general context, the notion of identity has been already been extensively problematized (for example see Hall 1996; Brubaker and Cooper 2000; Friese 2001). Supporting some of these critiques of the concept we argue that 'identity' has become something of a catch-all concept, which is used uncritically to support an untenably disparate range of claims; in actual fact the explanatory potential of 'identity' has been much diminished by such loose and over-generalized application. We believe that a point has now been reached where the concept of identity, without serious de- (and re-) construction, provides little of the theoretical or methodological precision necessary for engaged, critical research.

1  For a more thorough history of the semantic development of the term 'identity' see Gleason (1983). He situates the development of the word's popularity in the post-war writings on mass society that problematized the relationship between the individual and the social.

Brubaker and Cooper, in their influential article 'Beyond "Identity"', suggest that '[c]onceptualizing all affinities and affiliations, all forms of belonging, all experiences of commonality, connectedness, and cohesion, all self-understanding and self-identification in the idiom of "identity" saddles us with a blunt, flat, undifferentiated vocabulary' (2000: 2). Certainly the elastic nature of the term poses a large, some would say insurmountable, problem for anyone hoping to use the concept to provide analytical precision for theoretical or empirical research. Accordingly there have been some notable calls within the social sciences to either (i) instil the concept of identity with the clarity and 'analytical purchase' it is lacking, or (ii) abandon it altogether in favour of new terms and concepts that are less laden with diverse, contested and elusive meanings. Brubaker and Cooper (2000) have taken the second position, arguing that the concept of identity has ceased to serve a purpose and should be consigned to the theoretical dustbin. They have also suggested that even attempts to 'soften' the concept of identity by stressing the constructed and fluid nature of identities is futile, as we are then left with a concept devoid of the necessary 'analytical purchase'.

It is important to clarify from the beginning of this chapter that we are *not* calling for the 'end of identity', even assuming that such a call would be heeded, but rather we are urging a *conceptual unpacking* of a concept which has been taken for granted hitherto, but which is one of the most misunderstood in common academic usage. A central contention here is that identity is very often the wrong 'sized' concept to aid understandings and explanations of what are hugely complex, specific, context-sensitive and context-dependent, discursively constructed social processes, operative at both individual and collective levels. Identity is frequently objectified as a theoretical panacea, as if the very utterance of the word provides sufficient explanation of the hugely complex and contested processes that go towards the way individuals perceive themselves in relation to others. However, it is equally important to stress that we are not attempting a 'softening' of the term simply by qualifying or diluting some of its theoretical premises. Rather, by providing a differentiation of the notion of identity we want to present the need for 'internal classification' of the broadly understood – at present, too broadly understood –concept; we are arguing for an ordering of the broad conceptual and analytical scope of 'identity' by referring to the particular settings where identities are produced, contested and transformed. We believe that, although based on numerous theories on collective and individual identities proposed in the recent years, our approach differs in some vital respects from traditionally understood attempts. For example, we aim not only at a theoretical explanation of the constitutive processes related to

40

identity, but also provide empirical evidence of how the main concepts and categories postulated here operate in 'concrete' discursive contexts. Far from abandoning the concept of identity, we hope to demonstrate why it is vital to take account of the range of processes that contribute towards the formation of an identity. On this question we support Ian Hacking's work, inasmuch as he convincingly argues that it is not enough to suggest that aspects of social life are 'socially constructed'; rather the challenge for social scientists is to show how (Hacking 1999).

## Belonging and Migration

Given the frequency and the force of some of the criticisms concerning the lack of explanatory potential offered by the concept of identity, the emergence of attempts to unpack its meaning is perhaps unsurprising. In the context of increased mobility for some thanks to the many interconnections opened up by globalized communicative technologies, and the concomitant fixity and exclusion of a far greater number of others, there is still a pressing need for conceptual developments and theoretically informed debate in the general area of identity. The concept of belonging is increasingly included in such discussions, and in this chapter we hope to provide the concept with some of the 'analytical charisma'[2] that we feel that discussions around identity are, for the main part, lacking. At a superficial level we can say belonging connotes being at 'home', but exactly where do such feelings come from, and how are they codified in 'everyday' social practice? Who has power to define who can belong, and what are the conditions? Belongings, attachments and lived experiences can be highly contingent and thus, seem to be very difficult to grasp in any 'concrete' social-scientific analysis, and although at present 'belonging' lacks a clear and unequivocal definition beyond these relatively banal common-sense understandings, this can in fact be interpreted as a strength of the concept relative to 'identity', which due to (perceived) over-familiarity and imprecise application has become all things to all theorists (Crowley 1999). In applying our framework on the concept of belonging to the contemporary European perspective, and in particular to migrants' construction of their 'belongings', we would like suggest that the notion of belonging we develop below allows for an understanding of how transient, sometimes unclear relationships can contribute to an individual's position vis-

---

2 Yasemin Soysal used this phrase in her plenary lecture to the 6th European Sociological Association conference in Murcia, Spain (25–28 September 2003). In her address Soysal provided a critique of the conceptual tools she felt had been left behind by 'real-world' social developments. Perhaps unsurprisingly, the notion of identity was one of her targets.

à-vis a collective identity. We hope we have developed a model that facilitates empirical research into identities in a way that rests on theoretically secure foundations, at the same time avoiding a retreat to a socio-psychological analysis. One of the problems with many theories of identity is that they are posited on an overly strict delineation between self and other, which is seldom evident in the 'real world'.

For example, the boundaries between national identities are almost never as fixed and delineated as the majority of the literature would have us believe. We feel that there is a pressing need to develop a better understanding of the dialectical, contradictory processes often inherent in the construction of identities, while at the same time analysing how a range of attachments, subjective feelings, preferences and memberships can feed into a sense of belonging. Our contention here is that the concept of belonging allows a theoretical foundation for the analysis of how identities can be made up of seemingly contradictory positions or memberships. The collection of essays edited by Barnor Hesse, *Un/Settled Multiculturalisms: Diasporas, Entanglements, Transruptions*, underlines this point, demonstrating how identities have the capacity to incorporate other identities as part of the definition of the 'self'. While identities, almost by definition, do have boundaries, it is clear that while one may associate strongly with, for example, a particular collective identity, this may also include an attachment or belonging to another collective identity. Similarly Michael Waltzer, in his famous essay entitled 'What Does It Mean to Be an American?', posited that the notion of a north American identity was dependent on the agglomeration of pluralities of existing collective identities. Waltzer sees American identities as being organized as 'hyphenated identities', combinations of existing national identities with an 'American' identity (such as 'Irish-American' for example). A problem with Waltzer's position, and also with some multiculturalist literature, is that it assumes the existence of stable, hermetically sealed identities that can be either kept separate or 'hyphenated' with others. Developing this critique, we believe that one of the analytical strengths of the concept of belonging as developed below is that it can be defined with sufficient precision to take account of the transient nature of many of the processes associated with the formation of identities. The concept of 'identity' as it is commonly understood in the literature does not really facilitate critical enquiry of such discussions and is increasingly serving to close down theoretically grounded discussions rather than open them up.

In short then it is vital to stress that identities are not hermetically sealed entities that are internally consistent and which necessarily exclude other identities. Social life is far too complex to conceptualize the relationship between individuals and the collectives of which they are a constituent part in such a crude, reductionist way, and the case of migration certainly provides us with a clear reminder of these dangers; as such it is a particularly useful focus with which to contextualize theories of belonging. Indeed, many of the weaknesses of the aforementioned usages of identity are particularly evident in discussions of 'migrants', who are frequently referred to as a coherent, internally consistent group. Such reification is incredibly problematic in the case of migrants, who are a hugely diverse group of people divided along at least as many (if not more) lines as any national community (differing in terms of class, gender, ethnicity and so on). In this regard an important broader question concerns the extent to which the overarching – some may say objectifying – status of 'migrant' is inherently a reductionist category. A major problem associated with this tendency is the intentional or unintentional 'othering' of migrants in academic research. Indeed, while identity theory attempts an understanding of how we situate ourselves within the social world, we believe that researchers in this tradition often overlook the vastly complex and contingent nature of individual attachment and belonging. Attempting to theorize such complexities in terms of an undifferentiated 'identity' has ceased to serve even a useful descriptive function; it is vitally important not only to take account of the 'constructed' nature of groups, but also of their frequently dialectic constitution.

Mindful of Brubaker and Cooper's warning about the dangers of 'soft constructivism', we are not positioning identity as an end-state, but rather we are illustrating how constructive and dynamic processes inherent in identity formation can be represented and constituted in a discursive way. If, as we believe, identity is underpinned by a range of fluid processes which are discursively constructed, so the attachments and belongings, we are suggesting, are also (re)constructed and (re)interpreted by actors in a multiplicity of ways. Developing this argument, we can see that as individuals we have huge ranges of affinities and attachments that shape the way we perceive ourselves, and crucially, ourselves in relation to others (collective or otherwise). On this point we should also like to stress the importance of the 'mundane', day-to-day things that feed into ways of belonging. Billig's work shows how populations are reminded of their identities in everyday, seemingly 'banal' ways through the 'waving' of a range of symbolic 'flags' (1995). This idea is useful for present purposes in helping aid our understanding of the nature of attachments, which we are suggesting can operate in a similarly 'banal' way, but considered in their totality such attachments (for example, to food, accents, a place's 'feel' and so on) have significant input into how one defines one's belonging. Of course Billig does not deny the importance of

43

studying the more extreme expressions of nationalism, but he suggests that there exist other, equally pertinent, expressions of nationalism that are routinely 'flagged' every day, in the media and throughout society.[3] Similarly, we are not suggesting that the stronger forms of attachment, pertaining perhaps for example to family, are not significant, but rather that they are part of a repertoire of potentially conflicting attachments and memberships that add up to a sense of belonging (that in turn can be translated by the individual into a collective identity).[4] On this question we agree with Hedetoft's claim that 'attachment and identity, in whatever form, are inconceivable and inexplicable without recourse to a certain measure of irrationality, emotionality, sentiment and unselfish dedication' (2002: 8); Sicakkan and Lithman also further a similar argument when suggesting that '"belonging" makes it possible to include sentimental, cultural, and symbolic dimension in a discussion of what ties a collectivity together' (2005: 8).

Vitally then, belonging can be considered a process whereby an individual in some way feels some sense of association with a group, and as such represents a way to explain the relationship between a personalized identity and a collective one. In a purely conceptual way belonging is about the relationship between personal identity and a collective identity – there is *something* about one's personal belonging that is comparable to one's perception of the aims, constitution or values of a given collective. Clearly such feelings can be more or less transient, but it is precisely because identities are formed in such a way that they should not be conceived of as things that exist prior to, or outside of, social action; it is these positional and relational aspects of identity that we illustrate in the analysis below. As stated above, we feel that the 'unpacking' of identity into a theory of belonging facilitates investigation in specific, researchable contexts, within which individuals have to position themselves in relation to an existing collective or community. With this in mind we show how agency and the constructive processes associated with identity formation can operate in 'concrete' social contexts. Unlike a great deal of identity research, our model is illustrated and developed with empirically grounded research.

The theory of belonging outlined in Figure 2.1 posits that identities are constructed, both 'internally' – by us through our self (re)presentation and alignment with others – and externally – by the powerful 'other', such as institutional gatekeepers who can set threshold criteria for entry to groups

---

3  Interestingly Billig makes the distinction between 'waved and unwaved flags' (1995: 39–43) and suggests that some of the most potent symbols of the nation are 'unwaved'.
4  The relative weight of attachments is clearly a highly subjective thing, and is open to case-specific empirical enquiry.

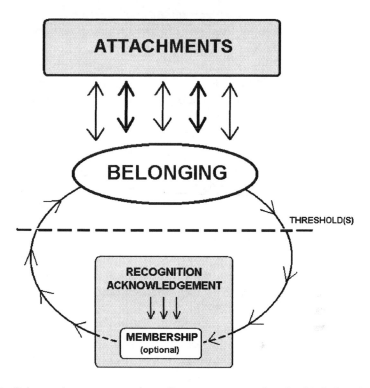

Figure 2.1. Schematic representation of processes associated with belonging

either through membership in a formal sense (such as with citizenship requirements, or in less formal or symbolic 'everyday' ways). This argument is predicated on a point we develop below, which concerns how an individual can end up with a sense of belonging that does not necessarily 'fit' with his or her collective identity – a key consideration in this enquiry is the relationship between personal identity and a collective identity. This model indicates how we take different routes to our collective identities and understand them in very different ways; belonging shows how difference can be incorporated into one group.[5] It is important to stress that belonging is not necessarily based on a distinction from a clearly defined 'other', as is the case to a greater degree with collective identities: on the contrary, individuals often express a sense of

5   EU attempts at developing an official European identity through cultural policy (Shore 2000) can be seen in this light. Attempts to 'celebrate difference', with slogans such as 'unity in diversity', are indicative of attempts to place a multiculturalism based on fixed identities (usually national) at the centre of an emergent EUropean identity (see also Busch and Krzyżanowski 2007).

belonging with an 'other', while remaining outside the bounds of the group. Such an approach helps guard against the reification of collectives while at the same time stressing the multiple and often contradictory nature of attachments that can go together to constitute a belonging (see also Krzyżanowski and Wodak 2007).

By the same token, while belonging can be predicated on relatively essentialized, 'fixed' or given understandings of membership (such as with ethnicities for example) it does not *have* to be. Belonging does not necessarily need to be based on 'objective', external sameness, but rather can be posited on a more fleeting solidarity. New forms of attachment can replace or supplement other forms of attachment, and we believe that the concept of belonging is at the right analytical 'level' to take account of this inherent fluidity. The migrant experience, as far as such an experience can be generalized, is revealing in this context, as collective identities are often be strengthened by dislocation from their (geographical) place of origin, with diasporic communities frequently reinterpreting or even reinventing national traditions in a new social setting (Hesse 2000). For example, cultural ceremonies can often be observed in a more strict fashion in the country that the migrant has moved to then they were/are in the country of origin. The tendency to conceive of the complex processes associated with identity formation in a uni-linear way, with identities either 'created' or 'discovered', overlooks these important questions of exactly how identities are constructed, frequently through contradictory, dialectical processes. However, belonging has to be based, to some extent, on elective attachments; it can only be understood in terms of an individual situating himself or herself in relation to a collective at some point. Of course, as is indicated by the thin arrows linking attachment and belonging, these can be relatively 'weak' attachments (for example, thinking a place would be nice to visit, supporting a sports team from a given city). However, it is important not to discount the importance of such seemingly 'weak' attachments, because they are vital in constructing a feeling of 'belonging', which we are suggesting is fundamental in understanding how individuals become a part of collective identities. The electivity of attachments and the further development of belonging may be seen as running parallel to the process of attitude formation. Teun van Dijk (1984) has made a very useful contribution to this discussion, by showing in his now classic work how the development of attitudes is based on socio-cognitive processes. Referring to 'schema transfer' he shows how an individual can perceive social and cultural groups in a very selective way, which, according to some goals, may be either negative (viz. stereotypes or prejudices) or positive (see also van Dijk 2006).

The development of belonging displays a similar mechanism in which negative information is rejected and positive experiences and views are aggregated so as to build up only positive information on the object of one's belonging while excluding and deleting negative information and experiences which would undermine or distort this positive image. Developing this suggestion we can see that attachments do not always proceed in a clear, linear way; our model takes account of the messy, complex and often contradictory attachments that go towards the make-up of an individual's identity. As suggested above, attachments can be very weak, and can feed into our sense of belonging in a range of ways. Clearly any feasible theory of identity formation must take account of the transient attachments that one can form in the context of social life, related to work, other relationships, cultural consumption and so on. Attachments are based on social action so accordingly are fluid and not fixed.[6] An important theoretical issue that is glossed over by much identity theory is an account of the complex processes that can lead to inclusion in or exclusion from a group, or an 'identity'. We believe our model of belonging has a useful contribution to make in this area, as it allows us to think about how 'thresholds' or 'barriers' to belongings are constructed and reconstructed by members of in- and out-groups. External definitions and elective attachments both play a part in the construction of a belonging. Another related theoretical issue with a great many of the studies on identity is the extent to which they objectify individuals, removing actors' sense of agency by categorizing them with reference to 'objective', external characteristics that take no account of the subtleties and complexities of belonging. Given these assumptions, an important issue is how far the 'other', or external recognition (see also Fraser 1995; Fraser and Honneth 2003; or Taylor 1994), is significant for definitions of one's own belonging.

An important consideration at this point is the extent to which a belonging can be imposed by the other, based solely on their interpretation of how one relates to a collective. Certain aspects of belonging can be imposed by an other (for example see Chapter 11 in this volume by Flam and Beauzamy), but there is also the suggestion in the above model that affiliations, whether weak or strong, can be supplemented by formal attachments of membership. It is important to stress that although aspects of belonging are not necessarily defined by the other, thresholds to belonging clearly do exist at both formal and informal levels. Of course, belonging is to some extent based on an exclusion of the other, but the theoretical model developed in Fig. 2.1

---

6 Of course this is not to say that attachments cannot be relatively stable and consistent over time, just that they are open to change.

illustrates how the extent to which one's belonging can be made up of a combination of elected attachments that sometimes do not need validation or endorsement by the 'in-group'. At this level belonging is, in part at least, dependent on someone making a 'choice' that they want to be included in, or align themselves with, a collective. It is important to separate these feelings from formal 'memberships'; the example of citizenship illustrates this point well, as it is not always synonymous with one's national identity. Indeed, many of the migrants who participated in the research highlighted elsewhere in this volume made a clear (discursive) distinction between their national identity – as a collection of loosely understood cultural practices, beliefs and so on – and their citizenship – the formal expression of political membership. Relatedly there is also a great deal of literature within globalization research that focuses on the related question of transnational associations beyond the physical and political borders of the nation-state (see for example Fortier 2000; Hedetoft 2003).

In fact Hedetoft has developed a framework on belonging similar to ours, but aims to assess the prospects for national identities in the context of the increasingly interconnected societies associated with globalization (2003: 13–32). However, Hedetoft's framework outlines a more 'fixed' notion of belonging than the one to which we subscribe, with his idea of belonging perhaps closer to traditional understandings of identity than is ours. For him belonging can be understood to do with sources (locality and familiarity), feelings (socio-psychological needs), constructions (e.g. nationalisms and racisms), and fluidity (globality cosmopolitanism) (2003). We depart from Hedetoft's definition primarily because we suggest that the fluidity can be in evidence in one 'coherent' identity, with individuals and even 'collectives' harbouring not only multiple attachments (to more than one nation, to more than one cause) but also sometimes (seemingly) mutually exclusive belongings. We would like to argue that identity can be and frequently is based on contradictory foundations of belongings. Whereas Hedetoft argues, relating to the sources of belonging, that 'belonging is conditioned by social and psychological concreteness… [t]hese are the materials, the building blocks of belonging' (2002: 3) we would rather suggest that there are many different attachments and memberships that feed into any emergent belonging (see Fig. 2.1). Membership can be understood as the more formalized requirements of such links, which – when relating to membership – can be formal, or less so relative to attachments.

So, even given the primarily elective nature of such belongings, clearly there can be many barriers to any belonging predicated on unvalidated attachments. Individuals frequently aspire to be a part of a collective, and interpret their own experience through the 'lens' of a (perceived) common frame of reference (for example, as a 'woman', as 'working class', as 'black'). It is clear that this self-understanding has to be, at some level at least, in line with the definition of that individual by the group. It is here that we need to examine the notion of *thresholds* (see Bauböck 1994) or barriers to full belonging to a community or collective identity. Such constraints can be normative, politically regulated areas of membership (for example, citizenship).[7] The extent to which thresholds are established is contingent on the 'rules' of entry – formal or otherwise. At some level belonging needs to be supplemented and recognized by the 'others', those who already belong to the group to which one aspires; denial of recognition can lead to exclusions and discriminations (see Reisigl and Wodak, 2001). In keeping with our general argument we believe that the level at which these thresholds operate is to be tested empirically. The Nationality, Immigration and Asylum Act 2002 in the UK clarified the 'threshold' for British citizenship, with applicants now required to sit a language test to demonstrate that they have sufficient language skills in English, Welsh or Scottish Gaelic.[8] Frequently these memberships are codified by cultural artefacts, such as for example passports, with the attainment of these artefacts more dependent on meeting formalized criteria of membership. Membership clearly introduces the issue of external constraints on one's self-definition. Of course, even those who are members can be differentiated by 'level' of membership ('full' or 'partial' citizenships),[9] and this further underlines the point that differences exist within collectives that are frequently presented as coherent and stable 'identities'.

Our model also allows us to theorize about the transformation of 'host' communities. It should be clear that we are not speaking about the kind of one-way process of assimilating migrants into the 'national culture' (whatever that means) of the 'host' society. Obviously as collective identities are transformed, so an individual's positional relation to the collective shifts. For

---

7   Frequently in the modern age it was in the interests of states to define identities of both self and other in coherent, bounded ways to allow for a mobilization against the other when politically expedient.

8   These language requirements may be waived on grounds of age or physical or mental condition. Exactly what level of competence is needed to pass such a test has been a matter of some debate. Home Office minister Beverley Hughes claims, for example, that 'sufficient' is enough linguistic ability to 'sustain unskilled employment'. This new language requirement is part of other measures in this act that have become widely referred to as the 'Britishness test', which also requires applicants for citizenship to be familiar with other aspects of 'British culture', in itself a highly contested concept. See David Ian Haneur's contribution in this volume (chapter 10) for a more detailed analysis of this policy.

9   As Sicakkan and Lithman point out (2005), the English language distinguishes between citizens and nationals – a discursive way of denoting membership and belonging.

example Tariq Modood has highlighted the fluid nature of national identities when addressing the question of how desirable it is for migrant communities to incorporate themselves into the ongoing construction of 'Britishness' (Modood 2000). From a similar perspective Maurice Roche has suggested that the internal fragmentation of national identities in a European context requires nations to 'periodically and profoundly, re-identify, make explicit and reaffirm their "common cultures" … to recognize the new "common conditions" and "ways of life" produced by culturalism, pluralism, co-existence and hybridization' (2001: 78). At an abstract level, then, actors can redefine or reappropriate collective identities in a way that facilitates their belonging, or not, as the case may be.

This scheme of belonging then provides a way for us to understand how internal(ized) process of belonging and the processes which exist outside the self (for example, why this group allows entry or not) can combine in multiple, complex ways. Denial of membership (for example, citizenship as symbolized by a passport or by papers) can clearly have significant effects not on the way in which an individual understands his/her personal identity, but vitally in how he/she *links* this personal identity to a collective. The logical extension of our argument is that it is foreseeable that people with very similar, developed forms of attachments, while sharing similar situation, background and conditions could develop entirely different senses of belonging. At some level belonging is a way of describing how individuals interpret a huge range of imagined and lived attachments and memberships. 'Identity' refers to the ways in which people link their complex range of belonging into an 'ideal-type' situation, in which all the multiple differences are incorporated into a collective identity, which can be seen as a proxy of infinitely complicated belongings. We conceptualize identity as a way in which individuals explain their complex belonging in a way that is understandable to others. Following on from this point, one of our main contentions is that collective identities represent an approximate translation of the infinitely complex, personalized and idiosyncratic belongings that are held by every individual. We believe our conception allows for a more 'researchable' model, which is especially important when attempting understanding of the very complex, myriad forms of belongings held by many migrants.

Indeed, in acknowledging these subtleties it is imperative that any theoretical model should support further empirical enquiry in the reflexive and context-sensitive way that Sicakkan and Lithman suggest is vital. Belonging allows for a more thorough assessment of how we define the 'self' in relation to (potential) 'others' – how far do we want to align ourselves with a given group? Some theorists have spoken of this process in terms of *identification* (Brubaker and Cooper 2000; Hall 1996; Hedetoft 2003; Rewers 2000), which involves a stronger emphasis on the object one is identifying with. The strongly positional basis of identification is emphasized in the work of Ewa Rewers, who has suggested that, although dynamic, identity is the outcome of other, constructive processes of identification that seldom lead to a 'full' identity. Rewers distinguishes between the two basic conceptions of identification. In the first one, identification takes place only on the basis of identifying oneself with someone/something else; such a conception does not allow one to sustain the already possessed identity, but only to identify with the new, 'other' identity. Such identification is characterized by 'uncertainty about still not being what one wants to become' (2000: 86),[10] and, in this process of identification, the return to the previous state, to the original 'self-identity', is impossible. On the other hand, in the second conception of identification, to identify oneself means 'to answer the question: with whom/what one can identify in order to emphasize one's own identity' (Rewers 2000: 87). Of course identification does not undermine the fact that identity is constructive and does not presuppose any essentialist visions.[11]

## Conclusions: Belonging in/and Discourse

It is certainly the case that '[t]he language of both politics and everyday life, to be sure, is rigorously categorical, dividing the population into mutually exclusive ethno-national categories, and making no allowance for mixed or ambiguous forms' (Brubaker and Cooper 2000: 27). However, not only do such categories both construct and maintain the exclusionary discourses directed towards migrants and other groups, they also fundamentally misunderstand the nature of social life by imposing overly strict delineations on groups. It is regrettable that many academic researchers have – in effect – served to maintain these 'mutually exclusive' categories, and we have argued that seeking to explain all the multiple, complex and contradictory associations that emerge from social action in terms of 'identity' only serves to cloud what is an already very complicated and nuanced terrain. Thus, we advance the concept of *belonging* as part of a differentiated theoretical language that we hope will help to advance theoretical discussion while

---

10 Our translation.
11 This, of course, is not the same as saying that they do not exist. It is clear that many feel their identities to be 'real' regardless of the fact that they were demonstrably constructed by agency at a definite historical juncture. A mistake that is often made with the interpretation of Anderson's work is to equate 'imagined' with 'false'; Anderson's central argument is that identities based around communities exist primarily in the imagination (1991).

providing a workable model on which to base empirical research into the question of identity. The concept of belonging allows a degree of methodological rigour within context-sensitive and empirically founded models of research. Since our model pertains chiefly, though not exclusively, to constructions of belonging in discourse, we have been able to achieve the previously elaborated 'conceptual unpacking' of the concept of identity, which, in turn, allows for the multiple, highly complex processes associated with identity construction to be revealed, analysed and scrutinized.

If, as we believe, identity is underpinned by a range of processes that are reproduced and/or sustained through a range of social practices, we can see that as individuals we have huge ranges of affinities and attachments that shape the way we perceive ourselves, and crucially, ourselves in relation to others (collective or otherwise). All those perceptions must be seen as inherently rooted in discourses of belonging/non-belonging which both create our social location and milieu, and are subsequently reproduced by discourses we produce ourselves as members or citizens, viz. as those belonging or non-belonging. In applying our framework on belonging to the contemporary European perspective, and in particular to migrants' belongings, it is necessary to develop an understanding of how transient, sometimes unclear relationships between self and other contribute to an individual's position vis-à-vis a collective identity. Thus, we have accordingly developed a model that facilitates empirical research into personal and collective identities in a way that rests on theoretically secure foundations, and avoids a retreat to socio-psychological categories traditionally deployed in the study of individual/personal identities. Our theoretical model represents an attempt to bridge a long-standing divide in the research on identity-constructions which have traditionally placed individual identities within the field of enquiry of (social) psychology, leaving 'only' collective identities to be scrutinized and explored within a variety of social sciences.

## References

Anderson, B. (1991) *Imagined Communities*. London: Verso.

Bauböck, R. (1994) *Transnational Citizenship: Membership and Rights in International Migration*. Aldershot: Edward Elgar.

Billig, M. (1995) *Banal Nationalism*. London: Sage.

Brubaker, R., and F. Cooper (2000) 'Beyond "Identity"', *Theory and Society* 29: 1–47.

Busch, B., and M. Krzyżanowski (2007) 'Inside/Outside the European Union: Enlargement, Migration Policies and the Search for Europe's Identity', in J. Anderson and W. Armstrong (eds), *Geopolitics of European Union Enlargement*. London: Routledge, pp. 107–24.

Crowley, J. (1999) 'The Politics of Belonging: Some Theoretical Considerations', in A. Favell and A. Geddes (eds), *The Politics of Belonging: Migrants and Minorities in Contemporary Europe*. Aldershot: Ashgate, pp. 15–41.

Fortier, A. M. (2000) *Migrant Belongings: Memory, Space and Identity*. Oxford: Berg.

Fraser, N. (1995) 'From Redistribution to Recognition: Dilemmas of Justice in a "Post-Socialist" Age', *New Left Review* I/212 (July–August): 68–93.

Fraser, N., and A. Honneth (2003) *Redistribution or Recognition? A Political-Philosophical Exchange*. London/New York: Verso.

Friese, H. (2001) 'Pre-judice and Identity', *Patterns of Prejudice* 35(2): 63–79.

Gleason, P. (1983) 'Identifying Identity: A Semantic History', *Journal of American History* 69(4): 910–31

Hacking, I. (1999) *The Social Construction of What?* Cambridge, MA: Harvard University Press.

Hall, S. (1996) 'Introduction: Who Needs "Identity"?', in S. Hall and P. du Gay (eds), *Questions of Cultural Identity*. London: Sage, pp. 1–17.

Hedetoft, U. (2002) 'Discourses and Images of Belonging: Migrants between "New Racism", Liberal Nationalism and Globalization', *AMID Working Paper Series* 5.

– (2003) *The Global Turn: National Encounters with the World*. Copenhagen: Aalborg University Press.

Hesse, B. (ed.) (2001) *Un/Settled Multiculturalisms: Diasporas, Entanglements, Transruptions*. London: Zed Books.

Krzyżanowski, M., and R. Wodak (2007) 'Multiple/Collective Identities, Migration and Belonging', in C.-R. Caldas-Coulthard and R. Iedema (eds), *Identity Trouble: Critical Discourse and Contestations of Identification*. Basingstoke: Palgrave Macmillan.

Modood, T. (2000) 'Anti-Essentialism, Multiculturalism, and the 'Recognition' of Religious Groups' in W. Kymlicka and W. Norman (eds) *Citizenship in Diverse Societies*. Oxford: Oxford University Press.

Probyn, E. (1996) *Outside Belongings*. New York/London: Routledge.

Reisigl, M. and R. Wodak (2001) *Discourse and Discrimination*. London: Routledge.

Rewers, E. (2000) 'Tozsamosc – utozsamienie – przywlaszczenie', in Z. Drozdowicz and Z. W. Puslecki (eds), *Przezwyciezanie Barier w Integrujacej sie Europie*. Poznań: Humaniora, 81–9.

Roche, M. (2001) 'Citizenship, Popular Culture and Europe', in N. Stevenson (ed.) *Culture and Citizenship*. London: Sage.

Sicakkan, H. G., and Y. Lithman (2005) 'Theorising Citizenship, Identity Politics and Belonging Modes', in H. G. Sicakkan and Y. Lithman (eds) *Changing the Basis of Citizenship in the Modern State: Political Theory and the Politics of Diversity*. New York: Edwin Mellen Press.

Taylor, C. (1994) *Multiculturalism: Examining the Politics of Recognition*, ed. Amy Gutmann. Princeton, NJ: Princeton University Press.

van Dijk, T. A. (1984) *Prejudice in Discourse*. Amsterdam: John Benjamins.

— (2006) 'Discourse, Context and Cognition', *Discourse Studies* 8(1): 159–77.

Waltzer, M. (1990) 'What Does It Mean to Be an American?', *Social Research* 57(3): 591–614.

# 3 'Us' and 'Them': Inclusion and Exclusion – Discrimination via Discourse

## Ruth Wodak

### Introducing Discursive Dimensions of 'Inclusion and Exclusion'

> Racial discrimination includes all acts – verbal, nonverbal, and paraverbal –
> with intended or unintended negative or unfavourable consequences for
> racially or ethnically dominated groups. It is important to see that
> intentionality is not a necessary component of racism.
>
> Essed 1991: 45

Philomena Essed (1991) has captured many aspects of contemporary
discrimination in this quotation: discriminatory acts may manifest themselves
on all levels of language; exclusion is linked to power; marginalized groups
tend to be discriminated against; and discriminatory acts may be intended or
non-intended. Discrimination may be legally legitimized, it may be structural
or it may occur in passing. In her seminal book *Everyday Racism*, Essed
focuses on 'everyday racism' in the Netherlands and in California (1991),
although her definition in its general and broad meaning covers many racist
and discriminatory phenomena, many dimensions of 'inclusion' and
'exclusion'.

Before elaborating on the concepts of inclusion and exclusion – and on their
application to discriminatory practices in the European Union and elsewhere
– it is necessary to state a caveat: one way of looking at discourses of
difference/discrimination is to examine the ways in which minorities or
migrants actually experience racial discrimination in European societies
today. However, such analysis cannot lead us to a causal explanation of racial
inequality, although it will provide relevant knowledge about the many facets
of racial discrimination from the perspective of the marginalized and
vulnerable – that is to say, an *'insider'* perspective (see Krzyżanowski and

Wodak 2007). In this volume we mainly focus on the 'insider perspective' in national, regional and local European contexts, while paying attention to structural conditions as well (see, for example, Chapters 8 and 9 by Burns and Flam).

The other way to proceed is from '*outside*', by investigating public arenas where politics are performed, such as in parliamentary discourses, election campaigns, public speeches, media reporting and so forth. In these cases, we study discourses *about* minorities, frequently embedded in the positive self-presentation of politicians which manifests itself, inter alia, in disclaimers and even in the denial of racism. Thus politicians from mainstream parties usually introduce discriminatory remarks by first presenting themselves in a positive way, for example as liberals, as tolerant and as democratic (see Wodak and Van Dijk 2000; and below). After such 'disclaimers', implicit or explicit discriminatory arguments may follow; often enough, especially in the rhetoric of the mainstream, various arguments and standardized themes which serve as warrants (*topoi*) are employed to justify and legitimize such opinions and beliefs (topoi of numbers, of criminality, of the abuse of social welfare systems, and so forth; see below for a more extensive discussion of arguments and topoi). This rhetoric, which typically includes disclaimers, specific topoi, and justification and legitimation strategies, implies that we are confronted with a gap between self-presentation and other-assessment which can only be bridged in small ways, but never in its entirety. Data triangulation (analysing various data sets and genres which all deal with the same object under investigation; see Cicourel 1974; 2007) allows for multiple perspectives; integrating various theories and methodologies from neighbouring disciplines also serves to differentiate a complex social problem (see Weiss and Wodak 2003).

Hence, we need to approach the processes of 'inclusion/exclusion' by carefully considering issues of power, in defining access *to* discourses and power *in* discourses. The first case relates to institutional/ structural inclusion/exclusion – who has access to which 'orders of discourse', to which genres, contexts, and in which roles? The second dimension concerns situated interaction and the ways dominance is negotiated – through knowledge, institutional roles, language, gender, ethnicity, social class or a combination of all these factors.

In other words, within the system of exclusion, this means that just like other discriminatory practices, discourse may be used to problematize, marginalize, exclude or otherwise limit the human rights of ethnic/religious/ minority out-groups. Moreover, discourses can be employed to legitimize the processes and decisions of the politically powerful and/or the state (see also

Chapter 5 by Lentin in this volume; Van Leeuwen and Wodak 1999). Such may be the case either by direct discriminatory discourse *in* interaction with 'Others', or indirectly by writing or speaking negatively *about* the 'Other'; the media, of course, have a decisive role here (see Van Dijk 2005a; Richardson 2004).

Hence, the starting point of a discourse analytical approach to the complex phenomenon of inclusion and exclusion is to realize that racism, as social action and as ideology, manifests itself discursively: on the one hand, discriminatory opinions, stereotypes, prejudices and beliefs are produced and reproduced by means of discourse, and through discourse, discriminatory exclusionary practices are prepared, implemented, justified and legitimated. On the other hand, discourse offers a space in which to criticize, de-legitimate and argue against racist opinions and practices, that is, to pursue anti-racist strategies (see Chapter 12 by Sawyer with Jones, in this volume).

Van Dijk (1984: 13) focuses on the 'rationalization and justification of discriminatory acts against minority groups' in detail. He labels the categories used to rationalize prejudice against minority groups as 'the 7 D's of Discrimination'. These are dominance, differentiation, distance, diffusion, diversion, depersonalization or destruction, and daily discrimination. These strategies serve in various ways to legitimize and enact the distinction of 'the other', for example, by dominating minority groups, by excluding them from social activities, and even by destroying and murdering them (Van Dijk 1984: 40).

This chapter proposes a framework that links different forms of (discursive) inclusion and exclusion to each other, thus elaborating the above-mentioned seven Ds, discriminatory practices which still hold true in many ways. More specifically, this chapter will focus on the discursive construction of exclusion which might serve any of the seven discriminatory functions. These functions usually appear in specific and context-dependent combinations.

Hence, phenomena that have traditionally been evaluated with different theories can be understood and explained as related to issues of inclusion and exclusion on various grounds. The public management of 'inclusion' and 'exclusion' is to be perceived as a question of 'grading' and 'scales', ranging from explicit legal and economic restrictions to implicit discursive negotiations and decisions. I assume that 'inclusion/exclusion' of groups, people, nation-states, migrant groups, changes due to different criteria of how insiders and outsiders are defined in each instance. In this way, various topologies, or group memberships, are constructed, which sometimes include a certain group, and sometimes do not, depending on socio-political and situational contexts and interactions (Wodak 2007; 2008a; 2008b).

Thus, a specific migrant status (coming from a certain host country) may serve as a criterion for exclusion; sometimes language competence is defined as salient (see Chapter 14 by Martín Rojo in this volume). Sometimes, however, all foreigners are assumed to belong to one single group and are classified as 'migrants or foreigners' although they arrive from different countries, with different motives and goals, with various educational backgrounds, religious and political affiliations, and (gendered) cultural traditions. Right-wing populist rhetoric attempts to merge all foreigners into one homogeneous group, which is subsequently stigmatized as a negative 'other' (Wodak and Pelinka 2002; Rydgren 2005). Sometimes, a specific job qualification may mean inclusion although the respective migrant comes from an otherwise excluded host country; in other cases, religion and gender are regarded as criteria which discriminate against specific groups (see Wodak 2008b, and below). The mere use of certain labels manifests the fluidity of definitions and membership categories; recent research on the British press has illustrated, for example, that the semantic concepts of 'migrant', 'refugee' and 'asylum-seeker' have become conflated and that all of these concepts are used in contemporary media to label all 'foreigners who are not welcome'.

In the following, after briefly defining the central concepts of 'difference'/ 'discrimination'/'racism' and summarizing some important interdisciplinary approaches, I will briefly present some linguistic indicators which have proved salient when analysing discriminatory language behaviour. I will focus on three manifestations of the rhetoric of exclusion while having to neglect the many other expressions of discrimination due to reasons of space:[1] on the *discursive construction of in-groups and out-groups* which relates to strategies of *positive self- and negative other-presentation*; on strategies *of justification and legitimation* of exclusionary practices through argumentative devices; and finally on the *denial of racism* which frequently accompanies and introduces discriminatory rhetoric. Thirdly, I will illustrate these discursive practices with two examples from a recent project which investigates British newspapers over the past ten years in their reporting on 'migrants' and 'asylum-seekers'.[2]

---

1  See Reisigl and Wodak 2001; Richardson 2004; Billig 2006; Van Dijk 2005a, b; Wodak 2008a, b; Chilton 2004 for extensive overviews. In this chapter I can only point to some linguistic manifestations in the brief illustration of exclusionary rhetoric in two examples. I refer readers to the literature referred to above.

2  The project on 'Asylum-Seekers and Migrants in the British Press' was funded by the ESRC (2005–2007). Principal investigators were Paul Baker and Ruth Wodak. The team consisted of Majid Khosravinik, Costas Gabrielatos and Michał Krzyżanowski. This project investigated the representation of asylum-seekers, refugees and migrants in ten years of British press reporting while applying corpus linguistic methods and qualitative critical discourse analysis (see Baker *et al.* 2006; 2008 for details).

## Inclusion/Exclusion – Discrimination, Racism

Rather than 'discrimination', 'difference' or 'racism', I have consciously chosen the concepts of 'inclusion' and 'exclusion' as relevant theoretical notions. All the former terms are heavily contested in the social sciences. For example, due to specific historical, linguistic and social developments, and ideologies, the concept of 'racism' is understood differently in Central Europe than in the US or UK. The radicalized 'race' theory of the German anti-Semites and National Socialists in the tradition of Arthur de Gobineau, Houston Stewart Chamberlain, and Georg Ritter von Schönerer tied together in a syncretic manner the religious, nationalist, economist, culturalist and biologistic racism and anti-Semitism, which then served as the ideology to legitimize systematic, industrialized genocide in the Holocaust. It was this use of 'race theory' 'that stimulated a more thorough critical appraisal of the idea of "race" in Europe and North America and the creation of the concept of racism in the 1930s' (Miles 1993: 29).

Since 1945, use of the term 'race' (*Rasse*) in the German-language countries of Germany and Austria has been strictly tabooed for politicians, for academics, and even for lay people in general. In France, the expression *relations de race* would also be regarded as racist (Wieviorka 1994: 173). Research must therefore take into account these differences in language use, as misinterpretations can lead to difficulties in translation and even to serious mistakes in shaping different analytical categories when dealing with racism (see Wieviorka 1994: 173). I have to neglect a more detailed discussion of the terminology here; suffice to say that this historical semantic tradition also accounts for major methodological difficulties in cross-cultural or cross-national comparison in previous studies (see Reisigl and Wodak 2001 for an extensive discussion).

The study of contemporary exclusion and inclusion is not straightforward and thus necessarily implies qualitative in-depth analysis: the ideological value of 'tolerance' is widespread in contemporary capitalist societies, so that the explicit promulgation of exclusionary politics conflicts with the generally accepted values of liberalism (Billig 1991; Van Dijk 1993; see above). Accordingly, discriminatory utterances tend to be 'coded' in official rhetoric so as to avoid sanctions; linguistic cues – such as insinuations – are frequently only comprehensible to insiders who 'know' what is implied by a given statement (Pelinka and Wodak 2002). Indeed, the very terms 'discrimination', 'exclusion' or 'prejudice' carry negative connotations. Few would admit, either in public or when interviewed, to excluding, being prejudiced towards or discriminating against minority groups. This is why the 'insider' perspective is of such importance as opinion polls and interviews are inherently doomed to fail when investigating racist belief systems (see Marin 2000; Wodak *et al.* 1990): Usually people deny these beliefs and present themselves in a positive, socially acceptable way; they are aware that such opinions are taboo or might even be associated with extremist right-wing political affiliation. Yet, structured inequality continues to exist.

For this reason, the study of exclusionary rhetoric has tended to attract critical analysts, who do not take what people say at face value but seek to examine the – often latent – ideological/discriminatory, complex nature of discourse (Van Dijk 1998). This means studying how discursive practices can accomplish exclusion in its many facets without the explicitly acknowledged intention of actors; exclusion seems to become 'normality' and thus acceptable, integrated into all dimensions of our societies. In some cases, exclusion occurs behind the backs of those who practise it. Alberto Melucci has summarized this phenomenon very clearly (1996: 66):

> Even marginality or exclusion are increasingly defined in terms internal to the system, the 'without' is 'within', the difference is denied and the unbalance of power is made invisible. The master codes tend to include the deprived or the potential opponent as a dependent participant. The traditional ways of dealing with the 'other' consisted in refusing and expelling him/her or, alternatively, resorting to inclusion and assimilation. Today these strategies, still in operation, are losing their effectiveness and are substituted by a growing tendency to set the formal pre-conditions for any discourse and practice, where even the excluded is already incorporated.

Norman Fairclough (2000: 66) also observes this important characteristic of 'social exclusion'. He notes that social exclusion has become part of the system of global capitalism, and that therefore the system has developed discourses and practices to cope with and justify social exclusion. He illustrates his view by analysing the policies of the Social Exclusion Unit set up by the Labour government in the UK in 1997. He concludes that both Social Democracy and Liberalism stress negative conditions rather than causative agencies as being responsible for social exclusion (although Social Democracy stresses redistribution, Liberalism self-transformation as ways of dealing with social exclusion). Such an orientation implies, of course, that a focus on agency and causality would be needed in a critical struggle against social exclusion.

In a similar vein, Niklas Luhmann (1997: 553) emphasizes that a differentiated description and analysis of processes of inclusion and exclusion are still neglected in the social sciences. He defines inclusion and exclusion as the two most important 'meta-distinctions' (*Meta-Unterscheidungen*), because they possess salience in our societies, in ways I have indicated above. Certain social groups lead 'parallel lives'; the social problems transcend the traditional values of justice and democracy. He states that only the people who feel included adhere to the democratic institutions of justice.

The British sociologist Anthony Giddens also points to the importance of the opposition pair 'inclusion/exclusion' (Giddens 2001: 323ff). He prefers the terms 'social exclusion' or 'social inclusion' over other theoretical approaches in sociology such as the concepts of 'class struggle' or 'social strata', defining social exclusion as 'ways in which individuals may become cut off from full involvement in the wider society'. Exclusion can be seen, Giddens continues, in economic, political or social terms. Giddens' choice of these terms could be seen as related to the policies of 'New Labour' adequately described above by Fairclough (2000) because Giddens was one of the major 'architects' of New Labour's political programmes.

In all cases, I claim, exclusion means *deprivation of access* through means of explicit or symbolic power (in Bourdieu's sense – see Chapter 11 by Flam and Beauzamy in this volume, which develops this perspective) implemented by the social elites: access to participation, citizenship, the media, information, language learning, power positions, important organizations, jobs, housing, education and so on.[3] Powerful elites frequently justify such exclusion in various ways; reference is made to status, belonging, ethnicity or gender, explicitly or implicitly, by discursively creating ever-new topologies. The modern and global form of 'inclusion' and 'exclusion' can be clearly and most acutely symbolized by somebody having or not having a 'passport' to enter countries of their choice. Hence, acquisition of citizenship becomes the legal means for inclusion, which, however, does not guarantee that migrants or refugees become accepted members of the respective host country when they actually have legally become citizens (see Chapter 2 by Jones and Krzyżanowski in this volume).

All nation-states practice policies of exclusion with respect to citizenship (Busch and Krzyżanowski 2007). In general, we can perceive nation-states as 'imagined communities' (Anderson 1985), which are (re)produced in everyday lives by banal forms of nationalism (Billig 1995; Wodak *et al.* 1999). This banal nationalism, for example, constantly uses specific forms of

---

3   Richardson (2004) has illustrated this exclusionary tendency and the problems of access by studying the representation of Muslims in the British media.

*deixis*[4] in newspapers, political discourse, news reports and so on, so that 'here' is assumed to be the national homeland and 'us' by inference the members of the imagined national community. The banal nationalism of nation-states is vague about who exactly 'we' are: sometimes the particular 'we' of the nation means the general 'we' of all 'reasonable people' (Billig 1995), in other cases the 'we' is very clearly defined and restricted to certain groups and group membership. However, nation-states also possess laws that enable discrimination to be practised with precision: Typically, as already hinted at above, nation-states will have laws that discriminate between those who are permitted citizenship of the state and those who are not. Similarly, they will have laws which grant residency to some non-citizens but not others, and now often linked to language tests (see De Cillia and Wodak 2006; Wodak 2007; Chapter 10 by Hanauer in this volume).

For the aforementioned theorists, inclusion/exclusion involves the control by gatekeepers over temporal and spatial processes – related to power and ideologies. Someone who is excluded now might be included tomorrow, and vice versa. Neither inclusion nor exclusion in our societies can or should be seen as static phenomena. Building on the theoretical approaches briefly summarized above, I propose the following definition of processes of inclusion and exclusion: 'inclusion' and 'exclusion' are to be understood as the fundamental construction of 'in-groups' and 'out-groups' in various public spaces, structurally and discursively, as the basis for, and with varying impact on conflicts, integration, negotiation, decision-making and the genesis of racism and anti-Semitism. These in-groups and out-groups may differ for the EU member states (historically and politically) and for different public spaces, such as media reporting, laws, access to positions, to policies, schools, housing, language, citizenship and so on – in sum, in relation to participation on all levels of society.

---

4   In pragmatics and linguistics, *deixis* (Greek for 'display, demonstration, or reference') is a process whereby expressions rely absolutely on context. The 'origo' is the context from which the reference is made —in other words, the viewpoint that must be understood in order to interpret the utterance. A word that depends on deictic clues is called a 'deictic' or a 'deictic word'. Pro-forms are generally considered to be deictics, but a finer distinction is often made between grammatical person/personal pro-forms such as 'I', 'you' and 'it', and pro-forms that refer to places and times such as 'now', 'then', 'here', 'there'. In most texts, the term 'deictic' implies the latter but not necessarily the former. (In philosophical logic, the former and latter are collectively called 'indexicals'.) In the context of 'inclusion/exclusion', deictic units are frequently used to construct boundaries and groups (inside/outside; us/them).

## The Discursive Construction of 'Us' and 'Them': Positive Self- and Negative Other-Presentation

According to Reisigl and Wodak (2001: 1), racism/discrimination/exclusion manifests itself discursively: 'racist opinions and beliefs are produced and reproduced by means of discourse... through discourse, discriminatory exclusionary practices are prepared, promulgated and legitimized'. Wetherell and Potter present a similar definition (1992: 4):

> [we] are not wanting to argue that racism is a simple matter of linguistic practice. Investigations of racism must also focus on institutional practices, on discriminatory actions and on social structures and social divisions. But the study of these things is intertwined with the study of discourse. Our emphasis will be on ways in which a society gives voice to racism and how forms of discourse institute, solidify, change, create and reproduce social formations.

Hence, the strategic use of many linguistic indictors to construct in- and out-groups is fundamental to political (and discriminatory) discourses in all settings. It is important to focus the latent meanings produced through pragmatic devices, such as implicatures, hidden causalities, presuppositions, insinuations and certain syntactic embeddings, as frequently manifest in the rhetoric of right-wing populist European politicians, such as Jörg Haider, Jean-Marie Le Pen or Silvio Berlusconi (see Rydgren 2005; Wodak and Pelinka 2002).

Haider's construction of rigid boundaries, for example, through implicit linguistic means was and is one of the reasons for his persuasive demagogic success. Through such discursive boundaries, 'others', be they foreigners, migrants or Jews, are excluded, as they are not 'real Austrians'. To analyse exclusion, therefore, it is necessary to examine those discursive practices in detail that promote and produce it (see Wodak and Iedema 2004)

The construction of in- and out-groups necessarily implies the use of strategies of positive self-presentation and negative presentation of others.[5] I am especially interested in five types of discursive strategies, which are all involved in positive self- and negative other-presentation. These discursive strategies underpin the justification/legitimization of inclusion/exclusion and of constructions of collective identities. 'Strategy' generally means a (more or

---

5    Here, I draw on the discourse-historical approach in critical discourse analysis, best summarized in Reisigl and Wodak (2001), which was first developed to study anti-Semitic rhetoric in post-war Austria (Wodak *et al.* 1990). Since then, this approach has been elaborated in a number of studies (see also Wodak and Krzyżanowski forthcoming).

less accurate and more or less intentional) plan of practices, including discursive practices, adopted to achieve a particular social, political, psychological or linguistic goal.[6]

First, there are *referential strategies* or *nomination strategies* by which one constructs and represents *social actors*, for example, in-groups and out-groups. This is done in a number of ways: membership categorization devices, including metaphors and metonymies, and synecdoches in the form of a part standing for the whole (*pars pro toto*) or a whole standing for the part (*totum pro parte*) are most relevant. Secondly, social actors as individuals, group members or groups as a whole, are linguistically characterized through *predications*. Predicational strategies may, for example, be realized as evaluative attributions of negative and positive traits in the linguistic form of implicit or explicit predicates. These strategies aim at labelling social actors more or less positively or negatively. They cannot be separated neatly from the nomination strategies.

Third, there are *argumentation strategies* and a fund of *topoi* through which positive and negative attributions are justified. For example, it can be suggested that the social and political inclusion or exclusion of persons or policies is legitimate. Fourth, one may focus on the *perspectivation*, framing or discourse representation by means of which speakers express their involvement in discourse, and position their point of view in the reporting, description, narration or quotation of relevant events or utterances. Fifth, there are *intensifying strategies* on the one hand and *mitigation strategies* on the other. Both of them help to qualify and modify the epistemic status of a proposition by intensifying or mitigating the illocutionary force of utterances. These strategies can be an important aspect of the utterance inasmuch as they operate upon it by sharpening it or toning it down.

Positive self- and negative other-presentation requires justification and legitimation strategies. Reisigl and Wodak (2001) define *topoi* as parts of argumentation which belong to the obligatory, either explicit or inferable premises. Topoi are the content-related warrants or 'conclusion rules' which connect the argument or arguments with the conclusion, the claim. As such they enable and justify the transition from the argument or arguments to the conclusion. Topoi are central to the analysis of seemingly convincing fallacious arguments which are widely adopted in prejudiced and discriminatory discourses (Kienpointner 1996: 562). The list below consists

---

6  All these strategies are illustrated by numerous categories and examples in Reisigl and Wodak (2001: 31–90). It would be impossible owing to space restrictions to present all these linguistic devices in this paper.

of the most common topoi which are used when writing or talking about 'others', specifically about migrants. These topoi have been investigated in a number of studies on election campaigns (Pelinka and Wodak 2002), on parliamentary debates (Wodak and Van Dijk 2000), on policy papers (Reisigl and Wodak 2001), and on media reporting (see below). Most of them are used to justify exclusion of migrants by quasi-rational fallacious arguments ('they are a burden on our society', 'they are dangerous, a threat', 'they cost too much', 'their culture is too different' and so forth). In this way, migrants are constructed as scapegoats, they are blamed for unemployment or for causing general dissatisfaction (with politics, with the European Union), for abusing social welfare systems or are more generally perceived as a threat to 'our' culture. On the other hand, some topoi are used in anti-discriminatory discourses, such as in appeals to Human Rights or to justice.

*Prevailing Topoi in Debates about Immigration*
1. Usefulness, advantage
2. Uselessness, disadvantage
3. Definition, name-interpretation
4. Danger and threat
5. Humanitarianism
6. Justice
7. Responsibility
8. Burdening, weighting
9. Finances
10. Reality
11. Numbers
12. Law and right
13. History
14. Culture
15. Abuse.

Similarly there is a more or less fixed set of metaphors employed in exclusionary discourse (Reisigl and Wodak 2001), such as 'migration as natural disaster', migration/migrants as 'avalanches or flood', illegal migration as 'dragging or hauling' and so forth.

Furthermore, Reisigl and Wodak (2001) draw on Van Eemeren and Grootendorst (1992, 1994) and Kienpointner (1996) when providing the list of general common fallacies, which serve transporting prejudices and thus construct exclusion. This list includes, among others, the following very frequently employed argumentative devices: *argumentum ad baculum*, which consists in 'threatening with the stick', thus trying to intimidate the opponent by using plausible arguments; the *argumentum ad hominem*, which can be defined as a verbal attack on the antagonist's personality and character (of his/her credibility, integrity, honesty, expertise, competence); and finally, the *argumentum ad populum* or *pathetic fallacy* which consists of the appeal to prejudiced emotions, opinions and convictions of a specific social group or to the *vox populi* instead of employing rational arguments. These fallacies frequently prevail in right-wing populist rhetoric (see Rydgren 2005).

## The Denial of Racism

Linked to positive self-presentation and the construction of positive group and collective identities is the denial of racism. Recall the well-known examples such as 'I have nothing against…, but', 'my best friends are…, but', 'we are tolerant, but', 'we would like to help, but'. All these discursive utterances, labelled as 'disclaimers', manifest the 'denial of racism or exclusion' and emphasize positive self-presentation (Van Dijk 1989; Wodak *et al.* 1990). By and large, speakers in such debates seek to justify the practices of exclusion without employing the related overt rhetoric. 'Prejudice' is to be denied or mitigated, as speakers claim for themselves an ethos of reasonableness. Hence, those who wish to criticize out-groups employ variants of the rhetorical device 'I'm not prejudiced but' (Wodak and Van Dijk 2000; Rojo-Martín and Van Dijk 1997).

Such an overt denial of prejudice basically involves two assumptions. First, it assumes the existence of 'real' prejudice. In this regard, the existence of extreme, outwardly fascist groups enables defenders of mainstream racism/ exclusion/discrimination to present their own rhetoric as being unprejudiced – by comparison. Second, speakers, in denying prejudice, will claim that their criticisms of minority group members are 'factual', 'objective' and 'reasonable', rather than being based upon irrational feeling, and will employ specific discursive strategies of legitimization accordingly (Van Leeuwen and Wodak 1999). Speakers can use similar denials of prejudice and arguments of reasonableness when talking about different forms of discrimination, such as sexism, racism, anti-Semitism or religious discrimination. Additionally, each type of exclusionary practice will integrate particular themes, stereotypes and argumentative devices (*topoi*), contributing to the syncretic nature of mainstream discriminatory discourses.

### Justification and Legitimation Discourses – The Quasi-Logic of Exclusionary Argumentation

In debates about migration and diversity or in media reporting, speakers/writers will often employ arguments about 'culture', depicting it as an essentially bounded entity whose integrity is threatened by the presence of residents supposedly belonging to a different 'culture' and not being willing to learn and adopt 'our' conventions and norms, or assimilate (see Richardson 2004); in these argumentative sequences, deictic elements acquire salience (see above). In this vein, Blommaert (2001) addresses the explicit inequality in the process of asylum application in Belgium, where the asylum seeker's narrative competence plays a decisive role and often does not adhere to expectations of cultural capital in the host country (see also Bourdieu 1999). The narrative that an asylum-seeker provides of his/her life story obviously presents the crucial source for bureaucratic decision-making. Blommaert discusses the role of such narratives as a localizing discourse and investigates the many miscommunications involved (2001: 414):

> My aim in this article is to document and discuss autobiographical stories told by African asylum seekers in Belgium ... Without resources to the long and detailed narratives about home, escape and travelling, asylum seekers cannot make their motives and causes for seeking asylum fully understood ... the problem I wish to address through an analysis of these stories is that of narrative inequality in the context of asylum applications in Belgium. The asylum procedure involves a complex set of discursive practices and language ideologies that are, in practice, being used as criteria for 'truth', 'trustworthiness' 'coherence' and 'consistency'. Such discursive practices require access to communicative resources that are often far beyond the reach of African asylum seekers not only linguistically but also normatively and stylistically.

He detects two main sources of inequality. The first one presupposes that the clients of an administrative procedure in a democratic society such as Belgium have control over the basic linguistic-communicative resources needed to participate fully in the procedures and thus to obtain justice and the benefits they are entitled to. This side of the problem could be argued to be a technical problem and could be tackled, for instance, by training programmes for interpreters.

The reason why power asymmetries and conflicts are invisible is, as Blommaert claims, their embeddedness in administrative procedures that are normalized for members of the autochthonous middle class. This observation leads us back to the assumptions about gate-keepers who regulate access, thus have 'power over discourse', and enforce dominant discourses (this is the second source of inequality). If migrants do not know the 'rules of the game', they are excluded from access. In such an arrangement every political crisis caused by incidents with asylum-seekers results in reaffirming the faith in 'our justice' and leads to a tightening and increase of the sophistication of the administrative procedure. Hence, more people should be hired and trained, the procedure should be accelerated, and handwritten documents should be replaced by computerized standard forms. The administrative text-making machinery is never questioned; on the contrary it is reinforced and enlarged.

Through this procedural shift of information from the context of person to person interaction to computerized forms another disciplining authority (in Foucault's sense) is developed, and with it the power asymmetry with regard to the production, treatment, ordering, and making sense of the migrants' narratives increases. Blommaert argues that such a shift is paramount in modern societies in different degrees based on the domains of social practice and that people and subjects are constructed, cases are judged and individual lives are being influenced based on second-hand narratives, their selection, their recontextualization and reformulation, and – most importantly – their interpretation and evaluation (2001: 446):

> As soon as we enter worlds in which talk and written text are seen as replicas of one another (and in which someone else's notes of what is said can be offered to me as 'my' story), we enter a world of differential power relations, which needs to be scrutinized in great detail ... The apparently small shifts our stories undergo as soon as they enter institutional text-making systems are instances of such practices of Foucauldian *savoir* in which social issues become individual yet standardized 'cases'.

Debates about migration and nationhood are also – as already mentioned above – crucially linked to assumptions about place, the second deictic dimension. 'Our' culture belongs 'here' within the bounded homeland, whilst the culture of 'foreigners' belongs 'elsewhere' (topos of culture; Billig 2006). The theme of place is particularly threatening to groups who are perceived to have no 'natural' homeland, such as the Romanies or other diasporic communities today (see Chapter 7 by Bellier in this volume) or the Jews in the first half of the twentieth century. Religion as a central condition for inclusion/exclusion, frequently triggered by indexical markers such as the 'headscarf' worn by Muslim women, has become dominant in some EU countries only in recent years (see Chapter 4 by Delanty in this volume).

Essed (1991) provides another example of the way that discursive

67

justificatory discourses and subsequent interactions can result in exclusion without conscious intention while analysing typical patterns of everyday racism. She examined interviews for a high-ranking civil service post in the Netherlands. The interviewer was a white male. In one interview the applicant was a well-qualified black woman. The interviewer began asking a series of questions that reflected his assumptions, or stereotypes, about black women. The interview did not run smoothly and the interviewer, judging that the candidate had not performed well, did not recommend appointment. The interviewer seemed unaware of the extent to which his questioning had produced in an almost self-fulfilling way the context in which the black female candidate was seen to perform less 'adequately'. No doubt, if challenged, he would have certainly denied any intentional exclusion due to stereotypes or prejudiced beliefs (see also Van Dijk 1993).

Similar observations were made by Van Leeuwen and Wodak (1999) when analysing official rejection letters from the magistrate of the city of Vienna, refusing 'family reunion', that is to say, rejecting applications of migrants who had already settled in the host country to have their families come and join them. In the latter case, a number of moral and rational legitimations were employed to justify exclusion by referring to statistics or to moral values (ethics, humanitarism, religion). The topos of culture was particularly salient in this case.

In sum, Billig (2006) suggests that such rhetoric points to four crucial factors about institutional discrimination and exclusion: (i) exclusionary practices typically occur in situations of differential power; (ii) the powerful actors need not possess a conscious goal or intention, indeed, they may deny that any discrimination/exclusion has occurred; (iii) the powerful actors are likely to consider their own actions 'reasonable' and 'natural', and justify them; (iv) the actions that lead to exclusion are typically conducted through 'coded' language and very seldom use overt exclusionary language.

## Perceptions and Constructions of Inclusion and Exclusion

*Some Examples from Recent Political Rhetoric*
The terms 'inclusion/exclusion' are also commonly used inside the European Union (EU), albeit with a different meaning. They were introduced by the so-called Eurocrats (bureaucrats employed in the European Commission). The European Commission, for example, has used the term 'inclusive society' in several documents since the late 1990s: the *Report on Education* from the Portuguese presidency (2001) and in the *White Book on the Cognitive Society*, September 2001. The *White Paper on European Governance* from July 2001

considers the 'opening' of European society as one of its most important goals.

The perception of a democratic deficit (to be regarded as one of, if not *the* typical and often-cited symptom of exclusion from EU policy and decision-making) was first noted in the *White Paper on European Governance* (Commission 2001). The document states that there is a 'widening gulf between the European Union and the people it serves' created by a perceived inability to act even when a clear case exists; when it does act it does not get credit for this, and when things go wrong 'Brussels is too easily blamed by Member States for difficult decisions that they themselves have agreed to or even requested'; that many people simply do not understand the mechanisms of the institutions; and all these factors lead to 'a lack of trust and disenchantment' (Commission 2001: 7–8). This analysis of the situation suggests that there are a number of democratic deficits including ones of knowledge, communication and trust, as well as a 'closeness' deficit, and that they are (i) not entirely of the EU's own making and (ii) not always fair.

The results of the referenda on the European Constitution in France and the Netherlands in May/June 2005 might be explained partially by the 'democratic deficit' and emphasize Euro-scepticism even more strongly. Other interpretations of these election results state that primarily internal French and Dutch governmental policies were the main cause of the election outcomes. Nevertheless, it is possible to state that the EU is in a state of crisis, because of the 'democratic deficit', i.e. the exclusion of European citizens from decision-making processes. Furthermore, the rise of right-wing populist parties in several countries in the European Union (for example, in Austria, Denmark, Italy, France, Poland, Belgium, Hungary and Bulgaria) can certainly be explained by EU-scepticism and the impact of exclusionary rhetoric which emphasizes 'inclusion' and 'exclusion' – migrants frequently serve as scapegoats in such discourses, the topoi of danger and threat seem ubiquitous (Rydgren 2005; Wodak and Pelinka 2002). Of course, there are many other reasons for the success of such parties as well, which are specific for each nation-state.

In this European context, 'social exclusion' is perceived to be linked to and often caused by poverty and unemployment: The riots in Bradford and elsewhere in the summer of 2001 (or in Paris in 2006 and 2007), for example, have demonstrated that violence from 'within', and mobilized by extremist rightwing parties such as the BNP, is possible as soon as 'parallel lives' exist (in Luhmann's sense as mentioned above). Different groups of our societies, such as unemployed youth and ethnic groups, are excluded economically and/ or educationally, and cannot participate in any mainstream activities at all. Such acutely experienced exclusion is bound to cause huge discontent, social fragmentation and the search for other means to survive. Many mainstream politicians have not succeeded in mediating such complex, often globally caused, problems and issues in a way that is comprehensible to their electorate. Simple answers, which necessarily imply the use of dichotomies – such as between the 'good guys' and 'the bad guys', the 'real Austrians, French etc.' and 'foreigners or others' or between 'those up there' and the 'man/woman in the street' – seem more persuasive and lead the to the above described exclusionary rhetoric. It thus seems much easier, obviously, to blame migrants for causing all these problems.

### Two Brief Examples from Media Reporting

The latter rhetoric relates well to some election slogans during the national election campaign in the UK in spring 2005. During this campaign, the Conservative party used linguistic devices similar to those of other European right-wing parties, in 'playing the race card' in its attempt to polarize and win voters. In a quite unusual genre for politicians – an open letter published in the *Daily Telegraph*, Sunday 23 January 2005 – Michael Howard, leader of the Conservative Party, employed a cleverly constructed exclusionary discourse (I reproduce a relevant part of this letter in the following):

### Extract 1

A Conservative government will set an annual limit on immigration and a quota for asylum seekers. We will put in place 24-hour security at ports to prevent illegal immigration. We will introduce an Australian-style points system for work permits – giving priority to people with the skills Britain needs. These policies will reduce immigration.

Some people say this is racist. It's not. It is common sense. Britain has always offered a home to genuine refugees and to families who want to work hard. I know – my family was one of them. We are a more successful country as a result.

But Britain has reached a turning point. Our communities cannot absorb newcomers at today's pace. Immigration must be brought under control. It is essential for good community relations, national security and the management of public services.

Without being able to go into all the argumentative and linguistic details, it is important to point to three salient exclusionary devices:

Mentioning refugees (asylum-seekers) and migrants throughout the letter in the same breath marks both groups as belonging together or even establishing and constructing them discursively as the same; such a semantic merger – of the concepts of asylum and migration – makes it easy, in a next step, to demand restrictions for both groups (referential and predicational strategies).

Moreover, a third group is discursively constructed: illegal migrants/illegal asylum-seekers [*sic*] who are presented as dangerous for the country, the economy and the communities. A fourth group is the group of 'real asylum seekers and migrants' where Howard uses the *argumentum ad exemplum* and the *topos of definition*, namely his own case as a positive example, leaving it unclear and unspecified whether his family was actually seeking asylum or came as migrants. His own case serves as *topos of authority*: referring to his own experience, Howard claims to be able to distinguish salient groups of 'Us' and 'Them', between the legal and illegal migrants, the real asylum-seekers and the illegal asylum-seekers. Moreover, this strategy contributes to the *positive self-presentation* of the Conservative Party – as a party responsible for the security and well-being of British citizens.

Secondly, it is important to point to the concept of 'community' used in this short letter, related to a restricted definition of the in-group, thus employing spatial deixis. Thirdly, the appeal to common sense (*argumentum ad populum*) is worth mentioning, a discursive pattern common to all populist political discourses and used to construct identification through an 'inclusive we'. Throughout the letter, the *denial of racism* is also apparent as a strategic device, as are the *topoi of responsibility and security*.

In a recent project on the reporting on migrants and asylum seekers in the British press (1995–2005), Baker, Wodak, Khosravinik and Gabrieletos (2006, 2008) have been able to detect the above mentioned tendency of merging the semantic concepts of 'migrants' and 'asylum-seekers' across the spectrum of the investigated media. I reproduce one example from *The Guardian*, a liberal, high quality newspaper, which illustrates the manifold use of the terms under consideration (3 September 2001, p. 17) (without being able to provide the detailed analysis due to space restrictions):

*Extract 2*

HEADLINE: Leading article: Tunnel escape routes: Asylum needs a European approach

BODY: There can be few more notorious examples of the way European nations 'pass the parcel' in handling asylum seekers than events in the Channel tunnel in the last five days. When 44 asylum seekers were caught six miles into the tunnel, they were detained and interviewed by the French police but then let go rather than prosecuted. Asked why this had happened, the French police said that as they had been unable to find an interpreter, they had been unable to continue with proceedings against them. In reality, French prosecutors have been systematically refusing to press charges against illegal migrants caught in the Calais docks or tunnel entrance.

Eurotunnel, which from October will face £2,000 fines for every asylum seeker who slips through, rightly complains that it is a transport company, not a frontier control point. But the principle of requiring carriers to act as immigration officers is now over a decade old. Lorries, ferries and airlines have all been penalised. Indeed, one reason why asylum seekers have turned to the tunnel, is because of the more effective security at the port. Eurotunnel is now calling for the closure of the Red Cross refugee camp at Sangatte, close to the tunnel and port. But the camp is a symptom, not a cause. The asylum seekers were there before the camp was opened – sleeping in parks or on pavements – and would remain there after closure.

There is only one way to stop France turning a blind eye to illegal refugees and that is a common European approach. European Union member states in the Schengen group do have a common policy but UK, Ireland and Denmark opted out. Now, thankfully, the European Commission, which is more liberal than member governments, is working on a directive to improve harmonisation. This is the only way 'pass the parcel' will be stopped. The EU moves are in line with yesterday's call from Ruud Lubbers, former Dutch prime minister and now UN high commissioner for refugees, for a more generous regional approach by the developed world: both in accepting more asylum seekers and in supporting third world countries like Pakistan and Iran which have large camps. Both moves are needed. One reason for the rise in illegal refugees is tighter restrictions in the west. But a more regional approach must not supersede the obligation on all states to consider individual asylum applications on an individual basis.

While focusing solely on *referential* and *predicational strategies*, one could conclude having read this article that the terms 'migrants', 'illegal migrants', 'illegal refugees' and 'asylum-seekers' are interchangeable, all having similar or identical meanings; thus, all 'foreigners' are perceived as threatening. No systematic discursive pattern can be detected when the one or the other concept is employed in the text. The mere concepts of 'illegal asylum-seekers' and 'illegal refugees' are paradoxical: while people are in the process of seeking asylum, it remains unproven whether they are fleeing from violence and torture in their host countries, or are voluntarily migrating to make a better life. Moreover, the question always remains of how such a danger is to be defined, which would then impact upon what would legally constitute a 'genuine refugee' or a 'genuine asylum-seeker'. Several different official and institutional voices are reported in this brief news report: on the one hand, emphasizing a more 'liberal tendency', on the other supporting 'tighter restrictions'. This tendency surprisingly prevails both in the tabloid press and in the high quality papers such as the *Guardian*, the *Daily Telegraph* and the *Observer*, albeit in different linguistic realizations and frequencies.

Quantitative analysis of the phraseology employed clearly demonstrates that the terms expressing a strong stance all contain an extremely negative bias. Figure 3.1 shows the frequency of the terms 'illegal refugees' and 'illegal asylum-seekers' in twelve national and three regional British newspapers. Some newspapers are clearly at the 'tabloid' end of the spectrum (*Sun*, *Star*, *People*, *Express*), while others are towards the 'broadsheet' end (*Guardian*, *Observer*, *Independent*, *Times*, *Herald*), with a group around the middle (*Mail*, *Mirror*, *Evening Standard* and – due to its political positioning – also the *Telegraph*). What should be noted, however, is that apart from *Business* and *Liverpool Echo*, which have no instances at all, and the four newspapers that show frequency of use significantly above the average, the rest show frequencies that are close together.

Only when the twelve national newspapers are grouped into broadsheets and tabloids according to conventional notions do differences become more clear-cut. Not only do tabloids use the word 'illegal' more frequently, but they also use it significantly more frequently to refer to refugees, migrants and asylum-seekers, in general, and in expressions referring to specific topoi in particular. This discursive change illustrates the (re)production of prejudices and beliefs throughout the press. It also exemplifies how public discourse in the media might influence everyday beliefs because of the almost monolithic belief system which is being constructed. Moreover, the analysis of media reporting and political campaigning (through media) demonstrates how public discourses reproduce exclusion and the construction of insiders and outsiders. In both instances, outsiders are foreigners, be they refugees, migrants or asylum-seekers. Through negative connotations and fallacious argumentation, these foreigners have been constructed and stigmatized as the archetypical 'Other'. The main argumentation and topoi used trigger fear and anxiety (see Introduction to this volume). It is to be expected that such media reporting across the whole political spectrum will most certainly be recontextualized in everyday beliefs and opinions, hence leading to further prejudice which is then functionalized to legitimize everyday and institutional practices of exclusion and discrimination.

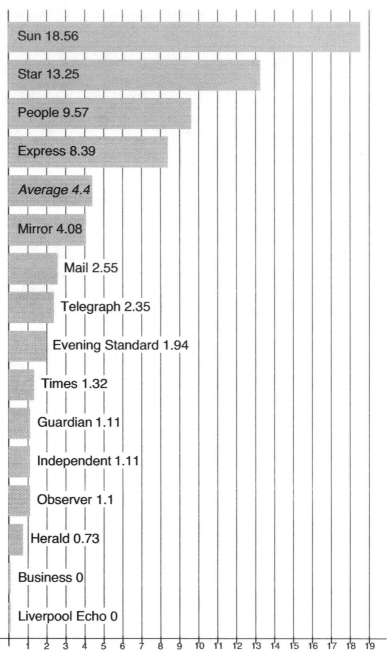

Sun 18.56

Star 13.25

People 9.57

Express 8.39

*Average 4.4*

Mirror 4.08

Mail 2.55

Telegraph 2.35

Evening Standard 1.94

Times 1.32

Guardian 1.11

Independent 1.11

Observer 1.1

Herald 0.73

Business 0

Liverpool Echo 0

1 2 3 4 5 6 7 8 9 10 11 12 13 14 15 16 17 18 19

3.1. Uses of the terms 'illegal refugees' or 'illegal asylum-seekers': total frequencies per million words in British newspapers, 1995–2005

## Concluding Remarks

The conflicting processes which define or change borders and which, for example, define who is 'inside' Europe or who stays 'outside' Europe can be labelled as 'inclusion' and 'exclusion'. These processes – as was demonstrated – relate to constructions of 'identity' and 'identity politics' in very complex ways and also reveal who (which person or group) has the power to define and construct such categories. The ongoing demarcation of 'us' and 'them' characterizes many debates in all European member states (such as polarized discussions on EU enlargement, gender mainstreaming, on definitions of citizenship, immigration and participation in decision-making, and many more). Inclusion and exclusion are important theoretical concepts to interpret new developments in our societies and to define the on-going global and local conflicts and struggles. The events since 11 September 2001, the war in Iraq and ethnic conflicts as well as the rise of right-wing populism, and the debate on reforming and enlarging the EU, point to the necessity of elaborating, refining, applying and validating this framework.

The power to provide and regulate access lies in the hands of bureaucracies and administrations, on a national and transnational level. The implementation of ever more restrictive immigration laws is accompanied by the coded exclusionary rhetoric described above: by constructing positive self- and negative other presentation, by employing strategies of justification and legitimation, and finally by denying racism.

The 'nomad' stands for a form of life, one that no longer seeks an anchor in a particular geographical space. Europe will soon be full of such 'nomads', with or without passports. Hierarchies of 'nomads' will be established, some more welcome than others. Thus, for some privileged migrants (academics, journalists, managers), mobility means cultural capital; for others, mobility is stigmatized and leads to the above elaborated forms of discrimination and exclusion. Mobility is one aspect of most new forms of life: the access to debate forums, to various jobs in different countries (new concepts of life histories and biographies), and lastly to (perhaps, new forms of) citizenship and civil rights in many countries. Participation and access are major factors, which have to be discussed when investigating inclusion and exclusion. Therefore, the analysis of the discursive construction of inclusion and exclusion and of the implied fluid and shifting but at the same time rigid boundaries presents a most important challenge to interdisciplinary research.

## References

Anderson, B. (1985) *Imagined Communities*. London: Verso.

Baker, P., R. Wodak, M. Khosravinik and C. Gabrielatos (2006) *Migrants, Refugees and Asylum-Seekers in the British Press*. Project Report, Lancaster University.

Baker, P., R. Wodak, M. Khosravinik, C. Gabrielatos and M. Krzyżanowski (2008) 'Studying Racism with Corpus Linguistics and CDA', *Discourse and Society* (in press).

Billig, M. (1991) *Ideology and Opinions*. London: Sage.

— (1995) *Banal Nationalism*. London: Sage.

— (2006). 'Discourse and Discrimination', in *Elsevier Encyclopedia of Language and Linguistics*, Second Edition, ed. K. Brown. Oxford: Elsevier, pp. 697–99.

Blommaert, J. (2001) 'Investigating Narrative Inequality', in *Elsevier Encyclopedia for Language and Linguistics*, Oxford: Elsevier, pp. 1036–38.

Bourdieu, P. (1999) *The Weight of the World*. London: Polity.

Busch, B., and M. Krzyżanowski (2007) 'Outside/Inside the EU: Enlargement, Migration Policies and Security Issues', in *Europe's Borders and Geopolitics: Expansion, Exclusion and Integration in the European Union*, ed. J. Anderson and W. Armstrong. London: Routledge, pp. 107–24.

Chilton, P. (2004) *Analyzing Political Discourse*. London: Routledge.

Cicourel, A. (1974) *Methode und Messung in der Soziologie*. Frankfurt: Suhrkamp.

— (2007) 'A Personal, Retrospective View of Ecological Validity', *Text and Talk* 27(5–6): 735–52.

De Cillia, R., and R. Wodak (2006). *Ist Österreich ein 'deutsches' Land? Anmerkungen zur Sprachenpolitik der Zweiten Republik*. Innsbruck: Studienverlag.

Essed, P. (1991) *Understanding Everyday Racism*. Newbury Park, CA: Sage.

Fairclough, N. (2000). 'The Discourse of Social Exclusion', in *The Semiotics of Racism: Approaches in Critical Discourse Analysis*, ed. M. Reisigl and R. Wodak. Vienna: Passagen Verlag, pp. 65–84.

Giddens, A. (2001) *Sociology*. London: Polity.

Joppke, C., and S. Lukes (1999) *Multicultural Questions*. Oxford: Oxford University Press.

Kienpointner, M. (1996) *Vernünftig argumentieren. Regeln und Techniken der Diskussion*. Hamburg: Rowohlt.

Krzyżanowski, M., and R. Wodak (2007) 'Multiple/Collective Identities, Migration and Belonging: Voices of Migrants', in *Identity Trouble*, ed. C. Caldas-Coulthard and R. Iedema. Basingstoke: Palgrave Macmillan, pp. 95–119.

Luhmann, N. (1997) *Die Gesellschaft der Gesellschaft*. 2 vols. Frankfurt: Suhrkamp.

Marin, B. (2000) *Antisemitismus*. Stuttgart: Campus.

Melucci, A. (1996) *Challenging Codes*. Cambridge: Cambridge University Press.

Miles, R. (1993) *Racism after 'Race Relations'*. London: Routledge.

Pelinka, A., and R. Wodak (eds) (2002) *'Dreck am Stecken'. Politik der Ausgrenzung*. Vienna: Czernin.

Reisigl, M. (2006) 'Argumentation in Political Discourse', in *Elsevier Encyclopedia of Language and Linguistics*, Second Edition, ed. K. Brown. Oxford: Elsevier.

Reisigl, M., and R. Wodak (2006). *Discourse and Discrimination*. London: Routledge.

Richardson, J. (2004) *(Mis)Representing Islam*. Amsterdam: Benjamins.

Rojo-Martín, L., and T. van Dijk (1997) '"There Was a Problem and It Was Solved!" Legitimation of the Expulsion of "Illegal" Immigrants in Spanish Parliamentary

Discourse', *Discourse and Society* 8/4: 523–67.

Rydgren, J. (ed.) (2005) *Moments of Exclusion*. New York: Nova.

Van Dijk, T. A. (1984) *Prejudice in Discourse*. Amsterdam: Benjamins.

— (1989) 'The Denial of Racism', in *Language, Power and Ideology*, ed. R. Wodak. Amsterdam: Benjamins, pp. 199–226.

— (1993) *Elite Discourse and Racism*. London: Sage.

— (1998) *Ideology: A Multidisciplinary Approach*. London: Sage.

— (2005a) 'Contextual Knowledge Management in Discourse Production. A CDA Perspective', in R. Wodak and P. Chilton (eds.), *A New Agenda in (Critical) Discourse Analysis*. Amsterdam: Benjamins, pp. 71–100.

— (2005b) *Racism and Discourse in Spain and Latin America*. Amsterdam: Benjamins.

Van Eemeren, F., and B. Grootendorst, B. (1992) *Argumentation, Communication and Fallacies: A Pragma-Dialectical Perspective*. Hillsdale, NJ: Lawrence Erlbaum.

— (eds) (1994) *Studies in Pragma-Dialectics*. Amsterdam: International Centre for the Study of Argumentation, Sic Sat.

Van Leeuwen, T., and R. Wodak (1999). 'Legitimizing Immigration Control: A Discourse-Historical Analysis', *Discourse Studies* 1(1): 83–118.

Weiss, G., and R. Wodak (eds) (2003). *Critical Discourse Analysis: Theory and Interdisciplinarity*. Basingstoke: Macmillan.

Wetherell, M., and J. Potter (1992) *Mapping the Language of Racism: Discourse and the Legitimation of Exploitation*. New York: Harvester Wheatsheaf.

Wieviorka, M. (1994) 'Racism in Europe: Unity and Diversity', in *Racism, Modernity & Identity. On the Western Front*, ed. A. Rattansi and S. Westwood. Cambridge: Polity Press, pp. 173–88.

Wodak, R. (2004) 'Discourses of Silence', in *Discourse and Silencing*, ed. L. Thiesmeyer. Amsterdam: Benjamins, pp. 179–209.

— (2007) 'Discourses in European Union Organizations: Aspects of Access, Participation and Exclusion', *Text and Talk* 27(5–6): 655–80.

— (2008a) 'Prejudice and Discourse', in *Handbook of Prejudice and Racism*, ed. A. Pelinka and K. Stögner. Vienna: Braumüller (in press).

— (2008b) 'Controversial Issues in Feminist Gender Studies', in *Methodologies in Gender Studies*, ed. J. Sunderland *et al*. Basingstoke: Palgrave Macmillan (in press).

Wodak, R., R. De Cillia, M. Reisigl and K. Liebhart (1999). *The Discursive Construction of National Identity*. Edinburgh: Edinburgh University Press.

Wodak, R., and R. Iedema (2004) 'Constructing Borders without Being Seen: The Case of Jörg Haider, Politician', *Revista Canaria de Estudos Ingleses* 49/2004: 157–78.

Wodak, R., and M. Krzyżanowski (eds) (forthcoming) *Qualitative Discourse Analysis in the Social Sciences*. Basingstoke: Palgrave Macmillan.

Wodak, R., J. Pelikan, P. Nowak, H. Gruber, R. de Cillia and R. Mitten (1990) *'Wir sind alle unschuldige Täter!' Diskurshistorische Studien zum Nachkriegs-antisemitismus*. Frankfurt am Main: Suhrkamp.

Wodak, R., and A. Pelinka (eds) (2002) *The Haider Phenomenon in Austria*. New Brunswick, NJ: Transaction Press.

Wodak, R., and T. van Dijk (eds) (2000) *Racism at the Top: Parliamentary Discourses on Ethnic Issues in Six European States*. Klagenfurt: Drava.

# 4   Dilemmas of Secularism: Europe, Religion and the Problem of Pluralism[1]

## Gerard Delanty

The question of the place and role of religion in modern secular societies has been a subject of much discussion in scholarly debates. Sociologists of religion have noted the increasing secularization of modern societies in terms of the separation of church and state and have noted the overall declining importance of religious belief and practice. Although the so-called secularization thesis has been much debated, since much of the decline of religion in fact amounted to the privatization of religious belief, there does appear to be widespread agreement that modernity entails the overall decline of religion (Bruce 1996; Norris and Inglehart 2004). This is not the place to enter into a detailed discussion of the secularization thesis, but it can be noted that the secularization of religion does not amount to the disappearance of religion. To take an obvious example, the USA is a highly secular society in terms of the role of religion in the state and the Constitution of the Unites States of America is one of the most secular constitutional documents in existence. However, American society is highly religious and there is in addition a certain cultural stream commonly referred to as civil religion, a sense of nationhood that has many features of religious worship (Casanova 1994, 2001; Madsen *et al.* 2002). In much of Asia and in most parts Africa, religion has become highly important to rapidly modernizing post-industrial countries that did not undergo a European-style reformation where major doctrinal change occurred before industrialization. The resurgence of religion is not in spite of, but because of modernity and is not easily explained in terms of the traditional secularization thesis, which for the greater part was concerned with the role of religion in the passage from pre-industrial to industrial societies. Secularization was once a vehicle of democratization while

1   This chapter was originally given as a lecture given at Koc University, Istanbul, 28 May 2005.

today popular democratic movements throughout the world have been allied to religion in many different ways (Castells 1997).

Europe is a different case. In comparison to other parts of the world and especially the United States, Europe is highly secular (Davis 2000; Remond 1999). Virtually every indicator – belief, church attendance, church–state relations – suggests an overall decline in religion and the tendency too has been towards the increasing separation of church and state. Most of the details of this will be examined later in this chapter, but it can be established that the general trend in European political modernity has been secular and that the privatization of religion has not led to a religious society within the bounds of a secular state, as has been the experience of the United States. It is not the aim of this chapter to doubt this but to raise new questions about the nature of secularism in Europe today, not least given the multi-ethnic nature of European societies today. The central question to be addressed is whether Europe can move from a secular to a post-secular conception of religion. There are several reasons why such considerations are timely.

First, while there can be no doubt that while secularism played a decisive role in democratization, Europe is now experiencing certain problems with the integration of ethnic minorities for whom the secularization of societies has resulted in degrees of marginalization. The issue here is the complicated relation of secularism to pluralism, for it cannot be automatically assumed that secularism leads directly to pluralism. Secularism concerns church–state relations; pluralism concerns the co-existence of culturally distinct social groups. Secularism of course too has often been linked with dogmatism and with intolerance of non-Christian religions (Keane 2000; Connolly 1999). As will be discussed in this chapter, there are different kinds of secularism in terms of church–state relations. One of the key challenges for Europe will be to devise secular relations that foster rather than undermine pluralism. Secularism was a development that preceded the democratization of European societies and while it was to become an important means of democratization it was not itself a democratic institution. It roots lie deep in the history of Europe and in one tradition it was connected with anti-clericalism, or anti-Catholicism. With the democratization of societies that are now multi-ethnic, secularism does not always lend itself easily to democratic pluralism. In short, a key question is the degree to which religion can be permitted in the public sphere.

Second, in the wider global public sphere religion has a greater presence than has been the case for much of the recent past. Religion was marginal to the social movements of the industrial and post-industrial age, but has become considerably more central to the social movements of the global information

79

age. It has also become increasingly linked to nationalism (Juergensmeyer 2006). The post-9/11 environment of security has been couched in the language of global anxieties about religiously inspired terrorism. Along with popular notions of a 'clash of civilization' by which the major world religions allegedly collide in a new age of cultural warfare, the global increase in Pentecostalism and various kinds of evangelical Protestantism, which has now spread into China, the growth of orthodoxy in eastern Europe and in particular in Russia, religion has become a significant part of politics. The funeral of Pope John Paul II in 2005 was a global mega-media event in which the Catholic church demonstrated its relevance for people throughout the world.

Third, specifically with regard to Europe there is the question of whether the cultural identity of Europe can be plausibly described as Christian. In this debate the Christian nature of Europe is often invoked as a part of the identity of Europe. Human rights, as in the debate over the Human Rights Charter, are held to be the universal products of the Judeo-Christian heritage. In this case there is the uncomfortable paradox of Europe being Christian but also secular. It is undoubtedly a problem that the global anxieties about religion are occurring at precisely the same time that multiculturalism has entered a critical period in Europe. In Europe religion has entered the public sphere around the question of Islam, which has witnessed global mobilization, and in many countries where Muslims live as large minorities there has been a process of Islamization (Esposito and Burgat 2003). In several countries there is controversy over headscarfs and religious symbols associated with Islam and since 2002 there has been ongoing debate about whether Turkey can join the European Union. These anxieties have been fuelled by the terrorist bombings in Madrid and London. The riots that occurred in French cities in 2005 are also a reminder of the degree of marginalization of Muslim minorities. But the reality is that Islam has become an integral part of Europe although this is not yet recognized on the level of cultural identity (Vertovec and Rogers 1998; Al Sayyad and Castells 2002; Goody 2004; Hussain and O'Brien 2000). Although Islam has now become the main focus of hostility, much of European religious intolerance has been exercised against the Jews and there has been an increase in cultural anti-Semitism – that is violence against symbols of Judaism – as well as in more physical forms in recent years, a situation that has of course been complicated by the consequences of the war in Iraq. Despite secularization, or possibly because of it, religious conflicts continue to play a major role in many European societies. The controversy in 2006 around the publication of satirical cartoons relating to the Prophet Muhammad is one such example.

Thus it has come about that the veil and the headscarf have become the embattled concerns of European identity in an age of global anxieties about religion. This chapter will address some of these issues in order to clarify the nature of secularism and its relation to pluralism. The chapter begins with a discussion of the historical context of secularism in modernity. On the basis of the analysis in this section, the next section develops the historical contextualization in a critical assessment of the extent to which Europe is actually secular. Here the main emphasis is on the different meanings of secularism and church–state relations in European countries, for European secularism does not take one form but many. The section discusses the different relations between secularism and pluralism and makes the argument that secularism does not necessarily entail pluralism. In the final section the notion of pluralism is developed around the idea of cosmopolitanism, which is in turn related to a different expression of cultural negotiation. The upshot of these considerations is that in normative terms secularism, modified by cosmopolitan pluralism, does not have to preclude the presence of religion from public culture.

## Modernity and the Forms of Secularism

It is helpful to begin with some consideration of the origins of secularism within the context of European political modernity, since the legacy of this tradition has shaped the current situation, presenting both opportunities and disadvantages for pluralism. The history of church and state relations in Europe was a struggle between two forms of authority, one religious and one political. This was one of the defining features of European history prior to the modern period. Neither church nor state ever succeeded in dominating the other. With few exceptions, and then only for short periods, European states were confessional states, but the principle of statehood was never subordinated to ecclesiastical authority, with the possible exception of some bishoprics in the Holy Roman Empire of the German Nation, but even in these cases theocracy never took root in Europe. In addition, the history of Christianity in Europe has been a history of its divisions. While many churches did gain considerable political and social influence, no church actually gained power over the state for long. This was due in part to the nature of the state but also to civil society as well as to divisions within the elites.

It was not until the principle of *cujus regio, ejus religio* whereby the ruler decided the religion of the population that political authority established its final superiority over clerical authority. Following the Peace of Westphalia in 1648, when the European states agreed not to wage war on another state on behalf of their co-religionists, the interstate system became anchored in secular politics. Thus the peculiar feature of European secularism is that the state, in establishing its superiority over ecclesiastical authorities, itself became the arbitrator of religion, for the ruler effectively decided the religion of the population. The history of Europe in the early modern period until 1648 was shaped by the conflicts and upheavals that resulted in changes in the religions of the elites and masses. Following 1054 there was no pan-European religion but three major religions: Catholicism, Orthodoxy and Lutherism. In addition, Judaism can be mentioned, although this was not a confessional geopolitical bloc. Today, it is possible to add Islam to the list of European religions (Goody 2004).

It would be a mistake to believe that Europe entered a post-religious age following 1648 with progressive secularization. For centuries it was the state that established religion, thus beginning the age of established churches, that is official state churches supported by state subsidies. Those countries shaped by the political modernity that arose from the French Revolution rejected established churches, but almost exclusively gave a privileged role to the religion of the majority of the population. On the whole it was the Protestant states that established a state church, while the largely Catholic countries embarked on a more radical separation of church and state. Thus it came about that two models of secularism were established from the late seventeenth century. The first was the constitutional conservative tradition whereby secularism entailed an official church established by the state and thus controlled by the state. The second, associated with the republican tradition, entailed the state separating the church from the public domain, in effect privatizing religion. European secularism is a product of these two traditions.

In both cases religion did not disappear from society, but was institutionalized, in the first case as an official religion and in both cases in the privatistic domains of family, education, and other social institutions, such as health. Indeed, the removal of religion from the domain of the state helped it to survive the transition to modernity. Churches also played a key role as charitable institutions. The Enlightenment itself was for the greater part fostered by the reformed Protestant churches in western Europe. It was only in France, with the Catholic Ancien Régime, that it took an anticlerical form. Although it was to be one of the signatures of the Enlightenment movement, the anti-Catholicism of the French Enlightenment intellectuals was an exception. It was not long after the French Revolution that Napoleon re-established Catholicism as a state religion. The Enlightenment, along with the movement we now call modernity, in which science and law were secularized, that is separated from religion, occurred precisely in order to preserve faith from the critique of science. Virtually all the major Enlightenment philosophers sought to place religious faith on a separate level from scientific reason or knowledge. This was encapsulated in the philosophy of Immanuel Kant, who argued that religious belief and ideas could not be justified on the basis of reason. In this, faith was protected from the critique of rationalists such as Voltaire, who argued that only reason was a criterion of belief.

The two pillars of modernity – belief based on faith and belief based on evidenced supported knowledge – have not always been equally acknowledged by the critics and defenders of modernity. The German philosopher Jürgen Habermas and Joseph Ratzinger, now Pope Benedict XVI, in a dialogue in Frankfurt in 2002 commented on this feature of modernity, which they both agreed cannot be reduced to the culture of rational science. However, it would be wrong to see religion and reason as separate and thus assume modernity has simply two faces that never interact. Max Weber discussed the mutual implication of religion and rationality in what he called the 'paradox of modernity', the paradox that the very rationalization or disenchantment that eventually eroded religion from society was actually produced by the tendency within Christianity, in particular in its Protestant forms, to intellectualize all traces of magic out of religious belief (Weber 1948). The progressive rationalization of religious belief as a result of the belief in salvation by a personal God, who awards worldly deeds, cultivated a rationalistic work ethic and a methodic approach to life that finally brought religion close to the capitalistic ethic. In Weber's view rationalism was present in all domains of life –law, economic activity, culture – and religion was not exempt from it. Hans Blumenberg offered a related argument, claiming that secularization operated within religious doctrine in a growing intellectualization and rationalization (Blumenberg 1983). In this sense one direction of religious secularization is its progressive intellectualization.

A further example of the religious origins of European political modernity is the somewhat extreme thesis, generally associated with Karl Löwith, that modernity is itself a secularization of Christianity (Löwith 1949). This is the view that modern western democracy derives from Christian ideas. Thus the liberty of the individual derives from the belief that all people stand equal before the eyes of God. This is questionable insofar as the claim is that there has been a direct transformation of a religious principle into a political one. More plausible is the view put forward by Max Weber that an inner rationalization is present in different spheres of life. Undoubtedly the values of solidarity and individual responsibility have a certain resonance in Christian ideas, but this does not mean that Christianity is the explanation. Many of these values can be related to pre-Christian traditions, such as the Roman and Greek traditions, and have been transformed in the course of history (Brague

2002). Indeed, S. N. Eisenstadt has made the claim that the key impulse of modernity – the notion that the world can be fashioned by human agency – was born with the great religions in the Axial Age with the discovery of transcendence and the desire to bring the kingdom of God onto earth (Eisenstadt 1986). All modern political movements, he has argued, have been driven by the numerous ways in which this antinomy can be worked out.

Finally, as regards the religious origins of European political modernity a different argument can be proposed which avoids some of the difficulties of the secularization thesis. There is much evidence to suggest that the modern quest for liberty was facilitated by – although not necessarily caused by – religious struggles. The political demands of dissenters and much of the Protestant reformation for freedom of worship provided the conditions for the recognition of other kinds of liberty, although largely only for Christian churches. While this took many forms – in England leading to an established church – the position that emerged from the end of the seventeenth century, while very far from late modern pluralism, was part of the movement towards the democratization of state power. Eventually, too, it led to the removal of the social and political exclusion of the Jews.

In sum, secularization means different things: it refers to the separation of the legal foundations of the state from religion, but it can also mean the separation of science and knowledge from faith, and it can mean the decline or rationalization of religious belief in terms of the erosion of the difference between the sacred and the profane.

The foregoing remarks serve as a background to the current situation in Europe. It has been argued that European political modernity has been influenced by religion to a very large degree and, as will be claimed below, the different forms of secularization – those associated with the constitutional conservative and republican traditions – did not eradicate religion from society but granted it a particular place and set conditions to its existence in the public domain. The separation of public and private was never complete and final in the way that it was in the United States and, as will be argued below, religion did exist within the public domain in most European countries. The result was that European secularism has been highly ambivalent; on the one side, the existence of either established churches or socially privileged churches often led to discrimination against members of other faiths, in particular Jews, while, on the other hand, European secularism has been such that there is no fundamental obstacle to a limited presence of religion in the public sphere and there has been a long tradition of the freedom of worship. This is one of the paradoxes of European secularism, which should be understood as the containment of religion. The main thesis of the chapter is that secularism is no longer adequate and instead a post-secular society needs to be created.

## How Secular Is Europe Today?

There has never been an American-style secularization of church and state in Europe. Contrary to a commonly held view, France did not separate church and state until 1905 in the wake of the Dreyfus Affair, although there was a gradual movement towards secularization from the late nineteenth century. Although the French Revolution was anticlerical, following the Concordat with the Vatican in 1801 Napoleon established Catholicism as the state religion. Only the communist countries were atheistic, in the sense of actively discouraging religion. The general European trend is one of neutrality, but this has been ambiguous since there has mostly not been a total separation of church and state and there are different interpretations as to the meaning of neutrality, ranging from non-recognition, to a principle of equality of all churches, to a position of privatization. In Ireland, for example, state neutrality was a means of maintaining the power of the Catholic church, especially in social policy, while in the Netherlands it has been a means of giving equal support to the main churches.

Many states support the main Christian churches and do so in different ways, even if it is only in the official recognition of religious funerals. Several states support the main churches with large subsidies, granting tax exemptions or, as in Germany, collecting taxes for the churches (see Madley 2003a and b; Madley and Enyedi 2003). This is also the case in Belgium, Denmark and the Scandinavian countries. Sweden has only recently disestablished its church and Germany is moving towards a position of greater neutrality. Austria, Netherlands and France remain strictly neutral. But this strict neutrality is relative. France, possibly the best example of republican secularism, provides limited subsidies for churches and for synagogues, tax exemptions for the clergy, allocation of TV time for religious broadcasts, and various minor concessions for religious education and the recognition of religious funerals (Safran 2003: 59). The French commitment to *laïcité* is not as inflexible as is often thought, and allows for a certain presence of religious symbols in schools (see Kastoryano 2002). In the case of the Netherlands, as noted above, state neutrality is intended to be supportive of all the major churches as opposed to non-recognition.

Although many countries, such as the UK, Norway and Denmark, have state churches, these generally have a weak function. Greece in contrast is a country in which religion has a strongly official function. The Orthodox church is the official established church, with the salaries and pensions of the clergy paid by the state, which appoints bishops and exempts clergy from military service (Pollis 2003: 158). It plays a leading role in Greek national identity comparable to the role of Catholicism in Croatia and Poland. In Poland, however, Catholicism was rooted in civil society, while in Greece Orthodoxy is firmly embedded in the state. There has been a general upsurge in religion in the former communist societies, which have moved from being atheistic to a position of neutrality, with many giving partial support for religion. Hungary is an exception in this regard. In particular there has been an increase in Orthodoxy in Romania and in Russia, although less so in Bulgaria. In these countries the Orthodox church has been successful in recovering property confiscated by the communist state. However, it should be noted that the increase in religious activity in post-communist countries is not greater than the extent of religious worship in western Europe (see Norris and Inglehart 2004).

The United Kingdom is an example of a country with an ambivalent tradition of secularism based on an established church, the head of which is the reigning monarch, and a constitutional arrangement enshrined in the Act of Settlement of 1701 which determined a line of succession that was designed to prevent a Catholic becoming the head of state. Yet the UK cannot be considered to be anything but secular in practice since the influence of the Anglican church has diminished to a largely ceremonial role and there is widespread recognition of the multi-ethnic nature of British society. Yet the secularism of British society has also been accompanied by a dogmatism and intolerance that may be precisely a product of secularism, as the controversy over Salman Rushdie's novel *The Satanic Verses* in 1989 illustrates. Further examples can be found in hostility to Muslims in the wake of the bombings in London in 2005. However, the variety of reactions of the British press to what has been widely regarded as a provocative decision by several European presses to publish satirical cartoons depicting the Prophet Muhammad as a terrorist suggests that there has been a learning process in coping with the politicization of Islam.

How secular is Europe then? It can be established that Europe does have different religious cultures with different degrees of secularization. There is no Christian unity to Europe, but there is evidence of a residual Christianity. Many countries have Christian political parties, and several have state churches, but throughout Europe there are Christian commemorations and festivities, which are all a reminder of the Christian background to European modernity. Most Europeans are affiliated to a church while being otherwise unreligious. The decline in religion in Europe is partly demographic in that the more traditionally staunch Catholic countries, Ireland, Spain and Italy, have lower birth rates than the Lutheran countries (Crouch 2000). Religious practice is predominantly a matter of formal affiliation around birth, marriage and death, but is relatively unimportant for identity for the vast majority of Europeans. Formal affiliation does not amount to identity or strong attachment of ideological conviction.

The privatization and disappearance of religion from the domain of the state has not led to the total disappearance of religion. Many of the Christian churches have become increasingly tolerant of dissent and have to varying degrees embraced the idea of a multi-faith society, often more so than political leaders. For this reason the resistance to religion that has been a feature of much of political modernity is less prevalent today and may even explain religious revival in many parts of the world. The funeral of Pope John Paul II in 2005 was a reminder of the global presence of the Catholic church and the adaptability of religion in the information age. It has been often noted that John Paul II created more saints than any previous pope, suggesting that modernity and religion are not irreconcilable (Madsen *et al.* 2002). One of the features of modern nationalism is the belief in personal selection, as is evidenced by the modern cult of the Virgin Mary and her apparitions (Skrbis 2005).

The question of Christianity has recently become an issue for the European Union. In order to articulate a European identity, a view has gained currency in recent years that Europe is rooted in Christianity and this is the basis of its identity (Seidentop 2000). Although attempts to place a special emphasis on Christianity in the proposed European Constitution were abandoned, this is an influential position (Schlesinger and Foret 2006). Joseph Weiler has argued strongly in favour of the official acknowledgment of the Christian heritage for the EU since, in his view, this would enhance the ideal of religious pluralism (Weiler 2003; Menendez 2004). The document 'The Spiritual and Cultural Dimension of Europe', although not an official statement of the EU, was commissioned by the President of the European Commission and argued that the public role of European religions is particularly important and that this includes Islam (Biedenkopf *et al.* 2004). There is also of course the role Christian values have played in shaping the EU. Douglas Holmes has commented that Christian social values have played a significant role in the making of the EU, in particular the tradition of Catholic social modernism (Holmes 2000).

The notion of a European Christian heritage has not been unconnected with the prospect of Turkey joining the EU and wider concern over the relation of Islam to Europe. With the waning of the Kemalist project in present-day Turkey, the strictly secular state created by Ataturk has reduced hostility towards Islam in the public domain (Özbudun and Keyman 2002). The decisive development was the election of the Islamic-based Justice and Development Party, a moderate Islamist Party which has been an agent of Europeanization, in the historic election of 2002 when it won two-thirds of parliamentary seats. It is clearly the case that the notion that Europe is Christian is invoked in order to express hostility to Turkey with its predominantly Muslim population. In this there is the interesting paradox of a Christian heritage defining a Europe that has become, we are led to believe, secular. In this debate views differ as to whether it is the distinctive nature of Europe that secularism precludes the existence of religion or, the position represented by Weiler, that it fosters tolerance.

One of the questions that this all raises is how secularism relates to the existence of a multi-faith Europe. Until recently, the challenge of religious tolerance was largely an issue that concerned the Christian religions and their relation to the state. It concerned issues such as the presence of religion in the public domain, the question of state churches, and where the limits of the public domain lie. The major exception to this was Judaism, which lay outside the secular politics of modernity. Today, in an age when non-Christian religions are becoming more important some of the assumptions of secularism need to be revisited. Islam is having a growing impact on Europe (see Bontempi 2005). The EU area has a Muslim population of 2.4% of the entire population. In France 6% of the population is Muslim, while in many other countries it is around 3%. The religious denominations within Islam also differ greatly. In the UK there is a wide variety of Muslim minorities while in France most are North African, while Germany's large Muslim ethnic group is almost entirely Turkish. In addition to Islam there are many other ethnic minorities, many of whom are defined by religion. This does not mean that all these groups are fervently religious in a way that the Christian population is not. It does appear to be the case that two trends are in evidence, especially with respect with Islam. There is a clear tendency towards the same kind of secularism within Islamic groups, who, it must be stressed, are not uniform, while on the other hand there is a marginal group within Islam, who range from young Muslims who have rediscovered strict Islamic teaching, to groups who are receptive to political radicalism. To this latter group belong supporters, who appear to be predominantly young male Muslims, for the actions of the suicide bombers in Britain in 2005.

## Secularism and Pluralism

Having outlined and discussed the historical and contemporary context concerning religion in Europe, we can now consider the actual mechanisms of secularism and their relation to the wider goal of pluralism in the context of multi-ethnicity. There are essentially three models of secularism operating in Europe, which are related to different conceptions of political community: the republican, liberal or constitutionalist conservative and liberal communitarian models.

The republican model has been central to church–state relations in many states and has also defined multicultural relations. The basic approach is a view of religion as a private matter. In the French variant religion cannot encroach on the public domain and there is no official recognition of ethnic groups or religious categories. The state recognises individuals as citizens, not as members of a social group. Although as noted above in actual practice most republican states are flexible when it comes to specific problems resulting from the exclusion of religion from the state, the republican model of secularism is not designed for multi-faith societies (see Kastoryano 2002). It derived from a historical context in which religion had to be banished from the state in order to reform the Ancien Régime. The republican mode of secularism related to the religion of the majority, but in the multicultural and multi-faith societies of today, the policy of strict legal neutrality and recognition only on the basis of the individual citizen is not compatible with pluralism, which requires an enabling approach by which the state must actively promote social inclusion. As a model for Europe it has its limits in that a strict secularism does not accommodate many of the needs of minorities.

The republican model can be contrasted to the liberal tradition in which the attitude to religion has been shaped by constitutional conservatism. The kernel of this is not the separation of religion from the state, but the principle of tolerance. The liberal tradition itself has been closely related to the Protestant tradition and the emphasis on the freedom of worship, while the republican tradition has been mostly influenced by the belief in the sovereignty of the people. Tolerance was not central to the republican tradition, which was often opposed to religious tolerance and, in the European state tradition, came to stand for a religiously neutral legal identity. If France is the paradigmatic example of the republican tradition, Britain is the classic example of constitutional conservatism. Other countries, such as the Netherlands and Germany, embody to different degrees a similar approach to religion but also include elements of the republican tradition. The private–public separation is common to most countries, even those that have official churches. The relation tends to be flexible and functional rather than being rigid. Possibly more significant than the principle of neutrality and the demarcation of public and private is the question of where the lines are drawn. Simply put, there are different notions as to the definition of the private and the public. In the Netherlands the general understanding of the private domain is that it consists of a larger space than in France, where a good deal of the domain of the state includes what in other countries would be the private domain.

There is much to suggest that the liberal/constitutional conservative approach to religion offers more scope for pluralism than the strict republican adherence to the principle of neutrality. This does not suggest that there are no problems with the notion of tolerance that underlies it. Tolerance can mean different things and does not necessarily entail pluralism. While the liberal understanding of tolerance is a largely negative view of liberty as the removal of unreasonable constraints, the version that has been influential in official policies towards religion is one that, on the one side, accepts the freedom of worship for all and does not require that this be confined to the private domain and, on the other side, recognises official churches. This recognition varies from official state churches to the Dutch practice of recognising the main churches in the policy known as pillarization. In these cases the principle of state neutrality effectively amounts to a policy of equal treatment. The Dutch case is a good example of the limits of this kind of liberalism, which was designed to accommodate the mainstream churches and was not intended to be applied to minority religions, such as those associated with migrant or ethnic groups.

There are two problems with the liberal approach to the creation of a secular society. The underlying notion of tolerance can mean different things and does not necessarily lead to pluralism. Tolerance is not the equivalent of acceptance and can simply mean indifference, but it can also mean the right to be different. In recent times, many questions are being asked about the meaning and limits of tolerance, such as the question whether intolerance should be tolerated. Is it merely a matter of 'we are all different'? A second problem with liberalism is the assumption of integration into a dominant, cohesive culture as the goal. Those who do not fit into this culture can be 'tolerated' within limits. The result is only a limited kind of pluralism.

Liberal communitarian is another model of religious secularization which has become an important aspect of multiculturalism, and in many ways it constitutes multiculturalism as opposed to the traditional republican and liberal conceptions of political community (Delanty 2000, 2003). Communitarianism, as used here to refer to the modification of liberalism proposed by a range of largely North American political theorists, is based on a stronger notion of community than in the liberal tradition, where the emphasis is on the individual. Liberal communitarians argue that democracy requires the empowering of minorities as a positive act, as opposed to a limited notion of liberal tolerance for difference. There are, broadly, two positions on this. One is the relatively narrow position associated with the Canadian theorist Will Kymlicka that only certain social groups should be empowered through special rights. The other position is one that is often termed radical pluralism, which demands a more general application of positive recognition of all social groups. Liberal communitarianism, which for the purpose of this discussion refers simply to the view that official state recognition of minority religion is an essential part of a pluralist democracy, is very strongly based on the belief in diversity in the public sphere itself. Some pluralists, such as radical multiculturalists, see diversity itself as the goal (Young 2000).

Liberal communitarianism offers an important alternative to the traditional secular practices of modern Europe in so far as it is explicitly addressed to the current reality of multicultural societies. Is this the alternative for Europe? The suggestion made in this chapter is that liberal communitarianism is not the ideal solution for the problems connected to secularism discussed above, in that the move towards pluralism requires a further development. The communitarian turn in liberal and republican theory is primarily based on the pursuit of diversity and has been particularly shaped by North American experiences. The US and Canada are societies formed out of successive waves of migration and in addition have pre-settler populations, whose concerns are quite different from migrant groups. Europe, on the other hand, is composed of societies that have far fewer migrants and a more complex mosaic of class and ethnic relations than is the case in North America, and there is the more or less total absence of pre-settler populations. The different colonial histories of European societies have led to different ethnic patterns of migration. However, the principal problem with liberal communitarianism as a multicultural practice is that it does not problematize religious/ethnic identities or recognize their hybrid nature. Religions and ethnic identities are largely accepted at their face value and the goal is simply the pursuit of diversity. This was the aim of Tony Blair's belief in a multi-faith Britain. This results in the abandonment of common ground and can also lead to an exaggeration of cultural differences between groups. For example, it does not accommodate the many Asian groups in Britain whose identity can be defined as British Muslim. The reality is that many ethnic groups have evolved identities that are not easily defined in terms of religion or a single ethnicity but are overlapping.

The upshot of liberal communitarianism is that the law becomes the site where society ultimately achieves recognition. As Elizabeth Povinelli has argued, legal recognition does not always translate into other kinds of recognition, such as solidarity, because social groups are forced to define themselves in the language of the law (Povinelli 2002). The general problem of multiculturalism conceived of as legal recognition is that it can mean quite different things depending on the conception of diversity that is invoked. Is the aim to reduce inequalities between different groups? Is the aim to promote diversity as a positive value? Is the aim the representation of different groups? Or is the aim to achieve integration or assimilation? What tends to be neglected in this is the process by which value systems, such as religion, change as a result of encounters with other value systems and as a result of the inevitable contestation that results from the public sphere. The modified position this suggests can be termed cosmopolitan pluralism.

## Cosmopolitan Pluralism

Cosmopolitanism is not merely about diversity or about the separation of the private from the public. Although cosmopolitanism is certainly concerned with secularism, it is not the main or only aspect: cosmopolitanism is not a generalized version of multiculturalism where plurality is simply the goal or a modernist drive to eliminate ethnic, religious and other markers of identity from the public sphere and the domain of the state.

The concept of culture underlying cosmopolitanism is different from that in liberalism and republicanism and its communitarian alternatives. Culture must be seen as a learning process; it is a developmental process entailing self-problematization and the discursive examination of all claims. This also pertains to ethnic groups and to religions. So this is not just a matter of liberal tolerance or the communitarian pursuit of diversity, and is also stronger than soft cosmopolitanism in the sense of the promotion of the awareness of otherness. A cosmopolitan approach differs from the established approaches, which are all based on keeping cultures separate, in promoting openness and public contestation.

Cosmopolitanism is not often related to questions concerning religion, but is highly pertinent to the predicament about religion in Europe today (see Turner 2001). Cosmopolitanism is compatible with secularism without accepting all the assumptions of secularism, such as the policy of an official faith or established church. Secularism in cosmopolitan terms moreover does not require the exclusion of religion from the public domain, which should be seen in more flexible terms in its relation to the private realm. A cosmopolitan approach suggests that all religions should be allowed in the public sphere but does not accept the constitutional conservative position that one religion be granted constitutional protection over others. Above all it is the basic tenet of cosmopolitanism that religion should not be protected from contestation in the public sphere and that cultural value systems undergo transformation as a result of dialogue and self-problematization. It is fundamentally opposed to the privatistic containment of religion that has been a feature of the republican tradition wherein religion is banished to the pre-political private domain. It is also in marked contrast to the implicit dogmatism in much of liberal and republican attitudes to religion. Cosmopolitanism is a position that is compatible with a view of the public culture as an ongoing site of contestation.

So rather than separate private and public, what is needed is a multiculturalism of mutual learning. This can include religion if the language used is compatible with public discourse. No religion or church can separate itself from modernity and the need to justify itself through argument. Thus, as Habermas has argued, the condition of entry into the public sphere should be willingness to engage in public discourse (Habermas 2005a, 2006). However, this does not mean that more extreme religious groups should be excluded, as Habermas suggests. The discussion about Islamic extremist groups that has come to the fore especially since the bombings in London in 2005 suggests the importance of public dialogue among all groups. The isolation that secularism demands in banishing religion from the public domain can create the conditions for militancy. Although many Muslim militants have been far from isolated in terms of education, and isolation alone does not explain radical political mobilization, cultural isolation in conjunction with other facts, such as access to a global web of Islamic communication, can create the conditions for a counter-consciousness.

A pertinent example of the cosmopolitanism of public culture in practice is the peace process that arose out of the Good Friday Agreement in Northern Ireland. What is illustrated by this is the dissolution of fixed identities rooted in primordial religious traditions and the cultivation of negotiated identities. While the peace process has a long way to go before significant progress will be evident, the fact that such a process is under way is an indication of the institutionalization of pluralism and the public recognition of the need to move beyond forms of identity based on exclusivist notions of statehood, religion and territory. To be sure, it is evident that the emerging pluralism is highly limited, confined as it is to the reconciliation of the dominant confessional groups, and there has been no attempt to extend the politics of recognition to other contexts. Although what is at issue here is not the recognition of minorities, but the accommodation of the dominant confessional groups, it is clearly the case that a significant dissolution of hegemonic national identities has occurred and with it a growing transgression of borders and the intellectual discreditation of confessional politics.

93

The presence of religion in the public domain does not amount to its acceptance. The role played by religion in people's lives varies in degree, from the level of purely formal affiliation, which is the case for many Europeans today, to a more central role, as it plays for others (including some migrant groups). The very terms inherited from an earlier modernity may be inadequate in comprehending religion today, since it is neither a question of churches nor of sects. The famous thesis of Ernst Troeltsch in the *Social Teachings of the Christian Churches*, one of the major works in the classical sociology of religion, that the conflict between church and sect that had been a feature of European history has given way to the collapse of a universal church, needs to be looked at in a new light (Troeltsch 1931; Turner 2005). The very category of the church, like that of the state, while far from irrelevant, does not explain the complex nature of cultural transformation in meaning, memory and identity that is a feature of the present day. The contemporary expressions of religious revivalism do not correspond to the model of the sect revolting against the institutionalized orthodoxy of a church; they are the products of a culture of individualized identities and the fulfilment of the impulse within modernity towards emancipation. Far from remaining purely traditional, religious movements have become central to the global information economy, providing meaning, self-expression and orientation to many people (see Hellas 1998). Such movements can be particularly attractive to those young migrants who are poorly integrated into local communities but highly integrated into a global communication community. As has been frequently noted, fundamentalist movements can occur within Christianity as much as in Islam, although the European experience of Christianity has not been in the direction of Christian fundamentalism (Buruma and Marglit 2004). However, the nascent Islamic fundamentalism in Europe, like all fundamentalist movements, is opposed to the traditional teachings of the past and is modernist in the pursuit of personal liberation.

Secularism in its conventional forms is inadequate when it comes to responding to the challenges of religion. Whether it is the presence of headscarfs in schools, state support for minority schools, the fine line between free speech, blasphemy and incitement to hatred, tax exemptions for churches, religious education in schools, or the exclusion of religion from the public sphere, the pursuit of policies aimed at the public neutralization of religion are doomed to failure and are ultimately contrary to the goal of democratic pluralism. This does not mean that a secular society is not possible; rather it means that the public culture must be able to address all kinds of cultural challenges (see Benhabib 2002; Gutmann 2003). It is in this sense that the term cosmopolitan pluralism can be used.

## Conclusion: The Post-Secular Challenge for Europe

The argument put forward in this chapter is that secularism is not an irreversible or clear-cut fact of European political culture (see also Eder 2002). It is, rather, a process, and one that is expressed in many different forms. While it is often argued that the secularization of modern society has led to a situation that is incompatible with the presence or recognition of religion in the public domain, the reality is that the European experience has been more flexible – in practice as well as in theory – when it comes to the public role of religion. European secularism has been characterized by dogmatism when it comes to non-Christian religions but the inherent ambivalence in the policies on neutrality relating to church–state relations is an indication of the mutual intertwining of religion and politics in European political modernity.

The challenge now for Europe is to articulate what in this chapter has been called cosmopolitanism (see Delanty and Rumford 2005). This involves moving from a secular understanding of the polity to a post-secular society. Europe is neither Christian nor simply secular, but post-secular. Islam has become an integral part of late European modernity, and is now more visible in Europe due to the presence of Muslim minorities and the Islamization of political discourse. It is possible to speak of a European Islam but this is, as yet, one that lacks a specific identity. Rigid adherence to a secularism that does not recognize the presence of religion in the public sphere cannot be the European solution to some of the problems of multi-ethnic societies. The argument advanced here in normative terms goes beyond communitarian and multiculturalist policies that simply demand the recognition and pursuit of diversity. It has been argued that a pluralist and cosmopolitan public culture can, and, indeed, must include the contributions of religion. The myth of secularism is often an obstacle in the path of creating a pluralist multi-ethnic society. This chapter has attempted to dispel some of these myths.

## References

Al Sayyad, N., and M. Castells (eds) (2002) *Muslim Europe or Euro-Islam*. Lanham, MD: Lexington Books.

Benhabib, S. (2002) *The Claims of Culture: Equality and Diversity in the Global Era*. Princeton, NJ: Princeton University Press.

Biedenkopf, K., B. Geremek and K. Michalski (2004) *The Spiritual and Cultural Dimension of Europe*. Vienna: Institute for the Human Sciences.

Blumenberg, H. (1983) *The Legitimacy of the Modern Age*. Cambridge, MA: MIT Press.

Bontempi, M. (2005) 'Religious Pluralism and the Public Sphere', in *Comparing European*

*Societies*, ed. G. B. Lattes and E. Recchi. Bologna: Monduzzi Editore.

Brague, R. (2002) *Eccentric Culture: A Theory of Western Civilization*. South Bend, IN: St Augustine's Press.

Bruce, S. (1996) *Religion in the Modern World: From Cathedrals to Cults*. Oxford: Oxford University Press.

Buruma, I., and A. Marglit (2004) *Occidentalism: The West in the Eyes of Its Enemies*. London: Penguin.

Casanova, J. (1994) *Public Religions in the Modern World*. Chicago, IL: University of Chicago Press.

— (2001) 'Civil Society and Religion', *Social Research* 68(4): 1041–80.

Castells, M. (1997) *The Information Age*, vol. 2: *The Power of Identity*. Oxford: Blackwell.

Connolly, W. (1999) *Why I Am Not a Secularist*. Minneapolis, MN: University of Minnesota Press.

Crouch, C. (2000) 'The Quiet Continent: Religion and Politics in Europe', *The Political Quarterly* 71(1): 90–103.

Davis, G. (2000) *Religion in Modern Europe: A Memory Mutates*. Oxford: Oxford University Press.

Delanty, G. (2000) *Citizenship in a Global Age*. Buckingham: Open University Press.

— (2003) *Community*. London: Routledge.

Delanty, G., and C. Rumford (2005) *Rethinking Europe: Social Theory and the Implications of Europeanization*. London: Routledge.

Eder, K. (2002) 'Europäische Säkularisierung – ein Sonderweg in die postsäkulare Gesellschaft? Eine theoretische Anmerkung', *Berliner Journal für Soziologie* 12: 331–44.

Eisenstadt, S. N. (ed.) (1986) *The Origins and Diversity of the Axial Civilizations*. New York: SUNY Press.

Esposito, J., and F. Burgat (eds) (2003) *Modernizing Islam: Religion in the Public Sphere in Europe and the Middle East*. London: Hurst.

Goody, J. (2004) *Islam in Europe*. Cambridge: Polity Press.

Gutmann, A. (2003) *Identity in Democracy*. Princeton, NJ: Princeton University Press.

Habermas, J. (2005a) 'Equal Treatment of Cultures and the Limits of Postmodern Liberalism', *The Journal of Political Philosophy* 13(1): 1–28.

— (2006) 'Religion in the Public Sphere', *European Journal of Philosophy* 14(1): 1–25.

Habermas, J., and J. Ratzinger (2005). *Dialektik der Säkularisierung. Über Vernunft und Religion*. Freiburg: Verlag Herder.

Hellas, P. (ed) (1998) *Religion, Modernity and Postmodernity*. Oxford: Blackwell.

Holmes, D. (2000) *Integral Europe: Fast-Capitalism, Multiculturalism, Neofascism*. Princeton, NJ: Princeton University Press.

Hussain, F., and M. O'Brien (2000) 'Muslim Communities in Europe: Reconstruction and Transformation', *Current Sociology* 48(4): 1–13.

Juergensmeyer, M. (2006) 'Nationalism and Religion', in *Handbook of Nations and Nationalism*, ed. G. Delanty and K. Kumar. London: Sage.

Kastoryano, R. (2002) *Negotiating Identity: States and Immigration in France and Germany*. Princeton, NJ: Princeton University Press.

Keane, J. (2000) 'Secularism?', *The Political Quarterly* 3(5): 5–19.

Löwith, K. (1949) *Meaning in History: The Theological Presuppositions of the Philosophy of History*. Chicago, IL: University of Chicago Press.

Madeley, J. (2003a) 'European Liberal Democracy and the Principle of State Religious

Neutrality', *West European Politics* 26(1): 1–24.
— (2003b) 'A Framework for the Comparative Analysis of Church–State Relations in Europe', *West European Politics* 26(1): 23–50.
Madeley, J., and Z. Enyedi (eds) (2003) Special issue on Church and State in Contemporary Europe, *West European Politics* 26(1).
Madsen, R., W. Sullivan, A. Swidler and S. Tipton (eds) (2002) *Meaning and Modernity: Religion, Polity, and the Self*. Berkeley, CA: University of California Press.
Menendez, A. J. (2004) 'A Pious Europe? Why Europe Should not Define itself as Christian'. ARENA Working Paper no. 10/04.
Norris, P., and R. Inglehart (2004) *Sacred and Secular: Religion and Politics Worldwide*. Cambridge: Cambridge University Press.
Özbudun, E., and F. Keyman (2002) 'Cultural Globalization in Turkey', in *Many Globalizations*, ed. P. Berger and S. Huntington. Oxford: Oxford University Press.
Pollis, A. (2005) 'Greece: A Problematic Secular State', in S. Safran (ed.) *The Secular and the Sacred: Nation, Religion and Politics*. London: Frank Cass.
Povinelli, E. (2002) *The Cunning of Recognition: Indigenous Alterities and the Making of Australian Multiculturalism*. Durham, NC: Duke University Press.
Remond, R. (1999) *Religion and Society in Modern Europe*. Oxford: Blackwell.
Safran, W. (2003) 'Religion and *Laïcité* in a Jacobin Republic: The Case of France', in *The Secular and the Sacred: Nation, Religion and Politics*, ed. S. Safran. London: Frank Cass.
Schlesinger, P., and R. F. Foret (2006) 'Political Roof and Sacred Canopy? Religion and the EU Constitution', *European Journal of Social Theory* 9(1): 59–81.
Seidentop, L. (2000) *Democracy in Europe*. London: Penguin.
Skrbis, Z. (2005) 'The Apparitions of the Virgin Mary of Medjugorje: The Convergence of Croatian Nationalism and her Apparitions', *Nations and Nationalism* 11(3): 443–61.
Troeltsch, E. (1931) *The Social Teachings of the Christian Churches*, vols 1 and 2. London: Allen and Unwin.
Turner, B. S. (2001) 'Cosmopolitan Virtue: On Religion in a Global Age', *European Journal of Social Theory* 4(2): 131–52.
— (2005) 'The Sociology of Religion', in *Handbook of Sociology*, ed. C. Calhoun, C. Rojek and B. Turner. London: Sage.
Vertovec, S., and A. Rogers (eds) (1998) *Muslim European Youth: Reproducing Ethnicity, Religion, Culture*. Aldershot: Ashgate.
Weber, M. (1948) 'Religious Rejections of the World and Their Rejections', in H. H. Gerth and C. Wright Mills (ed.), *From Max Weber*. London: Routledge & Kegan Paul.
Weiler, J. (2003) *Un' Europa cristiana*. Milan: Rizzoli.
Young, M. I. (2000) *Inclusion and Democracy*. Oxford: Oxford University Press.

# Part II

# Institutional Forms of Discrimination

# 5. Racism, Anti-Racism and the Western State

## Alana Lentin

Racism and ethnic discriminations are under continuous historical and sociological examination. But anti-racism is consigned to the status of a 'cause', fit only for platitudes of support or denouncement.

Bonnett 2000: 2

In his book, *Anti-Racism*, Alastair Bonnett points out the paucity of research into anti-racism. Indeed, the discourse and political practice of anti-racism has generally been considered to be the mere opposite of racism, and as such undeserving of specific attention. In this chapter, I argue that, contrary to such a view, understanding anti-racism is central to making sense of 'race' and racism in the West since the Second World War. The end of the last World War and the full unveiling of the Nazi 'final solution' is a key moment in this regard. In the years that followed, anti-racist scientists and thinkers developed explanations for racism and proposed solutions for combating its persistence. These precepts formed the backbone of the approach to racism, or the more acceptably termed 'discrimination', taken by governments, supranational institutions and 'mainstream' groups in civil society, such as trade unions, church and solidarity organizations.

The argument I make concerns western Europe generally: although national contexts and their varying histories of colonialism and immigration all differ, official discourses generally offer a similar interpretation of racism. According to this interpretation, racism is a perversion of the logical course of modern politics that comes to affect western political culture from beyond the pale. In mainstream thought, the origins of racism are rarely considered to be political. It is thought of as a pathology, that may infect politics – often through the extremes of a singular leader or party – but which does not emerge from political processes inherent to the state. Indeed, racism is often interpreted in

101

psychological terms that root it in the individual's mind: a victim of ignorance and consequent hatred. It is thought, therefore, that it may be expunged from the realm of mainstream politics and restricted to the maverick fringes.

Moreover, state discourses of anti-racism rest on a general presumption that the western, democratic European state is *de facto* anti-racist. France and Britain both claim to have enabled the abolition of slavery in the colonies. France's self-declared status as the birthplace of human rights makes it tautological to imagine the French state as anything but anti-racist in principle. Other examples, such as Ireland's own history of colonial domination under Britain making it impossible for the liberated Irish Republic to be racist, follow suit. As a result, official approaches to anti-racism are centred on the presupposition that the solution to racism may be found within the political and legal apparatuses of the state; not beyond it.

This parallel view of racism and anti-racism largely informed efforts, such as that of UNESCO, launched in the early 1950s, to find solutions to racism. Racism would be eradicated if an acceptance of cultural relativism and greater intercultural knowledge could be promoted among peoples of different ethnic or cultural – rather than racial – backgrounds. The idea that greater knowledge of the other can destroy the psychological roots of individual racism continues to inform many anti-racist campaigns, training courses and youth programmes to this day.

In contrast, an anti-racism grounded in the lived experience of those who face racial discrimination has, for a long time, challenged this depoliticized view of racism and argued for a recognition of the role of the state in its continued perniciousness. As a consequence, various governments have addressed racism as a phenomenon that is deeply rooted in society. Nevertheless, even when invocations of institutional racism have been taken seriously, as in the case of the 1997 Macpherson Report in the UK, the state's assumed commitment to anti-racist principles has never been questioned from within. Rather, particular institutions are seen to have become 'infected' with racism; once again supposing that racism evolves independently from political processes that are internal to the state.

Racism has been approached in two main ways in mainstream politics. Both approaches stem from the overriding view of racism as an aberration from the principles of modern democratic state politics. On the one hand, a so-called 'colour-blind' attitude purposefully overlooks differences between people and emphasizes the meritocratic nature of modern, ostensibly egalitarian societies. On the other hand, cultural, religious or ethnic differences between groups and individuals *are* recognized, and mechanisms for redressing discrimination based on these differences have been put in place. It is unnecessary to get into the merits of what may be loosely termed 'liberal' versus 'multicultural' approaches, to show that both methods are perceived to have failed today for two interlinked reasons. Firstly, governments claim that these are policies that promote integration and social cohesion or that tackle the 'problems' of immigration rather than racism. Secondly, therefore, racism is not necessarily seen as being related to the social unrest, discrimination and poverty that governments suggest emerge from a lack of 'integration'. As a result, racism – when it is accepted – is not considered a factor in socioeconomic problems that are considered to lie with the state. It is, rather, an external or additional factor (increasingly identified with 'inter-ethnic' hatred and not just with the extreme right), that hinders the efforts of an inherently anti-racist state to engender greater social cohesion.

This chapter sets out to question the supposition that anti-racism is synonymous with the principles upon which democratic state policies and practices are said to be based. I consequently argue that the effort to externalize racism from the realm of the state by psychologizing and thus depoliticizing it masks the embeddedness of the idea of 'race' (Voegelin 1933) in the structures of the modern state.[1] The argument that 'race' and the nation-state are in a relationship of what Etienne Balibar calls 'reciprocal determination' (Balibar 1991: 52) is common to several important authors (Balibar 1991; Bauman 1989; Foucault 1997; Goldberg 2002a). Goldberg, for the United States context in particular, has shown how the post-Civil Rights US constructed a fiction of colour-blind 'racelessness' that belied the persistence of racially based discrimination. The question posed by this chapter is what role anti-racism played, following the Second World War and the rise in large-scale immigration to Europe, in bringing about the dissociation of the once almost synonymous concepts of 'race' and state.

To understand the key role played by anti-racism it is important to recognize that the majority of the explanations of racism available to us have been formulated from an anti-racist perspective. They emerge from a concern with the effects of racism on society and a desire to explain it so as to rid us of the damage it causes. Nevertheless, the heterogeneity of anti-racism means that there is no agreement on either the history or the contemporary meaning of racism from a conceptual perspective. It is only through an analysis of the competing versions of anti-racism and the reasons for their disunity that we may start to understand how 'race' and state have become dissociated in hegemonic discourse.

---

1 Voegelin distinguishes between 'race' concepts, or the pseudo-sceientific theories of racial scientists, and the idea of 'race'. The idea of 'race' is inherently political and one of a set of 'body ideas' that are at the basis of a theory of state (Voegelin 1933).

To make this point, the chapter firstly lays out the theoretical underpinnings for viewing anti-racism as a heterogeneous political discourse and practice of state and supranational institutions, on the one hand, and non-governmental and grassroots organizations, on the other. I briefly outline the main historical reasons for this divergence and for the adoption of a specific form of anti-racist discourse by state and mainstream bodies. Based on primary research carried out into anti-racism in four European countries, the second part of the chapter analyses in more detail one of the main discursive divides in European anti-racist discourse. I demonstrate how this opposition between 'majoritarianism' and 'communitarianism' illustrates the way in which the state is perceived in divergent anti-racist discourses. I conclude the chapter by discussing the relevance of this unravelling of the history of European anti-racism for racism today. Focusing on the recent 'rioting' by French youth of immigrant origin in France, I show how, by dissociating itself from 'race', the state may – to put it simplistically – be both racist and anti-racist at the same time. How this bodes for the future of our diverse European societies and the possibility of activists to challenge received ideas about the history and nature of racism is the key question this chapter seeks to raise.

## Generating Anti-Racisms

Racism can be described as chameleon-like in nature, adapting itself to changing political circumstances. It is also heterogeneous, meaning that it may be better to talk about plural racisms with differing origins, targets and ways of functioning. For example, the distinction is often made between overt and covert, or between individual and institutional racisms. Whereas this is a generally accepted fact about racism(s), there has been a failure to reflect on the similar heterogeneity of anti-racism. Anti-racism is presumed, simply, to oppose racism. But, we should perhaps ask: *which* racism does anti-racism oppose? As soon as this question is asked, the diversity among various anti-racist discourses and practices is thrown into light. Because anti-racism has been so bound up with the interpretation and portrayal of the meaning of racism, the type of racism it counters is often evident in the type of discourse it promotes and the types of action carried out in its name.

Elsewhere, I have argued (Lentin 2004) that the heterogeneous nature of anti-racism can be conceived in terms of the degrees of proximity of various anti-racist standpoints to the public political culture of the nation-state. Public political culture, a term borrowed from John Rawls, refers to a set of 'familiar ideas' (Rawls 2001: 5), some 'more basic than others' (Rawls 2001: 5) that 'play a fundamental role in society's political thought and how its institutions are interpreted' (Rawls 2001: 6). In basic terms, I have argued that the various approaches to anti-racism taken by governmental and non-governmental actors may be seen as existing along a continuum. At one extreme of this continuum, anti-racism embraces elements of public political culture which are seen as anti-racist in essence. These include principles such as democracy, liberty, human rights, and solidarity. The presumption is that if these principles were adhered to, racism would be eradicated through a respect for both the rule of law and the progressive ideas upon which democratic states are assumed to be built. At the other end of the continuum, the state itself is seen as a source of racist discrimination, both as reflected in current policy and, structurally, as a consequence of the miring of western history in slavery, colonial domination and the unequal treatment of non-national Others.

The significance of this continuum explains the lack of unity which characterizes the anti-racist 'movement' in most countries and often hinders the possibility for transnational activism. It also explains how certain strands of anti-racism have themselves contributed to the prevailing understanding of racism as an aberration from public political culture. It is this form of anti-racism that I would like to focus on in this section of the chapter. What we may call institutional or mainstream anti-racism has dominated the fight against racism since the aftermath of the Second World War. In Europe, even when anti-racisms attempt to highlight state and institutional racism, they are often constrained by a mainstream approach that tends to dictate funding opportunities and access to the political debate at national and European level. Mainstream anti-racism has also, most importantly, to a large extent dictated the way in which racism is explained through its impact on education, policy-making and the media.

In the introduction I stated that mainstream approaches to anti-racism, even when they attempt to take on board the challenges posed by those who experience racism themselves, are unable to assimilate the interrelationship between 'race' and state. It may be accepted that state institutions operate racially discriminatory practices, yet this is seen as conflicting with the principles embedded in public political culture. The reason this is the case, I want to argue, is firstly that racism was not adequately historicized in official discourse. It was therefore not politicized and was, rather, reduced to its scientific pretensions. Second, much more emphasis was placed on searching for solutions to racism's persistence than on fully uncovering how and under what circumstances it evolved over time. To this end, the focus was placed on inventing ways of talking about human difference without evoking the taboo of 'race'.

## Institutional Forms of Discrimination

### The Influence of the UNESCO Tradition

One of the principal vehicles of this approach has been what Martin Barker (1983) has referred to as the UNESCO Tradition. The example of the project embarked upon by UNESCO in 1950 to develop a 'statement on race and racial prejudice' and an accompanying research and pedagogical programme is a good one. It contains the main elements that continue to inform the anti-racist practice of institutions, such as the various European bodies established to combat racism and discrimination,[2] as well as the agendas of a range of mainstream associations. The main problem created by the UNESCO Tradition for interpreting racism is that by reducing 'race' to its pseudo-scientific dimension and by attempting to propose a culturally relativist approach to living with diversity it encourages the idea that our societies are 'raceless' or at least 'post-race'.

As Goldberg (2002b) has argued, we can only talk about states without 'race' in the west once the privilege associated with whiteness[3] has been dismantled. Despite the scientific fallacy of the hierarchy implied by 'race', the structure that this idea has imposed through its historical entry into the political, social and economic spheres has made the *experience* (rather than the fact) of 'race' a reality for all those living in multi-cultural, post-colonial societies. Therefore, as Goldberg writes,

> a state without racism in the wake of the long and vicious racist histories of the present cannot simply be a raceless state. Post-racist (in contrast to merely post-racial) states must be those for which state agencies, and most notably law, are vigorous both in refusing racist practice and in public representation of the unacceptability of all forms of discriminatory expression... It would mean, in short, a very different sort of state personality, a different demeanor to those inside and outside the state cast(e), a different disposition to population definition and characterization, to law and law en*force*ment, to power and policy-making, to kith and kin, 'legitimate' family and the shape of class, to socio-spatial configurations and schooling, social engagement and accessibility, to national culture (most notably in and through language, the 'mother tongue') and historical memory.

2  These include various units of the European Commission, the Council of Europe's European Commission on Racism and Intolerance (ECRI), the European Monitoring Centre against Racism and Xenophobia (EUMC) and the European Network Against Racism (ENAR) among others.
3  David Goldberg writes from the perspective of the USA where black–white dichotomies more clearly define the state of racist play. In Europe, particularly since the fall of Communism, the association of racism with skin colour alone has been superseded by an acceptance of the racialization of non-Western-Europeanness regardless of skin colour.

Instead of addressing ra*cism*, the UNESCO Tradition, and the mainstream institutionally legitimated anti-racism to which it gave rise, propagates the thesis of 'racelessness'. It promotes the idea that we live in a post-racial world and, therefore, is incapable, to follow Goldberg, of effectively addressing the injustices of racism past and present. According to Hannaford, the UNESCO line can be said to promote the principle that 'all men belonged to the same species, *Homo Sapiens*, that national, cultural, religious, geographical, and linguistic groups had been falsely termed races; that it would be better to drop the term and use "ethnic groups" in its place; that the "race is everything" hypothesis was untrue' (1996: 386). The UNESCO project had two main aims: to disqualify the scientific validity of the 'race' concept, and to propose alternative ways of conceptualizing human difference that would not evoke the hierarchy implied by 'race'. Firstly, in order to disprove the scientific validity of 'race', it was imperative for the panel of experts brought together by UNESCO (mainly anthropologists, geneticists and sociologists) to diminish the significance accorded to it. This aim nevertheless resulted in a view of racism that denied its effects upon the state and politics, relegating it to the realm of misplaced pseudo-science. Point 3(b) of the statement they produced reads: 'The division of the human species into "races" is partly conventional and partly arbitrary and does not imply any hierarchy whatsoever. Many anthropologists stress the importance of human variation, but believe that "racial" divisions have limited scientific interest and may even carry the risk of inviting abusive generalization' (UNESCO 1968: 270).

Although the UNESCO project contributed to undermining the scientific credentials of the 'race concept' (Barkan 1992), it did not address the political implications of racism in the history of the West. It failed to deal with the important fact that while race-thinking may have had its beginnings in the scientific or philosophical domain, it was through the medium of politics that it had been given such significance. For example, while the Statement on Race and Racial Prejudice recognized that the colonial 'conditions of conquest' (UNESCO 1968) contributed to racism, the state is not analysed as having been an active agent of colonialism and racism. Furthermore, while admitting the historically rooted, rather than natural or universal, origins of racism, the Statement does not expand on the precise character of these origins. On the contrary, it skims over the history of colonialism and the resultant 'dependency' of the colonies to claim that progress had since been achieved due to the inclusion of many 'formerly dependent countries' (UNESCO 1968) in the international organizations. The formulation of the Statement ignores the power relations between large and small, western and 'developing' states that still define the workings of such institutions, as well as of the neo-colonial dependency that persists despite the official end of western domination.

This depoliticized approach to the origins and development of 'race' and racism was mirrored in the UNESCO proposals for combating racism in the post-immigration era. The influence of anthropologists on the panel's work, in particular Claude Lévi-Strauss, brought cultural relativism to the fore as a means both of conceptualizing diversity on a global scale and of promoting understanding between peoples. This culturalist interpretation of difference is epitomized by the assertion in the Statement that 'Current biological knowledge does not permit us to impute cultural achievements to differences in genetic potential. Differences in the achievements of different peoples should be attributed solely to their cultural history. The peoples of the world today appear to possess equal biological potentialities for attaining any level of civilization' (UNESCO 1968: 270). The main proposal made by UNESCO, and most forcefully by Claude Lévi-Strauss in *Race and History* (1961), was that human groups could be divided into cultures that are relative, and therefore equal, if not equivalent, to each other. The relativity of culture eradicated the hierarchical implication of 'superiority' and 'inferiority' built into the idea of 'race'. Therefore, Lévi-Strauss and UNESCO suggested replacing 'race' as a mode for categorizing human difference with 'ethnicity' or 'culture'. 'Racism' too is replaced by the term 'ethnocentrism' which, to Lévi-Strauss, more adequately describes the intolerance of different cultural or ethnic groups for each other. This inter-group mistrust is considered to be almost inherent, and therefore less dangerous.

The idea that each culture contributes to humanity 'in its own way' sought to counter the widely accepted belief that a hierarchy of 'race' divided Europeans from non-Europeans. Lévi-Strauss (1961) celebrated the diversity of humanity, demonstrated by what he called the 'distinctive contributions' of each cultural group. He stressed his belief that different levels of progress between such groups could not be attributed to any innate differences. Rather, progress comes about as a result of interaction between groups. The historical chance that led to the onset of modernity taking place in the West meant that the other cultures that rubbed shoulders with the Occident experienced more rapid progress. Those that remained isolated did not. In the culturally-relativist framework adopted by Lévi-Strauss which so greatly influenced the UNESCO approach and which forms the basis of a multiculturalist approach to the ongoing discrimination of non-Europeans in western societies, the differences between human groups are seen as fortuitous and almost arbitrary.

In making this point, Lévi-Strauss rightly critiques the Eurocentric notion of progress, which he sees as emerging from the evolutionist idea that all cultures are merely stages towards a single model of humanity epitomized by the West. Rejecting the idea of 'primitive' and 'civilized' cultures and the ideal of assimilation, Lévi-Strauss proposed that the only means to curb ethnocentrism was through the greater exchange of knowledge about different cultures among themselves. This interculturalist objective underpins the anti-racist policy of international institutions, such as the United Nations and the Council of Europe, to this day.

UNESCO's quest to wipe out 'race', to reduce it to the level of dubious science and to propose that all human cultures should be equally valued is not uncommendable in itself. The problem this approach entails, as I have briefly attempted to explain, is that it has been unable to cope with the realities of racism. It does not adequately explain how racism emerged and grew in political importance in relationship to the exigencies of nationalism (Balibar 1991) and the demands of colonialism.[4] Neither is it able to propose solutions that take into account the fact that, while 'race' as a concept may be easily disproved scientifically, the lived experience of racism, as Fanon (1967) so poignantly points out, cannot so easily be effaced. Therefore, the idea that encouraging understanding of 'other cultures' – or 'celebrating diversity' in contemporary terminology – is sufficient for wiping out racialized discrimination is unacceptable to those whose experience of racism, on a daily basis, reveals the contrary.

Be this as it may, it is precisely this approach to racism that dictates the strategies for opposing it taken by institutions. The goal of racelessness is declared reached although the criteria set out by Goldberg for a truly anti-racist politics at the level of states and supranational institutions are far from being in place. Indeed, this formula for anti-racism has filtered down to contribute to the disunity among non-governmental anti-racist associations. They are often pitted against each other around their attitude to the type of anti-racism set out by UNESCO. The depoliticized approach it takes to racism legitimates the idea of 'racelessness' and the culturalization of difference that underpins governmental and European policy on racism and discrimination.

For a contemporary analysis of racism, this means that institutions may be seen as being both racist and anti-racist. They make and enact policies that are experienced and analysed by many as discriminatory. Nevertheless, governments often present such policies as benefiting greater social cohesion in culturally diverse societies. At the same time they engage overtly in anti-

---

4 For a much more detailed account both of the political history of racism and the UNESCO Tradition, see Lentin (2004).

racism by funding governmental and non-governmental organizations committed to combating racism, and by passing anti-discrimination legislation. These dual actions have the effect of locating racism beyond the state: state-based discrimination, in immigration policy or policing for example, is said to ensure security and the peaceful co-existence of diverse groups within society; the racism legislated against and the anti-racism work that is funded target the actions of individuals and groups in civil society, or at best the institutionalization of racism within administrative sectors that is not, however, identified historically or politically with the political culture upon which states are built.

## Anti-Racists and the State

In this section of the chapter, I examine how the depoliticized and dehistoricized view of racism that dominates state and supranational institutional responses to it is played out at the level of anti-racist organizations. My main argument is that anti-racist approaches must be seen as being bound up with the emphasis placed upon public political culture as a source for the principles guiding anti-racism. This, in turn, reflects the degree to which varying anti-racist discourses see the state itself as central to the origins and persistence of racism. To put it simply, the closer an anti-racist discourse can be situated to public political culture, the less it tends to have a state-centred critique of racism. This type of approach can be summed up by a comment made in an interview by a representative of the French association SOS Racisme. The organization believes that it is by turning to the principles espoused by French republican ideology – *liberté, egalité, fraternité* – that the social exclusion of minority groups can be overcome:

> We knew that this failure at school, this poverty, this delinquency had also contributed to the rise of the *Front National*. And we wanted both to come to the assistance of the problem neighbourhoods – so, to help minorities, to guarantee them access to the best conditions of life – but also, because we knew that to convince French people tempted by the racist vote for the Front national that there were solutions to poverty, to the violence in the neighbourhoods and that there were human solutions that would lead to better living conditions for everyone. And in fact, it was simply the application of the Republic that could stop the process of ghettoisation in the neighbourhoods.
>
> Cited in Lentin 2004: 202

In contrast, organizations that can be located at a position of distance from public political culture develop an analysis of racism which focuses on the role of the state in maintaining the status quo of societies structured in racism. Whereas both types of organization may target institutional racism, the first considers the entry of racism into the practice of institutions the result of a 'few bad apples', while the latter point to the more deeply embedded, historically rooted nature of this type of racism. While the first focus more on the influence of individual prejudice on social, political and economic life, the latter see individual prejudice as a product of accepted norms about difference that are structurally built into these spheres.

An important element that I uncovered while researching anti-racism in four European countries is the extent to which mainstream or institutional anti-racist discourses are not, as may perhaps be expected, strangers to a particular form of nationalist rhetoric. This is not the commonly recognized virulent and exclusionary nationalism. Rather, it may be expressed through a commitment to the law of the land grounded in myths about the struggle for democracy epitomized by the French Revolution or the anti-fascist resistance. It can also be perceived in the 'better the devil you know' language to which anti-racists often have recourse when comparing racism in their own countries to that elsewhere. I called this (Lentin 2004) a 'national way of doing things' which impinges upon the possibility for anti-racism to take on a truly transnational dimension in the way of other progressive social movements. Perhaps the interwovenness of racism and nationalism causes anti-racism, in turn, to constitute itself in nationally specific terms. Nonetheless, when coupled with the constraints governing funding for anti-racist activities that often strictly curtail the possibilities for critiquing government policy, the degree to which some anti-racisms uphold the image the state promotes of itself as an anti-racist actor warrants attention.

In what way is proximity to the public political culture of the nation-state expressed in anti-racist discourse and practice? How does this positioning affect the possibilities open to anti-racisms that are founded upon a state-centred critique of racism? I would like to focus on a dichotomy I identified in anti-racist discourse that illustrates how anti-racisms struggle conceptually with the state. Consistent with the emphasis of the chapter so far, I will highlight the way in which this dichotomy is perceived from the perspective of mainstream anti-racism. I am calling this dichotomous couple majoritarianism/communitarianism. Using examples from the research I carried out with anti-racist activists, I shall briefly outline how this pair contributes to uncovering the complex interaction between anti-racism and the public political culture of European states.

# Institutional Forms of Discrimination

## Majoritarianism/Communitarianism

These strange terms are awkward translations from French in which they are commonly used by both activists and the general public. Nevertheless, they are useful because they sum up a central dilemma in anti-racist ideology that impinges directly on the relationship between anti-racism and the state. 'Communitarian' is used in France to refer to activities or attitudes that are restricted to minority groups. Most commonly, to be communitarian is popularly interpreted in terms of exclusivity or, still further, as a rejection of what are seen as being the universal principles of republicanism. In contrast, to be majoritarian or generalist is to be accessible to the population as a whole and to reflect what are portrayed as being the interests of society at large.

Translated into anti-racist terms, communitarian organizations are said to be those which are grounded in a specific community, of immigrant origin for example. It is assumed by those who hold a majoritarian stance that such groups are incapable of practising anti-racism. This is because anti-racism is seen as being a universal value with which everyone must be able to identify. According to the French organization SOS Racisme:

> Why teach the culture of one community to that community? We think that there shouldn't be specific teaching for Algerians of their Algerian culture at the secular schools but that there should be an education for everyone about Algerian culture … we don't want each community teaching its culture without the others being able to benefit. We don't support the idea that in a classroom they say: OK, the Algerians, you go to school with Mr A.N. Other who's going to talk to you about your culture of origin while the Chinese go with Mr Wong who's going to talk about the culture of the Chinese … It's against communitarianism. In fact, there is a real stake to stop communitarianism in school.
>
> Cited in Lentin 2004: 214

Beyond the French context, the distinction also has relevance. The idea of a majoritarian anti-racism is inextricable from the belief that anti-racist principles are part of the political culture of democratic countries. Where states do not practise anti-racist principles they should be reminded by activists of their responsibilities. This is done by recalling key texts, such as the Declaration of Human Rights or the national constitution, and evoking historical moments in the national struggle for freedom from domination, most commonly that against fascism and Nazism. For example, the Italian organization ARCI, a left-wing organization with over a million members, sees its involvement in anti-racism as a commitment to ensuring responsibility among its membership and across society as a whole:

We are not an association that, let's say, was born an anti-racist association. We are an association that was born out of the democratic culture of the Italian Left. So, we felt the necessity, in comparison to other anti-racist associations that are called anti-racist that were created in recent years, we need anchorage, to make our members understand – those who perhaps were partisans, or workers, or maybe had participated in the anti-fascist struggles of the seventies – to make them understand than they could not, on the grounds of their own history, be racist. We were very worried about this because the culture of intolerance is a culture that we felt ran the risk also of affecting our membership.

Cited in Lentin 2004: 200

The approach taken by ARCI, evoked by this statement, is concerned with making anti-racism relevant to its membership. It therefore tends to set the agenda on this basis rather than being led by the needs of those facing racism. Being anti-racist is portrayed as being part and parcel of what being left-wing is about, especially for an organization that prides itself on its roots in the partisan movement. The size and importance of ARCI in the Italian political arena enables it to take positions which feed the political agenda of the left and centre left. This majoritarian standpoint passes through the prism of anti-racism in order to connect a vision of the heroism of the Italian left's historical struggle against fascism to a present and future politics based on the principles of that laudable past:

We felt that there was a weak Italian national consciousness, a perception of history that was also weak. Luckily, the consciousness of the partisan fight against fascism was strong, on the other hand. So, that great struggle of the people was strong, one of the greatest stories of Italian history: the anti-fascist resistance. And beneath that anti-fascist fight is, therefore, the Italian constitution which was written on the basis of an encounter between Catholic culture, Liberal culture, Communist culture, Socialist culture: it is still a constitution that stands by those who suffer. It is a constitution that refuses war and refuses racism because the experience of antisemitism was seen by the partisans – and so by its authors – as a risk from which Italy could no longer hide.

Cited in Lentin 2004: 224

This recourse to the foundations of the contemporary state illustrates the fact that, for many mainstream, majoritarian organizations, the post-Second World War state is generically committed to democratic principles which are seen as being essentially left-oriented. This enables government policy to be distinguished from the public political culture of the state. While the first may instigate discriminatory policy, the latter can always be looked to for solutions to racism. As such, majoritarian organizations do not see it as contradictory to co-operate with state institutions or accept state funding.

The majoritarian approach to anti-racism contrasts with that which emerged from the struggle for justice of racialized peoples in colonial, postcolonial and immigration societies. Majoritarians argue that an anti-racism based upon the lived experience of racism can never be inclusive of the majority of the population who, though not suffering racism, feel committed to fighting it. This seems to confirm the argument for greater social cohesion in the face of failing multiculturalism that is increasingly being advocated by governments. This argument supports the idea that 'minority groups' ghettoize themselves by clinging to ethnic particularities, rather than focusing on the racism that often drives discriminated groups into enclaves. Majoritarian organizations, such as SOS Racisme, believe that it is imperative to avoid communitarianism in order to avoid what it sees as being the trap of ethnic attachments. This position leaves little room for imagining an anti-racism based on the lived experience of racism that is nonetheless inclusive and open to participation by all:

> From the moment that we would rely on a communitarian model, we'd lose all our power and all our force because we wouldn't be speaking to everyone's hearts. We would not be speaking to 60 million people, we'd be speaking to the victims concerned. And the victims concerned are not the main part of the activist force.
>
> Cited in Lentin 2004: 185

The same message is expressed by the British Anti-Nazi League which insists upon the necessity for anti-racism to bridge political divides and reach a wide target group:

> You could see that there was actually lots of opposition to the Nazis but it was like from all different parts of society, so it wasn't just the Left, there was other people who were a bit more conservative who were against the Nazis and we wanted to bring that all into the one kind of group and we needed a group that had a very narrow, narrow remit so it doesn't stop people from fighting the Nazis. Because what you would see was there was people ... there was revolutionaries and there was reformists and there was even people who were quite conservative and we wanted to unite all those people and that's when the Anti-Nazi League was initiated with different kind of MPs, different groups, celebrities and all that kind of thing.
>
> Cited in Lentin 2004: 204

The majoritarian position, by seeking to generalize its message as widely as possible, and by failing to recognize organizations grounded in the experience of the racialized as truly anti-racist, upholds the vision of anti-racism generally promoted by governments. The autonomous race committees (Gilroy 1992) that dotted the UK in the 1970s saw their activities curtailed in the 1980s when funding for cultural activities was prioritized over a politicized activism that linked 'race' and class. Similarly, the *Mouvement beur* that emerged in the 1980s in France failed when the Socialist government ploughed funding into the youth organization SOS Racisme as a means of ensuring that the anti-racist agenda remained under the auspices of a controllable organization with strong links to the ruling party (Malik 1990; Fysh and Wolfreys 1998). Many organizations in both countries have, as a result, resorted to operating at a much smaller scale and therefore run the risk of being labelled as communitarian or exclusionary.

While the positions taken by these organizations, despite the challenges they face, continue to contribute to setting the anti-racist agenda, the divisions summed up by the majoritarian/communitarian dichotomy entrench the disunity of the anti-racist movement in Europe. This disunity is evident in a variety of arguments central to debates on how to define and practise anti-racism. These arguments include the question of the autonomy of anti-racism from the state and its institutions, the degree to which anti-racism should be local, national or transnational in its orientation, the level to which lived experience should be a criterion for setting anti-racist agendas, and so forth. All of these arguments pertain to the relationship between anti-racism and public political culture and the positioning of various anti-racist discourses in relation to the state. As such they relate directly to the various ways in which racism itself is conceived, either as an aberration from the public political culture of European states or, in contrast, as specifically bound up with the political development of the western state. In the final section of this chapter, I shall ask how these disparities in conceptualizing racism influence interpretations of racism in Europe today. How do these disparities in approaching racism that emerge from the disunity at the heart of anti-racism itself affect a politicized and historicized analysis of the racism that continues to dog migrants and the racialized?

## Crisis Measures: Racism and Riots

In this chapter I have shown how the interpretations of racism that are available to us in European societies have been developed by anti-racists committed to eradicating the injustices brought about by racist discrimination. These explanations of racism and the solutions put forward to dealing with it have often been either directly commissioned by states and supranational institutions or harnessed by them for the development of institutional policy on the issue. The positioning of anti-racism vis-à-vis the state, I have argued, is fundamental, not only for understanding the disunity among anti-racists, but also for making sense of why there are simply so many different approaches to tackling racism. It should not be extrapolated from my argument that the blame for the persistence of racism should be laid at the door of anti-racism; quite the contrary. However, it is important to have a complete understanding of how various anti-racist discourses, albeit unwittingly, contribute to legitimating policies that bypass the central reasons for why racism persists; namely because it remains intertwined with state logics.

Since the end of the 1990s, voices have increasingly been heard decrying a crisis in multiculturalism or the failure of integration in societies of immigration. This can be witnessed in the attack on affirmative action in the United States, the criminalization of immigration in Europe, the change of citizenship criteria and ceremonies in several countries, the rise of Islamophobia, the rolling back of civil liberties as a fallout of the 'War on Terror' and the increased recourse to racial and ethnic profiling in the service of greater national security. One event in recent times demonstrates the link between this politics of greater social control, based on an orchestrated 'fear of the other', and racism. This event was the 'rioting' of French youth of immigrant origin for three weeks in November 2005.

These – at times violent – uprisings can be taken to be symbolic of the political failure of the declared commitment to the eradication of racism in postcolonial Europe. This event was just one among many of its kind since the beginning of large-scale non-European immigration following the Second World War. People of immigrant origin, most often black and brown, have periodically been led to radically draw attention to the inequalities they face in the democratic states of the First World. The rage expressed at the death of two teenagers in Clichy-sous-Bois on 27 October 2005, while fleeing the police, that triggered the rioting is part of a larger, collective rage felt by all those who experience the daily realities of structural racism. Nevertheless, the 'riots' have been largely treated as unprecedented in France, revealing both the shortness of political memory and the reluctance to view 'national problems' within a global context.

Looking to examples from other societies, however, would reveal that solutions to the persistent problem of racism are generally proposed only at times of crisis, as the response to the November 2005 uprisings in France has once again demonstrated.[5] In addition to the promise of increased budgetary expenditure to bandage the wounds inflicted by unemployment and public spending cutbacks, these solutions tend to revalorize both the instruments of state rule and the political culture from which they have emerged. Therefore, a commitment to an increase in community policing, for example, has been accompanied in the French case by a reaffirmation of 'French values'. President Jacques Chirac, in a televised address to the nation on 14 November 2005, claimed that the riots must be met by 'being firm, being just, and by remaining loyal to the values of France'.[6] The social exclusion that is recognized to have ignited the flames of the burning cars, shops and schools is rarely linked to an admission of the way racism has become embedded in modern state structures, making this exclusion an inevitability for the 'immigrant' underclass. While governments admit that it is no longer possible to argue that racist discrimination is the work of only a few 'bad apples', they still prefer to present the widespread nature of discrimination as the (almost justifiable) frustrated reaction of a threatened 'indigenous' population.

What an unravelling of the 'story' of post-war western anti-racism reveals is the paradoxical manner in which racism has been officially interpreted. As the French example shows, racism is both admitted and denied in an official discourse that, in turn, influences the wider societal interpretation of events such as the November 2005 uprisings. On the one hand, the facts are clear: people of non-white, immigrant origin with addresses that connect – and condemn – them to the 'sensitive neighbourhoods',[7] face poor schooling and healthcare and are often considered unemployable. They are regular targets of heavy-handed policing based on impromptu racial-profiling schema. On the other hand, it is proposed that this inequality may be overcome by adhering, not only to the law, but also to the ideology, of the land. Whether states propose a universalist or a multicultural model for the 'integration' of post-immigration societies,[8] the presumption is that the tensions given rise to by diversity can be overcome by a commitment to that model.

5  Similarly, the Scarman Inquiry which refused to consider the possible existence of institutionalized racism in Britain, was carried out in response to the 1981 Brixton riots.
6  Citation taken from the TF1 television station website: http://news.tf1.fr/news/france (last accessed 5 September 2007). This translation from the French original is my own, as elsewhere in this article, unless otherwise stated.
7  The French expression 'les quartiers sensibles' is euphemistically used to describe the poor suburbs populated mainly by families of Maghrebi and African origin.
8  A common opposition is made between the so-called Anglo-American multicultural model and the French universalist model for the organization of post-immigration societies. Stereotypically, the first model conceives of society as made up of an array of culturally different groups, co-existing under a common set of laws and duties. The universalist model emphasizes the seamless integration of cultural difference in public life

As this chapter has shown, the way in which a certain brand of mainstream anti-racism has given weight to this assumption is palpable. Since the end of the Second World War, governments in the West, and particularly in Europe, have had to prove their commitment to acting against racism. This is linked inextricably to the history of the Holocaust and the persistent imprint it continues to leave on European politics. Yet, crucial as it is to recall the horrors of that history, especially in the face of the threats to its memory, the Holocaust cannot be the only lens through which to understand European racism. In the multicultural, post-immigration societies of contemporary Europe, problems of 'race' and class, that have both local and globalized dimensions, result in the exclusion from political, social and economic life of a great number among our populations. The systematic discrimination that affects both new migrants and many among those whose grandparents were the original immigrants cannot be thought of as an anomaly. However, by thinking one-dimensionally about racism as uniquely synonymous with the genocidal Holocaust, the political mainstream in Europe does just that.

Because the Holocaust has always been explained as aberrant from the public political culture upon which modern democracies have been founded (Bauman 1989), it has in turn been impossible to face up to the relationship between racism and the European state and its history of slavery, colonialism, genocide and discrimination against minorities and non-national others. Because racism has consistently been held at a distance, the idea that we live in a post-racial age has become generalized despite the fact that, as Goldberg explains, we are far from having expunged 'race' from our midst. As a consequence, it is possible to reduce the contemporary experience of racism to the lesser evils of discrimination or intolerance. The debate following the French 'riots', by laying the blame on irresponsible hip-hop artists and polygamous families,[9] reduced the significance of the message behind the riots to the excesses of 'uncontrollable kids' out 'past their bedtimes'. This type of rhetoric infantilizes the rioters and their social milieus. The predominance of this type of response when added to the government's refusal of the link between social exclusion, unemployment, poverty and racism compounds the chasm between racism and anti-racism in state logic. According to this logic, democracies are theoretically committed to fighting racism, and indeed spend a great deal of money to this end on campaigns, programmes and inquiries.

9 The French Employment Minister, Gerard Larcher, claimed that polygamy among families of immigrant origin was one of the reasons for the November 2005 riots. The Minister was quoted as saying, on 16 November 2005, that 'as a part of society takes part in this anti-social behaviour, it is hardly surprising that some of them find it difficult to find a job' (http://news.tf1.fr/news/france/0,,3263446,00.html, last accessed 5 September 2007).

Yet the extent to which anti-racism itself has become institutionalized means that the interpretation of racism used by governments is often unable to take into account what is experienced as racism by real people. This chapter has attempted to demonstrate the heterogeneity of anti-racism in order to uncover the role that certain anti-racisms have had in entrenching the struggle between the state and its racialized citizens over what racism *is*. I might provocatively end by asking how many more schools have to be burnt before discussion begins.

## References

Balibar, E. (1991) 'Racism and Nationalism', in E. Balibar and I. Wallerstein, *Race, Nation, Class: Ambiguous Identities*. London: Verso, pp. 37–67.

Barkan, E. (1992) *The Retreat of Scientific Racism: Changing Concepts of Race in Britain and the United States between the World Wars*. Cambridge: Cambridge University Press.

Barker, M. (1983) 'Empiricism and Racism', *Radical Philosophy* Spring: 6–15.

Bauman, Z. (1989) *Modernity and the Holocaust*. Cambridge: Polity Press.

Bonnett, A. (2000) *Anti-Racism*. London and New York: Routledge.

Fanon, F. (1967) *Black Skins, White Masks*. London: Pluto Press.

Foucault, M. (1997) *Il faut défendre la société: Cours au Collège de France, 1976*. Paris: Gallimard Seuil.

Fysh, P., and J. Wolfreys (1998) *The Politics of Racism in France*. Basingstoke: Macmillan.

Gilroy, P. (1992) 'The End of Anti-Racism', in *'Race', Culture and Difference*, ed. J. Donald and A. Rattansi. London: Sage.

Goldberg, D. T. (2002a) *The Racial State*. Malden, MA, and Oxford: Blackwell.

— (2002b) 'Post-Racial States', *Janus Head* 5(1), Spring, http://www.janushead.org/5-1/goldberg.cfm, last accessed 31 August 2007.

Hannaford, I. (1996) *Race: The History of an Idea in the West*. Baltimore, MD: Johns Hopkins University Press.

Lentin, A. (2004) *Racism and Anti-Racism in Europe*. London: Pluto Press.

Lévi-Strauss, C. (1961) *Race et Histoire*. Paris: Editions Gonthier.

Malik, S. (1990) *Histoire secrète de SOS Racisme*. Paris: Albin Michel.

Rawls, J. (2001) *Justice and Fairness: A Restatement*. Cambridge, MA, and London: The Belknap Press of Harvard University Press.

'The Stephen Lawrence Inquiry' (1999) Report of an Inquiry by Sir William Macpherson of Cluny. Presented to Parliament by the Secretary of State for the Home Department by Command of Her Majesty. London: The Stationery Office.

UNESCO (1968) 'UNESCO Statement on Race and Racial Prejudice', *Current Anthropology* 9:4: 270–2.

Voegelin, E. (1933 [2000]) *Race and State*, trans. by R. Heim. Baton Rouge, LA, and London: Louisiana State University Press.

# 6 What Space for Migrant Voices in European Anti-Racism?

## Çağla E. Aykaç

The European Union (EU) positions itself as a rights-based union founded on the principles of liberty, democracy, respect for human rights and fundamental freedoms and the rule of law. It included anti-racism into its fields of competence a little before the end of the millennium and has, over the past decade, developed a set of tools and mechanisms to address issues related to racism and xenophobia on a European platform. As highlighted by Alana Lentin, anti-racism ought to be considered as a subject of study that bears political significance in itself, and involves more than a simple 'commonsensical' opposition to racism (Lentin 2004). As such, the discourse, activities and policies of the EU in the field of anti-racism need to be considered in light of their underlying assumptions and contradictions, and beyond the proclaimed European rejection of all behaviour and structures that perpetrate or encourage the development or persistence of racism and xenophobia in Europe. This chapter proposes to trace the position of anti-racism in a broader EU policy context through a brief historiography of the development of race matters in the EU. It critically assesses the policy priorities and the theoretical frameworks of European anti-racist activities. EU anti-racist policies will undoubtedly bear a growing influence on the experiences of those affected by racism in Europe as they are in constant interaction with member states' policies in the field of anti-racism and create new spaces for anti-racist action. This chapter does not give voice to migrants but proposes to think about whether the European Union, as a political project, contributes to doing so.

Racism was first addressed in the European institutions in 1986 when the European Parliament, the Council and the Commission put forth a Joint Declaration against Racism and Xenophobia. Various institutions of the European Union got involved in bringing racism and xenophobia on to the

European agenda in the mid-1990s, particularly in the fields of employment and education or as joint actions to combat racism and xenophobia and anti-Semitism. At the end of the decade, these actions were concretized through the creation of a legal framework to combat discrimination in general terms. Anti-racism thus officially figures alongside and in interconnection with the wider anti-discrimination concerns of the EU, which include the fight against discrimination based on ethnicity, age, disability, religion or sexual orientation. This anti-discrimination legislative framework was inspired by the EU gender equality legislation developed in the 1970s and continues to evolve as the EU gains competence and experience in anti-discrimination. The year 1997 marked a European threshold in the fight against racism as it was declared the European Year against Racism. The year also saw the establishment of the European Monitoring Centre on Racism and Xenophobia (EUMC) in Vienna, and the inclusion of article 13 in the Treaty of Amsterdam.

The EUMC holds a central position in the anti-racist activities of the EU as it is vested with the task of providing reliable and comparable research and data on racism and xenophobia. It works through the European Information Network on Racism and Xenophobia (RAXEN) designed to collect data and information through twenty-five National Focal Points (NFP), one in each member state. Each of the NFPs is commissioned to set up national information networks that include governmental institutions, NGOs and research institutes. All NFPs collect data and information through different channels and have varying degrees of proximity to the state. Most do not rely directly on information provided by migrants themselves but rather on police data, media coverage, state statistics or information provided by anti-racist organizations. The EUMC incorporates recommendations from (among others) the Council of Europe's European Commission against Racism and Intolerance (ECRI), the United Nations Committee on the Elimination of Racial Discrimination, and the Organization for Security and Co-operation in Europe (OSCE). The EU thus works in co-operation with international organizations. At the same time, it also aims to involve member states and civil society organizations working at the grassroots level. The EUMC was created and developed within the framework activities of the Employment and Social Affairs DG of the European Commission. In 2007, it will be detached from this policy framework and will fall within that of the justice, liberty and security affairs. It will then no longer be mandated to deal with racism and xenophobia alone, but will be converted into a wider Fundamental Rights Agency. As I shall discuss below, the shift is politically significant and signals continuities and discontinuities in the anti-racist activities of the EU.

Further, and most importantly, in 1997, the Treaty of Amsterdam extended the powers of the EU in the field of combating discrimination. In effect, the Treaty gives the EU powers to intervene in member states with regard to discrimination and to apply sanctions on those that do not adequately transpose and implement related legislation. It introduces a binding power that former resolutions and actions did not hold. Article 13 empowers the EU to take action in dealing with discrimination on grounds including racial or ethnic origin, religion or belief, age, disability and sexual orientation. Race matters thus fall within a wider anti-discrimination effort that takes into account multiple forms of discrimination. The inclusion of Article 13 in the Treaty of Amsterdam gave rise to two new Directives. The Racial Equality Directive (2000/43/EC) implements the principle of equal treatment irrespective of racial or ethnic origin. It bans direct and indirect discrimination as well as harassment and instructions to discriminate on grounds of racial or ethnic origin. It covers employment, training, education, social security, healthcare, housing and access to goods and services. The Employment Equality Directive (2000/78/EC) establishes a general framework for equal treatment in employment and occupation. It focuses on discrimination in employment and occupation, as well as vocational training. It also deals with direct and indirect discrimination as well as harassment and instructions to discriminate on grounds of religion or belief, disability, age and sexual orientation. The two directives are complemented by a community action programme (2001–2006) which aims at supplementing legislation, improving knowledge of phenomena related to discrimination, and developing policy and capacity to prevent discrimination on a European platform. The Directives were adopted around the same time as the Charter of Fundamental Rights of the European Union at the Nice European Council (December 2000) which further contributed to establishing equality as a constitutive element in the formation of the union.

In addition to the legal framework provided by Article 13 and the two Directives, racism and xenophobia became criminal offences with the 2001 Commission proposal for the criminalization of racism and xenophobia that was to be implemented by 2004. In 2002, the Framework Decision on combating racism and xenophobia criminalized 'racism and xenophobia' defined here as the 'belief in race, colour, descent, religion or belief, national or ethnic origin as a factor determining aversion to individuals'. Henceforth, public incitement to violence or hatred, public insults or threats, public condoning of racist or xenophobic purpose of crimes of genocide or crimes against humanity, public dissemination of material containing expression of racism and xenophobia became crimes in European Union member states.

These offences are punishable by sentences that range from extradition to deprivation of liberty or seizure of material.

Whether this legislative framework positively contributes to giving voice to migrants is a question that is seldom posed in academic and policy research on the directives. This said, in theory, the directives contribute to the creation or consolidation of means for migrants to voice their concerns through legal channels. In effect, the directives rely on individual complaints and thus imply the creation of a space for expression. Although this is not a negligible development, it is clear that numerous obstacles remain before migrants can have their voices heard. Among these, as the EUMC research on policing shows, is the position and role of the police. In effect, in most EU member states, the police hold responsibility for recording and evaluating racially motivated crime and violence. The ineffectiveness of police recording practices for racist crimes in Europe carries the potential of deterring victims of racism from filing complaints in the first place. In addition, difficulties in gathering evidence, providing sufficient financial resources, or holding sufficient information appear as additional structural impediments to the full use of this space for expression. It is worth noting here that positive action is sanctioned without appearing as an official policy recommendation in the Racial Equality Directive, Article 5: Positive Action: 'With a view of ensuring full equality in practice, the principle of equal treatment shall not prevent any Member State from maintaining or adopting specific measures to prevent or compensate for disadvantages linked to racial or ethnic origin.'

Beyond the establishment of legal structures to address issues related to racism, the EU is currently in the process of establishing mechanisms to try to understand, frame, and develop policy to address racism and other forms of discrimination. The development and standardization of data collection systems figures as one of the principal European policy priorities in the field. In effect, there are considerable differences and gaps in the data collection mechanisms of member states. The quality and coverage of the material provided by the National Focal Points varies greatly. Altogether, these pose real methodological problems. Illustratively, it is worth mentioning that each and every resolution or research project on racism and xenophobia produced by the EUMC highlights the tensions that are inherent in trying to define, quantify and qualify the issues and subjects at stake. The fact that terms and categories inevitably hold different meanings in different contexts brings into question the validity of research in which data is used comparatively and sometimes interchangeably in the effort to gain a European perspective. The comparative aspiration of the EUMC is further complicated by the fact that member states have very different histories in their relation to racism and anti-racism, as well as different contemporary political, economic, demographic, and social contexts. Europe is today admittedly struggling to overcome these inconsistencies.

The process of trying to establish common conceptual definitions as well as shared implementation methods holds the positive function of monitoring trends and levels of implementation in individual member states. It forces a certain level of transparency and accountability at a European level. Targeted reports on various forms of racism such as racist violence or institutional discrimination in employment, housing, and education present inventories of the nature and breadth of national data on discrimination currently available through governmental and non-governmental channels. The practice, from an EU perspective, aims not only to increase knowledge of the phenomenon at stake but also to evaluate best practices, and thus devise policies to combat racism and xenophobia that would be applicable at a European level.

At the same time, the process of collecting data implies categorizing individuals under labels that never seem to quite capture the complexity of contemporary European identities and forms of belonging. Multiple discriminations, for example, such as those faced by women, or the issues of generational differences, can hardly be incorporated in these targeted data. Further, today all member states have different modes of naming, quantifying and qualifying migrants and minorities that attest to their historical, political, social, economic and demographic particularities. Most are associated with member states' histories of migration and their 'integration' policies. Among the broad variety of terms used throughout member states one reads: immigrant, ethnic migrant, third-country national, foreigner, non-national, non-Western, alien, asylum-seeker, refugee, ethnic minority from non-Western countries, third-country (non-Western) immigrants, autochthonous minority, descendant, foreign-born, or foreign origin, among others. These categories, when they exist, hold more than a purely descriptive function. They attest to features that would make certain people or groups vulnerable to racism and they clearly do not refer to the daily experiences of those that are subject to racism. In other words, they primarily refer to the legal status of the potential victim of racism rather than their feelings of exclusion. By extension, they imply a hierarchy of rights whereby the right not be discriminated against is not granted equally to all individuals.

Today, the preferred terminology used at a European level is that of 'migrant and minority'. It understandably tries to reconcile and encapsulate a very wide range of terminologies that are used at national levels to refer to vulnerable groups. At the same time, it fails to account for – among others – those who were born and raised in Europe and continue to be discriminated

124

against. In addition, it involves related yet contradictory policy fields. On the one hand, minority policies aim to redress inequalities and discrimination among citizens who are considered to have equally legitimate claims to rights. The concept of 'minority' actually appears to be relatively marginalized in the work of the EUMC. On the other hand, that of the 'migrant' appears at the forefront. Racism in Europe is thus increasingly considered and explicated in light of twentieth-century migrations into Europe. Discrimination and racism are associated with the integration policies of various member states, and in light of the integration capacity of migrants, who are thus indirectly held partly responsible for the racism they encounter. In addition, current developments in the immigration policies of the EU increasingly portray the migrant as a threat to European security and social cohesion. Immigration policies in the EU involve co-operation on the surveillance and control of migrants who tend to be associated with crime and illegality. They increasingly contribute to the marginalization of migrants and reinforce their portrayal as social, political and economic threats. In such a framework, rights for migrants tend to be perceived as concessions rather than as legitimate rights. Their right not be discriminated against is set against the question of whether they truly 'deserve' to be in Europe in the first place.

Further, the increasing linking of racism with migration contributes to constructing and solidifying national and European senses of belonging to an imaginary European community which, if left to itself, could well be racism-free. This European community celebrates heterogeneity, but within certain limits. It is selectively inclusive and clearly tends to exclude all those that fall into the wide category of 'migrant and minority', whether it is by limiting the mobility of non-national residents, or through other means. Overall the singling out of the migrant as the victim of racism contributes to creating a sense of internal European unity and solidarity in the face of a threat that comes from outside. In parallel, it fails to reflect the multiplicity of forms of racism that exist in Europe today. Among these, one can cite that which exists between Northerners and Southerners in Italy, that between Flemish and Walloons in Belgium, the racism that Portuguese and Spaniards faced a decade ago and which persists today at different levels, the Roma who are known to face extremely high levels of discrimination throughout Europe, or more recently the overt racism expressed towards those who come from the 'east' and have become part of the EU through the last wave of enlargement. By extension, the creation of a quasi-natural link between racism and migration fails to account for the reality that racism, in Europe, is and has been in a reciprocal relation with nationalism and colonialism (Balibar 1988a). Racism in Europe is not a new phenomenon, a response to waves of invasions by migrants. It was and is a constitutive element in the formation and construction of the nation states that compose the Union. The failure to properly historicize racism in Europe bears on the political agenda of anti-racism and the forms of anti-racist activities (Lentin 2004). Last, it can hardly be said that the voices of migrants are being heard in the policy priority of the EU to collect data on racism. In effect, as underlined above, the process of categorization and quantification procedures have little, if anything, to do with migrants' daily experiences of racism or with their sentiments of belonging/non-belonging and exclusion.

As mentioned above, the inadequacies of the data at hand raise concerns about the comparability and the validity of material on racism. However, research compiled by the EUMC contributes to positing racism as a multi-layered contemporary reality in Europe. Research highlights the existence of both institutional and symbolic forms of racism. Racism, from an EU perspective, is not simply an ideology to which a number of extreme groups adhere. It is embedded in the institutional structures of European Union member states and also manifests itself through daily discourses, practices and violence. It is not monolithic; it has local and national particularities. It is not static, and does not evolve in a way that could allow imagining a Europe free of racism in the near future. Peaks taken into consideration, levels of racist violence have been a long-term concern in Europe and on the agenda of the EU since the mid-1980s. Racism in Europe is in constant dialogue with global social, economic, political and economic trends.

The structural aspects of racism that involve the functioning of institutions are addressed through a series of research activities on the situation of migrants and minorities in the fields of employment, education, and housing. These reports highlight the existence of forms of discriminations that are embedded in daily practices that interact and feed upon each other. The report on discrimination in housing highlights that migrants and minorities live in comparatively poorer housing conditions. The report on education shows that educational achievement among minorities is lower than that of the majority groups. Migrants and minorities tend to enrol in schools with lower academic credentials, and are over-represented in vocational tracks. The report on employment highlights the relatively disadvantaged position of migrants and minorities who are disproportionately employed in low-skilled, low-paid professions and hold precarious employment positions. 'Migrants and minorities' have higher unemployment rates than 'natives or migrants from other EU/EEA countries'. Tackling the issue of discrimination in employment was noticeably the topic of one of the first EU resolutions on racism and xenophobia in 1995. The 'Lisbon strategy for economic, social and environmental renewal' has anti-discrimination provisions. Programmes such as Integra, the EQUAL Initiative of the European Social Fund, or PHARE aim to 'integrate' minorities in the European labour market. Discrimination in employment is a priority concern that goes beyond ideals of social equity. It plagues the overall prospects for economic growth, dynamism and competitiveness of Europe and thus its overall performance. Different forms of institutional discrimination exist in all member states. They feed upon each other and contribute to the creation of a system in which exclusions need to be tackled on multiple grounds at the same time.

The concept of institutional racism has both strengths and weaknesses. Its strength lies in the fact that it recognizes that the absence of openly racist discourses, or their transformation, does not automatically imply the disappearance of discrimination and racist practices. It thus forces us to acknowledge the systemic aspects of discrimination. Its weakness or its insufficiency lies in its representation of discrimination as a reality in which actors are absent. Most relevant for this chapter, Michel Wieviorka argues that one of the strengths of the concept lies in the fact that it contributes to giving voice to migrants (Wieviorka 1998). According to him, it allows for a dialogue in which the ethical and moral 'integrity' of those who benefit from an unequal order need not figure as an obstacle to fostering political and institutional changes. It is an invitation to debate and to challenge discrimination and segregation, and an opportunity to foster changes. The EU recognizes and proposed to address forms of institutional racism that increasingly pose problems necessitating long-term solutions.

In parallel, the EUMC has set up a Rapid Response Force to address 'crises' of European dimensions. It was designed after the 11 September 2001 attacks in New York to evaluate possible repercussions of the terrorist attacks for Muslims in Europe. Since then, reports have been produced on immediately international 'crises' that might have bearing on levels of racism in Europe. Overall, National Focal Points stress that 'crises' lead to temporary rises in levels of racist violence. However, these peaks are not particularly significant in light of the already high pre-existing levels of violence and discrimination before the attacks. In other words, a simple cause/effect link between terrorism and racist violence should not be taken for granted. It can be argued that the attacks provided grounds for justifying and legitimizing opinions that were already widespread and well established. Yet it appears difficult to argue that they trigger a new form of racism that did not previously exist. Further, the reports underline an increase in the popularity of far-right movements while underlining that racist discourse is not limited to extreme fringes. Europeans appear to be increasingly tolerant in the face of racist behaviour or discourse, whether it is in the media, on the internet or in the discourse of mainstream political figures.

Muslims were expected to be particularly vulnerable targets to racist violence and discrimination after the attacks. Yet it is asylum-seekers, immigrants or 'foreigners' more generally that are targeted, irrespective of their religious beliefs or country of origin. Visual identifiers ranging from dress codes to physical appearance determine racist violence or harassment more than religious practice or degrees of religiosity. The work done by the Rapid Response Force illustrates the existence, reality and multiplicity of what was termed 'New Racism' by Barker in 1981 and was further theorized under the labels of 'symbolic racism', 'cultural racism', 'differential racism' or 'neo-racism' (Taguieff 1991; Balibar and Wallerstein 1988). While biological racism might persist despite having been discredited after the Second World War, 'new' forms of racism seek justifications beyond biological arguments. They legitimate racist behaviour through arguments based on 'culture'. Cultural forms of racism are based on arguments that posit culture, ethnicity or religions as having essential features that are incompatible with those of a majority population. The 'other' is different; his/her difference is recognized yet seen as irreconcilable with the identity of the dominant group. Moreover, he/she is seen as a threat to the identity, the values, the economic stability and the security of the majority population. Muslims in Europe are not alone in facing this kind of racism. Yet certain characteristics that are invariably attributed to Islam and by extension to all Muslims provide fertile ground to legitimize these forms of racism. The growing portrayal of all Muslims as being ill educated, prone to violence, particularly against women, lazy and inclined to abusing European social benefits, and more generally as being opposed to the values of liberty and democracy, provide arguments to justify racism against them. Overall, Muslims and more generally migrants in Europe are considered to threaten European values because their cultural charac-teristics are considered to be irreconcilable with a common European identity.

It is interesting to note that there are important inconsistencies between the outcome of the research on Islamophobia and the policy recommendations formulated to address the problems at stake. Most importantly for us, here, policy recommendations focus on giving voice to migrants. This might well be the only context in which giving voice to migrants appears to be a preferred policy option, where it is encouraged to the apparent exclusion of other forms of policy. In effect, policy recommendation here advocates increasing dialogue with between religious communities, encouraging the involvement of religious leaders in national and European public spheres, and the media. Increasing knowledge about the culture and traditions of Muslims, and spreading information about Islam, appear as a preferred policy with the ultimate aim of fostering intercultural dialogue.

The reports on Islamophobia show that all migrants are at greater risk of being subject to discrimination or racist violence, be it perpetrated by nation-states, institutions or individuals. They highlight that terror attacks perpetrated in the name of Islam provide fertile ground for the reinforcement of a climate of suspicion against migrants in general. Yet policy recommendation advocates intercultural and inter-religious dialogue with Muslims alone. In doing so, it reinforces the idea that the rise of levels of racism in Europe can actually rightly be attributed to the presence of Muslims. The trend holds the potential for belittling or bypassing the high levels of discrimination faced by other vulnerable groups in Europe. In addition, the policy recommendations focus on giving voice to Muslim leaders in their roles as religious leaders. The imam is thus considered to be qualified to address all problems faced by all Muslims living in Europe and to speak in their name. This approach not only assumes that all people originating from majority Muslim countries are Muslim, but also that they all identify in religious terms, that they form a homogeneous group, and that their concerns in Europe can be addressed primarily in religious terms. It contributes to depoliticizing a situation that obviously does not involve Muslims alone. Giving voice to migrants here implies separating them from forms of belonging and action that are not linked to religion. While reinforcing the idea that all Muslims can be considered to be part of a homogeneous entity, the process contributes to creating hierarchies among and between vulnerable groups – the idea of the 'good' migrants versus the 'bad' ones – as imams are chosen selectively with little regard to their representative quality. Giving voice to migrants selectively, in this perspective, also implies silencing many.

The policy recommendations formulated by the EUMC in the framework of the Rapid Response Force follow the lines of the UNESCO tradition launched in the 1950s which argues that greater intercultural knowledge and dialogue have the potential to eradicate racism. As Lentin suggests, the tradition psychologizes and depoliticizes racism; it marginalizes the role played by modern states in the development of racism. In light of the overview of the anti-racist activities of the EU described above, it would be simplistic and reductive to argue that Europe's approach to anti-racism in general terms is limited to one that is line with the UNESCO tradition. Rather, it seems that this kind of discourse is preferred for dealing with certain issues, such as those that are associated with Islam. This said, discourse and policy that build on ideas of equal opportunity and intercultural dialogue are gaining in popularity in Europe; the years 2007 and 2008 will respectively be the European Year of Equal Opportunity and the European Year of Intercultural Dialogue.

It is worth underlining that the trends and policy recommendations mentioned above are developed as responses to a general sense of 'crisis' in Europe. This crisis is presented as being triggered by international events that are seen as carrying the potential to increase levels of racism in Europe. The sense of crisis is thus related and associated with dynamics that are considered to be external to Europe, and thus are not considered to be linked to the long-term institutional forms of racism existing in Europe. In 1988, Balibar noted that the development of racism in France was presented as being related to a crisis, and underlined that the concept of crisis in itself could contribute to obscuring the debate on racism if not addressed in all its complexity (Balibar 1988b). He suggested considering a reciprocal relation between crises and racism rather than seeing them as being linked in a linear fashion. This approach would involve recognizing that 'crises' have two dimensions, one that involves a 'crisis of racism' and the other that he terms 'racism of crisis'. 'Crisis of racism' and 'racism of crisis', according to Balibar, are in a reciprocal relation and appear in their urgency when a certain threshold of tolerance has been transgressed. It can safely be said that, from both perspectives, thresholds have already been crossed in Europe and that it is today pertinent to speak both of a 'crisis of racism' and a 'racism of crisis'. In this vein, the EUMC reports on racist violence, on its yearly activities and on institutional forms of racism clearly posit the reality of a 'crisis of racism' where racism takes a systemic form that is embedded in the structures of member states. In parallel, the Rapid Response Force addresses the issue of 'racism of crisis'. Here, acts of terrorism and threats to security would constitute the main elements of the crisis and would translate into a reactive increase in Islamophobia as a dominant form of racism. Both a 'crisis of racism' and a 'racism of crisis' are thus clearly recognized through the anti-racist activities of the EU, yet their relation appears to be rather linear.

In effect, increasingly, the idea of a crisis in Europe comes to be exclusively related to questions of security. Europe is facing a security crisis today, and it needs to devise policies and develop mechanisms to address this crisis. The security crisis of Europe is associated with an 'immigration problem' which is, as we have seen, presented as one of the principal triggers of the 'crisis of racism'. On the other hand, the 'crisis of racism' appears to bear on the economic capacity of the EU and on its levels of social cohesion. It is not considered to be a determining factor in the portrayal of immigrants as potential criminals and threats; and the obviously discriminatory environment of most member states is not seen as bearing on increasing levels of street violence or riots.

This limited use of the concept of crisis can in effect, as foreseen by Balibar, dilute and blur the debate on racism. The above mentioned associations can best be illustrated by the changing position of the EUMC within European Institutions. The EUMC, since its creation in 1997, developed within the Social Affairs and Employment DG of the European Commission. This policy field involves, among others, issues of employment policies, job-creation measures, the free movement of workers, employment rights, social protection, equality between men and women, social inclusion and the fight against poverty, anti-discrimination and relations with civil society. By 2007, the EUMC will be converted into a Fundamental Rights Agency and will be transferred into the policy field of the Justice, Freedom and Security DG of the European Commission. The shift implies the elimination of a space in which race matters are treated independently from immigration and security issues. From an EU perspective the transfer will have minimal consequences for the efforts invested in combating racism and xenophobia in their multiple forms. This claim can hardly be taken for granted as the Justice, Liberty and Security DG is vested with the functions of building a common immigration and asylum policy, assuring police and judicial co-operation, border controls, data protection, prevention and combating of crime, international terrorism, and the respect of fundamental rights. Given the scope of this policy field, it is indeed clear that close monitoring on the part of a fundamental rights agency is necessary. However, the fusion of agendas dealing with racism, immigration and security could be quite perilous.

The end of the 1990s saw the establishment of structures for the development of the anti-racist agenda of the European Union. From an EU perspective, anti-racism and anti-discrimination were and are necessary to the emergence of a globally competitive European economic power, and the solidification of a political Europe that upholds human rights and dignity as its founding principles. The project bears inherent challenges and contradictions. The aim of developing common reliable European legal, conceptual and policy frameworks to address racism from a transnational and comparative perspective poses important methodological and political problems. The central policy efforts invested in standardizing definitions and data collection systems illustrate both a commitment to increasing the transparency and efficacy of national anti-racist policies, and the growing involvement of the EU in social control mechanisms and structures. The EU has a multi-layered understanding of contemporary forms of racism, ranging from institutional and structural forms of racism to racist violence, and new manifestations of racism. However, the EU fails to properly ground racism in European history and society, which contributes, along with the various discursive forms and terminologies used, to positing racism as something that is 'external' to Europe and can then be perceived as a reaction to migration. As migration is increasingly conceived of as a 'problem' in Europe and since it is questionably associated with security, the issues of racism, migration, and security come to be conceived as different manifestations of a single crisis. The overlapping of these agendas carries the potential of marginalizing actions that racism.

As we have seen, migrants' voices are seldom heard in the context of establishing the mechanisms and structures that ultimately aim to give them a voice and empower them. The anti-racist priorities of the EU have little to do with migrants' daily experiences and sense of belonging or exclusion. As an exception to this trend, one can underline the policy recommendation for intercultural and inter-religious dialogue in the case of Muslims in Europe. The selective nature of this policy recommendation runs the risk of silencing migrants while trying to give voice only to a restricted and carefully selected number of individuals. It is worth underlining that what could be called a democratic deficit of the EU is not a concern for migrants and minorities only. It has been voiced over the years by populations and groups throughout member states, and figured among the reasons for the rejection of the European Constitutional Treaty by France and the Netherlands. But Europe is a political project in construction. It aims, to a certain degree, to transcend national borders and nationalist modes of thinking that are closely related to and partly responsible for processes of marginalization and exclusion (Balibar 1988a). Europe reproduces inequalities and trends that exist at national levels and which have historically excluded migrants, while trying to pursue and enforce its anti-racist agenda.

## References

Balibar, E. (1988a) 'Y a-t-il un "néo-racisme"?', in Balibar and Wallerstein 1988, pp. 27–41.
— (1988b) 'Racisme et crise', in Balibar and Wallerstein 1988, pp. 289–302.
Balibar, E., and I. Wallerstein (1988), *Race, nation, classe: Les identités ambiguës*. Paris: Éditions La Découverte.
Barker, M. (1981) *The New Racism*. London: Junction Books.
Lentin, A. (2004) *Racism and Anti-Racism in Europe*. London: Pluto Press.
Taguieff, P.-A. (1991) 'Les métamorphoses idéologiques du racisme et la crise de l'antiracisme', in *Face au racisme 2: Analyses, hypothèses, perspectives*, ed. P.-A. Taguieff. Paris: Éditions La Découverte, pp. 13–64.
Wieviorka, M. (1998) *Le Racisme, une introduction*. Paris: Éditions La Découverte et Syros.

## Primary Sources

Council Decision 2000/750/EC of 27 November 2000 establishing a community action programme to combat discrimination (2001–2006) (published in OJL303 of 2 December 2000).
Council Directive 2000/43/EC implementing the principle of equal treatment between persons irrespective of racial or ethnic origin (published in OJL180 of 19 July 2000).
Council Directive 2000/78/EC establishing a general framework for equal treatment in employment and occupation (published in OJL303 of 2 December 2000).
European Parliament Resolution of 27 April 1995 on racism, xenophobia and anti-Semitism (Official Journal C 126, 22 April 1995).
European Parliament Resolution of 26 October 1995 on racism, xenophobia and anti-Semitism (Official Journal C 308, 20 November 1995).
Joint Action to combat racism and xenophobia 96/43/JHA 15 July 1996.
Proposal for a Council Framework Decision on combating racism and xenophobia (Official Journal C 75 E/269, 26 March 2002).
Resolution of 5 October 1995 on the fight against racism and xenophobia in the fields of employment and social affairs (Official Journal C 296, 10 November 1995).
Resolution of the Council of 23 October 1995 on the response of educational systems to the problems of racism and xenophobia (Official Journal C 312, 23 November 1995).

## EUMC Reports (www.eumc.eu.int)

Annual Report 2002 – Parts 1 and 2.
Annual Report 2005 – Part 1: Activities of the EUMC.
Annual Report 2005 – Part 2: Trends, Developments and Good Practice.
Breaking the Barriers – Romani Women and Access to Public Healthcare.
Comparative Report: Migrants, Minorities and Education.
Comparative Report: Migrants, Minorities and Employment.
Comparative Report: Migrants, Minorities and Housing.
Comparative Report: Migrants, Minorities and Legislation.
Comparative Report: Policing Racist Crime and Violence.
Comparative Report: Racist Violence in 15 EU Member States.
Country Studies on Anti-Discrimination Legislation in EU Member States.
The Fight against Antisemitism and Islamophobia: Bringing Communities Together (European Round Tables Meetings).
The Impact of 7 July 2005 London Bomb Attacks on Muslim Communities in the EU.
Majorities' Attitudes towards Migrants and Minorities. Annual Report 2003, 2004.
Manifestations of Antisemitism in the EU 2002–2003.
Reports on Anti-Islamic reactions within the European Union after the Acts of Terror against the USA.
Situation of Islamic Communities in Five European Cities – Examples of Local Initiatives.

# 7 Multiculturalization of Societies: The State and Human Rights Issues

## Irène Bellier

Twentieth-century 'developed' societies are part of a world that is generally considered to be characterized by a range of mobilities, with such societies frequently attempting to define themselves as 'open' to a range of flows. In the case of the European Union project, attempts to build up an economic system based on a 'knowledge society' – facilitated by the present regulations on tariffs, taxes and visas – are not simple measures contributing unproblematically to member states' national growth: they are unequally distributed over the regions and sometimes counter-oriented. Indeed, in all the countries, internal socio-economic inequality contributes to an uneven access to – and relationship with – 'knowledge', an inequality that challenges the very notion of 'open' societies. However, even with this unequal context, multiculturalization remains a process which attempts to open societies to a 'world society' (Habermas 2001). If we accept the concept of a world society, it assumes no territorial borders of the sort that define the nation-state's sovereignty, national identity and culture. Hence the question is not so much to qualify multiculturalism but to see how it develops and how the different cultures and languages manage to co-exist in one society and to share political and economic resources. We must consider the question of political organization and that of the orientation and mandate of these institutions at the same time.

In that respect Europe is an interesting place to think about multiculturalism, simply because its political project is based upon 'unity and diversity' but also because at the same time there is no possible way to dispute the existence or the centrality of national cultures: this existence is mentioned in Article 1–4 §2 of the draft treaty establishing a constitution, which states that 'any discrimination on grounds of nationality shall be prohibited'. Europe is multinational, multilingual, multicultural by definition and, at the discursive, legal and institutional level, all national cultures and individuals are allowed equal rights. Under the EU's remit therefore, dominant cultures are shifting positions from absolute domination within the national context to relative equality on the European stage. Does this mean that European individuals and peoples, entitled to enjoy similar rights, are *de facto* equal when it comes to the consideration their cultures, languages and practices deserve? After the fall of the Berlin Wall, with the end of the Cold War, the EU decided to enlarge itself by incorporating the members of the 'European family' that socialist regimes had prevented from developing Western-style liberal democracies. This prompted a turn in the domain of human rights policies and legal frameworks. A number of declarations, conventions and charters have been signed by the members of the Council of Europe (CoE), the Organization for Security and Co-operation in Europe (OSCE) and the General Assembly of the United Nations to consider the issue of minority peoples' rights in a new way, with the intention of contributing to the pacification of a world whose numerous conflicts can be related to the unsatisfactory resolution of minorities' issues. In this chapter, after briefly considering the issue of cultural pluralism or of multiculturalism, I examine the particular situation of two categories of peoples that, after having been marginalized, have been involved in attempts to improve their respective positions in social and political structures, assessing the problems their situation and mobilization causes to the state. The 'minority issue' that I introduce centres on a case study of the Roma people in Slovakia, as well as the indigenous peoples issue whose particular relevance is under discussion in the frame of the European co-operation to development policies.

## Cultural Pluralism or Multiculturalism?

Social and cultural differences are continuously constructed and deconstructed in the social body, hence the basis for de-essentializing cultures, considering that they are not always seen as 'closed systems saturated by meanings' (Bonte et Izard 1991) but rather as stages where competitive modes of interpretations reign (Geertz 1973). This perspective cannot be reduced to the debate between 'unity and diversity', an up-to-date motto through which federal structures such as the EU – but interestingly also India, Indonesia and South Africa – defines their political structures. Nor can it be reduced to a view that opposes holism to relativism the way universalism is opposed to cultural singularity. In theory, 'developed' societies do not rely on one or the other version as exclusive positions, but rather on the combination of views in particular places of state and society. Therefore we do not have to think in terms of unity or diversity, universalism or relativism any more, but rather in terms of the mechanisms that allow diversity to be part of unity and the values of universalism to be fully compatible with the expression of cultural singularities. We must also look at how the ideological discourse on liberalism that seems to spread over the world as a discourse on freedom, grounded on universalism, masks the various mechanisms for imposing new forms of social and individual controls that shape the present constellation of powers (Bayart 2004). New trends in political domination generate new forms of contestation whether we think, in Europe, about the discourses underpinning the so called alter-globalization movement, or about the religious discourse of the fundamentalist type that aims at destroying the other (that 'other' being alternatively the person belonging to another religion, or the system based on a democratic distribution of powers).

If we follow Benedict Anderson's analysis of 'imagined communities' (1986), the present context leads us to try to understand what multicultural perspectives, associated with the flux of peoples and the circulation of images and imaginaries, could mean for nation-states that are, historically at least, constructed around common views of a homogeneous nation (Arendt 1951). How do states adapt the legal and political structures to take account of emergent diversity? Do they attempt to capture the shifting mosaic of people through bureaucratic tools such as surveys, polls, statistics and so on? How do dominant and subaltern cultures co-exist and in which areas of social interaction and political action? How is the cultural pluralism that constitutes social diversity reflected in, for example, schools, justice and the police (three institutions which are of particular relevance for social cohesion)? Clearly all societies and cultures are not similarly 'open' to the rest of the world; there are significant differences of perceptions as to what diversity means, and it is necessary not to reduce the question to the debate between included and excluded social groups, since there are serious discrepancies among nationals and migrants according to their geographical origins, gender and socio-economic status. Differences of integration – constructed by several modalities and varying according to historical periods – are reproduced over the years, only partly generating complete integration for some people who in most cases disappear as culturally different from the majority or dominant society.

In France, for instance, integration is understood through the constitutional principle of citizens' equality, a model that does not contemplate the actual inequalities of status existing between the different groups as collective entities, as long as individuals are entitled with the same formal rights. In real life, there are *de facto* differences between nationals born within the nation, naturalized French nationals who had to apply for French citizenship, and first/second/third-generation migrants who may or may not have adopted

French nationality, even though all of these people are given the possibility to identify with the unitary model of the Republic – although it must be said that this requires a lengthy process. This model corresponds to a process of assimilation that leads to the progressive disappearance of cultural differences as group differences, at the same time allowing state structures to combat the discrimination produced by society against individuals.

But the Republican model is regularly confronted with demands emanating from fragments of the nation (Chatterjee 1993) to be recognized and guaranteed the exercise of a cultural difference. Some of these are acceptable within agreed boundaries: for instance, relating to religious and spiritual practices, the 1905 French Law on the Separation of Church and State, among other things, distinguishes the public sphere (where strict neutrality is the rule) from the private domain where the freedom of cultural practices is respected (including religion). Other claims, for instance those conveyed by regional autonomists, are rejected when they pertain to the contested domain of political autonomy and self-determination. Some progress has been made since the 1970s concerning the cultural and linguistic rights of regional minorities such as the Basques, the Corsicans and the Alsatians, whose languages were admitted in schools, while a double linguistic regime was accepted in public advertisement (road signs for instance) together with an emphasis on all kinds of regional products and know-how that helps to develop tourism in these regions.

Modern, post-modern or post-colonial societies have been characterized by internal heterogeneity for a very long time but it is only quite recently that they have started to face new forms of diversity such as undocumented migrants joining social demonstrations in the streets to get residence and work permits and citizenship rights, or community leaders pleading in the court of justice for their linguistic rights or traditions to be respected, or indigenous people's representatives fighting at UN level for the definition of collective rights. Dominant societies and nation-states are confronted with a growing pressure emanating both from within the national territory and from outside. Migrants and minority peoples may find solutions to some of their problems within the legal framework of the European charter for the protection of regional and minority languages (1992), the European frame convention for the protection of national minorities (1995), the United Nations' declaration of the rights of persons belonging to national, ethnic, religious and linguistic minorities or on the elimination of racism and discrimination (1992), or through a number of declarations and instruments developed by the OSCE and NATO in the 1990s. But indigenous peoples, who have been particularly marginalized by the development of states and national societies, remain unsatisfied by these legal instruments, particularly because they are based on the universalism of individual human rights, which they cannot see as preventing their marginalization and extermination as peoples. They fight politically and legally to advance the concept of collective rights that could, in their view, help preserve the integrity of their cultures, languages and political systems.

What is extremely interesting here is that the nation-state, as the primary legitimate territory for political action, is not the only space worked out by individuals and minority groups. There are different sources for legitimating and developing political actions that confront states with the need to open themselves to – and train their elite for – respecting different socialization forms including languages, rituals, kinship patterns, trade and legal systems. They should also develop a better understanding of the cultural minority patterns and the multiple links possibly uniting a particular minority to a kin-state (like national minorities in Central and Eastern Europe), to another minority group in other states. They should also understand better the patterns of cultural identification that may, despite the lack of a direct connection, oppose entire segments of social groups who identify with particular religious communities in reference to an external conflict (such as the Israeli–Palestinian conflict). States may have to explore further the consequences generated by the possibility for individuals to be part of several imaginary communities at the same time (see for instance Appadurai's definition of the ethnoscape, 1996), in such a manner that we can no longer think in terms of a single identity.

Members of a diasporic culture may identify with the country they have left in a similar fashion to the country they have joined (see Chapter 2 by Jones and Krzyżanowski in this volume). At a distinct – yet still meaningful – level, a similar division can be observed in the case of the European civil service, with national experts sent to the European Commission to work with EU civil servants, expressing their feelings of belonging to both their home state and the EU. Every EU civil servant may experience such ambiguous feelings, but in the particular situation of the EC co-exist a complex issue of power and a game of influences that induce value judgments and contest the legitimacy of double belonging. The peer solidarity that emerges from the fact of 'working together' may break on particular occasions and a colleague's attitude, behaviour, or incapacity to stick to the common ideological frame will be pointed out and criticized through the notion of 'double loyalty'. Using a profane word, these national experts are called 'submarines', a word taken from the intelligence service glossary that serves to criticize those individuals who give priority to their home state's interest instead of to the common EU interest (see also Bellier 2000).

Could the difficulty posed to the integration of migrants and minority groups in dominant society derive from a similar pattern? Or could it not result instead from the difficulty the dominant society experiences in accepting its mutation? With the diversification of the sociological and cultural mosaic and the growing complexity of political claims and possible identifications, what does 'integration' mean in the context of a multicultural society? If we think it is solely a question of sharing language or following a common cultural behaviour, then what we have is an extremely basic view of what culture and identity mean, not dissimilar to the 'assimilation' that underpinned nineteenth-century nation-state building in Europe as well as the homogenization of the nation in the Americas.

After the Jewish and Roma Holocaust most policy-makers and researchers – as well as the majority of European societies – rejected the concept of assimilation as it leads to an eradication of human diversity. But the assimilation ideology, based on the hierarchy of peoples and the dominance of whites, remains developed by far right political parties, their idea being that homogeneity must prevail inside the national territory and heterogeneity outside. Such a differentiated treatment of people, according to where they come from and what they represent, is in fact furthered by the democratic European states when they police their borders, allowing in some categories of migrants and excluding others through a process of classification that is contested by human rights organizations (O'Leary 1992). Eventually, in a democratic society where different regimes of culture are at work – since individuals may find their aspiration beyond several definitions of borders (geographical limits, state border, intellectual milieus) – the main question relates to the constitution of the national body both in legal terms (citizenship rights) and in affective terms (feeling of belonging).

## Multiculturalism in the EU

Multiculturalism is one of the 'European values' that has been celebrated and fostered by the European Commission in co-ordination with other legal developments put forward by the Council of Europe. As an anthropologist, I am particularly interested in exploring the ways in which the decisions adopted by the European institutions to reach all European societies influence and are influenced by the working conditions of the European civil servants who have the capacity to contribute to their implementation.

### *The European Commission Experience of Multiculturalism*
Multiculturalism is a normatively desirable value for EU civil servants,

especially because they all come from different member states to work in the sectors of their competence (for instance, agriculture, trade policies, development and co-operation) with nationals from all the regions of the world (see Bellier 1997). They are confronted with cultural and linguistic differences in their day-to-day life, an experience that leads them to consider that multiculturalism is the 'wealth' of the EU, even though it entails a number of concrete difficulties to be solved, especially as regards the production of a 'unique' European culture. Sharing cultures and languages is one way to make Europe, but the process of 'building Europe' (Bellier and Wilson 2000b) creates specific tensions between the move towards 'unity' ('We are all Europeans') and the defence of national diversity which is promoted by many different sources, including the very active political family of conservative politicians, the so-called 'sovereignists' in France.

In the European Commission, there is no difficulty in the co-existence in the same space of all modes of being and behaviours, as well as cultural practices related to family values, food, authority structures that are differentiated according to the national backgrounds but also, and it should not be forgotten, according to ideological self-identification (political, spiritual and religious values), gender and generations. A case study undertaken in the early 1990s also shows that multiculturalism induces a kind of instability of the system that nonetheless survives mainly because of the strength of professional identities. The fact that Euro civil servants share an imagined 'community of destiny' helps them to adjust to their multicultural environment. Repressing differences as if they were not active does not help – especially because the EU has not successfully forged an image of what Europe should be – but there is an understanding that it does not correspond exactly to existing national imaginaries based on the state (see also chapter 1 by Stråth in this volume).

On the one hand, the non-recognition of the cultural dimension of the construction of the EU led the European Commission to commission a team of anthropologists to better understand how cultural and linguistic differences operate in the system (Abélès, Bellier and McDonald 1993). One of their conclusions was that cultural differences survive as a reference for civil servants, despite the efforts made by the authorities since 1958 to play down their existence (no mention of national identity is attached to the staff lists and offices charts, there is no quota policy for recruitment, no career profile according to national origins and so on). Cultural differences are so continuously operative throughout the European project that the political compromise, which characterizes the EU decision-making system, derives from the cultural compromise whose basis was prepared in the EC (Abélès and Bellier 1996). Multiculturalism affects Europe-building, a conclusion that led the Secretary General of the EC to admit that EU civil servants should be trained in these aspects, and to organize such training.

On the other hand, a number of media – mostly in the UK – whose 'Euro-scepticism' is well known, have developed a set of negative stereotypes that present the 'perfect EU civil servant' like an alien, thanks to the compilation of all national stereotypes in a reverse distribution: he/she is generous like the Dutch, calm like an Italian, flexible like a German, nervous like a Dane, drives like a French person and cooks like a Briton… The case study reveals of course that stereotypes do circulate in the EC (the French are arrogant, the Spanish talk endlessly but never do anything, Italians are *mafiosi*, Greeks are lazy…), especially when in a competitive situation. In a power organization that is made of hierarchies, individuals are competing to access a better professional situation and their strategies are often analysed as national signs of influence on the European organization. The reconstruction of national dividing lines can be observed, mostly because the home states (communities of affect) acting as member states (political structures) are competing powers. But it is, by and large, maintained within the limits defined by the ideal construction of a common European project. As a result, an equality of cultural status is assumed, even though the language in use does noticeably induce some effects of cultural domination, since the European Commission admits three working languages only (English, French and German). With tolerance considered as a central value, negative stereotypes are kept under control and a progressive education in the culture of the 'other' develops progressively, through which national stereotypes dissolve. This process is well exemplified by civil servants who state that 'after some time I do not think of the other in terms of nationality any more, but as a colleague'. Working together is what makes the model of European identity different from the construction of national identities. Stereotypes do not constitute the basis of the cultural compromise that affects the writing of policies; rather, their often poor intelligibility relates more to their form – their meaning changes due to the translation of key words, and an excessive respect for the principle of additionality leads to the compilation of lengthy texts and multiple references rather than to a clear revision of the documents.

What is actually practised as the day-to-day experience of the civil servants serves as a model of what Europe could be. Such a relation can be observed for instance in the project for a knowledge society that is based on the 'three languages' formula (that is experienced in the EC) and the role of education. The problem is that exporting such a model without developing a social Europe based on active practices of re-equilibration of the different social status of the cultural groups in question seems counter-productive. European societies are indeed evolving under European laws but the implementation of these depends on national political and administrative cultures. Although 'Europeanness', understood as a common state of feeling and perception, is based upon the dissolution of the cultural competition that leads to war between nation-states, the European Union is supposed to develop as a result of 'a fair and undistorted competition' (article 1–3 §2 of the Constitution) that does not exist in the 'real world'. There is a clear contradiction in the process, as cultural differences do not count in the European institutional documents, beyond the fact that they must be respected and that cultural reconciliation, the rule of law and the respect of human rights are fundamental in a harmonious development. Paradoxically, 'Europe at the top' also defines a model for the 'Europe at the bottom'.

## Multiculturalism and Policy-Making: The Minority Case of the Roma

'Multiculturalism', albeit without a particular definition, has been introduced as a value to be respected in the Central and Eastern European Countries when these states were negotiating their accession to the EU through the PHARE programmes, and in several European policies directed at improving the social conditions of the individuals affected by the economic and political changes due to the endorsement of the *acquis communautaire* (Bellier 2004), 'Europeanization' and inclusion in the western European family of values and principles as specified in the Copenhagen criteria (stable institutions guaranteeing democracy, the rule of law, human rights and respect for and protection of the minorities – see Bulletin of the EC 6–1993). It is interesting, in that general framework of a West-to-East-oriented action, to note that the EU project is equated to 'a project of civilization', but that it has had to face particularities inherited from the past of Central and Eastern European societies, that is the recognition of national, ethnic, linguistic and religious minorities. One of those minorities constitutes such a problem for all the nation-states in which it is included that the European Council and the European Parliament have declared it the European minority par excellence: these are the Roma, who are diversely known in their countries as Gypsies, Tziganes, Gitans, Manouches and Travellers.

On the one hand, the EC has put forward different programmes aimed at improving the situation of the Roma as regards their access to education and health, in order to desegregate them in economics and political life. On the other hand, and this is a demonstration that the EU is bound to be a melting pot, these countries, led by Hungary in that case, succeeded in incorporating the minority issue in the preamble of the European Constitution among one of the human rights to be respected. Even though 'the rights of the persons belonging to a minority' fits in with the EU's self-defined European project, particularly with the Copenhagen criteria that were defined in 1993 to politically align the EC systems with Western union values and principles; they nonetheless oblige member states to adapt their own constitutions to that principle, opening room for interesting discussions between constitutionalists. France is again an interesting example in this regard, as the constitution stands for and advocates the unity of nation, people, language and territory, with no differentiation according to ethnicity.

In this context, without entering into details, it is clear that all minorities should not be treated through only one policy frame, as there are clear differences between national minorities that benefit from a kin-state support on the one hand, such as Hungarians in Slovakia, Romania and Ukraine, who are supported by Hungary (which passed a status law to rule on their rights), and non-state minorities on the other, such as the Roma, who not only lack a reference to a territorial anchorage, but also share a history of experiencing discrimination. In Slovakia and Hungary, despite several centuries of assimilation, differences have long existed in the treatment of the Roma: Empress Maria Theresa (1717–1780) outlawed their nomadic habits; the Nazis sent them to concentration and extermination camps; and the Communist regime obliged them to work and live in particular buildings. Nowadays, despite the positive incentive given by the international community, which subsidizes education and anti-discrimination programmes, the dominant society still does not respect the Roma. Claims are made, racist attacks are reported in such a fashion that a decade has been declared in Sofia (in February 2005) to mobilize the World Bank, the EU, and eight countries which participated in the inaugural meeting in order to improve the situation of their respective Roma communities.

In Slovakia, for example, multiculturalism would concern the recognition by the dominant society of the different cultural biases that limit equality, to develop integration and anti-discrimination policies. As a political project, it is self-reflective, and it concerns mainly the integration of Roma communities. The situation of that particular group of people is dealt with in such a manner that one may wonder what implicit model lies behind the new policies: is the aim integration or assimilation once again? The transition to west European modernity divided the Roma group in two parts: the assimilated Roma, approximately two-thirds of the population, mainly diffused in the cities, and the segregated ones, one-third of the group, who live in settlements – not to say 'ghettos' – in absolute poverty, experiencing overt racism and the day-today problems associated with social exclusion. Ten years after the EU interest in the Roma started to develop, a better knowledge of their situation exists, but two problems have emerged for considering the group objectively. One concerns the census of the population, whose size varies from 350,000 to 500,000, according to whether each Roma individual chooses to declare an identity that is the source of their marginalization (Roma people have not forgotten that being in the list led them to the gas chambers), and also according to the way the inspectors determine who is Roma, Slovakian, Hungarian or whatever better-off identity (cases have been proved of racial discrimination by inspectors declaring someone to be Roma without even asking the question, based on appearance and social criteria only). Competing identities based on status inequality are *de facto* making it impossible for the state to have a fair 'countable' view and to be capable of implementing a non-discriminatory control of the population (see Foucault 1979 for the disciplinary aspect of these state activities). Another problem in this regard concerns the 'reinvention' of a Roma identity, language and culture when and where there are multiple Roma/Gypsies/Manouches/Lovar identities, communities and social practices.

Under the auspices of the EU, with the help of the Soros Foundation, the World Bank (all of them of course motivated by 'good intentions'), the 'Roma Issue' is being addressed in such a fashion that an invented, abstracted Roma identity progressively takes the place of real Roma people. New forms of invisibility are developing, not as the result of racial policies leading to assimilation, as used to be the case, but as the product of anti-discrimination policies that in effect attempt to erase cultural differences through social measures. There is a consensus that the Roma problem derives from their social marginalization, hence desegregation policies should solve the problem. During research fieldwork in this area, I wanted to understand what 'multiculturalism' meant when applied to the specific case of Slovakian policies directed at the Roma population. I did my research through face-to-face interviews, in which it commonly appeared that, based on the perception of cultures as 'essences', it was considered enough to have two Roma children in a school to have a multicultural education. No major efforts were made to include in the national school curriculum the content of Roma cultures and languages, the different perceptions of life and the world (even though a university started to develop a department on Roma culture with the intention to train teachers and produce material for education). The material that will be delivered to Roma schools, Roma children and Roma teachers will certainly contribute to improving the self-perception of that group and its demands of dignity. But nobody thought it would be necessary to produce similar material directed at the dominant society that does not have the knowledge to fight stereotypes and combat prejudices. A change can be observed as programmes are developed with several components for training Roma assistant teachers to mediate in schools and social workers to help Roma parents to bring children to schools, providing them with food and an adapted education (with a high degree of practical training in hygiene and domestic skills for the women, sport and technology for the teenagers).

What became important was to provide Roma children with pedagogical tools in the Romany language, a language that is progressively being standardized, so that they can access in one stage of their 'development' dominant language and social semiotics and may consider the possibility of getting a job in mainstream society (see chapter 14 by Martín Rojo in this book). They can learn language and history and begin to consider themselves as 'equal'. In the dominant society, however, media campaigns aimed at preventing racism and anti-Roma discrimination do not provide the references to consider Roma people as equally and positively equipped with cultural artefacts. There remains a consensus that leads Slovakians to continue to state simply 'they [Roma] do not live like us [integrated Slovaks]', 'they do not care for their children', 'they exploit them', 'they do not want to work' and so on. 'Cigan', from which derives the French word 'tzigane', means 'to lie' in Slovak.

The prevalence of such stereotypes not only reveals the unequal status of Roma and other minorities in Slovakia, it also reveals the necessity to reverse centuries of negative perceptions that led to the separation of dominant and minority societies. The key to the problem can be found through an analysis of the economic situation and racial discrimination that contributes to the 'Europeanization' of this issue. It does not act directly to promote the re-foundation of the nation for the dominant society to accept its Roma dimension. There are huge difficulties 'integrating' Roma in the new model of society related to joining the EU. At present, it is impossible to imagine the complete integration of the Roma in the political system, both because of the inadequacy of the measures taken to favour the political organization of the various Roma communities, and because of the difficulty the Roma people have imagining their destiny in a representative democracy.

Roma cultural specificities are at odds in the European market, even though one might consider their cross-border aptitude as a sign of Europeanness. The Roma nobility that used to be admitted in the courts and cities, like the musicians, may benefit from a better visibility with their capacity to make a name for themselves in the European and world cultural market. But the modernization of societies leads to the destruction of the skills and professions that used to be the domain of Gypsies, such as horse-training, iron-manufacturing and so on, leaving them with no particular tools in their hands for their children to access the labour market. Fighting exclusion in schools and launching vocational training is the beginning for the Roma to improve their future, but such policies are not combined with any coercive measure to force companies to employ Roma people. The liberal view of economics is hardly compatible with the means that should be taken to improve Roma employability; no one wants them in the service industries, they are kept out of the dominant society's homes, they have a hard time entering the electronic/computer universe. The banking system does not 'trust' them with micro credits to develop their own businesses, and that limits their capacity to tender for work, as I could see at the level of the municipality regarding a job preparing land ready for the construction of an industrial zone.

A new social stratification derives from the economic changes. The assimilated 'Roma' continue their journey towards becoming invisible (they change their names, do not remember the language, consider themselves as part of the national state). The segregated ones are targeted for new public policies which are controversial among non-Roma members of the dominant society who are objectively in the same situation, at least in terms of wealth. As a consequence, the European focus on the integration of Roma people shifted in 2000 to fighting social and economic exclusion so that poor non-Roma people do not resent the flow of PHARE money going to the Roma for housing, education, health and employability.

## Multiculturalism and the Notion of Collective Rights

The experiences of indigenous peoples are different from those of other minorities for several reasons not easily perceived by most Westerners. The main differences relate to the process of their marginalization within the state, where they are not recognized as citizens (not because they come from abroad and need time to be assimilated or integrated, but because a dominant society has developed which relegates them to the margins). In such societies, their languages, cultures, ethos and physical integrity are not respected and are devalued. This process may be the consequence of the conquest undertaken by European soldiers, clergy and civilians, such as in North, Central and South America, Northern Europe, Australia and New Zealand. It may result from several successive waves of migration by dominant groups, or social groups that progressively became dominant and tried to impose their religion, social and political organization, contributing to the formation of states, as has been the case in Asia, Africa and Russia. What does multiculturalism means in societies which accept ethnic discrimination even when they forged the concepts of human rights and fight for citizens' equality?

Indigenous subordination does not proceed only from a racial discrimination based on their phenotype, even though most indigenous peoples actually suffer at the hands of this form of racism, but also because of the distinctiveness of their economic, social, cultural and political systems. This fact has not been properly recognized. As stated by Martinez Cobo, who wrote an expert study for the UN in 1986: 'they constitute today non-dominant sectors of society and are determined to preserve, develop and transmit to the future generations their ancestral territories and ethnic identity on the basis of their continuous existence as peoples, in agreement with their own cultural systems, their legal systems and their social institutions'. Whether we consider them – as the United Nations agencies does – as victims among the victims, or the poorest among the poor, a noticeable change in their political organization and visibility leads me to study their discourses of the last two decades in favour of the construction of an international indigenous movement, which is a universal movement covering all continents. These discourses are to be analysed in relation to the acts they perform, from local to world levels, to put an end to a long story of marginalization and benefit from the present-day concern for cultural differences.

Through their representatives in the UN, and their observers at the Organization of American States and the African Commission for the Human Rights, among other organizations, and in every political arena of global and regional governance, such as the Earth or the Millennium world summits, indigenous peoples want to be recognized as a people and fully identified as such, to have the capacity to enjoy the right of self-determination that is given to peoples as defined by the UN charter and the two 1966 international covenants on civil and political rights, and social and economic rights. But this is a right that is denied to all of them, on the grounds that it may affect state sovereignty and territorial integrity, even those who had signed treaties with the conquerors, a situation that exists in North America and New Zealand, or other similar agreements according to a variety of situations in the world. Although there is no space here to describe in detail the content or the form of their movement (see Bellier 2004), I argue that it is indigenous peoples' ability to word their claims at different levels to raise awareness on the part of state representatives, NGOs, global activists and the civil society at large that constitutes them as political actors, endowed with their own subjectivity.

This process, although not always peaceful or entirely successful, induces a number of changes in the states and societies they are living in. The point of discussion today, for this movement and its many components, is to express

147

the indigenous peoples' desire to be considered capable of taking their future into their own hands, instead of being submitted to national and global processes based on a system that caused the loss of their territory and dignity. Indeed, there are many differences and discrepancies to be observed between the indigenous movement at world level, which benefit from a certain status, and the local communities that suffer concrete experiences of marginalization, the two levels being affected and particularized by a variety of ideologies ranging from Marxism to Christianity. But together they carry the idea that a democratic society cannot develop without the consent of its fragments, among which figure the indigenous peoples who have specific relations to the land and territory and attest of the rich diversity of humankind (being the representatives of the 5000 languages spoken in a world managed by only 192 states).

As compared to the previous centuries or decades, a change is to be observed as well in the dominant societies, which, under the pressure of international human rights organizations, are progressively becoming sensitive both to such rights issues and to their own diversity, a situation that forces democratic states to adjust their policies to avoid the massacres and despoilments that are part of indigenous peoples' lives, and to diminish the pressure on their forced assimilation. The direct influence of international organizations to adjust the economy, determine policies, and build ecological programmes, but also of NGOs that introduce new practices and references, has a slow but continuous impact that leads to a view of indigenous peoples as persons that may benefit from particular programmes in health, education and economics, or may even contribute to implementing a better protection of the world's biodiversity. Constitutional changes have taken place in South America during the 1990s, after centuries of a complete denial of the 'humanity' of indigenous peoples who, at best, were accepted if they assimilated to the *mestizo* nation, and at worse were hunted and killed in the jungle. The national constitutions of Colombia, Ecuador, Peru and Bolivia now admit the existence of 'first peoples' or 'first nations' and define the states as plurinational, pluricultural and plurilingual, thus creating the basis for a complete redefinition of the national discourses. This is how, in the UN headquarters, I have heard that '[indigenous] identities and rights are a positive value for the peace of the whole society', according to the words of a Guatemalan representative in 2004. Such words could never be imagined during the civil war that took indigenous people hostage. Since then, Rigoberta Menchu has received the Nobel Peace Prize and a Commission for Forgiveness and Reconciliation has been instituted to define a new social and political equilibrium.

Against this background, tough negotiations are taking place internationally, at the level of both the OAS and the UN, for the definition of indigenous peoples' collective rights. Most of the states participating in these negotiations – members of the UN Human Rights Commission who attend the indigenous working group on a voluntary basis – are in agreement to acknowledge cultural and linguistic rights to indigenous peoples, based on the freedom of individuals and the legal documents that contribute to protect it. But they resist the emergence of other collective rights that could effectively contribute to safeguarding cultural diversity, such as land rights or political rights, arguing that such rights would be contrary to the interests of the individuals and the third parties that the state is supposed to protect as well. This is where the real interests compete. I do not have space here to go into this argument, which relies on two systemic convictions that strengthen the Western model of domination: property rights are individual, private and contractual; representation is the mechanism that stabilizes democracy. The arguments are varied and sophisticated but it is salient from the state's point of view that the rights of individuals are the only ones that could be protected since collective rights given to ethnic groups or minorities are considered a menace to law and order.

However, several powerful states, such as the USA, Canada, Australia and France, are now confronted with the need to modify a status quo settled by force, which introduced a legal system operating to the constant detriment of indigenous peoples. These groups, which can be demographically dominant as in Bolivia or in Guatemala, are nowhere near the political majority and they do not constitute a 'real menace' for most states – therefore such states are not confronted with the risk of secession. But globally, nation-states are reluctant to apply the right to self-determination that is claimed by indigenous peoples, and limit the application of the concept of 'free prior and informed consent' to be taken from the peoples before any act can be performed on their territory. With the evolution of international standards and the emergence of the so-called civil society, it becomes acceptable to protect indigenous peoples in the name of humankind; but the nineteenth-century model of protection is no longer acceptable, since it led authorities to treat indigenous peoples like children, depriving them of their sense of responsibility, as well as individual and collective autonomy, a process that allowed the conquest of land and resources and the marginalization of indigenous communities.

## Conclusion

This chapter has briefly considered different cases in which multiculturalism can be both observed and questioned critically. A common conclusion is that the word 'multiculturalism' is frequently used to introduce a context in which multiple competing identities, cultural references and practices are at stake. This is in contrast to the version of multiculturalism that is taken to refer to particular modalities of policy-making that would for instance be different from national politics and policies. Multicultural policies can be national politics and policies that intend to address the variety of cultural, regional and ethnic groups in one state. Another general conclusion is that multiculturalism might compose a rich environment for individuals or the groups they belong to, but it is often associated with complexity and the fear that such competing identities could lead to the destruction of the national body. However, it is crucial to note that national bodies are not as homogeneous in the twenty-first century as they were in the nineteenth; multiculturalism has become part of our lives in most places in the world because of globalization, the new forms of capitalism and the effect of the associated circulation of peoples and images. The problem that has only been introduced through three cases (the European civil servants, the Roma minority and indigenous peoples) is that multiculturalism does not imply that all cultures are considered on an equal basis. Prejudices remain strong and the idea that the culture one belongs to is the reference point for evaluating other cultures is equally dominant.

Multiculturalism refers to the principles that may lead a particular society to accept several languages, cultures, social and political organizations, but it does not imply that an equal interest will lead each representative to defend the common interest, or that the political representatives of the dominant society will perform their duties with respect to the minorities. For an anthropologist, multiculturalism is better seen from the viewpoint that education and knowledge are what allow the tenants of a particular culture to understand and respect the representatives of other cultures, and the mobilization of the state and social institutions required for that perspective is coherent with the project to develop knowledge societies. But the formation of knowledge does not ensure the respect of the other if it is not associated with the propagation of values based on human rights principles, and if states do not engage in active policies to redress historical situations and combat prejudice. Multiculturalism cannot be seen from the cultural viewpoint only, since what needs to be explored is, concretely, the subtle mechanisms within nation-states which help stimulate social competition for power, contributing to the creation of subordination and marginalization.

## References

Abélès, M., and I. Bellier (1996) 'La Commission européenne: Du compromis culturel à la culture politique du compromis', *Revue française de Science Politique* 46:3: 431–55.

Abélès, M., I. Bellier and M. McDonald (1993) *The Anthropological Approach of the European Commission*. Brussels: Mimeo.

Anderson, B. (1986) *Imagined Communities*. London: Verso.

Appadurai, A. (1996) *Modernity at Large: Cultural Dimensions of Globalization*. Minneapolis, MN: University of Minnesota Press.

Arendt, H. ([1951] 1973) *The Origins of Totalitarianism*. New York: Harcourt.

Bayart, J.-F. (2004) *Le Gouvernement du monde: Une critique politique de la Globalisation*. Paris: Fayard.

Bellier, I. (1997) 'The Commission as an Actor', in *Participation and Policy Making in Europe*, ed. H. Wallace and A. Young. Oxford: Clarendon Press, pp. 91–115.

— (2000) 'The European Union, Identity Politics and the Logic of Interests' Representation', in Bellier and Wilson 2000a.

— (2004) 'The European Commission: Between the *acquis communautaire* and the Enlargement of the Union', in *The Changing European Commission*, ed. D. Dimitrakopoulos and J. Richardson. Manchester: Manchester University Press.

Bellier, I., and T. Wilson (ed.) (2000a) *An Anthropology of the European Union: Building, Imagining, Experiencing Europe*. Oxford, New York: Berg.

Bellier, I., and T. Wilson (2000b) 'Building, Imagining, Experiencing Europe: Institutions and Identities in the European Union', introduction to Bellier and Wilson 2000a.

Bonte, P., and M. Izard (1991) *Dictionnaire de l'ethnologie*. Paris: Presses Universitaires de France.

Chatterjee, P. (1993) *The Nation and Its Fragments: Colonial and Post-Colonial Histories*. Princeton, NJ: Princeton University Press.

Foucault, M. (1979) *Discipline and Punish: The Birth of the Prison*. New York: Vintage.

Geertz, C. (1973) *The Interpretation of Cultures*. New York: Basic Books.

Habermas, J. (2001) *The Postnational Constellation, Political Essays*. Cambridge, MA: MIT Press.

Martinez Cobo, E. (1986) *Study of the Problem of Discrimination against Indigenous Populations*, E/CN.4/ sub 2/1986/87 add 1-4, UN.

O'Leary, S. (1992) 'Nationality Law and Community Citizenship: A Tale of Two Uneasy Bedfellows', in *Yearbook of European Law*, ed. A. Barav and D. A. Wyatt. Oxford: Oxford University Press.

# 8 Towards a Theory of Structural Discrimination: Cultural, Institutional and Interactional Mechanisms of the 'European Dilemma'

## Tom R. Burns

Structural discrimination consists of both institutional discrimination based upon norms, rules, regulations, procedures and defined positions that determine access to resources, and also a broader cultural discrimination based upon widely shared social paradigms and related systems of categorization that both constructs and devalues the 'other'. In the case of institutional racism, the suggestion is that norms and other rules may operate in so-called 'indirect' ways; that is they are not necessarily discriminatory in intent but nevertheless may motivate exclusion of those who deviate from or challenge the norms in other ways. Crucially, institutions construct and maintain categorization systems, cultural stereotypes and attitudes that frame discriminatory ways irrespective of the intentions, personal attitudes, or beliefs of the individuals involved. In any given institution there are established organizing principles, rules and regulations, procedures, role definitions and so on, which discriminate against individuals and groups that do not 'belong' to majority society. Such frameworks are reflected in shared cultural elements in society such as established and legitimized category systems, concepts, stereotypes, judgment principles, generalized strategies, and societal norms that of course also cut across institutions. These are 'societal in character'. For present purposes, an analytical distinction is made between two general institutional forms of discrimination, which can both be investigated and analysed using the tools of institutional case studies. Firstly, structural discrimination (institutional and cultural forms of discrimination) entails the automatic operation of rules and procedures – including informal ways of doing things – in ways that disadvantage migrant groups. Secondly, institutional agentic discrimination describes discriminatory behaviour of agents in organizationally powerful positions. Here I am particularly interested in agents who play gatekeeping roles, that is who determine life chances of migrants in institutional contexts such as markets, workplaces, schools, political parties, state agencies and NGOs.

An institutional approach emphasizes the fact that social institutions embody power and have real exclusionary consequences – albeit in some cases unintended – for minorities and migrants as well as for different host populations. For instance, state power is used (or not used) through law and the exercise of administrative and statistical power in such a way as to normalize discriminatory or exclusionary practices. Institutionalized categorization systems and stereotypes define migrants as the 'other'. Key mechanisms identified in existing research are: legal restrictions – laws and policies, procedures; universal application of particularistic norms; biased application procedures; assumed hierarchy in judging non-national experience and certification; agents in key positions of power and authority who exercise discretion: school counsellors, co-ordinators, labour-market mediators, personnel office chiefs and staff; gatekeepers concerned with the 'reactions of customers or clients' or other employees; normalization of discriminatory discourses; denial and lack of self-reflection. In sum, European societies can be characterized as robust discriminatory systems with multiple exclusionary mechanisms.

## A Structural Approach to Discrimination

In a structural approach to ethnic, racial, national or religious discrimination, there is a stress on enduring structures and trends across society. For its part institutional racism is often implanted in routine practices and the functioning of organizations (Wieviorka 1995). In the structural perspective, discrimination, stigmatization, inferiorization and exclusion operate not only in particular interpersonal encounters but also in and through institutions and other complex systems of social relationships.[1] Discriminatory practices produce and reproduce differential access to resources, positions, careers,

---

1 Pettigrew and Taylor (2002: 2) point out the biases here: The broadest definitions of discrimination assume that racial minorities have no inherent characteristics that warrant inferior social outcomes. Thus, all inequality becomes a legacy of discrimination and a social injustice to be remedied. Favoured by the political left, to many this view appears too sweeping. By contrast, political conservatives favour a narrow definition that limits the concept's scope by including only actions *intended* to restrict a group's life chances.

153

etc.; thus any given society consists of an elaborate 'web of institutions', all of which discriminate in ways that make for unequal life chances. Structural discrimination consists of institutional discrimination (through operative norms, laws, regulations, procedures as well as defined positions that determine access to resources and the exercise of 'fate control') and cultural discrimination (through widely shared systems of categorization, stereotypes and us–them paradigms). Institutions together with cultural formations may operate in discriminatory ways irrespective of the intentions, personal attitudes, or beliefs of the individuals involved. In general, there are institutionalized tendencies to reject, and to discriminate against those who do not know, understand, or accept the 'host society's' code(s).

Among the contributions of a structural approach are the following: that it disassociates 'discrimination' (and racism/otherism) from individuals and treats such patterns as (possible) features of social institutions, cultural formations and broader societal arrangements. As such, this approach breaks the tendency to view discrimination and racism largely in terms of individual psychology, or attitude and simple intentionality. In particular, an intentionality perspective reduces the problem to one of psychology or social psychology and deflects attention away from institutional arrangements that constrain, select, and discriminate against particular groups (Pettigrew and Taylor 2002: 2; Burns and Kamali 2005a, 2005b). Structural discrimination may operate independent of a person's attitudes and awareness. Hence, models based primarily on individual prejudice, whether psychological or economic, will uniformly understate and oversimplify the phenomenon of discrimination and racism (Pettigrew and Taylor 2002: 2). In order to determine whether or not structural discrimination is operating, one examines the ways that particular arrangements as well as cultural components operate and/or their discriminatory/exclusionary consequences. Ethnicity (and other objects of otherism such as 'race',[2] 'nationality' and religion may be included here) is not a matter of shared traits or cultural markers, although these play a role also, but rather the social practices of classification and categorization (Barth 1969).

In sum, many of the major forms of discrimination are institutional in character. In any given institution there are established organizing principles, rules and regulations, procedures, role definitions and relationships, which may discriminate against individuals and groups that do not belong (fully) to majority society, or are marginal to it. Also, there are cultural elements shared

---

2 'Race' has increasingly come to be seen as a manner of dividing and ranking human beings by reference to selected embodied properties (real or imputed) so as to subordinate, exclude and exploit them (Wacquant 1997).

in the majority society such as established and legitimized category systems, concepts, stereotypes, judgment principles, generalized strategies, and societal norms that cut across institutions and discriminate against those with migrant background. They are 'societal in character'; they are carried and reproduced by particular institutions, professional groups and networks. The model shown in Figure 8.1, which is developed in the rest of the chapter, identifies key concepts in an investigation and analysis of structural forms of discrimination.

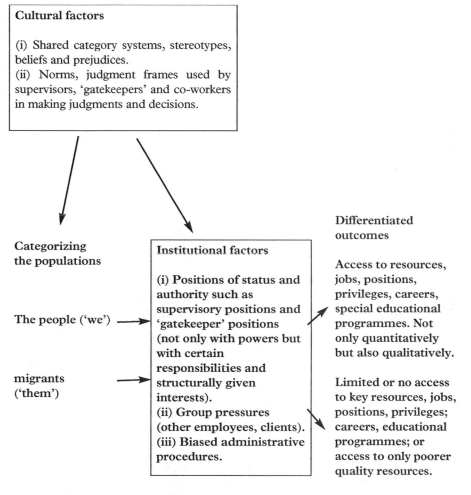

Figure 8.1. Institutional arrangements, cultural factors and mechanisms of structural discrimination

## Forms of Institutional Discrimination

Institutionalized forms discriminating against those of migrant background entail routine, systematic and sustained denial of respect and dignity, denial of opportunities, privileges and positions generally available to members of the majority population. Such discrimination may result from a dominant group applying automatically or unthinkingly the existing organizational and institutional rules, regulations, procedures and laws. For this reason, blatant racism or prejudice, stereotyping and hostility need not be present for unequal treatment or in unequal distribution of life chances. Here we can distinguish two general types of institutional forms of discrimination, which can be investigated and analysed using the tools of institutional case studies: 'pure' institutional discrimination entails the automatic or routine operation of rules and procedures – including informal ways of doing things – in ways that disadvantage migrant groups, while institutional 'agentic' discrimination focuses on the agents who play gatekeeping roles, determining opportunity structures and life chances. First, we shall examine institutional discrimination before subsequently addressing institutional agentic discrimination.

### Institutional Discrimination

Institutions embody power and have real consequences. For instance, state power may be used (or not used) through law and the exercise of administrative and statistical power in such a way as to normalize discriminatory or exclusionary practices. Institutionalized category systems, stereotypes, and models define 'others'[3] in settings such as public agencies, labour markets, housing and education and inform how decisions are made, resources allocated, and opportunities given or denied. Indeed, across Europe there is much evidence of discrimination and exclusion practices in key institutional areas with respect to new migrants (Burns and Kamali 2005a, 2005b; Castles 1984; MacEwen 1995; Pettigrew 1998; Pettigrew and Taylor 2002: 4). Controlled tests reveal the full litany of discriminatory forms concerning

---

3 Brubaker *et al.* (2004: 34) point out that 'recent works have examined how censuses inculcate the idea that national societies are founded wholes, composed of discrete, mutually exclusive ethnic, racial, or cultural groups. Even when census categories are initially removed from prevailing self-understandings, they may be taken up by cultural and political entrepreneurs and eventually reshape lines of identification. Especially when they are linked through public policy to tangible benefits, official census categories can have the effect of "making up people" or "nominating into existence," creating new kinds of persons for individuals to be. Such categories...are central to the state's exercise of "racial governmentality": censuses have constituted a "formative governmental technology in the service of the state to fashion racialized knowledge – to articulate categories, to gather data and to put them to work".'

employment, public accommodations, housing, the courts, insurance and banks. Employment discrimination poses the most serious problem; in almost every European Union nation, migrant groups have markedly higher unemployment rates than natives, frequently arising from the inability or great difficulty in obtaining citizenship; this restricts migrants' ability to get suitable housing, employment and schooling. Castles (1984) contends that the guest-worker system that brought many of the migrants to Europe was itself a state-controlled system of institutional discrimination that established the newcomers as a stigmatized 'out-group' suitable only for low-status jobs but not citizenship and the associated full access and full participation in society.

The structural approach to investigating discrimination is less concerned then with personal attitudes of hostility or rejection, but rather with institutional mechanisms of discrimination, such as those operative in labour markets, workplaces and educational systems. When apparently neutral requirements for recruitment or routines affect certain ethnic groups more than others, or more generally when certain rules, instructions or everyday practice within an institution have systematic intended (or unintended) discriminating consequences (Augustsson 1996: 26), we may talk about institutional discrimination. When they are of marginal importance to job performance, language requirements are a clear example (Lindgren 2002) and one of the most common types of institutional discrimination in European labour markets.[4] These requirements are sometimes justified, but often are not. As Knocke and Hertzberg (2000) show in the case of Sweden, there are sometimes requirements of having fluent Swedish for cleaning jobs. We also see examples of this mechanism in the interviews with work managers reported by Augustsson (1996: 88):

> Everybody that works on the production lines can apply to this new organization [which is generally seen as more attractive for workers]. As shown elsewhere, there are actually quite many Finns, Turks, South Americans, and Hungarians engaged. But then there are certain requirements that have to be met: to write and speak Swedish. ... Quite many come up short on these requirements.

---

4   As Bourdieu and Wacquant (1992: 56–7) put it, 'The position which the educational system gives to the different languages (or the different cultural contents) is such an important issue only because this institution has the monopoly in the large-scale production of producers/consumers and therefore in the reproduction of the market without which the social value of the linguistic competence, its capacity to function as linguistic capital, would cease to exist.' Those who lack command of this legitimate competence will be *de facto* excluded from the social domains in which this competence is defined as necessary, or are condemned to silence (Alexander 2001: 8).

Moreover, as stressed above, discrimination can also be a result of unmotivated, exaggerated and/or vague and perfunctory criteria for 'social and communicative competence', which are often conflated with 'Swedish social competence' (Höglund 2000: 27).

Such mechanisms entail discrimination in one institutional realm of society that produces negative secondary effects in other realms: for instance, when discrimination in the school system creates problems in the labour market for those of migrant background (Lindgren 2002). One particularly important form of spill-over discrimination is network recruitment – although this is partly also a mechanism of its own. Individuals holding gatekeeper positions (that is, who are in a position to employ people, to promote people and so on) are likely to choose someone belonging to their own network. Moreover, information about job vacancies tends to spread through key networks of the dominant population. Since actors holding strategic gatekeeper positions in such networks tend to be 'natives', this leads to a situation in which migrants are disfavoured. Consequently, migrants have – on average – fewer social resources, because of, among other things, a lack of network ties to high-status persons holding positions of power (Lin 1999). In short, institutionalized categories, rules and practices provide a basis for systematic forms of discrimination, marginalization and exclusion of persons and groups that deviate from ethnocentric value-laden constructions.

### Institutional Agentic Discrimination and the Power of Gatekeepers

Teun van Dijk (2000: 15–16) stresses that

> even if prejudice and discrimination occur at all levels of dominant group structure, unequal treatment by some members has more impact than when it is practiced by others. Ordinary people, for example, may discriminate against their Turkish, West-Indian or North-African neighbour in many overt and subtle ways; however, they will generally be unable to affect seriously the socio-economic position of these neighbours.

It is safe to say that prejudice, discrimination and racism would be significantly less influential if it were limited to common feelings of resentment against the newcomers. Indeed, these very common feelings are largely a reflection of broader social and institutional power arrangements (a position that is developed elsewhere in this volume). Discrimination is often inherent in category systems, laws and regulations, institutional policies and practices. In this sense, the problem is not simply a perception or a way of categorizing and stereotyping those of migrant background, but also a basis for action, for discrimination, for the exercise of institutional power over them.

Addressing the collective classifications and stereotypes which prevail in all social life, Brubaker *et al.* (2004: 43–4) emphasize that these not only entail classifying social actors in ethnic terms but viewing – and acting in – the social world, which means that

> relevant questions are not only about how people get classified, but about how gestures, utterances, situations, events, states of affairs, actions, and sequences of actions get classified (and thereby interpreted and experienced)... Much knowledge (in the broadest sense) that is relevant to – indeed partly constitutive of – race, ethnicity, and nationhood is embedded in such event schemas.

In the context of all forms of institutional power, 'discrimination' takes place as certain judgments and actions are carried out – or not, as the case may be – in relation to differentiated individuals and groups. Actions are predicated on distinctions between situations, agents, types of conditions. There may or may not be discrimination on the basis of ethnicity, 'race', religion, class, or gender, but institutions and their agents are typically required to make distinctions – to differentiate and categorize – for purposes of judgment and action. One creates simplicity, reduced heterogeneity and order through the use of abstract categories (Schauer 2003). However, as a result of discriminatory judgments and actions, certain individuals and groups may be disadvantaged (or advantaged). There are systematic biases in the allocation of premiums and penalties through institutional mechanisms.

The structural approach to institutional agentic discrimination stresses then the cognitive-normative basis for judgment and action on the part of those with authority or power to make a difference ('fate control over life chances'). So, two major structural components are identified in this conceptualization: institutional arrangements and positions (such as gatekeepers and policy-makers) and the socio-cognitive models or paradigms utilized by those in such positions. As pointed out earlier, the institutional mechanisms of discrimination need not be 'intentional' or conscious on the part of those carrying them out. However, particular actors, or groups of actors (such as professions) occupying key decision-making roles or positions, can exercise 'fate control' and determine access to resources. These gatekeepers occupy institutional positions where they can grant formal or informal entry and access to specific resources, positions and opportunities to participate. Obviously, such positions of power allow the incumbents to impose conditions for access. These positions may be official, such as the management of an organization, or unofficial, namely those incumbents who might have no formal gatekeeping function but have through their network connections substantial influence to help gain (or to deny) access to resources. Gatekeepers might believe – or act in such a way – that institutional objectives are given priority over individual interests or needs, for instance denying migrants positions because they might disrupt established teams or disturb clients. Or, powerful gatekeepers may see applicants as unsuitable for organizational purposes, because of ethnicity, religion, appearance or patterns of behaviour.

Categories, stereotypes, schemas and related concepts such as cultural models and paradigms are mental structures in which knowledge is represented and reflected materially. They range from the universal to the idiosyncratic; most, however, are neither but are culturally (more or less widely) shared mental constructs (Brubaker *et al.* 2004: 41). Such constructs are not simply abstract representations; they structure and process information; they play a role in judgment, decision-making and action; they guide perception and recall, interpret experience, generate inferences and expectations and organize action (Brubaker *et al.* 2004: 34; Burns and Carson 2002, 2005; Carson 2004). As Brubaker *et al.* emphasize, a 'cognitive construction *is* social construction: it is only in and through socio-cognitive processes and mechanisms that the social construction of "race", ethnicity, and nation can plausibly be understood to occur' (2004: 34). Furthermore, rather than take 'groups' as basic units of analysis, cognitive perspectives shift analytical attention to processes of 'group-making' and 'grouping' activities which occur through classification, categorization and identification. By their very nature, these structuring processes construct groups and assign members to them; groups do not exist independently of the myriad acts of classification, categorization and identification through which they are sustained from day to day (Brubaker *et al.* 2004: 45).

It is worth bearing in mind that majority groups may stress cultural, physical or religious characteristics of people for opportunistic reasons (to mobilize support, gain legitimacy, violate legal constraints) in discriminatory ways. At the same time a cognitive-normative approach enables us to avoid over-rationalistic assumptions (Brubaker *et al.* 2004: 51):

> There is a recognized cognitive mechanism tending to 'naturalize' and 'essentialize' racial, ethnic, and national categories – and this may be grounded in the human cognitive apparatus ... Rather than attribute the naturalization of social differences to vaguely conceived emotional commitments, to an irreducible sense of 'identity', or to 'a certain ineffable significance ... attributed to the tie of blood, cognitive perspectives provide potentially powerful explanations for this tendency ... cognitive research

indicates that much cognition (and schema-governed cognition in particular) is unselfconscious and quasi-automatic rather than deliberate and controlled. This suggests that the explicit, deliberate, and calculated deployment of an ethnic frame of reference in pursuit of instrumental advantage may be less important, in explaining the situational variability of ethnicity, than the ways in which ethnic – and non-ethnic – ways of seeing, interpreting, and experiencing social relations are unselfconsciously 'triggered' or activated by proximate situational cues.

Decisions are based on the employer's beliefs about typical characteristics of the group to which the individual belongs or is believed to belong to (certain migrant groups are defined as 'unproductive', or 'they are too often absent because of illness', 'they lack the capacity to work in teams'). More specifically, a stereotype can be defined as a highly stylized and simplified image of the characteristics of a social group or category. Stereotyping is a process by which someone attributes to another person characteristics 'which are seen to be shared by all or most of his or her fellow group members' (Brown 1995: 82). Individual characteristics that are easy to observe, such as name and appearance (for example, skin and hair colour), are used as data instead of achieved skill-related characteristics which may be more difficult to observe at first sight.

Stereotyping by race, religion, education, gender, age or any other characteristic is commonplace. But when it is considered relevant and accepted or legitimate by those exercising institutional power, then it is likely to become pernicious – and potentially illegitimate in an egalitarian society. Employers assume that certain characteristics, for instance, 'Swedishness', a degree from a Swedish (or European) university, or employment in a highly qualified position with a reputable Swedish firm, for example, will predict successful job performance. The formula in this case is the following:

Institutional power or authority + consequential, widely shared stereotypes = discriminatory decisions or actions (determining 'life chances') with respect to people of migrant background

Irrespective of whether the beliefs are true or false, stereotypical judgments and decisions are often based on group belonging and not on the individual's demonstrated characteristics or skills (Arai *et al.* 2000: 9). Stereotypical discrimination works in a patterned way as the following quotation from an interview with a Swedish foreman illustrates (Augustsson 1996: 81):

You could put it like this, as a foreman you'll get a lot of preconceived ideas about migrants, and about certain migrant groups. Because it is always the fact, there are exceptions, that if you have had two persons of a nationality that haven't been good, then I, as a foreman, do not want to have two new of the same nationality.

Hence, as in all such discrimination, this way of thinking allows very little room for within-group variation for the out-group (that is, 'they are all the same', whereas the in-group, e.g, native Swedes, implicitly or explicitly is seen as much more heterogeneous (that is, the interviewed foreman has probably had a number of native Swedes who were not very good). Hence, as Paulsson (1994) puts it, 'if Johansson is late to job, he is a problem. If Stojanovski is equally late to the job, the Yugoslavs are a problem' (Paulsson 1994: 150).

Language problems are frequently singled out as the reason why employment of migrants should be avoided (see chapter 11 by Flam in this volume). One of the foremen, for instance, says in the interview (Augustsson 1996: 83):

The public authorities think we should throw in heavily with migrants, but we cannot do that. We have to consider the fact that we will develop our organization. If we should throw in heavily with migrants here who don't know Swedish that good, I don't think we will be able to develop these organizations.

Hence, the 'fact' that migrants applying for jobs cannot handle Swedish competently enough is taken for granted, as a prejudged fact rather than as an open empirical question that varies from individual to individual. Also in this case, real or perceived group-specific characteristics rather than individual characteristics inform the ways that gatekeepers and other agents with authority may perceive and judge. There are numerous examples of stereotypical discrimination. As Knocke and Hertzberg (2000) show, in conducting in-depth interviews with labour agency officers, migrant-sounding names are often a sufficient cause for discrimination, even when the person in question speaks Swedish fluently. Most of the officers avow that employers commonly say that the place is already taken when migrant youths with foreign-sounding names call.

### Actuarial or Statistical Discrimination

Actuarial or statistical discrimination is a special case of stereotypical discrimination, which occurs when decisions are based on an employer's beliefs about typical characteristics of the group to which the individual belongs or is believed to belong to. For instance, 'certain migrant groups are not particularly productive, because they are absent too often due to sickness', or 'they lack the capacity to work in teams'. Irrespective of whether these beliefs are true or false, actuarial discrimination is always stereotypical: decisions are based on group belonging and not on the individual's skills (Arai *et al.* 2000: 9). Not all members of the group have the characteristics or engage in the behaviour attributed to the entire group. These are actuarially encumbered with the 'traits' of a few or even many in a class; there is attribution to the entire category certain characteristics (criminality, untrustworthiness, cultural incompetence, low motivation, low technical competence, etc.) that are statistically indicated by membership in the category, but are not possessed by the majority of members of the category. Labels are applied in arbitrary ways, unfair to some or many, because one condemns or distrusts all members of the group on the basis of group characteristics not held by all members.

Stereotypes are often employed when people feel the need to form a quick social category in order to process incoming information. Being stereotypical, actuarial discrimination may hence be a 'rational' way for employers to economize the decision-making process, because it saves them time from gathering individual-specific information (see also Arrow 1972; Phelps 1972). Hence, the theory of actuarial discrimination assumes that this kind of behaviour is more common in situations of uncertainty, when employers or other gatekeeping agents have only imperfect information about applicants' skills and productivity. Examples may be the ethnocentric interpretation of education/qualifications/training undertaken in the country of origin, another may be the pragmatic difficulty of obtaining references from previous employers abroad (see Le Grand and Szulkin 2002).

However, normally this type of stereotypical thinking focuses only on one salient group characteristic (for example, ethnicity) while it disregards others (social class, religion, urban/rural distinction). It moreover tends to overestimate within-group homogeneity ('all Turks are...'). Even if a particular ethnic group in fact has, on average, higher sick leave rates than natives, there is likely to be an enormous within-group variation, which means that all individuals who deviate from the mean in the direction of low sick-leave rates will be unjustly treated. Furthermore, actuarial discrimination is often based on false and erroneous beliefs (social representations). Frequently not only stereotypes but also prejudices are involved. A prejudiced stereotype can be defined as an attitude or set of attitudes held towards a group or members of a group, encompassing over-simplified beliefs and a set of negative feelings and judgments (see also Operario and Fiske 1998: 45).

The importance of this mechanism – actuarial discrimination based on stereotypical thinking – is due to the fact that stereotypes underpin much of everyday thinking, which means that people use them, and rely on them, without much reflection. As socio-cognitive theory has stressed repeatedly, reality is usually too complex to be perceived and apprehended without the help of social categorizations (Augoustinos and Walker 1998; compare Boudon 1994; Schauer 2003). Hence, employers and other actors holding gatekeeper positions in the labour market, workplaces and other institutional domains often engage in actuarial discrimination and make decisions based on over-generalization and prejudiced stereotypes without being aware of it. Under conditions of high uncertainty – and high costs of obtaining information to reduce uncertainty – such over-generalization is cost-efficient and rational.

There are diverse examples of a 'rational' type of discrimination, underpinned by the fact that private companies pursue profits above all and, therefore, adopt an overwhelmingly instrumental approach that assesses the 'cost' and 'benefit' of recruiting (or promoting) migrants (Rydgren 2004). As one salaried employee puts it, 'the reason why you don't employ migrants is that you are afraid. I would never employ a Turk. We have had Turks here, and I think that none of them worked here after they became 45–50 years of age. And then they have long absences due to illness' (cited in Augustsson 1996: 96). Hence, employers want to be as sure as possible that workers will stay a long time, so they get returns for their investment. In assessing the likelihood of this, knowledge about how long different (ethnic) groups stay on average often enters into the reasoning process. In every society there is a collective repertoire of stereotypes to draw upon, which implies that stereotypes are often socially shared in a more or less consensual way (Gardner 1994; see also Lamont 2000). But more importantly, the modern organization of society presupposes some uniformity, some willingness to suppress much diversity in the service of large-scale homogenization. At the same time that we honour the individual, we fight for the concept of diversity ('good' forms of diversity), and reject certain forms of deviance or variation (the 'bad' or 'evil' ones).

## Multiple Structural Mechanisms: Research and Policy Implications

The structural perspective has immediate implications for research design as well as policy-making. It aims to identify and analyse major institutional mechanisms underlying discrimination in diverse institutional domains: labour markets, workplaces, schools, universities, housing markets, clinics and hospitals, social service and police encounters. Categories are central to social life, as 'without the ability to categorize, we could not function at all, either in the physical world or in our social and intellectual lives' (Brubaker *et al.* 2004: 37) and institutionalized category systems and stereotypes are widely and persistently applied to migrants and migrant groups. Stereotypes, like other categories, entail some combination of prototypical features, concrete exemplars, and theory-like causal knowledge. They obey the principle of cognitive economy, generating inferences and expectations that go 'beyond the information given' with minimal cognitive processing. As Brubaker *et al.* emphasize, 'Like other categories, stereotypes work largely automatically. They can be primed or cued subliminally, and can influence subjects' judgments without their awareness ... stereotyping is deeply rooted in ordinary cognitive processes and countering or correcting stereotypes is effortful and costly' (2004: 39). Thus, ethnic and other differentiated and discriminated-against groups are socially constructed. Structurally oriented research is focused on 'group-making' and 'grouping' activities as a function of classification, categorization, and identification in institutional settings. In these processes, ethnic groups, races, religious groups and nationalities come to be treated as things-in-the-world, as real, substantial entities with their own cultures, their own identities and their own interests.

*The application of established norms of language, appearance and behaviour* is a common basis of differentiation and discrimination with respect to those with migrant background (as well as within other groups of course). These norms are often applied in relation to job recruitment and career advancement, even when, for instance, high language competence is not especially relevant to the type of job or career. Less than perfect language competence, however, is seen as an indicator of poor cultural competence, inability to fit in, or unpredictability of behaviour (although it is typically a poor indicator of the particular job performance expected). Furthermore, *legal and normative restrictions* discriminating against migrants are widespread across Europe, relating to (among other things) employment and careers (although itself no leading light, Sweden is probably better in this respect than most of the other European countries) (Flam 2005). Formally or informally, natives tend to be favoured ahead of migrants. This is particularly the case in economies with tightly regulated wage structures. Under such conditions, there can be little difference between the labour costs of natives and migrants, which tends to reinforce the selection of natives. In systems allowing more variation in wage setting, for instance England and Italy, recruitment conditions for migrants are more open and favourable. A number of EU countries (for instance, Austria, France, Germany, Italy and Poland) have laws giving a certain priority for jobs to natives or to EU citizens. For instance, employers or work mediation officials have the burden of proof to show why recent migrants or non-EU migrants should fill a vacant position before a native.

*Biases in judging experience and certification* are a concern when applying for jobs or applying to admission to educational systems. There are often legal requirements for certification for many jobs or academic purposes but there are multiple constraints on certifying migrants (legal, resources, lack of interest or good will) and in admitting qualifications acquired abroad (whether education or work experience). For instance, degrees and diplomas may not be legally recognized; similarly, work experience abroad may be ignored. There is a widespread tendency to favour education and work experience gained in the host society. *Biased procedures*, for instance in job interviews, test-taking, encounters with medical personnel, social workers, police or dealings with other authorities, exist in part because people of migrant background are insufficiently familiar with the 'proper' procedures, which often imply a wide range of 'framing' cultural and social assumptions.

We also find *direct discrimination* on the part of institutional agents, that is gatekeepers who utilize category systems, stereotypes and value judgments that are differentiating and discriminatory towards groups with migrant backgrounds. Such agents are found in all institutions including government agencies and political parties. Officials granting work and residence permits are among the most powerful agents from the viewpoint of migrants (Flam 2005). Of course, the degree of discrimination (particularly arbitrary discrimination) varies across institutions, contextual settings and countries. *Actuarial discrimination* is also exercised by gatekeepers (it is also exercised by everyday people as they generalize from a few persons or experiences to entire classes or categories of persons, but this is largely without major consequence). Gatekeepers may generalize on the basis of a few cases or experiences to an entire class of persons about their cultural competence, lack of skills, improper value orientations (for example, 'they' are not interested in education, hence 'They don't do well as academic subjects'). This mechanism may work in the opposite way in the case of a migrant population of which some members achieve particular success, which can lead to a generalization about the extraordinary capabilities of the entire group. Likewise, *derived or indirect discrimination* can take place when gatekeepers pre-empt the projected reactions of clients and/or employees. Work groups may complain that those with migrant backgrounds 'don't fit in', 'don't know or understand national codes', 'lack cultural competence'. Derived discrimination reflects a type of 'collective gatekeeping' (and may be justified in the name of workplace 'democracy').

All of these forms of discrimination can result in *spill-over mechanisms*. Because of limited educational opportunities, selective channelling and differentiated programmes of study, job opportunities and career possibilities are narrowed. Or, only finding housing in certain stigmatized areas may limit job access and opportunities, as employers (and employees) react negatively to persons coming from certain areas.

*The formulation and diffusion of denial discourses* (Mulinari 2002; Van Dijk 2002) is a major mechanism which tends to block awareness and reform efforts. 'Of course, we do not discriminate; we are not racists'; 'we always apply our norms, laws, procedures and programmes in a fair and proper way'. Across countries, institutions, workgroups and other groups, denial and distorted or low reflectivity are commonplace. Discriminatory judgments and patterns are revealed through contradictions in statements and the astute observations on the part of some persons (migrant as well as non-migrant) in positions to know or observe. Typically, the biased attitudes, stereotypes and negative talk and actions towards migrants contradict the norms and values of 'equality', 'democracy' and 'humanitarianism' that are part of the positive self-conceptions of modern Western societies and of most of their citizenry (Van Dijk 2002: 323). Van Dijk points out (2002: 323):

> Disclaimers, mitigations, euphemisms, transfers, and many other forms of racism denial are the routine moves in social face-keeping, so that in-group members are able to come to terms with their own prejudices. At the same time, these denials of racism have important social and political functions, e.g., in the management of ethnic affairs and the delegitimation of resistance. We have seen that, especially in elite discourse, for instance in the media and in the legislature, the 'official' versions of own-group tolerance, and the rejection of racism as an implied or explicit accusation, are crucial for the self-image of the elite as being tolerant, understanding leaders. However, we have also seen how these strategies of denial at the same time confirm their special role in the formulation and the reproduction of racism.

This complex of mechanisms is a highly robust system operating within modern institutional arrangements – the apparatus of modern society. If one mechanism is blocked or fails to operate, there are others filling the functions. It is in this sense that we speak of robustness. There are redundant and reinforcing mechanisms discriminating against and excluding those with migrant backgrounds. General pronouncements, information campaigns and anti-discrimination legislation are not likely to move such a system far – although such gestures are important in terms of expressing interest and normative concern. But more radical types of policies and regulations are called for.

## Concluding Remarks

Much valuable research has been devoted recently to analysing and explaining forms of institutional discrimination. Institutional arrangements, power relationships and cultural components including category systems, stereotypes and ideologies, among other factors, explain to a greater or lesser extent the systematic discrimination against and exclusion of those with migrant backgrounds (for example see Operario and Fiske 1998). Such factors go some way to explaining the great difficulty in bringing about effective reforms (Feagin and Eckberg 1980; Knowles and Prewitt 1969; Ohri *et al.* 1982; Williams 1985; Wilson 1973).[5] If ethnic boundaries, as Barth (1969) says, are sustained by processes of categorical self- and other-description, then this is no less true for racial, national or religious boundaries. The processes of classification and categorization, formal and informal, that systematically divide 'us' from 'them'; the forms of social closure that depend on excluding certain groups as 'outsiders'; the schemas, scripts and cultural models that allow one to perceive, experience or interpret situations and sequences of action in standardized racial, ethnic or national terms; the cognitive biases in the retrieval and processing of information that lead to evaluating evidence in selective ways tending to confirm prior expectations and strengthen stereotypes – all of these and many more cognitive and socio-cognitive mechanisms and processes are involved in phenomena conventionally coded in terms of race, ethnicity and nationality (Brubaker *et al.* 2004: 48–9).

Brubaker *et al.* (2004: 39–40) conclude that

> stereotypes are no longer defined in terms of cognitive deficiencies – in terms of false or exaggerated or unwarranted belief – but more neutrally as cognitive structures that contain knowledge, beliefs, and expectations about social groups. Nor are stereotypes seen as the distinctive and pathological propensity of particular kinds of personalities (the 'authoritarian

---

5  Brubaker *et al.* (2004: 40–1) point out: 'Stereotyping is, of course, one key aspect of social categorization, but is by no means the only one. Other aspects have been explored by the largely European tradition of research known as "social identity theory" (or in some later variants as "self-categorization theory") ... the mere perception of belonging to two distinct groups – that is, social categorization per se – is sufficient to trigger intergroup discrimination favoring the in-group.' The differences *within* categories – and indeed between different categories – is exaggerated in exclusionary discourse. When the categories at hand are categories of 'human kinds', the overestimation of inter-category differences and of intra-category (especially out-group) homogeneity facilitates the reification of groups. Ethnic classification depersonalizes individuals by transforming them from 'unique persons to exemplars of named groups [which also] explains the resilience of "groupist" representations of the social world.'

personality' or 'high-prejudice' individual, for example), but rather as *rooted in normal and ubiquitous socio-cognitive mechanisms*. There is no need to postulate special 'needs' – for example the alleged need to feel superior to others – to explain stereotypes; they are more parsimoniously explained as an outgrowth of ordinary cognitive processes... there is nothing intrinsically individualistic about the study of cognition. The domain of the 'mental' is not identical with the domain of the individual. Indeed, the kind of knowledge in which we are interested – the schemes of perception and interpretation through which the social world is experienced in racial, ethnic, or national terms – is social in a double sense: it is socially shared knowledge of social objects ... Because they are not the products of individual pathology but of cognitive regularities and shared culture, stereotypes – like social categories more generally – are not individual attitudinal predilections, but deeply embedded, shared mental representations of social objects.

The structural approach investigates stereotypes and patterns of judgment and rejection as socially constructed and reproduced in diverse institutional contexts. Racism practised by public authorities, political parties, private enterprises and other institutional agents often finds informal support in the dominant community. There is tolerance of discriminatory attitudes and practices rather than pressures to challenge negative stereotypes and practices against migrants and other dominated groups (Essed 1991: 42). Elites might, of course, use their authority to reinforce tolerance and to reduce or block the circulation of stereotypes and prejudices and the discrimination against migrants and minorities, exploiting the opportunities to produce and develop alternative, non-racist conceptions of society and power relationships.

## References

Alexander, N. (2001) 'Language, Education, and Race Relations', Paper prepared for the United Nations Research Institute for Social Development (UNRISD), Conference on Racism and Public Policy, Durban, South Africa, September 2001.

Arai, M., L. Schroder and R. Vilhelmson (2000) *En Svartvit Arbetsmarknad: En ESO-rapport om vägen från skila till arbete*. Stockholm: State Department Report Ds 2000:47.

Arrow, K. (1972) 'Models of Job Discrimination', in *Racial Discrimination in Economic Life*, ed. A. H. Pascal. Lexington, MA: DC Heath.

Augoustinos, M., and I. Walker (1998) *Social Cognition: An Integrated Introduction*. London: Sage.

Augustsson, G. (1996) *Etniska Relationer i Arbetslivet. Teknik, Arbetsorganisation och Etnisk Diskriminering i Svensk Bilindustri*. Umeå: University of Umeå, Department of Sociology.

Barth, F. (ed.) (1969) *Ethnic Groups and Boundaries: The Social Organization of Cultural Difference.* London: Allen & Unwin.

Becker, G. (1957) *The Economics of Discrimination.* Chicago, IL: University of Chicago Press.

Billig, M. (1985) 'Prejudice, Categorisation and Particularisation: From a Perceptual to a Rhetorical Approach', *European Journal of Social Psychology* 15: 79–103.

Boudon, R. (1994) *The Art of Self-Persuasion: The Social Explanation of False Beliefs.* Oxford: Polity Press.

Bourdieu, P., and L. Wacquant (1992) *An Invitation to Reflexive Sociology.* Chicago: University of Chicago Press.

Brown, R. (1995) *Prejudice: Its Social Psychology.* Oxford: Blackwell.

Brubaker, R. (1996) *Citizenship and Nationhood in France and Germany.* Cambridge, MA: Harvard University Press.

Brubaker, R., M. Loveman and P. Stamatov (2004) 'Ethnicity as Cognition', *Theory and Society* 33: 31–64.

Burns, T. R., and M. Carson (2002) 'Actors, Paradigms, and Institutional Dynamics: The Theory of Social Rule Systems Applied to Radical Reforms', in *Advancing Socio-Economics: An Institutionalist Perspective,* ed. R. Hollingsworth, K. H. Muller and E. J. Hollingsworth. Oxford: Rowman and Littlefield.

— (2005) 'Social Order and Disorder – Institutions, Policy Paradigms, and Discourses: An Interdisciplinary Approach', in *A New Agenda in Critical Discourse Analysis: Theory and Interdisciplinarity,* ed. P. Chilton and R. Wodak. Amsterdam and Philadelphia, PA: John Benjamins Publishing Company.

Burns, T. R., and H. Flam (1987) *The Shaping of Social Organization: Social Rule System Theory and Applications.* London: Sage.

Burns, T. R., and M. Kamali (eds) (2005a) *Work Places and Labor Markets: Institutional Patterns of Discrimination.* EU Xenophob Report. Uppsala: Uppsala University, Multiethnic Centre.

— (eds) (2005b) *Institutional Patterns of Discrimination in School Systems.* EU Xenophob Report. Uppsala: Uppsala University, Multiethnic Centre.

Castles, S. (1984) *Here for Good: Western Europe's New Ethnic Minorities.* London: Pluto Press.

Ekberg, J., and M. Hammarstedt (2002) '20 år med allt sämre arbetsmarknadsintegrering för invandrare.' *Ekonomisk Debatt* 4: 343–53.

Essed, P. (1991) *Understanding Everyday Racism: An Interdisciplinary Theory.* Newbury Park, CA: Sage.

Faist, T. (1993) 'Ein- und Ausgliederung von Migranten: Türken in Deutschland und mexikanische Amerikaner in den USA in den achtziger Jahren', *Soziale Welt* 44(2): 275–99.

Feagin, J. R., and D. L. Eckberg (1980) 'Discrimination: Motivation, Action, Effects, and Context', *Annual Review of Sociology* 6: 1–20.

Fiske, J. (1994) *Media Matters: Everyday Life and Political Change.* Minneapolis, MN, and London.

Flam, H. (in collaboration with B. Beauzamy, T. R. Burns and M. Kamali) (2005) 'On Institutional and Agentic Discrimination: Migrants on the Labor Market', Paper presented at the Xenophob Workshop organized by the EU Commission, Brussels, Belgium, 27 January 2005.

Gardner, R. C. (1994) 'Stereotypes as Consensual Beliefs', in *The Psychology of Prejudice: The Ontario Symposium*, vol. 7, ed. M. P. Zanna and J. M. Olson. Hillsdale, NJ: Lawrence Erlbaum Associates.

Höglund, S. (2000) 'Reflektioner kring mångfald och diskriminering i arbetslivet', in *Mångfald, Diskriminering och Stereotyper: Tre Forskaruppsatser om Mångfald*, ed. P. de los Reyes. Stockholm: Rådet för arbetslivsforskning.

Kamali, M. (1997) *Distorted Integration: Clientization of Migrants in Sweden*. Uppsala: Multiethnic Centre.

Knocke, W., and F. Hertzberg (2000) *Mångfaldens Barn Söker Sin Plats. En studie om arbetsmarknadschanser för ungdomar med invandrarbakgrund*. Stockholm: Svartvitt förlag.

Knowles, L. L., and K. Prewitt (eds) (1969) *Institutional Racism in America*. Englewood Cliffs, NJ: Prentice-Hall.

Lamont, M. (2000) *The Dignity of Working Men. Morality and the Boundaries of Race, Class, and Immigration*. Cambridge, MA: Harvard University Press.

Le Grand, C. (1999) 'Empiriska problem och möjligheter med att belägga diskriminering i arbetslivet.' *Diskriminering i Arbetslivet: Normativa och Deskriptiva Perspektiv*. Stockholm: Socialvetenskapliga forskningsrådet.

Le Grand, C., and R. Szulkin (2002) 'Permanent Disadvantage or Gradual Integration: Explaining the Migrant–Native Earning Gap in Sweden', *Labor* 16:1: 37–64.

Lin, N. (1999) 'Social Networks and Status Attainment', *Annual Review of Sociology* 25: 467–87.

— (2001) *Social Capital: A Theory of Social Structure and Action*. Cambridge: Cambridge University Press.

Lindgren, C. (2002) *Etnisk Mångfald i rbetslivet i Norden*. Norrköping: Integrationsverkets rapportserie 2002/10.

MacEwen, M. (1995) *Tackling Racism in Europe: An Examination of Anti-Discrimination in Practice*. Washington, DC: Berg.

Miles, R. (1993) *Racism after 'Race Relations'*. London. Routledge.

Mulinari, D. (2002) 'Det är inte rasism – om facket och invandrarna', in *Det Slutna Folkhemmet: om etniska klyftor och blågul självbild*, ed. I. Lindberg and M. Dahlstedt. Stockholm: Agora.

Nieke, W. (1991) 'Benachteiligung ausländischer Jugendlicher im Zugang zur Berufsausbildung', in *Ausländische Jugendliche in der Berufsbildung – Auf dem Weg zur Chancengleichheit?*, ed. W. Nieke and U. Boos-Nünning. Opladen: Leske-Budrich.

Ohri, A., B. Manning and P. Curno (1982) *Community Work and Racism*. London: Routledge and Kegan Paul.

Operario, D., and S. T. Fiske (1998) 'Racism Equals Power plus Prejudice. A Social Psychological Equation for Racial Oppression', in *Confronting Racism: The Problem and the Response*, ed. J. L. Eberhardt and S. T. Fiske. London: Sage.

Paulsson, S. (1994) 'Personlrekrytering: en nyckelfråga', in *Arbetets Etniska Delning*, ed. C.-U. Schierup and S. Paulson. Stockholm: Carlssons.

Pettigrew, T. F. (1998) 'Reactions toward the New Minorities of Western Europe', *Annual Review of Sociology* 24: 77–103.

Pettigrew, T. F., and M. C. Taylor (2002) 'Discrimination', in *The Encyclopedia of Sociology*, ed. E. F. Borgatta and R. J. Montgomery, revised edition. New York: Macmillan.

Phelps, E. S. (1972) 'A Statistical Theory of Racism and Sexism', *American Economic Review* 62:4: 659–61.

Porter A. (1998) 'Social Capital: Its Origins and Applications in Modern Sociology', *Annual Review of Sociology* 24: 1–24.

Priester, K. (2003) *Rassismus*. Leipzig: Reclam.

Rydgren, Jens (2004) 'Meso-Level Causes of Racism and Xenophobia: Some Converging and Diverging Effects of Radical Right Populism in Sweden and France', *European Journal of Social Theory* 6(1).

Schauer, F. (2003) *Profiles, Probabilities, and Stereotypes*. Cambridge, MA: Belknap Press.

Van Dijk, T. (2002) 'Denying Racism: Elite Discourse and Racism', in *Race Critical Theories*, ed. P. Essed and D. T. Goldberg. Oxford: Blackwell.

Wacquant, L. (1997) 'For an Analytic of Racial Domination', *Political Power and Social Theory* 11: 221–34.

Wieviorka, M. (1995) *The Arena of Racism*. London: Sage.

Williams, J. (1985) 'Redefining Institutional Racism: Theoretical, Empirical and Political Issues', *Ethnic and Racial Studies* 8: 323–48.

Wilson, W. J. (1973) *Power, Privilege and Racism*. New York: Free Press.

# 9  On Institutional and Agentic Discrimination: Migrants and National Labour Markets

## Helena Flam

The purpose of this chapter is to analyse the sources of discrimination operating at the entrance to and within the labour market in eight different European countries: Austria, Cyprus, France, Germany, Italy, Poland, Sweden and the UK. The findings presented here draw on approximately 65 expert interviews conducted by various members of the project team with teachers, managers, workers, trade union and/or work council representatives, officials at employment mediation offices and various NGO representatives in each of these countries in spring 2004. The interviews concerned with the labour market focused on various aspects of the hiring, work and layoff proccsscs in two diffcrcnt towns in cach country, whcrc at lcast onc public and one private firm was to be investigated. Although caution is advised given the problems of access, uneven willingness of firm representatives to answer our questions and the qualitative nature of our data, some insights into commonalities and differences in European patterns of discrimination can be offered. Before presenting them, let me briefly and roughly position our approach to labour market-related discrimination.

Human capital and the organizational-structural perspective dominate current debates about inequalities in the labour market. The first perspective takes a look at job applicants – either directly or through the eyes of the employer (see, for example, Kalter and Kogan 2002 but also Harzing 1995). The proponents of the human capital approach initially proposed by the economist Gary Becker in 1964 look at the supply side of the hiring process. They see disadvantages to which women or migrants/minorities are subject on the labour market as entirely of their own making. Women and migrants/minorities, it is argued, are less qualified than their competitors.

They have fewer skills and educational credentials and/or poorer motivation and therefore face higher unemployment rates, worse work positions, less authority and lower pay than white males (Tomaskovic-Devey 1993: 4–5; Ruwanpura 2005: 4–7). This approach links the qualifications of job applicants directly to their labour market situation. When a conceptual concession to the idea of discrimination is made and the hiring process becomes examined from its demand side, it either still takes the form of Becker's 'taste for discrimination', understood as an employer aversion to specific groups which are therefore granted access to fewer jobs and/or lower wages than other groups, or it takes the form of Phelps' and Arrow's concept of 'statistical discrimination' which says that employers discriminate against specific groups based on their conviction that these groups on average are less productive than others (Moss and Tilly 2001: 86; Tomaskovic-Devey 1993: 7–9; Ruwanpura 2005: 4–7). Employer discrimination then explains why different groups receive unequal treatment on the labour market.

The second major perspective takes a look at the structural and organizational factors delineating and forming the labour market. From this perspective individual characteristics of job applicants cannot explain labour market inequalities. Nor is it sufficient to measure discrimination as a ratio between the numbers of successful applicants and job-eligible members of a given social category (Kanter 1979: 52–3). To demand proportional representation on the job market is unrealistic. As Kanter (1979), Rosenbaum (1979) and Feagin and Feagin (1978: 63–72) have stressed, a closer look at the structure of work organizations is necessary, since these differ in their opportunity and power structures which determine differences in their hiring, employment and career rules and thus discriminatory outcomes. Like Piore and Doeringer, they pinpointed the existence of internal labour markets, which skew not only hiring criteria but also career paths to the advantage of (male) whites, regardless of the general distribution of qualifications (Feagin and Feagin 1978: 63; Ruwanpura 2005: 9). A complementary argument is that the segmented structure of the labour market causes gender and racial inequalities. White males with high educational credentials are in demand for the best jobs in resource-rich organizations located in booming economic regions. As the critics of this explanation argue, this indeed leads to, but does not satisfactorily explain, gender and race discrimination (Tomaskovic-Devey 1993: 5–6; Milkman and Townsley 1994: 610–12; Moss and Tilly 2001). Employer and manager stereotypes as well as professional, management and organizational discourses do their share to bias hiring to the advantage of white men (Kanter 1981 [1975]; Feagin and Feagin 1978: 66; Lovering 1994; Carrington *et al.* 1996; Harzing 1995: 65; Moss and Tilly

2001; Wharton 2002: 264). To explain the inequality of outcomes, moreover, it is not enough to consider mere proportions between 'dominants' and 'tokens' within a given organization or its departments; one also has to take into account the influence of sex- and race-typing on particular jobs – the gendering or racializing of work means, for example, that (i) the characteristics of employees become defined in terms of their gender or 'race', (ii) specific jobs and career paths become associated with specific gender/race stereotypes and only seemingly neutral job requirements, (iii) women and nonwhites usually encounter more hostility when they enter predominantly white male jobs than the other way around, and (iv) as the proportions of women or nonwhites increase in these jobs, the pay and working conditions deteriorate (Kanter 1981 [1975]; Feagin and Feagin 1978: 66; Tomaskovic-Devey 1993: 6, 12–13; Milkman and Townsley 1994: 604–5, 610–12; Lovering 1994; Carrington *et al.* 1996; Wharton 2002: 259–61). Not to be forgotten, gendered, racialized and emotionalized on-the-job interactions add their weight to the reproduction of the established inequalities within work organizations and consequently on the labour market (Carrington *et al.* 1996).

Our research goal was to explore institutional discrimination in eight European countries, looking for similarities and contrasts. The research framework posited discrimination as rooted first of all in the general laws and regulations barring access of migrants to the national labour markets. We also explored other basic dimensions of institutional discrimination, such as organizational rules, procedures and practices, including informal ways of doing things, to identify those which exclude or disadvantage migrants. Finally, we paid attention to institutional agentic discrimination, focusing on the incumbents of positions of authority within organizations who can make decisions or carry out actions with discriminatory consequences. We were particularly interested in public and private agents who play gatekeeping roles.

Our approach was much indebted to the classical essay by Robert Merton and to the early American research on institutional discrimination. In Merton's answer to Gunnar Myrdal's 'The American Dilemma', in which Myrdal raised the issue of the gap between the creed of equality and ethnic/racial prejudice in the US, we find for the first time the argument that people's beliefs and practices do not necessarily coincide. Merton argued that discrimination rates are not shaped so much by the negative or positive belief in the creed of equity,[1] but rather by individuals' fear of legal sanctions/group disapproval, on the one hand, and by their search for social status, votes or

---

1 The Declaration of Independence, the Preamble to the American Constitution and the Bill of Rights assert 'the human right to human equity – the right to equitable access to justice, freedom and opportunity, irrespective of race or religion or thnic origin' (Merton 1973: 367).

175

profits, on the other (Merton 1973 [1949]: 1–371). In his view, interpersonal dynamics, institutions, power structures and 'the legal machinery' (Merton 1973: 377) are powerful forces supporting or counteracting individual beliefs and so either facilitating or constraining individuals' ability to act upon these beliefs.[2] Early American research on institutional discrimination also worked with the profound insight that focusing on individual prejudice (and its psychological or societal causes) is insufficient to explain societal rates of discrimination. Such early proponents of this approach as, for example, Feagin and Feagin (1978: 46–77) argued that one should instead concentrate on (i) laws, (ii) recruitment practices, including advertisements, word-of-mouth recruitment networks and reliance on unions or work mediation offices, and (iii) screening practices, such as requiring credentials or qualifications unnecessary to the role and difficult for migrants/minorities to acquire, or job interviews, which allow stereotypes to influence the hiring outcomes, making sure that one distinguishes the intended from the unintended discrimination. Our interest in the decision-makers' beliefs, stereotypes or thought categories leading to discrimination follows a number of American sociologists, ranging from Kanter 1981 [1975] to Moss and Tilly 2001.[3] In contrast to the US, research of this kind is, for example, extremely scarce in Germany (but see Räthzel and Sarica 1994; Biller 1989; Fijalkowski 1990; Gillmeister 1994; Velling 1994; von Freyberg 1994) and rapidly expanding in the UK. Comparative European research on migrants in contrast to women is still infrequent (but see Zegers de Bejil 1991; García-Ramon and Monk 1996; Van Doorne-Huiskes, Van Hoof and Roelofs 1995; Wrench, Rea and Ouali 1999; EUMC 2003; on migrant/minority women, see chapters 8–11 in Afshar and Maynard 1994).

Our own research provides comparative information about the typical 'stations' or 'stages' in an career (Goffman 1991 [1961]) of a legal migrant,

2 Interestingly, to account for why the initimidated fair-weather bigot may come to act in a non-discriminatory manner, Merton names the pressure of 'powerful countervailing forces, institutional, legal and interpersonal' (Merton 1973: 371–2). Also to account for why a confirmed bigot acts in a prejudiced manner, Merton points to 'the [supportive] local mores, the local institutions and the local power-structure', while to explain why he/she acts against his/her own prejudice Merton points to his/her social isolation (Merton 1973: 372).

3 Our approach was not structural in the sense that we largely ignored the extent to which legal status as a non-citizen, the frequent low socio-economic location of migrants and their children in the social structure or their usually densely concentrated residence patterns affect the general position of disadvantage in the institutions of a given country (see also Castles and Davidson 2000: 75–9, 114–15). This is, however, not to say that we are not aware of the extent to which for most migrants the mere fact of being a migrant and belonging to the lower social classes, having hard, dirty and low-paying jobs and living in a migrant ghetto determines being subjected to discrimination defined in cultural, ethnic-national or racial terms.

such as the application for a work and residence permit, first perusal of advertisements or contacts with the work mediation offices, foremen or employers, efforts to have one's credentials recognized in the host country, renewal of work and residence permits and so on. It thus expands the usual perspective on discrimination by taking a look not only at work organizations and the structuring of the labour markets, but also at the gatekeepers guarding and shaping access to these markets.

Like Robert Merton and the early research on the institutional discrimination, we also distinguish intended from unintended forms of discrimination. Unintended discrimination may result from decision-makers applying automatically or unthinkingly the existing laws and institutional rules to outsider groups which – here Bourdieu's distinctions are useful – lack what the decision-makers (and well-positioned insiders) define as economic, social, cultural or political capital. In such a case, not blatant prejudice, stereotyping, and hostility but the sheer indifference of seemingly universal laws paired with the naivety or indifference of decision-makers are the factors leading to unequal treatment and unequal distribution of life chances. Reality being complex, in practice we find discriminatory and non-discriminatory rules combining with prejudiced and prejudice-free decision-makers, so that 'out there' some happy racists get to implement racist laws, while the unhappy racists have to implement non-racist laws. 'Indifferent' and 'ignorant' functionaries, depending on their workplace, implement both discriminatory and non-discriminatory laws. By changing laws and institutional rules we can constrain the ability of happy racists and indifferent functionaries to assert themselves. But to know how to do it, we need to analyse how institutional discrimination works.

## Institutional Discrimination

Institutional discrimination and exclusion take place daily in labour markets, in housing, education, and politics. In such settings, decisions are made, resources are allocated, opportunities given (or denied), persons granted or not granted voice, entire groups included or excluded. Our questions pertain to the labour market and are: which migrant groups are being discriminated against and excluded; where; and through what mechanisms.

The principal result of the national case studies is that in each of the eight European states one can speak of a segmented labour market in which migrants tend to be employed in positions characterized by low wages and low status, no matter in which sector of the economy (see Figure 9.1; see also Castles and Davidson 2000: 74–5, 114; EUMC 2003: 27–50). Even in high-

| | Low-status job / low wages | Seasonal | Highly qualified | Exoticism | Highly qualified | Self-employment (employment of migrants, illegal networks) | Marginal or deviant sectors | Public services |
|---|---|---|---|---|---|---|---|---|
| Tertiary sector | Gas stations (I) Taxi drivers (S, UK, D) Hairdressers (D) **Outsourced** Cleaning business Catering business (I) **Casual, insecure, part-time** Restaurants **Female** Food distribution Geriatric care (I, D) **Family care** Domestic: assistance/cleaning child-/geriatric care (I) | Tourism (I) | Medical services (S, F) physicians and nurses Massage services (P) Para-medical (P) | Restaurants | | Service sector (I) Building trades (I) Restaurants (S, UK) Food distribution (UK) | | 'Cultural mediation' (I) |
| Secondary sector | **Unskilled positions** Automotive and electronics industry (D) **Manual work** Shoe-making (I) **Dangerous/dirty** Construction work | | | | **Highly qualified** Multi-national companies: (D, F, P) | Arts and craft (I) | | |
| Primary sector | | Agricultural work (I, C, D) | | | | | Seasonal (I, F) | |

Figure 9.1. Migrants' positions in the labour market. Key: A= Austria, C = Cyprus, F = France, D = Germany, I = Italy, P = Poland, S = Sweden, UK = United Kingdom

tech industries, they are as a rule employed as unskilled workers for hard, inconvenient, dirty or dangerous jobs. In general a majority of migrants work on short-term contracts in precarious, part-time positions in agriculture, heavy industry and the service sector. In this sense we can speak of migrant-typing of the hard, low-wage, low-status jobs running across economic sectors.

Many of the migrants are also employed at the fringe of legality. In particular, the domestic service and care sector (domestic help, geriatric care and childcare) appears to be the stronghold of the employment of female migrants, with a high rate of illegal work (cf. Westwood and Phizacklea 2000: 131–7; see also Castles and Davidson 2000: 122–4). Although it can be assumed that the household work sector is primarily targeted at illegal migrants,[4] foreigners with work permits can also be found there due to the many barriers in access to other forms of employment.

The general equation of migrant work with low-skill, hard, low-paid and low-status jobs should not lead us to disregard the fact that some migrants are highly educated. Earlier research points out that migrants do not stem from the poorest social strata, whose members have insufficient resources to finance migration (Westwood and Phizacklea 2000: 122, 126, 135–6; Velling 1994). It also indicates that since about 1974, due to restrictive immigration policies, professionals with valuable skills actually predominate among legal migrants from the South to the North. Specific types of migrants, for example, Filipina and Central European domestics, are very well educated, but do not find jobs reflecting their education. Starting in the mid-1980s East–West migration became more important than the South-North migration, but the trend remained the same: the average migrant from Russia and Eastern Europe moving to Western Europe after the collapse of the Soviet bloc in 1989/1990 has been better educated than a typical member of the host society. The overall situation of these well-educated migrants can be illustrated by doctors from Iraq, Palestine or Afghanistan whose credentials are not recognized and who are very much in demand as nurses in severely understaffed French hospitals, or by Russian and Bulgarian doctors who are sought after in Milan as poorly paid home carers.

Large multinational companies are more likely to hire such employees

---

4   In particular the Italian, French and Polish research teams highlighted the exploitative and abusive role of employers, sub-contractors or foremen in the illegal labour market. Often the sub-contractors and foremen belong to the same ethnic group as the employees, rely on network-hiring and are often as abusive and exploitative as the bosses. Illegality makes migrants vulnerable. Part of their income is kept by their employers, sub-contractors or foreman on the grounds that they hire them in the first place, help them with the formalities or provide them with housing.

despite their migrant background either because they fill quotas defined by anti-discrimination procedures or because it is their multicultural background which is needed for a particular position. Managers of the multinationals think that migrants possess 'expertise in two cultures' which will be helpful to the company. Migrants often have to emphasize their 'exotic' skills to achieve success – in multinational enterprises as well as when they try to escape discrimination by becoming self-employed businessmen running 'ethnic' restaurants, supermarkets, furniture stores or translation offices.

In what follows I will try to explain the main research result – the migrant-typing of the lowliest jobs across economic sectors. To signal very briefly what is to come: of the eight case countries, six have discriminatory laws and/or regulations barring migrants from access to work and/or residence permits. Seven countries reserve their civil service sector for citizens only, six by law and one *de facto* (Sweden). Only in two countries (Sweden and the UK) are there no explicit discriminatory laws keeping migrants away from the national labour market, and instead it is agentic discrimination (by authorities and/or employers) which plays a major role in barring migrants from access to jobs. In all countries that we studied (but perhaps less so in the UK where the anti-discrimination laws and supervision are very strong) the official authorities granting work permits and job access are the major institutions of discrimination.

## Laws and Institutional Rules with Institutional Consequences

### Priority Laws and their Equivalents

As Fig. 9.2 shows, the most important discriminatory factors are laws and regulations barring migrants from access to the labour market and the civil service sector. Although several European countries legislated bans on migration by the mid-1970s, their motives differed and so did the restricting rules. The racist intent to reduce (post)colonial nonwhite migration and to reserve 'belonging' or true citizenship for natives and their descendants informed the 1968 and 1971 Immigration Acts in Britain and the 1974 and 1977 bans on immigration in France (Travis 2002; Hampshire 2006; Atkinson 2002; Hamilton and Simon 2004: 2). In Britain the 1971 Act made a right to entry and abode in Britain dependent on a prior work contract even for the New Commonwealth citizens. In France the distinction between legal/free/privileged migrants, and illegal, 'wild', to-be-controlled (either to be expelled or legalized) migrants has shaped government migration policy from 1946 on. Today the privileged group no longer embraces Algerians and francophone Africans – or (post)colonials in short – but instead only EU citizens and – at least on paper – long-term legal residents. Illegal, 'wild', to-be-controlled migrants are defined as those who come from Turkey or Africa. In the course of the 1960s France successively curtailed the freedom of Algerians to work or settle. In 1974 it put an official end to its labour migration programme and ten years later it introduced a new law which allows for migration only when the labour market situation calls for it. In contrast to the British and French racist intent, the Swedish decrees of 1967 and 1972 requiring all non-Scandinavians to secure employment and work permits before entering Sweden (Gustafsson 1980: 149) were supposedly motivated by the integrationist desire to protect the employed, no matter where they came from, while the German 1973 ban on further work-related migration was motivated by an unmitigated nationalism – the wish to protect native workers against unemployment. Today in six of the eight case countries – France, Germany, Austria, Poland, Italy and Cyprus – laws or regulations grant natives, EU nationals and long-term residents privileged access to jobs, while excluding other groups. In these countries employers and/or work mediation officials have the burden of proving that no person privileged by such law or regulation can fill the vacant position before they inform a person without such a priority about this position (see also Castles and Davidson 2000: 86–102). These laws and regulations exclude recent migrants, non-EU migrants, and 'illegals' from access to the national labour markets. In Germany as early as 1965 one type of work permit for foreigners could only be granted if no native interests were threatened. The so-called 'priority law' passed in the mid-1970s generalized the principle of priority being granted to Germans. In 1998 a modified German law was passed denying migrants work permits, unless no Germans, EU citizens or long-term migrants could be found for the job. It became part of a new Immigration Law in 2005. A similar law, Bossi-Fini, was passed in Italy in 2002. Austria, Cyprus and Poland have similar regulations. Although on the surface equivalence between natives, EU citizens and long-term migrants is called for, a hierarchy which (re-)asserts native rights is a matter of actual practice.

Moreover, migrants and/or their employers carry the burden of renewing their work permits, as well as residence permits which can be received only when a work permit is in place. Both permits have to be renewed at frequent regular intervals. The renewal process is extremely cumbersome and uncertain. Permit-granting institutions with intricate rules and procedures, as well as their discriminating decision-makers, make their own contribution to discrimination. They make applicants extremely vulnerable to exploitation by employers and middlemen.

# Institutional Forms of Discrimination

| Discriminatory Laws and Regulations | Institutional Discrimination |
|---|---|
| **Work permit/residence laws:** | **Employment Mediation Offices and Residence Permit Authorities** (D, I, F, C) slowness/obstruction, outright discrimination |
| **Germany**: Priority Law (1975) no work permit is to be granted to a foreigner unless it is proven that no natives (or their equivalents 1998, 2005) are available to fill a position; residence permit attached to work permit or EU-status | |
| **Italy**: Bossi-Fini Law (2002): work permit granted only if the employer can demonstrate that no Italian, EU citizens or long-term migrant-residents can be found; residence permit attached to work permit; employer has to provide housing and cover repatriation costs | **Employer Application**: cumbersome, repetitious, 'same procedure next year' (D, I, P) |
| **UK**: 1968 and 1971 right to entry dependent on work even for the citizens of the New Commonwealth | |
| **France**: Bans (1974 and 1977) on immigration, linked to labour market (1984) | |

**Job access laws or regulations:**

Citizens, EU citizens and long-term migrant residents are to be given priority in access to jobs: **A, D, C, F, I, P** — **Employment Mediation Offices** application forms/handling internet

Civil service – access granted to natives only: **A, F, I, C, P** and some *BL*/Germany — **Public Institutions as Employers of Natives Only** (even Sweden)

## + Restrictive Naturalization Laws: A, D, (F)

| **Title-recognition laws:** | **Title Recognition Authorities** |
|---|---|
| (**D**): title non-recognition: local and regional authorities decide whether and which foreign qualifications are granted recognition | (**D**) dispersed professional bodies, chambers of commerce and industry, universities |
| (**S**): nobody knows where to apply | (**D+S**) authorities unknown |
| (**I + A**): title non-recognition | |
| (**F**) : no recognition for some skills such as medicine | |

**Laws/rules regulating job announcements:** — **Job advertisement**: language, medium (UK, D, S, C)

**COUNTERMEASURES :**

| | | |
|---|---|---|
| Anti-discrimination laws: | A, F, UK, S | (D) – *only in workplaces!* (C) – *only in private workplaces!* |
| Anti-discrimination rules for ads | S, D, I, F | |
| Laws legalizing illegal labour, 2002/2003 | I | |
| Supportive Trade Unions: | UK, I | (S) – *nat'l level only; (C) – only a minority* |
| NGOs: | I, UK | |

Figure 9.2 Discriminatory factors in the workplace.

182

| Gatekeepers | Discriminating belief patterns |
|---|---|
| Public servants | 'native rights should be protected'<br>'laws protecting native rights are good'<br>'foreigners cheat/claim what is not their right'<br>'we cannot host the whole misery of the world' |

**Decision-making about job access:**
**Officials in work mediation offices**
Bosses – all countries
**Human resources managers (S, A, F)**

**(D): Hiring managers**
**(UK): Selection panels, senior managers**
**(S) Supervisors, heads of personnel office,**
**key union functionaries, key employees**
**(I) Manager or foreman (many foreign**
**themselves) or sub-contractor/assocn**
*+ special problem of abusive employers*
*on the informal labour market*
**(A) Dept. managers and co-workers**
**(P): Labour office and NGO officials:**
*discrimination against Easterners,*
*positive discrimination of Westerners*

**All countries – ethnocentrism:**
'language comptence is crucial' – for each job
'our educational system is best'
'work experience from our country is necessary'
'well-written, well-structured CV' and interview
'professional skills and orientation are a must'
'have to fit in/possess social competence'
'capacity for teamwork is essential'
'communication skills are of great importance'
'bad experience with migrants before'

UK: 'local accents are preferred'; 'local
knowledge is crucial'; 'lacking local
knowledge blocks careers'
S: 'knowledge of Swedish social codes is a key';
'in times of high unemployment CV is a key'
D: 'our own people have to get jobs first'; 'too
many migrants would upset our employees';
'mixing cultures creates conflicts'
D + I: 'poor knowledge of labour contracts and
of safety laws/regulations'
I: 'blacks upset clients and patients'; Filipinas
are 'nice and obedient'; 'sub-Saharan blacks
are suitable for hard work in manufacture'
F: 'diversity in a team may be an asset, but it
may increase conflicts'
C: 'they will get our jobs'; 'ethnic minorities
don't want to fit in'; 'Pakistanis smell bad';
'Polish women are dirty'

**AND INSTITUTIONS**

**Minority and migrant networks:**
**D, UK, S, A, C, P, I, F**

**MITIGATING FORCES:** occasional helpful public servants, migrants on workers' councils,
NGOs, exemplary employers, firms with labour shortage, employers accused of discrimination in
the past

Key: A= Austria, C = Cyprus, F = France, D = Germany, I = Italy,
P = Poland, S = Sweden, UK = United Kingdom

## Institutional Forms of Discrimination

*Job Access Laws – Civil Service*
Secondly, we note that in six of our case countries – Austria, France, Italy, and (with some minor exceptions) Poland, Germany and Cyprus – by law or regulation (France) only citizens are entitled to work in the civil service (see also Castles and Davidson 2000: 75, 92–7). In a seventh country, Sweden, this is the case *de facto* rather than *de jure*.

Since citizenship is a key precondition for access to the labour markets in six of the case-study countries, and also to public service in six of the case-study countries, it has to be noted that restrictive naturalization laws, which grant more weight to citizenship by descent (*ius sanguinis*) than to citizenship by birthplace (*ius soli*), reinforce the intent to exclude non-citizens and non-EU nationals. Such restrictive naturalization laws are most pronounced in Austria and Germany but even in France in 1993 the Pasqua Laws abolished the long-standing right of every child of foreign parents born and living (for at least five years) in France to automatic citizenship. Instead a special declaration had to be filed (Brubaker 1996 [1992]: 151–4; Bizeul 1997: 96; Wodak and Van Dijk 2000; Castles and Davidson 2000: 91–4). The law of 1998, however, made the acquisition of French citizenship at the age of eighteen once again automatic (Hamilton and Simon 2004: 4). In Germany and Austria restrictive naturalization laws pose obstacles to acquiring citizenship even for the children and grandchildren of migrants and thus make their access to national labour markets more difficult while barring them completely from the civil service. In France the opposite trend can be noted: since discrimination in the labour market is severe, while acquiring citizenship is still easy, comparatively speaking, naturalized children and grandchildren of migrants seek employment in the public sector. In Italy, since naturalization is officially possible after two years (although it is usually closer to four years in practice, due to bureaucratic obstacles and resistance), a 'French' trend of the offspring of migrants taking up public-sector employment can therefore be expected.

*Title (Non-)Recognition*
The next piece of influential legislation concerns title recognition. We discovered that in at least five of our eight cases – Germany, Austria, Italy, France and Sweden – either law requires and makes difficult the conversion of qualifications acquired abroad (Germany, Austria, Italy, France) or this is a standard national praxis (Sweden). This accounts for the difficulties migrants have in translating their diplomas. This barrier applies also to EU citizens, and not just to non-EU citizens such as Turks or Moroccans. It constitutes one factor which contributes to extremely low occupational mobility within the EU itself. In 2001 no more than 1.5% of the entire EU

working population worked in another EU state – just as in any other year so far (European Commission 2004: 40).

*Laws and Regulations Pertaining to Job Advertisements*

Laws regulating job advertisements leave room for discriminatory practices, if they do not contain anti-discriminatory clauses. In Cyprus the mere fact that an advertisement is in Greek discriminates not only against various types of migrants, but also against the largest minority, Turkish Cypriots. An advertisement asking for citizenship, proficiency in the native language, or domestic graduation is also discriminatory. Anti-discriminatory laws, which put a legal ban on such practices, help to limit them. Noteworthy perhaps is that only five of the eight case-study countries have specific anti-discrimination advertisement laws or regulations: France, Sweden, Italy, the UK and Germany.

Concluding the section on labour market institutions, it is important to note that only four of the eight case-study countries – Austria, France, Great Britain and Sweden – had anti-discrimination laws in 2005. Cyprus has an anti-discrimination law only for the private sector, Germany has an ineffective company-focused anti-discrimination law (*Betriebsverfassungsgesetz*) that seeks to combat inequality and racism in private and public companies (at least in principle if not in practice). The EU anti-discrimination law is supposed to cover other aspects of life in these countries, but in Germany, for example, not even the representatives of anti-discrimination and anti-racist NGOs (100 of which responded to our survey in 2004) were aware of this. They expressed frustration with the fact that no German anti-discrimination law helps protect migrants. Only after repeated reminders to pay heed to the EU directives did Germany finally pass an anti-discrimination law in July 2006, calling it the General Equal Treatment Law (AGG) probably to fend off any further outcries against it (Flam 2007: 33).

## Institutional Agentic Discrimination

Turning now to institutional agentic discrimination we can recall that one goal of this research project was to identify decision-makers in key institutions, such as work mediation officers or work enterprises, whose routine decisions lead to discrimination against or exclusion of migrants and their children. These decision-makers can be conceptualized as gatekeepers. They have the power to categorize human beings and decide which categories of persons will or will not gain access to specific resources, such as work permits, jobs or training programmes. It is when they exercise their agentic power that these gatekeepers create certain excluded or disadvantaged groups, and their decisions create systematic biases in the allocation of premiums and penalties through institutional mechanisms.

As Figure 9.2 shows, as far as the labour market is concerned officials in charge of granting work and residence permits play a major role as discriminatory agents in six of the eight countries we studied: Sweden, Germany, France, Italy, Austria and Cyprus. Based on this and another research phase (focus group interviews) we can say with a reasonable degree of certainty that they serve as the major gatekeepers who work to exclude migrants and their children from the mainstream of national institutional life. The Polish case is mixed: Westerners encounter positive discrimination and Easterners from the Ukraine, Lithuania or White Russia negative discrimination. In the UK the anti-discrimination laws and supervision are extremely strong, so that such gatekeepers' ability to act in a discriminatory manner is much reduced.

An equally important role is played by businesses: Figure 9.2 shows that there is some national variation in who the key decision-makers in enterprises are. In some countries, such as Italy, only the managers or their foremen have a say about hiring, in others, such as Sweden, several decision-makers, such as supervisors, heads of personnel office, key union functionaries, and key employees decide who will be hired. This shows that while in some cases only personal prejudice of the manager or his/her representative has to be included in the equation leading to discrimination, in others the orientation of the entire decision-making body has to be investigated and taken into consideration, since it is the collective orientation of this body (or the dominant actors within it) which is crucial.

## Beliefs and Belief Patterns

In everyday interactions migrants (and/or members of some minorities) are stereotyped as lacking language, technical or cultural competence, or as being unreliable, lazy, devious or criminal. Employers and managers rely on such negative stereotypes, but they also link positive traits with specific minority or migrant groups. They use these stereotypes to sort the individual representatives of these groups into unacceptable and acceptable job candidates, and to allocate the acceptable candidates to the available jobs. As briefly pointed out at the outset, in Europe migrants are most often sentenced either to unemployment or to menial, hard, repetitive, dirty and badly paid tasks. In both these ways they are denied equal opportunities with natives when it comes to access to jobs or positions. Stereotypes play a very efficient role in defining positions in which the presence of a migrant will be acceptable, and even expected.

To cite one well-researched example: in their multi-city, large-scale surveys of US employers, Moss and Tilly (2001: 44, 49, 79, 83) distinguish hard skills, which refer to cognitive and technical abilities, from soft skills, which refer to interactive and motivational factors. Their literature review and their surveys showed that for low-skill entry jobs a moderate rise in demand for both hard and soft skills has taken place. This rise works mostly to the disadvantage of high-school dropouts, African-Americans and Latino men in city centres. Moss and Tilly (2001: 97, 100, 102) reported that in general employers see blacks' hard and soft skills as particularly poor, while in about 50% of firms at least one manager depicted black people as 'lazy, unmotivated, or undependable'. Positive statements came from about 2% of the respondents who categorized blacks as perhaps 'just a little more testy', but – out of need – more dependable and willing to work hard, do menial tasks and stay at a job longer (Moss and Tilly 2001: 103). Some saw them as more inclined towards friendly customer service. The point is that irrespective of whether blacks were seen in a positive or negative way, they were either refused jobs or hired to do hard, menial, long-hour labour. Their chances of being positively evaluated and hired were much greater at the city periphery than in its centre.

As this US example shows, at best, specific 'skills' or 'talents' – such as being flexible, being able to take on hard workloads or the worst working times – become attributed to the US minorities. As our research indicates, in Europe too the imagined 'skills' or 'talents' of specific migrant groups are evoked to justify sending them to the worst jobs – which hardly any natives want to do. Tilly and Tilly (1994: 300–1) as well as Moss and Tilly (2001) demonstrate that American employers mix the attributions of specific skills, work experience and traits/stereotypes to specific ethnic groups and based on these attributions they decide against hiring them at all or assign them to different departments in their enterprises, which results in ethnic segregation within these enterprises. Comparable to this would perhaps be the conviction spread throughout much of Europe that Turks are only suitable for unskilled, heavy jobs in industry, while Poles are reliable in backbreaking, low-paid seasonal jobs in agriculture (picking strawberries, grapes, asparagus or apples). Another belief which is currently in vogue in Europe is that women from the Philippines are ideal as caring babysitters.[5] As these examples show,

---

5  National stereotypes about migrant women differ strongly, however: in Sweden and Britain Polish women are believed to make excellent nurses, but in Cyprus they are seen as dirty and therefore unsuitable for domestic tasks. In Italy East European women are believed to be serious, patient and honest which makes them ideal for housekeeping or the care of the elderly. Filipina women are thought of as nice, obedient and, when beautiful, appropriate as a status symbol. They are employed as domestics.

individuals become associated with specific nations and allocated to different jobs based on the collective characteristics associated with these nations. Gender-typing accompanies nation-typing. This suggests that as well as the migrant-typing of the hard, low-wage, low-status jobs across various labour markets sectors, we can speak of nation-typing of particular jobs, which sometimes follows tradition (see also Sassen 1999: 15–31, 45–51, 54–81) and sometimes rather short-lived fashions and fads.

Only in Cyprus, Germany and Italy[6] were the gatekeeper beliefs truly explicated, and not only nation-typing but also cultural and biological racism[7] surfaced. While in Cyprus gatekeepers spoke of 'smelly Pakistanis' and 'dirty Polish women', in Germany they argued that people with a different 'mentality', 'culture' or 'skin colour' should be kept apart since bringing them together only causes conflicts (see Flam 2007; Gillmeister 1994: 153). Polarized images of superior Europeans were posed against deficient, strange or threatening non-Europeans – one gatekeeper argued that Arabs and black Africans with their different-from-European mentality just cannot be as reliable as German (and other European) workers, while another savoured the image of the integration-resisting Turks, with their 'pasha mentality' and their submissive, veiled, 'tiny goosefeet' Turkish wives, thus bringing up to date the colonial image of the 'oriental woman' who was seen as exotic, yet dependent, oppressed and in need of (forced) liberation, so as not to undermine superior Western values (Brah 1994: 157–8). In Italy it was reported that Arabs but not sub-Saharan Africans are accepted for work in pizza parlours because employers believe that customers find black people handling food offensive. Similarly, blacks are barred from hospital nursing and geriatric care, since many patients feel fearful and suspicious towards them.

Most often, however, gatekeepers in enterprises stated that their hiring decisions are based on such criteria as 'good self-presentation', 'good manners', 'good work motivation', 'work qualifications', 'fitting in', 'communicative skills', 'well-structured CV and interview'. For the US, Feagin and Feagin (1978: 52–3) argued that such requirements express a middle-class bias which serves to exclude lower classes and minorities, since these usually have a lower-class background, from access to (good) jobs. Yet these criteria as such appear rather innocent. Even the statements smelling most strongly of prejudice were rather innocuous and 'common sense':

---

6 A single case of direct racial discrimination was reported from Sweden, where a company did not hire a black woman as a cashier 'to protect her' from troublesome clients.

7 We can suppose that the norm of political correctness silenced open expressions of even more racial prejudice and stereotyping. Nevertheless to label everything that we heard as racist would be akin to squaring a circle.

experts and gatekeepers all agreed that language competency is a must. Such demands are clearly discriminatory when directed at street sweepers or garbage collectors, but they seem reasonable enough when applied to, for example, clerk jobs which call for extensive report-writing. In this second case, the claim to own linguistic and so implicitly cultural-national superiority has to be read into this job requirement, since it is not explicit. Yet, even if the demands for language competency as well as those for native educational titles and work experience seem innocuous, their effects are discriminatory. They make the practice of setting a priority on hiring citizens legitimate at the same time as they legitimate rejecting non-citizens and long-term residents lacking domestic qualifications. Although discriminatory, it would be incorrect to claim that these criteria are inherently racist. To describe much of Europe today as racist would be jumping to conclusions. The aforementioned evidence speaks instead for a strong case of nativism.

As far as hiring criteria are concerned, we need to know the characteristics of a job candidate, also in comparison with others, to decide whether specific selection criteria are neutral or discriminatory, nationalist or racist. Consider the case of a discriminating mind irritated by and rejecting anything unfamiliar. It is offended by a trace of an accent or suburban origin (F) and insists on 'local knowledge', 'fitting in', 'team spirit' (UK) or familiarity with 'national cultural codes' (S) from an otherwise suitable job candidate.[8] Some of these selection criteria, such as 'fitting in' or 'team spirit', in and of themselves do not even seem discriminatory. Others do not tell us whether racism or nationalism is at work. Given the current demand for national credentials, domestic work experience and national cultural codes, one could argue that they just specify in even more detail the general demand for native labour. However, to the extent that demands for 'local knowledge' or 'national cultural codes' or 'fitting in' are directed at migrants or minorities who are citizens and do have domestic qualifications, ethnic/racial factors – and thus racism – are at issue rather than issues of nationality. In such a case what appears as nationalism at first sight should be understood as racism.

Our perhaps most important finding is that national slurs are rare these days. They were directly made in Cyprus and reported for Italy. Secondly, only in Germany was nativism an open reality, taken for granted. It could be

8 One could argue that the demand for credentials and work experience constitute 'hard data' whose comparability can be defined. The second, subtle set of requirements, calling for 'local knowledge' or the knowledge of 'national cultural codes', is more discriminatory because it makes the possession of non-tangibles into a job prerequisite. This kind of discrimination is harder to prove and to counteract. It resembles the soft-skill discrimination which Moss and Tilly investigated in the US (for their policy recommendations, see 2001: 253–74).

seen as 'defensive' nationalism: over and over again experts and key gatekeepers in eastern Germany asserted that the German priority law is a good law since it protects Germans against outsiders during times of high unemployment. Their counterparts in western Germany offered no enthusiastic support for the priority law, but nor did they express any criticism. At an eastern German branch of a multinational company the manager, who all along argued that nationality does not play a role in hiring, added twice that migrants 'are also people after all'. The turn of phrase indicates a defensive posture – an awareness of a discursive field in which hiring foreigners is unwelcome and in which doubt prevails as to whether foreigners do indeed belong to the category of people. In the western German branch managers admitted that they thought it would not be desirable to hire more Turks for their company since this would upset their German employees.[9] In the same firm Turkish foremen are unimaginable because of their 'macho' characteristics. France could perhaps be classified as a case of 'assertive' nationalism, but the French experts disagree about whether or not French businesses in fact openly demand what they call BBR, or 'bleu blanc rouge' – that is, native – employees. If this demand for BBR is indeed as omnipresent as some experts claim, then the French businessmen display to an extreme the nativist trend which seems typical of Europe today.

After reviewing the material about expectations and stereotypes it seems then that although racist beliefs can be found in Cyprus, Italy and Germany, nationalism – understood as a conviction about the superiority of one's own educational and cultural achievements and work patterns – plays a role everywhere as a key discriminatory factor. Subtle demands for local or cultural knowledge play perhaps a *decisive* role as a factor of discrimination mostly in Sweden and the UK, where (i) the naturalization laws are liberal (Sweden) or post-liberal (the UK), (ii) priority laws or regulations do not prevent giving jobs to migrants, and (iii) strong anti-discrimination laws exist.

## Conclusion

To summarize our key findings, the case-study countries can be divided into two categories with two different discrimination emphases. Germany, Austria, Italy, Cyprus, Poland, and France have explicit discriminatory laws

9  Gillmeister's survey of 79 factories in Berlin revealed that a substantial number had a hiring quota by which foreigners should constitute 5% or, where this was unrealistic, 30% of the workforce. These personnel policies were dictated by the need to feel 'like the boss in your own house' but often could not be implemented for lack of applicants for jobs which offered little status or pay for much hard labour (Gillmeister 1994: 156). Some employers tried to counteract the dominance of Turks among employees by focused recruitment of Yugoslavs, Vietnamese or Lebanese workers.

or regulations concerning work and residence permits which bar new migrants from access to the national labour markets and make it difficult for older migrants to stabilize their work and life conditions. Great Britain and Sweden have no such laws and so the legal context sets up the gatekeepers (hiring committees in Britain and Sweden) and their beliefs as the major factors of discrimination. Finally, in all countries (except Britain) institutions granting permits or mediating jobs, such as the police, the *Ausländerbehörde* or the work mediation office, play a clearly discriminatory role.

Our material suggests that only self-help, in the form of 'ethnic networks', mitigates the worst types of discrimination in hiring. 'Ethnic networks' help migrants access jobs. They spread information about openings and support hiring members of their own group for certain jobs (see also Ruwanpura 2005: 20). As opposed to, for instance, trade unions, NGOs or anti-discrimination laws, networks were said to play a key countering role in all eight case studies. But they usually channel migrant workers into the low-paid menial work sector where they are already predominant. In our research we have not come across the 'US' type of 'ethnic networks' which, as Tilly and Tilly (1994: 302) show, reverse the discrimination criteria and monopolize control over hiring for certain jobs, departments, trades or professions. The presence of such networks – mostly 'white ethnic networks' organized by Italians, Irish, Poles or Jews – in specific trades and professions in the US led Alejandro Porter (1998: 15) to speak of ethnic groups as possessing certain – positive or negative – social capital. We have not come across such networks but instead the fear of such networks, as when, for example, German managers feared that Turkish networks might actively try to expand the number of Turks working for their company. It can be concluded then that 'ethnic networks' at present reinforce the underprivileged position of migrant groups in the labour market and in the host state rather than improving it. They should thus be seen in contrast to opportunities for escaping migrant-typed niches provided by new training or employer demand, setting up non-ethnic businesses or acquisition of rights through naturalization or the accession of one's nation-state to the EU.

Many academics today speak of racializing of the 'outsider'/'Other' and of cultures as such, the effect of which is portraying migrants as coming from a different 'race' and 'culture', even if they come from the same geographical region (Sassen 1999: 135; Castles and Davidson 2000: 80, 170; see also Miles 1993: 36–52 for some early biological and constructivist views on 'race'). This trend is said to intensify discriminatory practices leading to the exclusion of minorities/migrants from the labour markets or sentencing them to hard, low-prestige, low-paying jobs. If one takes a look only at the unemployment figures and at the labour market segments in which migrants and minorities are overrepresented, then one could at first indeed conclude that race-typing is going on – minorities, migrants from south-eastern Europe and migrants from outside Europe are put into a single cultural-racist category of aliens/*Fremde* and are pushed into unemployment, or the worst jobs. But neither unemployment nor poor jobs is reserved only for minorities or migrants (see Phizacklea and Miles 1980: 10–14). Although it is true that there are more unemployed or employed in unskilled positions among these groups than among the natives, and most have been pushed to take on lowly jobs, it cannot be claimed that they have been turned into 'disadvantage monopolists'. We should not forget that many natives are also unemployed or work in low-skill/low-pay occupations.

And the reverse is also true. Not all minorities and migrant groups are crowded out from the labour market or forced into the worst labour market sectors. As far as both minorities and migrants are concerned, European employers are inconsistent: different groups fare differently across Europe and even in the same country over time. For example, migrant women in France, but not in Germany or Great Britain, improved their employment situation in some respects compared to native women between the 1980s and the 1990s, as Phizacklea showed (1994: 176–7). As research indicates, moreover, it would be false to equate migrant or minority labour with the unskilled labour segment or to reduce it completely to the so-called 3D jobs: dirty, dangerous and demanding (EUMC 2003: 47, 27–51). Just as some natives have 3D jobs, so, for example, Antillean and Surinamese women in the Netherlands are found in the same sectors as Dutch women, while West Indian women are employed as nurses and West Indian men in skilled manual jobs in the UK (Harzing 1995: 59–60; see also Phizacklea and Miles 1980: 14–25). In such cases discrimination cannot be equated with being crowded into unemployment, the unskilled or the 3D sector. As a rule it means heavier and lower-paid jobs within the same sector as natives, although exceptions can be found even to this rule, such as when a specific minority group of women earn more than their native counterpart.

I do not wish to deny many obvious discriminatory practices and their consequences. I only wish to stress that our research, like some of the examples provided by Castles and Davidson (2000: 80, 170), points to the nationalization as well as the racialization of cultures, whereby the national culture rather than one's own 'race' becomes equated with the superior language, education or customs. Although as Miles (1993) and Priester (2003) argue, racism can also be directed against 'whites' (the Jews, the Irish) and the lower classes of the same nation, we should not forget that racists think primarily in terms of 'race' and not 'nation' as a category, and distinguish anything between two and seven 'races'. However, 'race' is not the (thought) pattern dominating the European labour markets today. Instead we hear demands for native educational titles and domestic work experience, which are believed to be superior to 'foreign' titles and experience in every case-study country except Poland, where a dualistic pattern preferring Western but downgrading Eastern qualifications is much more pronounced than in the West. Nationalism and not racism seems to prevail.

Moreover, it is important to stress that many migrants escape 'racialization' sentencing them to the worst jobs, if it is indeed going on. At the moment, especially in those European countries where unemployment is high (10%) or unemployment among migrants is very high (Sweden), migrants and minorities are turned into the labour reserve army of the unemployed. But when labour market demands cannot be satisfied by natives, employers are willing to offer jobs to 'outsiders', even skilled ones, in engineering, medicine (doctors, nurses) or computers (EUMC 2003: 41). Exclusion from the labour market is far from permanent; rather it is demand-driven.

Most migrants already residing in Europe have two self-chosen means of avoiding the clutches of permanent 'racialization'. Some escape the worst, migrant-typed sectors of the labour market by establishing their own businesses, even if their goal is only to flee unemployment or low-paid, dirty or demeaning jobs (EUMC 2003: 37–40, 43). Although in many cases their 'profit' levels bring them close to starvation, at least nobody orders them around. Some migrants and migrants' children, moreover, manage to overcome the existing institutional barriers and attain decent educational qualifications and occupations: national school systems vary considerably in the extent to which they block this particular avenue of upward mobility (EUMC 2003).

Yet another, and perhaps the most important, means of avoiding permanent 'racialization' is currently working to the advantage of East European migrants. Their nation-states have by now almost all joined the EU, so that – at least by law – they are already (as in, for example, Britain, Finland, Ireland and Spain) or will be in at the most four more years (as in, for example, Germany or Austria) entitled to a native-like access to all national labour markets within the EU, no longer subject to the obligation to constantly renew their work and residence permits, and allowed to move freely within the EU.

In sum, many migrants naturalize, (re-)educate themselves, become self-employed and/or claim rights in their host countries as the citizens of the new EU member states. In all these ways they counter any processes of racialization they might encounter. Just as it was in the US, where the Irish and the Jews as well as the south-east Europeans started their migrant lives as members of the 'lower races', but (in contrast to the American blacks and American Indians) managed by the middle of the twentieth century to acquire the status of 'white', 'prefixed', ethnic American (as in 'Jewish-American' or 'Italian-Americans') (Roediger 2002), so it will be in Europe with many current migrant groups, such as Italians, Portuguese, Greeks or Poles.

In contrast to the mass media and politicians, who lump all migrants, minorities and asylum-seekers together and 'racialize' them, putting them into a separate – threatening, alien and opposite to the natives – cultural category (Wodak and Van Dijk 2000; Van Dijk 2005: 113–37), labour markets in Europe today do not so much race-type as nation-type jobs. Internal European discrimination is mostly related to nativist and less often to explicit racist trends. If there is race-typing going on, it is not permanent, at least for the citizens of the EU.[10] Even if the Portuguese, Spaniards, Greeks and Italians were 'dark' when they were signed on as 'guest workers' by Western Europe, the accession of their countries to the EU has 'whitened' them. The same pattern can be expected for the ten new EU members from Eastern Europe. It is only in Europe's relationship with Turkey and Africa that a contrary pattern can be found. Considering the effort which is being put into the construction of 'Fortress Europe' aiming at keeping out the so-called third-country nationals, for the time being we should not be surprised that Turks and Africans will remain 'dark' – a stain of shame on Europe's 'white' map.

### References

Afshar, H., and M. Maynard (1994) *The Dynamics of 'Race' and Gender: Some Feminist Interventions*. London: Taylor and Francis.

Atkinson, J. (2002) 'British Immigration Policy, Race Relations, and National Identity Crises', http://www.jimmyatkinson.com/papers/british.html, last accessed 5 September 2007.

Biller M. (1994) *Arbeitsmarktsegmentation und Ausländerbeschäftigung*. Frankfurt am Main: Campus.

Bizeul, Y. (1997) 'Die französische Debatte um Alterität und Kultur', in *Vom Umgang mit dem Fremden*, ed. Y. Bizeul, U. Bliesener, M. Prawda. Weinheim: Beltz Verlag, pp. 94–115.

10 Even in countries such as Austria or Germany where the definition of nation and citizenship implies shared descent by blood or racial ties, and where the nationalization and racialization of culture overlap to a great extent, there is no empirical evidence to support the thesis that all non-natives end up unemployed or lowest in the job hierarchy. For such countries it is easier to assume a correlation between nation- and race-typing of jobs and specific labour market sectors, but empirical evidence is lacking. For instance, Sweden, Austria and Germany currently have the highest rate of self-employed migrants in Europe (EUMC 2003: 38–9).

Brah, A. (1994) '"Race" and "Culture" in the Gendering of Labour Markets', in Afshar and Maynard 1994, pp. 151–72.

Brubaker, R. (1996 [1992]) *Citizenship and Nationhood in France and Germany.* Cambridge, MA: Harvard University Press.

Carrington, W., K. McCue and B. Pierce (1996) 'Black/White Wage Convergence: The Role of Public Sector Wages and Employment', *Industrial and Labour Relations Review* 49(3): 456–71.

Castles, S., and A. Davidson (2000) *Citizenship and Migration: Globalization and the Politics of Belonging.* New York: Routledge.

EUMC (2003). Migrants, Minorities and Employment: Exclusion, Discrimination and Anti-Discrimination in 15 Member States of the European Union. Equality & Diversity for an Inclusive Europe. EUMC Comparative Study. Data analysed by the International Centre for Migration Policy Development on behalf of the European Monitoring Centre on Racism and Xenophobia.

European Commission (2004) *Bericht über die Umsetzung des Aktionsplans der Kommission für Qualifikation und Mobilität.* KOM (2002) 72 endgültig. Brussels.

Feagin, J., and C. B. Feagin (1978) 'Discrimination in the Economy: A Focus on Employment', in J. Faegin and C. B. Faegin, *Discrimination American Style: Institutional Racism and Sexism.* Englewood Cliffs, NJ: Prentice-Hall, pp. 43–84.

Fijalkowski, J. (ed.) (1990) *Transnationale Migranten in der Arbeitswelt.* Berlin: Edition Sigma.

Flam, H. (ed.) (2007) *Migranten in Deutschland: Statistiken – Fakten – Diskurse.* Konstanz: Universitätsverlag Konstanz.

García-Ramon, M. D., and J. Monk (1996) *Women of the European Union.* London: Routledge.

Gillmeister, H. (1994) 'Nationalität als Einstellungskriterium', in *Gewerkschaften und Einwanderung: Eine kritische Zwischenbilanz*, ed. P. Kühne, N. Öztürk, K.-W. West. Cologne: Bund-Verlag, pp. 150–63.

Goffman, E. (1991 [1961]). *Asylums.* London: Penguin.

Gustafsson, M. (1980) 'Mein Kater ist mit einer Maus verheiratet. Ein Blick auf das "schwedische" Modell', special issue 'Vielvölkerstaat Bundesrepublik', *Kursbuch* 62: 147–56.

Hamilton, K., and P. Simon (2004) 'The Challenge to French Diversity', http://migration information.com/Profiles/display.cfm?id=266, last accessed 5 September 2007.

Hampshire, J. (2006) 'Citizens Who Do Not Belong: Political Membership and Immigration Policy in Britain', Presentation in the session on 'The Politics of Belonging in Europe' organized at the 15th International Conference of the Council for European Studies, Chicago, IL, 29 March – 2 April 2006.

Harzing, A.-W. K. (1995) 'The Labour-Market Position of Women from Ethnic Minorities: A Comparison of Four European Countries', in *Women and the European Labour Markets*, ed. A. van Doorne-Huiskes, J. van Hoof and E. Roelofs. London: Paul Chapman Publishing, pp. 53–71.

Kalter, F., and I. Kogan (2002) 'Ethnic Inequalities at the Transition from School to Work in Belgium and Spain: Discrimination or Self-Exclusion?', Paper presented at the tenth annual workshop of the European Research Network on Transitions in Youth held in San Domenico di Fiesole, Florence, Italy, 5–7 September 2002.

Kanter, R. M. (1979) 'Differential Access to Opportunity and Power', in *Discrimination in Organizations*, ed. R. Alvarez, K. G. Lutterman. San Francisco, CA: Jossey-Bass Publishers, pp. 52–68.

— (1981 [1975]) 'Women and Structure of Organizations: Explorations in Theory and Behavior', in *The Sociology of Organizations: Basic Studies*, second edition, ed. O. G. and G. A. Miller. New York: The Free Press, pp. 395–424.

Lovering, J. (1994) 'Employers, the Sex-Typing of Jobs, and Economic Restructuring', in *Gender Segregation and Social Change*, ed. A. MacEwen Scott. Oxford: Oxford University Press, pp. 329–55.

Merton, R. (1973 [1949]) 'Discrimination and the American Creed', in *The Study of Society. An Integrated Anthology*, ed. P. I. Rose. New York: Random House.

Miles, R. (1993) *Racism after 'Race Relations'*. London: Routledge.

Milkman, R., and E. Townsley (1994) 'Gender and the Economy', in *The Handbook of Economic Sociology*, ed. N. J. Smelser and R. Swedberg. Princeton, NJ: Princeton University Press; and New York: Russell Sage Foundation, pp. 600–19.

Moss, P., and C. Tilly (2001) *Stories Employers Tell: Race, Skill and Hiring in America*. New York: Russell Sage.

Nieke, W. (1991) 'Benachteiligung ausländischer Jugendlicher im Zugang zur Berufsausbildung', in *Ausländische Jugendliche in der Berufsbildung – Auf dem Weg zur Chancengleichheit?*, ed. W. Nieke and U. Boos-Nünning. Opladen: Leske and Budrich, pp. 9–32.

Phizacklea, A. (1994) 'A Single or Segregated Market? Gendered and Racialized Divisions', in Afshar and Maynard 1994, pp. 172–81.

Phizacklea, A., and R. Miles (1980) *Labour and Racism*. London: Routledge and Kegan Paul.

Porter, A. 1998. 'Social Capital: Its Origins and Applications in Modern Sociology', *Annual Review of Sociology* 24: 1–24.

Priester, K. (2003) *Rassismus*. Leipzig: Reclam.

Räthzel, N., and Ü. Sarica (1994) *Migration und Diskriminierung in der Arbeit: Das Beispiel Hamburg*. Berlin and Hamburg: Argument.

Roediger, D. (2002) 'Whiteness and Ethnicity in the History of "White Ethnics" in the United States', in *Race Critical Theories: Text and Context*, ed. P. Essed and D. T. Goldberg. Oxford: Blackwell, pp. 325–43.

Rosenbaum, J. E. (1979) 'Career Paths and Advancement Opportunities', in *Discrimination in Organizations*, ed. R. Alvarez, K. G. Lutterman. San Francisco, CA: Jossey-Bass Publishers, pp. 69–85.

Ruwanpura, K. N. (2005) 'Exploring the Links of Multi-Discrimination: Considering Britain and India', International Institute for Labour Studies, DP/157/2005.

Sassen, S. (1999) *Guests and Aliens*. New York: New Press.

Tilly, C., and C. Tilly (1994) 'Capitalist Work and Labor Markets', in *The Handbook of Economic Sociology*, ed. N. J. Smelser and R. Swedberg. Princeton, NJ: Princeton University Press, pp. 283–312.

Tomaskovic-Devey, D. (1993) *Gender and Racial Inequality at Work: The Sources and Consequences of Job Segregation*. New York: Cornell University Press.

Travis, A. (2002) 'Ministers Saw Law's "Racism" as Defensible – Powell Wielded Influence over Bill's Direction', *The Guardian*, 1 January 2002, http://www.guardian. co.uk/guardianpolitics/story/0,,626266,00.html, last accessed 5 September 2007.

van Dijk, T. (2005) 'Elitdiskurser och institutionell rasism', in *Bortom Vi och Dom:*

*Teoretiska reflektioner om makt, integration, och strukturell diskriminering*, ed. P. de los Reyes and M. Kamali. Rapport av Utredningen om makt, integration och strukturell diskriminiering. States Offentliga Utredningar, SOUR 2005:41, pp. 113–37.

van Doorne-Huiskes, A., J. van Hoof and E. Roelofs (1995) *Women and the European Labour Markets*. London: Paul Chapman Publishing.

Velling, J., 1994. 'Zuwanderer auf dem Arbeitsmarkt: Sind die neuen Migranten die 'Gastarbeiter' der neunziger Jahre?', *ZEW-Wirtschaftsanalysen* 2(3): 261–95.

von Freyberg, T. (1994) 'Betriebliche Konfliktpotentiale zwischen Ausländern und Deutschen', in *Gewerkschaften und Einwanderung: Eine kritische Zwischenbilanz*, ed. P. Kühne, N. Öztürk, K.-W. West. Cologne: Bund-Verlag, pp. 259–73.

Westwood, S., and A. Phizacklea (2000) *Trans-nationalism and the Politics of Belonging*. London: Routledge.

Wharton, A. S. (2002) 'Gender, Institutions, and Difference: The Continuing Importance of Social Structure in Understanding Gender Inequality in Organizations', in *Structure, Culture and History: Recent Issues in Social Theory*, ed. S. C. Chew and J. D. Knottnerus. Lanham, MD: Rowman & Littlefield, pp. 257–69.

Wodak, R., and T. A. van Dijk (2000) *Racism at the Top*. Klagenfurt: Drava Verlag.

Wrench, J., A. Rea and N. Ouali (1999) *Migrants, Ethnic Minorities and the Labour Market: Integration and Exclusion in Europe*. London. Macmillan.

Zegers de Bejil, R. (1991) *Although Equal before the Law... The Scope of Anti-Discrimination Legislation and its Effect on Labour Market Discrimination against Migrant Workers in the United Kingdom, the Netherlands and Sweden*. Geneva: International Labour Office.

# 10  Non-Place Identity: Britain's Response to Migration in the Age of Supermodernity

## David Ian Hanauer

Becoming a British citizen is a significant life event. The Government intends to make gaining British citizenship meaningful and celebratory rather than simply a bureaucratic process. New citizenship ceremonies will help people to mark this important event. We want British citizenship to embrace positively the diversity of background, culture, and faiths that living in modern Britain involves. The Government is also concerned that those who become British citizens should play an active role, both economic and political in our society, and have a sense of belonging to a wider community.

The Home Secretary the Rt Hon. David Blunkett, MP,
9 September 2002 (Home Office 2004: 3)

The acquisition of citizenship, the bureaucratic process of changing the legal status of residency in an institutionally defined territory termed a nation, is usually perceived in legal, societal and personal terms as a major repositioning of the individual. Research in response to the changing realities and experiences of migration in the age of globalization has focused on the definition of transnational citizenship and posits as a basic premise that all citizenship questions rest on the interaction between legal rights and personal membership (Fox 2005; Stokes 2004). In the above quotation, from the then British Home Secretary David Blunkett, the repositioning of the self in relation to the nation is presented as a 'significant life event' which should be 'meaningful and celebratory' and should lead to a 'a sense of belonging to a wider community'. At least from the perspective of this specific political discourse, the two basic concepts of citizenship – legal rights and collective membership – are fused into a single entity. This linking of the personal, societal and the legal is based on the concept that the acquisition of citizenship is also the acquisition of a new identity, usually conceptualized in idealized language as a national identity. In this conceptual, ideological context becoming a citizen is operationalized as a bureaucratic legal process but is conceptualized as a process of internalizing national identity. Recent changes to British citizenship law (the Act of 2002) which require applicants for British citizenship to be tested on 'a sufficient knowledge of English, Welsh or Scottish Gaelic' and also 'a sufficient knowledge about life in the United Kingdom' (Home Office 2004: 11) are an attempt to operationalize the national identity internalization issue in British citizenship acquisition. By requiring a test of citizenship, British legislators are demanding that applicants study in order for them to take on the 'identity' of British citizens.

Within the applied linguistics framework, a lot of attention has been addressed to the discriminatory usage of language tests in situations of migration and citizenship acquisition across the world (Shohamy 2001). Less attention has been directed to the general idea of a test of citizenship. Utilizing a theoretical, anthropological frame of reference termed supermodernity, to reconceptualize contemporary migration trends, this chapter draws out the underlying assumptions of the British citizenship test and ultimately proposes an alternative to understanding the issue of migration and identity, termed non-place identity. Following previous work on transnational and 'flexible' citizenship (see Ong 1999 and Baubock 1994), the concept of a non-place identity questions the assumed link between the legal and the personal-societal aspects of migration and posits the option of cognitive, pragmatic citizenship without deep identification (also see chapter 2 by Jones and Krzyżanowski in this book). Within a non-place identity acceptance of citizenship on the part of the applicant does not require anything beyond the acceptance of the legal requirements of the community; territory does not dictate identity or identification. This concept of identity posits a shift in locus from static physical existence in time and space as required by modernist concepts of national identity to a more individualized conceptualization based on available semiotic resources as described by supermodern understandings of the world. In this sense, the concept of non-place identity differentiates between the core components of citizenship – rights and membership – and offers the individual migrant the option of only being concerned with the establishment of legal rights while ignoring heritage, ethnic and assimilatory cultural identities.

This chapter has two interconnected aims: (i) the discussion of the British citizenship test; and (ii) the discussion and explication of the concept of non-place identity. These two aims are linked in that the analysis of the British citizenship test reveals that the test does not actually test community membership and thus facilitates in its implementation the option of a non-place identity. As will be seen below, in the British citizenship test extensive life experience in Britain is superseded by the requirement for explicit knowledge; evidence of 'national identity' is acquired through literacy. Ironically in relation to the aims of the British government, a non-place migrant identity manifest in the British citizenship test does not necessarily involve identification with the wider community but rather only verification of shallow, explicitly stated and testable knowledge of community practice.

## Time and Place in the Nation-State

The idea that the acquisition of citizenship involves the internalization of national identity is based on the concept of the nation-state that can be first historically situated in Europe of the nineteenth century (Keane 1994) and has continued to be used right up to the 1980s (Sassen 2003). In this formulation, citizenship consists of a collective national identity that is situated in a defined physical territory in which a common language is spoken; customs, belief in a historical narrative and values are shared; and emotional ties to perceived landscapes and pride in the nation exist. Within this construct, loyalty to the nation and a single fixed citizenship are fundamental requirements enacted in law and socially conditioned.

The role of this conceptualization of citizenship has been explained in military, economic, educational and societal terms. For Turner (2000) the welding of citizenship to national identity allowed the creation of armies of faithful, unquestioning soldiers unified in the solidarity of their national identity and pride. For Marshall (1950) the construction of a unified nation allowed the working class access to social rights, creating a situation in which citizenship and national belonging were strengthened. For Gellner (1983) the modern nation and its corresponding definition of citizenship allowed an industrial nation to emerge by overturning localized ethnicities and facilitating a universal education system. In these different explanations, the specific construction of citizenship which linked citizenship with national identity was crucial in supporting the existence and operation of the modernist nation-state and a central component in allowing it to fulfil its self-defined mission.

The modernist construct of citizenship, which is indivisible from a unified concept of national identity (see Kamali's conclusion to this volume), is dependent, from an analytical perspective, on a specific understanding of the semiotic value of space and time. In order for a mental picture of a unified cohesive nation-state clearly demarcated from other nation-states to emerge, physical and temporal boundaries had to be clearly marked and conceptually policed. Narrative, specifically the historical national narrative, offers a central mode of conceptually controlling time (Bhabha 1990). In narrative the temporal aspect of individual and collective existence is made meaningful through embedded positioning: your life as citizen of a nation is explained in terms of your position in a historical narrative, historically situated and progressing towards a better future. These narratives build upon a desire to 'recover a lost national origin' which is then utilized to structure a national mission that designs future actions (Pease 1997: 4). In this sense national narratives allow the state access to and control of the individual psyche: the narrative defines both the collective mission and the individual's role within this wider mission (Bhabha 1990; Pease 1997). In an interesting semiotic shift, the national narrative creates a concept of collective unity by situating and defining the situated characteristics, values and aims of the individual within its structure of past and future events.

Place, particularly as conceptualized as borders and landscapes, provides the symbolic representation of national unity and as such is a central component in the national narrative (Sheldrake 2001). The national narrative takes place in relation to a defined territory, with nostalgic references to characteristic landscapes, towns, cities and individual dwellings. The national landscape and all its components are infused with symbolic meaning. This transforms space (geographic location) into place (meaningful territory). Many modernist national narratives describe the pre-nation state of space as wilderness uncontrolled by humans. The nation-state with its historical conception overturns the wilderness of space and transforms it into a place in which meaningful human interaction takes place. In this sense, place defines participation and belonging.

This concept of place within the national narrative is clearly summarized through the use of the terms 'homeland', 'motherland' and 'fatherland', the linguistic remnants of the patriarchal nature of European monarchies. Through these metaphors the national territory takes on its symbolic meaning as the historical, parental source of meaning. The national territory is your home with all the related emotional attachments and meanings that this entails. Thus space is layered with deep emotional meaning creating a connection between the individual and the landscape of the 'homeland'.

The benefit accrued by the individual who conceptualizes him- or herself within the confines of national identity are belonging and meaning. Belonging is normalized to those individuals who are defined according to national identity and are within the national territory (or a representative space that symbolically functions as national territory). You feel at 'home' with those individuals who both manifest the defined qualities of national identity and implicitly accept them as natural attributes. The benefit of meaning results from the relatively transparent negotiation of human interaction and the environment within the national territory. Comprehension of the world, defined from within the national perspective, seems natural and effortless. You implicitly understand the positions expressed by fellow citizens of the nation-state. Meaning is also achieved on a more significant level. Situatedness within the national narrative through internalization and the implicit acceptance of national identity brings with it an inherent sense of purpose. The reason for your life and existence can be explained in relation to the needs and definitions of the wider collective. This in many ways is the true power of nationalism (and, in its extreme forms, fascism): the ability of national identity to give individuals a sense of belonging, personal purpose and meaning (see chapter 1 by Stråth in this volume).

## Migrant 'Otherness' in the Nation-State

The same (modernist) concept of citizenship infused with a specific national identity that provides the conceptual and emotional groundwork for a sense of belonging to a wider collective unity underpins the concept of the alien other. 'Otherness' is the situation of being beyond the conceptual definition of national identity in legal, societal or personal terms. Since national identity is dependent on a specific semiotic understanding of time and place (a narrative extending from the historical past into the future and physically situated within specific borders and nostalgic landscapes), individuals who manifest a different temporality and physicality are beyond the conceptual boundaries of national identity and are thus perceived as alien others.

The infused nature of citizenship and national identity and its semiotic value is made explicitly clear in the response naturalized citizens often experience from other citizens within the nation-state. Legal citizenship does not mean acceptance within the nation-state. For example, many migrant populations who are legally naturalized within Britain live within ethnically defined territories in close congregation with other migrants from the same heritage country and region. This situation of British multiculturalism has been described by some critics as the 'ghettoizing of migrants' (Rex 1996). On an analytical level, what is happening is that these communities of legal migrants are perceived in terms of their heritage nations. This is the idea of a diaspora, in which congregations of migrants from the same heritage country and within a defined territory have set up what are perceived to be representative territories of other nations within the wider collective of the nation-state (Rex 1996). These territories are often given linguistic indicators clearly defining the national otherness of the territory, whether through the use of streets signs, shop signs or graffiti. Through their presence and social action, migrants have turned the land of the host nation into a new place that is representative of the heritage nation. Migrants in these territories and their children live (and may even have been born) in a new country but are defined in essentialist terms as representatives of their heritage countries. They are symbolically returned to their native lands. Although these may be legal migrants they do not have the characteristics of the constructed, collective national identity and thus they are treated as outsiders. This type of interaction with these groups of migrants is within the context of modernist definitions of citizenship and national identity. The legal status of citizenship is irrelevant because it is seen as a hollow entity when it is divorced from the characteristics of national identity.

The presence of a national narrative situated within the physicality of a specific nation-state makes acceptance and self definition a site of serious contention for the migrant. The migrant is faced with a series of forces within the symbolic and bureaucratic structure of the host nation that situate, constrain and limit self-positioning by the migrant. The migrant's cognition and intention plays a role in that choices can be made but these 'choices' are bureaucratically constrained with an economic and legal power structure and subtly influenced by the insidious and seductive nature of symbolic hierarchical authority. For example, the Runnymede Trust Report (2000), *The Future of Multi-Ethnic Britain*, makes clear that migrant identity formation within the United Kingdom needs to contend with a historical consciousness of white 'Britishness' focused on a past that excludes even historical entities such as the Scots and Welsh, let alone newer arrivals from Bangladesh or Pakistan. To become 'British' under these circumstances is not only a matter of migrant choice. Existing forces both real and conceptual often lead the migrant through a series of contortions of self-positioning before settling on an identity schematically defined as an option within the symbolic and bureaucratic structure of the host nation. Thus migrant 'choice' of identity is made against the pervasive backdrop of existing power structures and not within a vacuum.

These forces are particularly powerful when the battleground of self positioning is situated on the acceptance of the modernist assumptions of the semiotics of time and place as defining qualities of national identity. Migrants functioning on this modernist platform define themselves in relation to a collective national identity. On this basis three options exist: they can define themselves according to the heritage nation; they can define themselves in relation to the host nation; or they can define themselves as bi-nationals with bi-cultural identities. These three options can be seen as a modernist continuum of attachment to national identity. At one end of the continuum is the home nation option of attachment to the heritage nation. At the other end of this modernist continuum is the nationalist option of attachment to the host nation. In the middle between these two poles is the option of a double attachment to both host and heritage nation.

The first option is the diaspora model of migration (Rex 1996). A migrant keeps the heritage identity and creates physical enclaves that allow the construction of a surrogate heritage national society and culture. Migrants in these mini-nations may keep ties with the original heritage nation, may institute the core societal, cultural and religious functions of the heritage nation and create situations in which the heritage language can be used, maintained and promoted. In other words, the diaspora migrant model continues the ties of narrativity and physicality with the heritage country through the creation of a surrogate, symbolically representative place in the host country. As in the British case, these same enclaves may also be the site of racist opposition as they may be perceived by other British citizens as evidence that these 'citizens' have ungratefully rejected national identity and values. These types of enclave and the migrants who live in them are often the source of negative stereotypical understandings of how the migrant group is perceived.

The second option is the assimilationist (monocultural) model of migration in which the migrant is required (or 'chooses') to forego any personal historical connections and recreate him- or herself in line with the characteristics, beliefs, values and narratives of the national identity. From the modernist ideological perspective of citizenship and the nature of the nation, assimilation is usually presented as the best and only way to construct society. The idea of 'otherness', a presence which is distinct from the schema of the national historical narrative and displays evidence of a different physicality, is viewed as an attack on the unity of the nation and a disintegration of values. For example, French policies on migration have long proposed that migrants need to assimilate into French society. Basically the idea is that new migrants should change to the degree that they become undifferentiated from other citizens.

As testified in recent violent demonstrations in the French capital, this transformation is never a mere technicality either for the migrant or for the more established citizens of the host nation. For the migrant, ties to a historical identity are difficult to sever and even if this is possible a change in deeply held beliefs and in-depth acquisition of new personal characteristics, knowledge of narratives and a change in belief system are lengthy and problematic tasks. For those migrants who have this desire the question also becomes what does this do to their own sense of personal history: Will they deny their own historical reality? Will they conceptually, emotionally and physically divorce themselves from the people they grew up with? Will they ever really feel united and comfortable with a new identity that denies the historical reality of their past? From the perspective of the semiotics of time, the assimilationist model of migration as in France requires a complete rewriting of personal history so as to match the host narrative. This may manifest itself as the migrant's search for historical ties, ancestors or more abstract thematic relations to the host narrative. This rewriting of history may also include the denial of personal history.

Ironically, for the established citizens of a nation assimilation may enhance rather than decrease racist responses to migrant groups and may lead to a tightening of the semiotics of time and place in definition of national identity. The case of the Jewish population in Germany at the beginning of the twentieth century is a case in point. Although this community was on the whole fully assimilated within German society and accepted national identity, the wider population saw this as a subversive act that was all the more problematic because the 'otherness' of Jews could not be seen immediately (or at all in some cases). The requirement that Jews wear a Yellow Star was to make sure that Jewish 'otherness' was marked in a place where as a result of assimilation it was nearly impossible to notice difference in any other way. This process was justified through the redefinition of the historical essence of German (Aryan) identity and a redefinition of place through the historical pattern of migration patterns.

Even beyond extreme examples of national identity as in the case of Nazi Germany, the schema of national identity often includes criteria that just cannot be attained by migrants. While there is the potential to acquire the conceptual components of national identity, it is very difficult if not impossible to relive your childhood, change your physicality, transform your linguistic self and reinvent your family. This creates a situation in which while migrants might have legal citizenship, without undifferentiated compatibility with national identity, they are still basically evaluated as aliens. Thus while the ideology of modernism, as enacted in some European nations at different historical periods (such as France through the twentieth century), would prefer an assimilationist outcome to migration, the inherent problems in assimilating a foreign identity, the devastating personal price of assimilation and the latent fear that assimilation raises in established citizens make this option extremely difficult to actually enact.

The third option of bi-nationalism and bi-culturalism is usually understood within the context of multicultural responses to migration. Multiculturalism situated within a postmodern philosophical orientation devalues unity, values difference and accepts multiplicity (Kincheloe and Steinberg 1997).

Postmodernism, as a collection of philosophical approaches, places discourse at the centre of the question of identity (Benhabib 1992). Migrant identity in this formulation becomes an issue of competing discourses. The host country with its narrative of national identity is seen as a dominant discourse that marginalizes other potential discursive positions that exist within the same physical and conceptual arena. By deconstructing the presumed universalism of the dominant discourse (in this case national identity), competing discourses were allowed to enter the discussion of national citizenship. Under the heading of identity politics marginalized groups of various kinds were legitimized in their search for voice and presence within public discourse. From a postmodern perspective, identity, whether in relation to the host or the heritage nation, is the acceptance of a discursive position. Thus while the postmodern sensitivity is more attuned to the marginalized identity, this is still seen as the result of presence and discursive exposure within the physical location of the nation and acceptance of the dominant discourse of that nation. As such both the heritage and host nation identities are discursive constructs.

The outcome of postmodernism in the social realm of migration was the localization to communal constructs of the question of identity. Identity became linked to ethnicity which presented a thinly veiled cover for exploring original heritage identities. Under these conditions, migrants who bore with them the historical reality of their exposure to national identities were required to value them. Thus bi-nationality and bi-culturalism became an option within the social realm as the historical reality of the past (the heritage nation) and the present (the host nation) and the discursive influences of each were seen to play a role in constructing the migrant as a subject. This duality of identity is seen as an option that allows the different historical components of the migrant to co-exist. From a phenomenological migrant perspective the phenomenon is experienced as a double presence that includes two physical locations and two (often disjointed) narratives. Migration becomes the beginning of a new narrative in a new locale. A positive manifestation of this concept is a dual identity that sees each national identity as a resource that can be used in a wide range of cultural situations; a negative manifestation of this concept is when this double identity is perceived as a split in which one identity cannot interact with the other. From the modernist national perspective, dual nationality has the same restrictions and complications as the diaspora model of migration. The migrant who holds onto another identity is by definition an 'outsider' way beyond the confines of a monocultural national identity.

The child of postmodern and postcolonial perspectives – identity politics – forms the basis of most multicultural propositions, and pushes migrants into the modernist trap of ethnic identity defined according to national identity (whether historic or present). Even more current proposals for transnational identities, that is identities that transcend a single national identity by keeping ties with more than one country, are also a twist on the same importance placed upon the nation (or nations) in what are basically essentialist terms (although conceived as exposure to significant discourse in particular physical locales). The bi-national option widens the realm of identification but still situates signification with national boundaries. Thus although the proposal for a bi-national identity finds its source in postmodern philosophical analyses of dominant discourse and identity, in the final analysis it situates migrant identity within the modernist boundaries of national time and place.

In broad terms the modernist concept of the nation disallows the definition of citizenship to be infused with anything but national identity. While the presence of migrants may be accepted for pragmatic reasons, on a basic conceptual and affective level, these migrants are not considered to be an inherent part of the nation. Their presence is seen as conditional and transitory. In other words, as they are not perceived to have historical justification within the nation's narratives and borders, their presence in the future is seen as temporary. Multicultural politics situated within nation-states assumed that acceptance of the presence and identity of migrant groups would ultimately lead to changes in the national identity in such a way as to include a wider range of options for national identity, the idea being that since national identity is discursive it is open to dynamic development and contestation. Ironically the acceptance of the discursive nature of national identity also empowered the re-emergence of virulent nationalism. Opposition to multicultural politics led to the rise of new nationalism in the form of anti-migrant legal, educational, linguistic and economic policies designed to strengthen the perceived threat to national identity posed by ethnic minorities. The dynamic nature of the discursive entity of national identity means that it is open to movement in both directions: it can lead to a widening of categories included under the heading of national citizenship but more often than not it reverts to a forceful reaffirmation of a restrictive definition of national identity.

Within the context of the modernist concept of citizenship, infused with a national identity controlled by the specific semiotics of time and place, belonging for a migrant group is problematic and racism a consistent problem. By definition, all three migrant options of diaspora, assimilation and bi-nationalism situate belonging within dual national boundaries. As it is virtually impossible to acquire an undifferentiated version of the national identity of the host nation, deep and comprehensive acceptance within the host society is a distant option. Thus many migrants working within the confines of the semiotics of time and place associated with national identity are forced in the direction of the heritage identity as a source of acceptance and belonging. In the diaspora model, they actively pursue the promotion of a specific heritage identity; in a bi-national, multicultural model they actively conceptualize the advantages of both the host and heritage identities. The most problematic form of belonging is that of the assimilationist model of migration. The migrant may 'choose' to internalize the national identity, but within the modernist concept of citizenship, undifferentiated national identity is a near impossibility, forcing the migrant into the situation of constantly explaining his/her position of acceptance while simultaneously actively repressing personal history.

## Globalization, Citizenship and the Nation-State

Since its inception in the 1990s the process of globalization has raised significant challenges to the nation-state and its modernist definition of citizenship (Menyhart 2003; Sassen 2003). The revolution is one of perspective. While the modernist world saw the nation as the major source of meaning and belonging, globalization looks beyond the nation to international/transnational/global relations and within the nation to smaller ethnic, religious and professional communities (among others) to create meaning and belonging. Thus, the perspective of globalization is paradoxically wider and at the same time more focused than that of the modernist nation-state. The new perspective weakens the importance of the nation as an identity marker and maker.

At the centre of this process of change is the legal definition of citizenship. As analysed by Menyhart (2003), multiple and dual citizenship are on the increase and have become widespread. The modernist assumption of single citizenship and the associated concept of loyalty to the state have been significantly eroded. Many nations who naturalize citizens allow those same individuals to retain their original citizenship or at least do not actively inquire or act against the presence of dual citizenship. Many nations have pragmatic criteria for allowing citizenship based on economic ability, professional knowledge, artistic or sporting achievement. International law, in many cases, accepts dual and multiple citizenship and does not see this as any danger to the stability of international relations. Even when citizenship is not bestowed, migrant workers with limited degrees of residency and working rights have been established. The H1B alien worker programme in the US or Germany's *Gastarbeiter* system confer certain rights directly or indirectly on their alien working populations. While these workers may be second-class citizens they still have some legal status within the nation-state. Whether the rhetoric of political discourse reflects this change or not, the international and national legal systems of many countries, building on the needs of the global economy, have weakened and transformed the legal concept of citizenship (Menyhart 2003).

This shift is perspective is clearly marked in relation to the concept and actuality of citizenship in the European Union and specifically in relation to the debate over European citizenship. The presence of the European Union places a very real supra-structure on the individual nation-states of the Union and citizenship law does not escape its reach. While nation-states may still consider the definition of a citizen the sole right of the nation, under certain conditions, the European Court of Justice utilizing European legal agreements can change residency rights for economic reasons (Guild 2003). Guild (2003) analyses the case of a British citizen who fought for the right of British citizenship for his Filipina wife against British citizenship law in the European Court of Justice. Using the wider definition of citizenship rights based on migration for economic reasons of the European Union, Mr Carpenter successfully managed to gain the legal right to live with his wife in the United Kingdom. In other cases, it has become common practice for British citizens who have been refused permission to live with their spouses in the United Kingdom to move to Ireland for six months, claiming work requirements for migration, and then use European Union law to return to the UK with their spouses (Guild 2003). The importance of these cases is that citizenship and residency are contested not only on the national level of the member nations but also on the wider and more accessible level of European Union rights.

The cases cited above result from a widening of the perspective in relation to citizenship law. The nation-state is not considered the single body that has jurisdiction over the legal definition of citizenship rights within the wider structure of the European Union (Guild 2003). However, it should be noted that like many other phenomena of globalization, it is the economic potential that directs the process of change and has forced governments to recognize the need for increased legal mobility for professional economic actors. While the nation-states and the transnational companies may be thinking of economic competitiveness, the ramifications of these changes are also on the level of identity, attachment and belonging. To a certain extent the outcome of these economic changes to citizenship law is that profession becomes more important than nationality. If you have a desirable profession and/or the ability to increase directly or indirectly the wealth, prestige and competitiveness of the nation then legal residency and citizenship are attainable. National identity, while still of importance, is countered by the option of attaining other citizenships through professional activity. The presence of multiple citizenships allows the individual to use that framework to achieve his/her personal agenda. The legal systems of national and supra-national entities become a 'supermarket' of options that can be manipulated to serve one's own purposes. Mono-citizenship and dedicated loyalty to a single place in this context seems on a practical economic level to be a very limiting choice.

These changes in legal status in relation to national citizenship have led to an extensive literature on new options for defining the cultural aspects of citizenship. These discussions are usually situated within the framework of the explication and definition of transnational options for citizenship (Vertovec 2001). As a basic definition Stokes (2004) defines transnational citizenship as citizenship that transcends the nation-state. This transcendence can in his terms be cosmopolitan (primarily interested in the individual's rights) or internationalist (primarily concerned with the establishment of international bodies to regulate global responsibilities). In these frameworks, as stated by Yuval-Davis (1999), citizenship becomes a 'multilayered' construct that crosses national, ethnic and local boundaries. Ong (1999) explores the transnational migrant situation of Chinese entrepreneurs who are members of specific cultural communities but do not partake in the wider political community of the host country. These migrants have a 'fluid' and 'flexible' concept of citizenship that allows them to reposition themselves in relation to the needs of their business opportunities (Ong 1999). Appadurai (1991), through the term 'translocal', has pointed out that territory in a globalized world may not be a useful underpinning concept for the investigation or understanding of migrant identity. The presence of tourists, migrants and refugees within and beyond a specific locale blurs the role of place and distance.

## Non-Place Migrant Identity

The emphasis on mobility and interconnectivity in the globalized economy has led to the creation of an ever-growing number of spaces which are radically different from the modernist concept of place. Airports, railway stations, McDonald's (and other fast-food) restaurants and shopping malls are all examples of these new spaces. These places have been termed *non-places* by the anthropologist Auge (1995) and what characterizes them is a very basic reconceptualization of the semiotics of time and place. In Auge's (1995) analysis these spaces are constituted as transitory and ahistorical. While the modern concept of place is a defined, bordered territory within which a narrative provides identity, belonging and meaning through historical positioning, a supermodern non-place is divorced from the history and narrative within which it is physically situated. The non-place has its own autonomous identity that rises above the national context. The airports in Newark, Tel Aviv, Frankfurt and Birmingham are nearly indistinguishable. What characterizes them is their 'airportness' and not the national locale of the airport. One can walk into a Starbucks anywhere in the world and find products that one recognizes and knows. In the case of Starbucks even a specific linguistic aspect of how to order coffee is copied across global outlets and it is a linguistic usage that represents a conglomerate of different 'right-sounding' terms that are unique to Starbucks.

These non-places, while easily recognized, do not in themselves require any depth of identification. Non-places tend to be generic and repeatable; places evoke a narrative of historical uniqueness and irreplaceability. It would be difficult to find someone who would cry over the destruction of a McDonald's restaurant due to a fire, as the assumption would be that another that is exactly the same could be built. However, the destruction of a historical site, for example the Wailing Wall in Jerusalem, would bring tears to the eyes of many people who identify with the narrative that constitutes this historic place and consider it to be unique as a result of its historical positioning. The presence of a situating historical narrative generates a process of identification with specific places that infuses that place with a special meaning for anyone accepting the narrative. The paradox of non-places is that for foreigners and outsiders distant from national identity, the non-place is comforting in its anonymity, ahistorical presence and non-intrusiveness. Like the migrant, the non-place is beyond the time and place of the physical site. Weak identification based on usability is preferable to alienation within another's historical narrative. For the outsider, these non-places also provide a very basic sense of meaning. Within them the ways of conducting life and social interaction are codified and well known since they have been transported between the different locales of non-places. One does not have to learn a new airport; all the same functions of every other airport are replicated and thus very quickly recognized. In these non-places the significance of national identity as a source of meaning in everyday action is erased; foreigner and local have the same access to the limited meaning resources that are present within the non-place. In many cases these resources of meaning making are marked through visual and not verbal literacy, widening even further the options for recognition.

The non-place utilizes a functional identity that is detached from any historical, national identity. Identity within the non-place and for the economic purposes of the non-place is left on the level of official documents, identity cards, passports, credit cards and debit cards. You are who your papers say you are and what you pay with. In these non-places, your network of identification – your sense of self-identity – is separate from your legal identity. This non-place identity is comforting in that you are not required to fit any historical constituted identity. As such, non-place identity is an open group that is very easy to join – all that is required is legal documentation from somewhere (and it really does not matter from where) and proof of economic viability. The issue of belonging and attachment is moved out of the social realm and into the personal realm. No one and everyone is an outsider (or perhaps a limited insider) in a non-place. Your options for belonging are more connected to your professional and economic interests than to your historical birthplace. The nation-state and its citizenship seems more of a pragmatic requirement than a source of essential identity. Your personal identity becomes an issue of your decision on the levels of attachment that you wish to apply to the different options for identity that exist within your life.

The non-place has also extended into our homes. Popular television programmes such as *Friends* create an intimacy that is not based on a physical or historical presence; the internet, defined by its global and personal perspectives ignores physicality and thus makes the nation irrelevant as a meaningful concept. While nations worry about keeping their boundaries safe, the internet creates networks of attachment that are bound only by technology and personal interest. This interconnectivity in communications allows working professional relationships to travel across the globe and into the most intimate spaces of the home. When you are on the internet, you are by definition in a transitory non-place where your attachment is only as deep as the next click of your mouse. Literacy in this context takes on a very special meaning. The ability to read and write verbal and visual signs replaces the need for actual physical experience. It is through the mediated experience of presented information that we define ourselves, create networks of meaningful interaction and fulfil our personal needs.

Auge (1995) in his analysis of the features of supermodernity specifies three main characteristics of the new world we live in: the contraction of space; the acceleration of time; and the elevation of the importance of the individual. Rapid transport and extensive technological development in communications have made the world much more accessible. Space has contracted through the ease of travel and the multiple images and information sources from all over the globe that consistently flood our televisions, radios and computers. The over-abundance of events from around the world has overturned any vestige of the concept of history. The news of today, however major and traumatic it may seem, is superseded by the events of tomorrow. The concept of history is trivialized by this acceleration of time measured through short-lived and quickly forgotten events. The ramifications of these changes are the elevation of the centrality of the individual and the individual's diversified life. It is the individual that is bombarded by a mass of personalized and disembodied information. This supermodern individual does not position him- or herself through the external narrative of national identity situated within defined territories as suggested by modernist conceptions or postmodern identity politics. This individual finds meaning through self-construction and belonging through attachment on the professional and personal levels of networks of interaction mediated in many cases through literacy and technology.

In the supermodern world some migrants have a changed perspective. Beyond the options of assimilation, diaspora and bi-nationalism, the option of non-place, migrant identity exists and seems attractive as a philosophical alternative and a practical solution. Non-place migrant identity views national citizenship in pragmatic terms as a practical way of widening a person's economic, intellectual, cultural and personal potential. Receipt of national citizenship includes full recognition of the legal aspects of citizenship but does not necessarily involve identification with national identity. The question of identity is personal and involves utilizing a wide framework of communication technologies that allow the generation of a continuing network of relations uninhibited by physical presence. From within a non-place migrant identity, every place is viewed as transitory, serving a pragmatic purpose, offering potentialities, and allowing the comfort of anonymity. Belonging to the nation and acceptance by the mono-national citizens is not a major concern of the non-place migrant. Attachment and belonging are situated as aspects of the individual's professional life, family bonds, personal interests and networked relationships.

This definition of non-place identity builds upon previous definitions of identity specified within the literature, especially the concepts of 'flexible' citizenship (Ong 1999) and translocal identity (Appadurai, 1991). A non-place identity has some of the economic opportunistic characteristics of flexible citizenship and definitely changes the value placed upon distance, as in translocal concepts of belonging. In the terms of the literature on transnational citizenship, a non-place identity comes as a second stage following acceptance of legal status. Its focus is on the issue of how identity is formed and the options that exist for this identity. As opposed to a lot of the literature that falls back on some heritage or ethnic culture which at its core still values place as a semiotic resource for the definition of self, non-place identity in the same way as non-places creates its own 'shallow' identity without reference to any specific place or locale, preferring an emphasis on functional utility. This is not a cosmopolitan identity concerned with human universal rights or a multicultural identity concerned with the promotion of a local, ethnic identity within a wider societal framework. This is the option of opting out of the question of placement altogether, focusing exclusively on full legal rights as a national citizen while keeping the question of personal identity separate from the realm of placement, whether in relation to heritage, ethnic or assimilatory identities in the host country. To have a non-place identity means not to consider place as the basic semiotic resource through which the meaning of identity is constructed. Place of birth may be a historical fact but it does not necessarily have to be used by the migrant as a marker of individual identity. The acceptance that you can be from nowhere can under certain circumstances and for specific migrants be a liberating experience, avoiding the limiting oppression of the need to be placed within a physical or conceptual narrative of inclusion and exclusion.

### The British Citizenship Test: Promoting Functional Identity

As stated at the beginning of this chapter, the United Kingdom has initiated a new test to evaluate the worthiness of a candidate for British citizenship. This test should be seen as the outcome of a series of contradictory motivating factors. Basically, British citizenship law is the recognition that within the globalized economy migration is a desirable process. As clearly contextualized by the British government, migration is justified on an economic basis. Britain needs migrants to counter the 'diminishing work force amid a healthy population living longer into retirement and away from the world of work' (Home Office 2004: 9). This migratory workforce should be able to fulfil the economic needs of the United Kingdom through a carefully managed migration policy. Thus the test is part of a wider process aimed at normalizing migration for those applicants who are considered to be advantageous for Britain's economy.

However, while the idea of economic migration might be acceptable in principle, the idea of a test of citizenship can be seen as a response to the fear of migration. It seems common sense to many Britons working within the modernist concept of a citizenship infused with national identity that new citizens should acquire linguistic, cultural and historical knowledge of the United Kingdom and should fully accept the core values of Britain. The presence of the test of citizenship makes studying 'Britishness' a requirement; in principle, the aim of the test is to make sure that new citizens adapt to British society and assume a simulacrum of national identity. In this sense the test guards the symbolic continuation of British national identity against potential dilution by migrant identities.

In its role as guardian the test is supposed to promote national identity. A close look at the content of the test reveals that the test designers have chosen to focus on functional knowledge far more than on core values. The material for the exam covers a brief review of history, a profile of ethnic diversity in Britain, an overview of British government, basic legal concepts, issues of everyday life such as housing, education and health, and employment. As described by the Minister for Immigration, Tony McNulty, the test is not actually a test of Britishness at all but rather it is designed to measure immigrants 'preparedness to become citizens, in keeping with the language requirement as well' (quoted in Soriano 2005). Thus while the test does introduce very basic concepts that can be related to national British identity, it essentially avoids historical controversy and presents instead practical knowledge that highlights employment.

In its implementation the test is designed as a multiple-choice 24-item test that takes 45 minutes to complete. Migrants can take the test as many times as they like and are required to get 75% of the items right in order to pass. A booklet of 143 pages has been prepared by the Home Office to help migrants prepare for this exam. The booklet contains all the required knowledge and for any adult with good literacy skills in English studying the booklet and passing the exam should not take longer than a few days. Passing the British citizenship test is more dependent on English literacy than it is on knowledge of Britain, proximity to British national identity or lived experience of Britain.

The British citizenship test emphasizes a functional identity directed at successful economic activity and is independent of lived experience. The test replaces the requirement of experience with that of literacy. While it may stem from a fear of migrants and the influence they may have on national identity, in its manifestation this test is more attuned to non-place migrant identity than it is to the modernist concept of citizenship infused with national identity. The test allows migrants to pass without requiring a depth of knowledge or identification.

## Situating Non-Place Identity: Concluding Remarks

The British citizenship test manifests one paradox of the supermodern world – because of the globalized world economy there is a necessity, recognized by nation-states, for accessible migration for qualified professionals; but the option of migration and the functional weakening of the concept of citizenship create concern over the loss of a major source of meaning and belonging –

national identity. In the British case, this need and concern produced a requirement for citizenship testing that is biased towards economically useful migrants and replaces national identity with economic functionality. The test itself exchanges life experience for explicit knowledge expressed through literacy. Although the rhetoric of public discourse usually contextualizes the Britishness test as a move towards the enhancement of meaningfulness in terms of national identity, the emphasis on mobility for economic reasons and decontextualized explicit knowledge of national life is actually conducive to a non-place migrant identity. For those who adopt the concept of non-place identity, the test and the changes to British citizenship laws create a situation in which it is possible to divorce legal citizenship from personal identity. The form of citizenship which emerges is not infused with the significance of national identity.

The concept of non-place identity developed within this chapter is based on the notion that place (and its inherent signification of time, narrative and identity) does not have to be the primary source for identity construction. This critique is equally relevant to current discussions of national, transnational, ethnic and community-based perceptions of identity formation in migration, all of which base themselves on the consideration that identity is tied to current, past or transitory placement. As argued by Aksoy and Robins, the discussion of migrant identity needs to move beyond the 'categories of collective attachment and identification' (2002: 20). The potential for a non-place identity involves moving beyond identification with either source or host identifications and focusing on personal interests and functions. These identities may be shallow and shifting. While many migrants who function within a nationally situated identity will not be able to access this option of identity, for the qualified, travelled professional, non-place migrant identity is a philosophical perspective that reduces the significance of place (and nation) by centralizing the individual as the nexus of meaning construction. New, non-place citizens respect the law; but consider personal identity, attachment and belonging as private matters divorced from the significance of place as a primary identity marker.

## References

Aksoy, A., and K. Robins (2002) *Banal Transnationalism: The Difference that Television Makes*, http://www.transcomm.ox.ac.uk/working%20papers/WPTC-0208%20Robins.pdf, last accessed 7 September 2007.

Appadurai, A. (1991) 'Global Ethnoscapes: Note and Queries for a Transnational Anthropology', in *Recapturing Anthropology*, ed. Richard Fox. Santa Fe, NM: School of American Research Press, pp. 191–210.

Auge, M. (1995) *Non-Places: Introduction to an Anthropology of Supermodernity*, trans. by J. Howe. London: Verso.

Baubock, R. (1994) *Transnational Citizenship: Membership and Rights in International Migration*. Aldershot: Edward Alder.

Benhabib, S. (1992) *Situating the Self: Gender, Community, and Postmodernism in Contemporary Ethics*. New York: Routledge.

Bhabha, H. (1990) 'Introduction: Narrating the Nation', in *Nation and Narration*, ed. H. Bhabha. London: Routledge.

Fox, J. (2005) 'Unpacking "Transnational Citizenship"', *Annual Review of Political Science* 8: 171–201.

Gellner, E. (1983) *Nations and Nationalism*. Oxford: Blackwell.

Guild, E. (2003) 'Developing European Citizenship or Discarding It? Multicultural Citizenship Theory in Light of the Carpenter Judgment of the European Court of Justice', *The Good Society* 12(2): 22–5.

Home Office (2004) *Life in the United Kingdom: A Journey to Citizenship*. London: HMSO.

Keane, J. (1994) 'Nations, Nationalism and Citizens in Europe', *International Social Science Journal* 46(2): 169–84.

Kincheloe, J. L., and S. R. Steinberg (1997) *Changing Multiculturalism*. Buckingham: Open University Press.

Marshall, T. H. (1950) *Citizenship and Social Class*. Cambridge: Cambridge University Press.

Menyhart, R. (2003) 'Changing Identities and Changing Law: Possibilities for a Global Legal Culture', *Indiana Journal of Global Legal Studies* 10 (2): 157–99.

Ong, A. (1999) *Flexible Citizenship: The Cultural Logics of Transnationality*. Durham, NC: Duke University Press.

Pease, D. E. (1997) 'National Narrative, Postnational Narration', *Modern Fiction Studies* 43(1), 1–23.

Rex, J. (1996) 'National Identity in the Democratic Multi-Cultural State', *Sociological Research Online* 1(2), http://www.socresonline.org.uk/1/2/1.html, last accessed 7 September 2007.

Runnymede Trust (2000) *The Future of Multi-Ethnic Britain: The Parekh Report*. London: Profile.

Sassen, S. (2003) 'The Repositioning of Citizenship: Emergent Subjects and Spaces for Politics', *The New Centennial Review* 3(2): 41–66.

Sheldrake, P. (2001) 'Human Identity and the Particularity of Place', *Spiritus* 1: 43–64.

Shohamy, E. (2001) *The Power of Tests: A Critical Perspective on the Uses of Language Tests*. London: Longman.

Soriano, C. G. (2005) 'New Citizenship Test Ignites UK Culture War', *USA Today*, 2 November.

Stokes, G. (2004) 'Transnational Citizenship: Problems of Definition, Culture and Democracy', *Cambridge Review of International Affairs* 17(1): 119–35.

Turner, B. (2000) 'Cosmopolitan Virtue: Loyalty and the City', in *Democracy, Citizenship and the Global City*, ed. E. Isin. New York: Routledge.

Vertovec, S. (2001) 'Transnationalism and Identity', *Journal of Ethnic and Migration Studies* 27(4): 573–82.

Yuval-Davies, N. (1999) 'The "Multi-Layered Citizen": Citizenship in the Age of Globalization', *International Feminist Journal of Politics* 1(1): 119–36.

# Part III

# Cases of Belonging and Exclusion

# 11  Symbolic Violence

## Helena Flam and Brigitte Beauzamy

In this chapter we want to investigate the ways in which the everyday encounters between 'natives' and 'foreigners' affects the ways in which migrants think and feel about themselves. In particular, we are interested in the non-physical hurt experienced by migrants: daily and routinely migrants confront different forms of rejection that can be intimidating, humiliating and incapacitating; repeated experience of such rejections causes feelings of fear, inferiority and reserve. We wish to explore these feelings, leaving for the next chapter the task of analysing subterfuge and resistance. The interview material that we draw upon shows that some people in the street, neighbours, sales clerks as well as the public authorities and the police sometimes do their utmost to make migrants feel miserable and undesired. We will focus on how 'natives' – including public officials and police – communicate their hostility towards migrants relying on the gaze, the body and the simplest forms of verbal communication.

## Two Meanings of Symbolic Violence

When Pierre Bourdieu introduced the term 'symbolic violence', he referred to positive, status-upgrading naming and bonding practices which concealed the true face of exploitation and domination in a Kabyl society he studied – a society which could not rely on the money economy, courts, police or politics to legitimate, conceal and reinforce the prevailing forms of domination (1991 [1972]: 21–31,188–92). His concept stood mainly for status upgrading through bonding and symbols. Since our contribution focuses on the negative aspects of the interactions between 'natives' and 'foreigners', it does not seem to fit Bourdieu's original concept. Instead of taking departure directly from his concept, then, our chapter is informed by a second concept of symbolic violence which was developed by feminist research. It redefined symbolic violence to stand for denying the presence, skills or contributions of the other, calling attention to real and symbolic status downgrading. This research showed how a male-dominated society denigrates women, renders their multifaceted contributions virtually invisible, while turning down their demands for equal rights and social recognition (for example, see Krais 1973). Both Bourdieu's and feminist concepts of symbolic violence assume that its victims remain unaware, passive (for criticism, see McNay 1999) and by implication 'unhurt'. In contrast we will show that victims are often both aware and hurt, sometimes managing to strike back – a theme to be elaborated at length in the next chapter by Sawyer and Jones. We will also introduce and develop Foucault's concept of disciplining and Bourdieu's concept of symbolic violence by connecting them both to real violence.

### The Power of the Human Gaze: Stares and Scrutiny

Since we want to address the ways in which the human gaze is employed in the communication between natives and migrants, let us recall a few classical statements about its constitutive power. Our self-definition and emotional well-being is a composite of how we see ourselves, how others see us and how we think others see us, constituting our identity as a 'looking-glass self' (Cooley 1970). Since our interactions with others have become more frequent in industrial societies, a dramaturgical 'as if' acting, meant for the eyes of an audience, has become a mass phenomenon (Goffman 1959; Riesman 1977). Both our self-definition and our other-oriented dramaturgical acting are unthinkable without the constituting human gaze. But this gaze can turn into an instrument of superordination, superiority and contempt, of surveillance, control and discipline. Sartre (1994) proposes a conflictual battle between 'I' and the 'Other' as a basic premise of social life. The gaze of the 'Other' simultaneously constitutes, judges and, in the very act of judgment, subordinates 'I' to the 'Other'. To reclaim the lost freedom 'I' must look back and thus acknowledge and seek to subordinate the 'Other' (Yar 2002: 60–1). In his pessimistic view, human beings mutually affirm, but also subjugate and instrumentalize each other. Their freedom and activity is only possible at the price of subjugation and passivity of the other. Writing about Jeremy Bentham's *Panopticon*, Foucault (1975) stressed that surveying and disciplining modern institutions bestow an absolute power on the observer, while disparate industrial sociologists analysed factory and office rooms in which a single supervisor takes in all present with a simple gaze and so turns into the ruler of an entire work universe. The constituting, disciplining, subordinating and/or contemptuous gaze that we are concerned with is premised on nationalism. It is directed by 'natives' at 'foreigners' and is meant to reinforce the symbolic boundaries between nations and nationals – boundaries which have become increasingly attenuated in the contemporary world by the fact of mass migration.

## Banal Nationalism

In his now famous argument, Michael Billig suggests that nationalism should not be reduced to its extreme expressions – wars, separatists or chauvinism – and that equally important are its daily, 'banal' expressions – the flag, hymn, national news, monuments or football matches (Billig 1995: 6–7). These 'everyday' flaggings create the ideological habit of nationalism, and thus reproduce nations and their members. Everyday nationalism is banal, but hardly innocent or benign, since, as Billig argues, it creates a general preparedness for war.

We contend that banal nationalism is malignant for yet another reason – it becomes expressed in injurious everyday encounters between 'natives' and 'foreigners'. In these encounters natives assert their knowledge and feelings about who rightfully belongs to a nation, its territory and its state while denigrating those who do not (see Hedetoft 2002: 5; Karst 1989). These encounters, which convert streets, supermarkets, nurseries, schools, workplaces, neighbourhoods and administrative offices into a battleground, can be understood as sites of preparatory warfare, of a routine, yet inconspicuous training for war. They are not just about cognition, but also about emotions. As miniature exercises in preparatory warfare they mediate between the rather passive intake of daily national symbols and the sudden, active mobilization for war. Every victorious encounter between 'natives' and 'foreigners' – whether it expresses indifference, hostility or pity, whether discursive or sub-discursive – re-asserts the 'native' right to belong and to exclude. It delineates anew the body of a nation.

These encounters leave scars, as any form of rejection does. As Essed (1991: 113, 170, 180–1, 189–203) and this chapter show, rejection takes many forms, ranging from rendering one invisible to negative singling out, from averted gaze to bodily attack and outright violence. The end effect is daily, massively felt exclusion of 'outsiders' from the community of belonging. This exclusion either reinforces or runs counter to the official definition of citizenship, but is a reality *sui generis*. It gives a new meaning to Renan's famous 'daily plebiscite' through which citizens express their will to belong to their nation (Renan 1990). Not only in Eastern or Southern, but also in Western Europe racism takes a form of (white) ethnic nationalism directed against civic nationalism, 'against the very idea of a nation based in citizenship rather than ethnicity' (see Ignatieff 1993: 8, 91–102; Delanty 2002: 105–6).

## Cases of Belonging and Exclusion

Every day, disparate individuals confront each other over the issue of belonging. These confrontations render the excluded more vulnerable and scar them more deeply than is the case when larger groups, growing in awareness, organization and strategy, 'make home' by usurping urban spaces, building up their associational and political life or using law to combat various forms of discrimination (Westwood 2000: 64–9; Karst 1989). Both types of confrontation produce casualties, even though a mere unexpected retort or a joke helps the 'outsider' to leave the encounter without a sense of total powerlessness.

### Glaring and Staring

In the encounters between 'natives' and 'foreigners' the human gaze plays a powerful role as an instrument of control, domination and rejection. Even in those European countries where it is not habitual to look directly at others in public places, 'natives' allow themselves the liberty of unrestrained staring at the migrants. Native glaring prevents migrants from feeling 'really at home'. It forces them to feel 'uncomfortable', 'unwelcome', 'afraid':

> It can be hard to feel really at home in Britain... people look at you sometimes like you shouldn't be there and like they don't want you there.
>
> UK, Pakistani female, 42 years old

> When you walk around the city people look at me. They do not want migrants to be seen... Sometimes you are afraid to go out
>
> Sweden, Turkish female

> Lots of young people were standing around us and just looking at me with my pitch-black hair tanned skin [laughs] and dressed like ah a southerner and then it got really uncomfortable suddenly so we left the fair pretty quickly and drove back to the youth hostel and I didn't dare go out on the street anymore I couldn't wait for the day that we drove back two days later it was not a great, great, great time.
>
> Germany, Italian male, 31 years old

Migrants feel that natives distrust and fear them in part because they associate migrants with an immediate threat to their bodies and property:

> My son sometimes sees an old woman and she is struggling with a trolley and he goes to help and she is like [acts shocked] 'oh he's coming to mug me because he's black'.
>
> UK, Senegalese female, 51 years old

This young lady came and asked me what I was doing there what did I want to steal there I showed her the keys told her that I didn't come to steal that I had the keys to this house she went on saying that it wasn't true.

Italy, Cameroonian female, 40 years old

Very often staring and ignorant, hostile or explicitly racist comments come together:

I have another colour of skin and it's evident. When I'm in a good mood I just laugh because it's really, I think it is ridiculous and stupid [laughter] and when I have a bad day I get really angry I just want to buy something and not to hear 'Oh, God' 'Oh, my!' [laughs]. Once [a woman] was talking on the 'phone and she said 'Oh, my! A Negro came in.' I hate us [being called] Negroes. I prefer they call me Black. Because I am black, that's all. That's that, I'm black and not some Negro.

Poland, Zimbabwean/UK female, 25 years old

A friend in my class she is from Somalia, and lived in [a suburb in Stockholm]. She said that there were only Swedes there she moved from there. She and her family, they were not accepted simply. They got racist comments and gazes and such. So they moved to [another suburb in Stockholm].

Sweden, Turkish female

If migrants respond in the native language or local dialect, they truly upset the hostile natives, since they demonstrate through their language skills that far from being strangers they in fact belong. They turn the everyday native assumptions on their head:

When you is with the family in stores or on the street then you often sense that you're stared at and my boys very often make a game out of it – they speak Polish for a while and when a stupid remark comes they then turn around and give an answer in beautiful Saxonian.

Germany, Polish female, 55 years old

*The Averted Gaze*
The averted gaze, most often employed by salespeople, constitutes the opposite of the unrestrained glaring and staring, since it renders migrants invisible. The sales clerk, considering it below his or her dignity, serves everybody but the migrant. In refusing to acknowledge the presence of the migrant, the salesperson hurls an ultimate insult at the migrant. The

implication is that the migrants are so inferior to everybody else that one does not even wish to waste a glance and so to constitute them in a Sartrean manner. The message is lost on no migrant. Each migrant senses the intended contempt and hostility, even if they remain uncertain about its source. The averted gaze makes a migrant feel powerless, worthless:

> I was first in line but a German simply went ahead of me and the saleslady served him first. She treated me like thin air and then I asked: 'excuse me am I invisible?' or something. In such situations I feel so powerless. Powerless.
>
> Germany, Cuban female, 28 years old

Or one's neighbours may treat one as if invisible. They seem to be unwilling to acknowledge the very fact that migrants not only live in the same neighbourhood but in the same building as they do. Similarly to the salesperson who refuses to offer the services for which they are paid, neighbours refuse to offer the migrant the simplest gesture of civility, like keeping the doors open for their cars:

> We always have often problems with people who lived around us with the parking of the car. Always a problem. They always claim that the buildings belong to them, and we are, we are supposed to park the car there so it's always a [unread] somebody and he's just opening the gate to leave you know they close it even if he sees you coming.
>
> Austria, male

### Bodily Rejection

Communicating rejection or hostility with the help of the body takes many forms. For example, German university students move to another part of the laboratory to avoid contact with foreign students, or an Austrian man bumps into a foreigner on purpose in a tram:

> I was sitting in the tram, lop-sided, and there was an old man and he was Austrian and he kicked my feet down and I didn't react because he was old and there were also a bit there were two people in front of him and ok I thought ok maybe he did this unintentionally and I took a short look at him wondering if he excused himself and afterwards he looked at me like this and said what what why do you stretch out your legs like this and I say no no for sure not I was putting down my legs in order to make it more comfortable for you to pass and there were two other Austrians as well and who started to argue with him why he acts in such a xenophobic way

because they exactly did see that he was bumping into me on purpose.

Austria, female, 17 years old

The most extreme examples of rejection associated with both verbal and bodily aggression can be seen in this example from Italy:

One time ... a lady said to me openly to my face I don't want to see people like you ... every time she heard the bell to my house she looked outside the window to see who was there one time someone came to bring me some bottled tomatoes she came straight down and bumped into her in such a way as to make these tomatoes fall on the floor and all the bottles were broken one of my friends asked her why she had made them fall down the lady responded because I don't want to see you here.

Italy, Beninese male, 37 years old

we were living in houses that were basements without windows and proper toilet facilities one night some people using a piece of iron as big as this finger blocked the outside door the next morning we could not go out ... another time they put a strong chain but they did not lock it ... this used to happen at night only at night.

Italy, Moldovan male, 30 years old

This kind of direct aggression and violence directed at migrants in Italy appears mild compared to arson attacks suffered by Turkish migrants and mixed groups of asylum-seekers in several towns in Germany in the early 1990s. While the victims of arson experience real, direct violence, many fellow migrants, who partake in the event through the media, feel shocked, disheartened, hurt. Their status as undesired strangers becomes paramount while their fear for their own safety intensifies.

## Varied Forms of Verbal Rejection

### *Infuriating Questions*

Rejection is also often communicated by such a simple question as 'Where do you come from?' To most migrants the native asking this question wishes to impose on the migrant one's own definition of the migrant's person solely as a 'foreigner'. The migrant becomes reduced, diminished, boxed in. This 'native' exercise of the self-awarded prerogative to name and define things, this sudden assumption of definitional power, to borrow briefly Foucault's concept, feels like a slap – an act of bodily violence. With this one question one's past and present – all one's accomplishments – are annihilated, only one's status as an unwelcome, rejected visitor, who does not and cannot belong, is brought into relief. It provokes a sense of helplessness, irritation or fury, depending on temperament, and, for certain, a deep sense of humiliation. One has heard this question many times before (Essed 1991: 190–1). One's stomach turns at being so reduced. A native would not dare to pose this question to anybody else, not the least because it is ultimately very personal:

> I think that that question is the same as asking what colour underwear I have on me.
>
> Sweden, Russian male

For a new arrival, this question is still understandable, but to a migrant who has for long lived, worked and been naturalized in his/her host country, this question is simply shocking, a throwback to the original lowly migrant status. It is shocking to discover that after all these years one should still be considered an outcast. A second question which is extremely irritating because of its presumption and ambivalence is 'Aren't you happy to be living here?' On the one hand, like any question directed to a migrant, it deserves gratitude for a crumb of interest thrown to him or her since it seems to indicate the native's interest in the person of the migrant and so to rescue the migrant from the sea of anonymity into which he or she is usually immersed upon arrival into a new country. On the other hand, it implies arrogance, since it communicates a felt sense of superiority and pride in the accomplishments of one's own country and also the belief that anybody fortunate to be living in it just has to be happy about it:

> Just this here impertinent [*fräcka*] question 'where do you come from?' I mean you are born in America do people ask black people in the street 'where do you come from?' Though they come originally from Ghana or not? But here they still ask after 30 years they ask in the subway 'where do you come from?'[with a mocking voice] 'Are you happy to be living here?' Yes it is clear I am happy. Of course I am not happy when you ask like that! It is not easy.
>
> Sweden, Polish male

Strangers, acquaintances, even 'friends', display hostility by accusing the migrant's country of origin of human rights violations or criticizing its current or past politics as if the person they addressed were responsible. This infuriates when addressed to somebody who was born, raised and educated in the same country and in fact feels she belongs. It means fully-fledged rejection, a refusal to recognize this person's right to be(come) naturalized, while pressing the other to assume an unfamiliar, undesired identity. It also means a lack of interest in the actual problems that this person may have, here and now:

> I am born and raised here. I am made responsible for what happens in Turkey I must justify myself I must say 'we' provide justifications.
>
> Germany, Turkish male, 26 years old

Some 'natives' are even more explicit in their rejection. What they ultimately want to know is when the migrant they address will disappear again:

> they will ask you from where you are coming from and the second question why you chose Austria (3.0) and ah and the third question is when you plan to go back to your country.
>
> Austria, Sudanese male, 36 years old

The two questions 'Where do you come from?' and 'When do you plan to go back?' are posed tediously often, and, though they can be asked separately, they in fact constitute a typical 'nativist' query pair. Many migrants hear the second question only after the first, which causes anger.

*Name-Calling and Insulting Tirades*

Any of the subtler forms of symbolic violence discussed so far can also take on more pronounced forms. A passer-by, a salesperson, a neighbour or a superintendent of the apartment building in which one lives can take to status-degrading. They might call a migrant a 'foreigner' [*Ausländer*] (Germany), a 'bloody foreigner' (the UK), or an 'evil foreigner' [*djävla utlänning*] or 'black skull' [*svartskalle*] (Sweden). They might also tell one to go back to one's own country; the worst is the unpredictability of it. One never knows when one will become a target of a hateful verbal assault:

> There was the tram I wanted to take and he was in front of the door I only I only touch him slightly and he said 'you fucking foreigner'.
>
> Austria, female, 17 years old

In a southern Swedish university town natives named a certain city bus the 'garlic bus' and in Berlin Charlottenburg is now called 'Russianburg' to pejoratively refer to the high concentration of Russian migrants in it. This is part of the folklore, but folklore that hurts, especially when a migrant, in an effort to blend in, gave up eating garlic a long time ago. A favourite native pastime is to deliver monologues about an especially obnoxious and barbaric migrant group or talk badly about a 'terrible' migrant natives know personally while having another – a 'friend', a workmate or a client – as a captive audience. The speaker often inserts a disclaimer such as 'I don't mean you, of course' or 'You are different, of course' (for more on such disclaimers see chapter 3 by Wodak in this book). The disclaimer, instead of softening the insult, makes it even more painful to a migrant, since it connects pejorative ideas about migrants to the so-addressed migrant (Essed 1991: 174).

Natives also typically attribute the 'odd' living rhythm, large families, bad smells, noise and dirt to migrants (Bourdieu *et al.* 1997; Essed 1991: 201, 172–5). Some migrants find these stereotypes particularly hard to take. Their sense of self and their moral sense are offended when they hear ethnic jokes or are exposed to ostracizing ethnic stereotypes according to which Poles are thieves and drunkards, Greeks are only good for dancing syrtos and drinking ouzo and Muslims violate every possible human right. Some migrants work out a personal rule about how to react to negative stereotyping. They decide to ignore such overtures, to counter with a put-down or to act as 'ambassadors of their countries' whose task it is to 'enlighten' the ignorants. Others let the hurt eat them up.

### Everyday Scapegoating Discourses

Symbolic violence takes also place when natives blame migrants for some real or imagined general wrongs, such as run-down neighbourhoods, poor schools or high unemployment rates. Reflecting current national discourses, many natives see migrants as parasites who either live off welfare or take the natives' work away from them. They see them as competitors for scarce resources. These days legal migrants are often lumped together with illegal migrants and 'fake' asylum-seekers to constitute a category of immoral, foreign people endangering one's nation and its welfare state (Wodak and van Dijk 2000). These discourses bestow visibility on migrants, but at a very high price.

The following Swedish migrant wonders at the natives who send a double message. They expect migrants to live off welfare so that they can put them down as dependent parasites. When migrants defy their expectations by working and managing well on their own, Swedes feel let down for they are denied the pleasure they normally take in pitying and inferiorizing 'those helpless foreigners':

> The double message is what I do not understand. If you are a welfare taker one says 'Ah! She is a migrant who lives on our taxes this kind'. If you work then you meet some of these looks [*blickar*]. What should one do then? What should I do then? Even now, I meet these *eyes*: 'she is making it even if she is a migrant'.
>
> Sweden, Kurdish female

A Turkish truck-driver, a divorced mother of four, living in Germany also points to the no-win situation in which 'natives' place 'foreigners'. More confident in her rebuttal, she turns the tables on 'natives', arguing that in fact it is the latter who are amoral – lazy and unwilling to work:

> They say that we are lazy excuses. I took work as a garbage collector then they said foreigners take our jobs away. If you want to work you can find work it is nonsense [*Quatsch*] when the Germans say that we take their jobs.
>
> Germany, Turkish female

## Verbal Rejection and Distributive Consequences

Natives use accent, a foreign-sounding last name and appearance to identify foreigners (Essed 1991: 202). Very often these suffice to reject a person as unworthy of an interaction on equal terms with a native. Instead migrants face prejudice, rejection and scorn. Typically natives will decide that any of these traits disqualifies a person from access to a job or an apartment:

> You can feel comfortable if you speak English and you don't have an accent. I know people who have been on buses for example are they are treated like they are nothing because they have a slight accent. That really upsets me.
>
> UK, Pakistani female

> [In] [Swedish town] she was a doctor but she was forced to change her name. Now she is named [Swedish name] and is married to a Swede and she is lucky now since they called her to an interview and when they saw her they [looks with eyes shocked up and down at imaginary paper and back at an imaginary friend] 'Oh! [Swedish name].' Every time, the same thing happens.
>
> Sweden, Moroccan female

> My friend, who speaks German even better than I do, without an accent, called to make an appointment when she was looking for an apartment and they had immediately told her yes and when she said her name which is a foreign name they said I'm sorry the apartment is already taken, although before they had confirmed her appointment so…
>
> Germany, Italian female, 45 years old

> When they see that I am black they tell me that there the house is no longer available when they see my face they say I am sorry but it has already been taken. If you a few minutes later send an Italian the lady will give him the apartment.
>
> Italy, Cameroonian woman, 40 years old

231

### The Unseen: A Special Case of Illegal Workers

Whenever human labour becomes commodified, human beings who have to sell their labour as a commodity to the employer become ignored at some psychic cost to themselves. This process of commodification is perhaps the most acutely felt by the migrants, especially illegal labourers who enjoy no institutional protection whatsoever. Their employers simply do not see them. The indifference of the employers who openly discuss their most intimate problems in front of them as if they did not exist intensifies the hurt caused by homesickness and loneliness, a sense of having been cut off from one's past, earlier societal position and its joys:

> I don't know how many times in huge apartments when I saw this – believe me it was a shock for me and what these ladies talk about in front of us – although we also have a life, we were also wealthy, we had a childhood. But the bottom line is when you get there so that Madam can cross her feet and we bring her a glass of water it hurts us somewhere because we realize that we feel really low – only because of an administrative paper – the person inside starts to boil. That's the problem.
>
> France, Algerian female, 45 years old

The problem of invisibility overlaps with the broader issue of lacking social recognition. Neither one's own community nor the host government takes notice. Illegal workers look into unseeing eyes:

> We undergo a lot of suffering even people who know you they are cold. Even from your own community they cannot help you, they ignore you as if you were nothing.
>
> France, Malian female, 39 years old

> The government has to have a look we only ask for a quick look that's all. We are not respected, as if we didn't exist, but they need to have a look at us to know we go through terrible times.
>
> France, Malian female, 39 years old

### Conditional Forms of Acceptance

At the most extreme we find forms of acceptance which are conditioned upon accepting a slave- or servant-like status. Two such dramatic examples come from Italy. In the first case a Ukrainian domestic worker is allowed to eat together with the family but the lady of the house serves her substandard food on a separate plate. In the second case the lady of the house tells her domestic worker from Cameroon that she is her slave and has to obey her. Such experience scars for life:

> The lady uses a plate just for me I don't know why even the type of food is different. She prepares paste or beans – always the same things. I eat with them but different food. In my country I was an elementary school teacher.
>
> Italy, Ukrainian female, 35 years old

> She came to me and said 'you have to do what I say because you are my slave and I am the master. I pay you and you have to do what I tell you'. She made me cry many times and she never lets me telephone.
>
> Italy, Cameroonian female, 40 years old

As well as presenting migrants with upsetting, distorted images of themselves, such stereotypes keep specific work – and even entire city areas – closed to them. In the best case migrants can get access to specific work areas at a price of imposed invisibility or as token 'ethnics' on display. In Austria, for example, the local hotels may hire a foreigner as a night porter, while in Sweden an owner of a fancy boutique may just decide to hire a token black person, but as a rule veiled women, men in turbans or dark-skinned people are banned from 'representative' jobs.

Another form of conditional acceptance is shown when natives engage in a relationship with migrants on the condition that the latter accept the natives' superiority. The patronizing trend is displayed by Austrians when they teach migrants how to polish a car or by Swedes when they show migrants how to celebrate Swedish Midsummer. In the view of these patronizing natives, there is only one way to live – their own. Underestimating the skills and capabilities of migrants is a rule. A rare migrant has the insight and strength to cry out 'stop putting us down, it hurts':

> We are like you look at the way you live: we live the same way. We had a misgiving in life which made us the way we are today that's all and it will work out. Stop putting us down. It hurts. It hurts somewhere, all this. You read French so do I; you write it so do I. You do something, I know how to do it as well you do.
>
> France, Malian female, 39 years old

## Institutional Scrutiny

Many migrants reported having difficult experiences with the administration of the host country. They are forced into regular contact with these authorities, since they must go through complex, long and repeated procedures to obtain

233

work and residence permits. How can one explain these burdensome and painful encounters with the administration? Common sense says that administrations cannot cope efficiently with an increasing number of people demanding their services. They treat migrants poorly simply because they are overwhelmed. Yet traumatic encounters with administrations are not painful exceptions to the rule, but instead reveal a pattern of institutional discrimination. Migrants or people of migrant origin are increasingly controlled and disciplined by institutions. Both welfare administrations and repressive apparatuses are said to use new tools of surveillance, such as file-keeping and data cross-checking, to make their control policies more efficient (Bonnelli 2001; Bigo 2001; Foucault 1975). In particular, the police practices and attitudes towards migrants are biased. Police officers not only enforce repressive policies but become involved in producing information on the 'dangerous' population which is being monitored. As we will show next, although in principle correct, this argument over-simplifies the complex web of power relations in which migrants are embedded.

### Administrative Disciplining through Classifying, File-Keeping, Interactions and Criminalization

Where universal or anti-discriminatory laws apply, discrimination operates through institutional norms, procedures and minuscule daily practices (Foucault 1975: 210; see Topper 2001: 43). Legal or institutional discrimination becomes reinforced by the actual interactions between migrants and public servants. Public servants take the liberty of showing anything from disrespect to deep hatred and contempt for migrants. They intimidate and discourage migrants from staying by displaying negative emotions and uttering short statements. The migrants are often very unsure as to whether public servants are acting according to the law or just their own whim. They feel defenceless and uncertain about their rights to self-defence:

> Like a beaten dog, people dare to tell her 'Listen, go home'. You are not there to say that you are there to follow a given law, you are there to welcome people and not to do that.
>
> France, Algerian female, 45 years old

> But you will never get your papers things like that. Really when you come in they tell you this but maybe it's written there that they should discourage people right.
>
> France, Madagascan female, 30 years old

These administrations exercise 'disciplinary power' – one of their key

234

functions is to categorize migrants (Foucault 1975: 213), first of all by defining them as such and then sorting them into different categories using legally prescribed filing systems. The country of origin determines to which procedures migrants will be subject. It decides about their 'career' (Goffman 1968) over time. The documents which instantiate the very identities of migrants, and which they are asked to show on numerous occasions, make a great difference in their everyday lives. Depending on the nature of these papers, migrants will be turned into 'no paper' illegal migrants, acquire one of the possible legal statuses evidenced by a corresponding document or, finally, be granted a passport of the host country. Migrants are strongly aware of these distinctions:

'Mrs No-paper' that's my name [laughing].

France, Malian female, 39 years old

The imposed classification often has traumatic consequences for its 'naïve' objects:

I have for example a son who was born here he had to apply for a residence permit the other day well for me it was understandable but for the child it was a traumatic experience suddenly he understood he is a foreigner here this is a mess [*eine Schweinerei*].

Germany, Greek male, 54 years old

These status distinctions, in turn, are constitutive of the many degrees and nuances of experienced discrimination. Below an Iranian woman comments on the status-upgrading difference naturalization makes:

when I first had my German ID my German citizenship and one day I had to go to the post office to pick something up until then I always had my foreign passport and then every time it got such funny looks every time I got a package or a registered letter every time they wanted to see my ID or passport and every time they looked at it really funny and paged through it and no one could understand a word of it and only this time when I was there for the first time with my German ID did I notice how differently the people all of a sudden they were very polite and were like huh then I thought have I until now been treated as a second-class person by all these institutions ... then I could apply for anything I wanted and had fewer problems as I had with my foreign passport it was the same thing at the bank ... and then I noticed what a difference [it makes].

Germany, Iranian female, 41 years old

Contrary to Foucault's view on disciplinary power, which associates surveillance with maximizing the productivity of the monitored, the disciplinary power applied to migrants does not aim at enhancing their productivity. Administrations treat them not as (a potential) resource but as a burden, a people in need of assistance. Even worse, reflecting current public discourses, but also their own sentiments, public servants often criminalize the migrants. They demonstrate in many ways their suspicion that they (falsify their status in order to) claim resources to which they are not or should not be entitled.

> The public servant simply just say looks at you like sometimes those looks say more than a book like when they just like toss the papers at you.
>
> Germany, Iranian male, 45 years old

> But I think it is really hard because I always have the feeling no matter where I am in each institution that one is somehow checked out from the very beginning foreigners are immediately *immediately* treated worse. Immediately. Somehow like I want to get something that's not my right to have and that I want to cheat.
>
> Germany, Polish female, 27 years old

Administrations handle migrants as two different types of diseases – these which must be kept at a distance and those which are subject to crisis management: new surveillance institutions, procedures, experts and control measures (Foucault 1975: 228–33). The resulting policy mixture subjects migrants to constant surveillance and checks, but keeps them at a distance and so considerably limits their access to and use of the welfare state.

### Encounters with the Police

As experiences, symbolic and overt violence are clearly separable. To their migrant victims symbolic hurt differs from pain or injuries caused by physical violence. To perpetrators inflicting physical violence on others implies modified subjectivity which becomes increased through the enjoyment of cruelty or a feeling of invulnerability, or decreased when the perpetrators feel that they are doing nothing more than obeying orders (Wieviorka 2004). Even if symbolic and physical violence are distinct, one can analyse how they are connected at a structural level. Addi (2001: 951, 953) argues that the state establishes a monopoly on legitimate physical violence, but cannot achieve a monopoly regarding symbolic violence. In their encounters with administrations migrants experience mainly discrimination – legal, institutional, interactional – which entails both scrutiny and rejection. However, in their encounters with the police they experience mainly brutality and violence.

Physical violence is an ultimate means of both disciplining and keeping at a distance when symbolic violence fails to obtain this result:

> In the administration's headquarters [*préfecture*] you see an administrator who searches through your life. And higher up they examine your file among themselves. Very well. They say and judge that this person does not fit into the criteria it's rejected. And when you ask for your file to be reconsidered but listen, it's easy go home. Now they dare to say it out loud. 'Go home we have other problems to deal with we have other things to think about. There are enough foreigners.' It's crystal clear the administrator talks to you this way, you are there, sometimes you don't understand what's happening sometimes you understand and you say 'I don't want to get into an argument' otherwise the police will intervene. Because the police is always there in the headquarters. Automatically they only need to press a button and they are here behind you. And you cannot talk. They dare to talk to you in a very mean way and sometimes they are very impolite because they are angry. It's true they are there from morning till evening. But all those people who are here they need to be. They are here because they want a residence permit.
>
> France, Algerian female, 45 years old

State policies aimed at controlling migrants entail the use of both symbolic and even physical violence (Addi 2001: 956). What marks the everyday experience of discrimination at the hands of the police is the constant control of identity cards and residence permits which affects primarily migrants with high visibility (Bonelli 2001; Bigo 2001). Checking out IDs is not only a matter of surveillance. It also serves to intensify migrants' feeling of estrangement in the host country. However, the conduct of the police towards migrants also involves a 'costly' (see Foucault 1975), dramatic display of authority based on the potential and actual use of overt violence:

> I mean, I had some contacts with a policeman I cannot say, it's too personal I went through a shock I was treated like a whore, they said such things. I then had to attend a psychologist, there was an incident.
>
> Poland, Ukrainian female, 31 years old

> There were five policemen in front of me. So they came into my room. 'Pack your bags! Hurry up!' They pushed me around. I told them 'Easy. I will come out. You told me to come out. I will come out, but I have to pack my bags'. With a [police] dog making noise, jumping here and there I didn't even take my bags. I was upset. More than 40 dogs more than 50 policemen

to make women leave – because we were only women – for the illegal immigrants who were there.

France, Malian female, 25 years old

As this material shows Foucault's concept of 'disciplinary power' does not suffice to describe the real life experiences of migrants, who are exposed to various harsh forms of administrative discrimination and police harassment, to physical as well as symbolic violence. Contrary to Foucault's arguments institutional surveillance is neither economical nor diffuse, nor does it exclude resorting to physical coercion. The concept of power exercised over migrants by the state administrations and the police needs to be broadened beyond his definition of disciplinary power.

## Conclusion

This chapter demonstrates that migrants are denied recognition on a daily basis and also barred from access to resources they badly need to make a decent living. Even if they are legal residents or citizens, they are refused a friendly, constitutive, native gaze. This unwillingness to bond, indeed, the unmitigated hostility directed towards migrants in Western societies, denies a factual relationship of dependence. Our expanding, but ageing and demoralized societies are dependent on migrants for much labour, taxes, contributions to the state pension plans, and the willingness to take on the menial jobs very few natives accept. Instead of showing hostility, the members of these societies should in fact be grateful to the mass of migrant labourers who take care of their children and homes (see, for example, Gottschall und Pfau-Effinger 2002; Hochschild 2001), dispose of the street and industrial garbage, and take on heavy industrial jobs. But most are not. And many want to send the migrants back home. Anti-migrant discourses help them to ignore the obligation to express well-deserved gratitude. They reverse causality, portraying migrants as exploitative and dependent.

Instead of displaying gratitude, natives take to blatant staring, averted gaze, various verbal and bodily forms of rejection, and demeaning anti-foreigner discourses to communicate their hostility. These basic elements of interaction ensure that many migrants feel that they will never be accepted, will never have a sense of belonging. Subject to constant institutional scrutiny which shades over into various forms of police violence, migrants become objects of unceasing harassment. Not for them or about them are the abstract discussions about recognition and redistribution (Fraser 2002; Honneth 2002) and romantic visions of multiple belongings to various cultures and places (Hedetoft 2002: 6). Rather than developing several belongings, migrants may end up with none – the new denied, the old long lost. Not only do they constantly confront misrecognition and suffer from hurt in a part of the world which boasts of its humanitarian achievements, but in some countries they find no laws, public institutions or émigré communities willing to help them in their struggle for access to basic human rights. Within Europe, migrants are currently among the most vulnerable people, and the most exposed to a wide range of hurts, both physical and symbolic.

## References

Addi, L. (2001) 'Violence symbolique et statut du politique dans l'œuvre de Pierre Bourdieu', in *Revue française de science politique* 51(6): 949–63.

Bigo, D. (2001) 'Identifier, catégoriser et contrôler: police et logiques pro-actives', in Sainati and Bonelli 2001.

Billig, M. (1995) *Banal Nationalism*. London: Sage.

Bonelli, L. (2001) 'Des populations "en danger" aux populations "dangereuses": les logiques de gestion policière et judiciaire des quartiers populaires', in Sainati and Bonelli 2001.

Bourdieu, P. (1991) *Outline of a Theory of Practice*. Cambridge: Cambridge University Press. First published in 1971 as *Esquisse d'une théorie de la pratique*. Geneva: Droz.

— et al. (1997) *Das Elend der Welt*. Konstanz: Universitätsverlag Konstanz.

Cooley, C. H. (1970) *Human Nature and the Social Order*. New York: Schocken Books.

Delanty, G. 2002. *Citizenship in a Global Age: Society, Culture, Politics*. Buckingham. Open University Press.

Essed, P. (1991) *Understanding Everyday Racism: An Interdisciplinary Theory*. London: Sage.

Foucault, M. (1975) *Surveiller et punir*. Paris: Gallimard.

Fraser, N. (2002) 'Recognition without Ethics', in *Recognition and Difference: Politics, Identity, Multiculture*, ed. S. Lash and M. Featherstone. London: Sage, pp. 21–42.

Goffman, E. (1959) *The Presentation of Self in Everyday Life*. New York: Anchor.

— (1968) *Asiles*. Paris: Les Editions de Minuit.

Gottschall, K., and B. Pfau-Effinger (eds) (2002) *Zukunft der Arbeit und Geschlecht*. Opladen: Leske & Budrich.

Hedetoft, U. (2002) 'Discourses and Images of Belonging: Migrants between "New Racism", Liberal Nationalism and Globalisation', *AMID Working Paper Series* 5.

Hochschild, A. R. (2001) 'Globale Betreuungsketten und emotionaler Mehrwert', in *Die Zukunft des globalen Kapitalismus*, ed. W. Hutton and A. Giddens. Frankfurt am Main: Campus, pp. 158–75.

Honneth, A. (2002) 'Recognition or Redistribution? Changing Perspectives on the Moral Order of Society', in *Recognition and Difference: Politics, Identity, Multiculture*, ed. S. Lash and M. Featherstone. London: Sage, pp. 43–55.

Ignatieff, M. (1993) *Blood and Belonging: Journeys into the New Nationalism*. New York: Farrar, Straus and Giroux.

Karst, K. L. (1989) *Belonging to America: Equal Citizenship and the Constitution*. New

Haven, CT: Yale University Press.

Krais, B. (1993) 'Gender and Symbolic Violence: Female Oppression in the Light of Pierre Bourdieu's Theory of Social Practice', in *Bourdieu: Critical Perspectives*, ed. C. Calhoun, E. LiPuma and M. Postone. Cambridge. Polity Press, pp. 156–77.

McNay, L. (1999) 'Gender, Habitus and the Field, Pierre Bourdieu and the Limits of Reflexivity', *Theory, Culture and Society* 16(1): 95–117.

Renan, E. (1990) 'What is a Nation', in *Nation and Narration*, ed. H. K. Bhabha. London: Routledge.

Riesman, P. (1977) *The Lonely Crowd*. New Haven, CT: Yale University Press.

Sainati, G., and L. Bonelli (eds) (2001) *La Machine à punir: pratiques et discours sécuritaires*. Paris: L'Esprit Frappeur.

Sartre, J.-P. (1994) *Der Blick: Ein Kapitel aus das Sein und das Nichts*, ed. W. van Rossum. Mainz: Dieterichsche Verlagsbuchhandlung

Topper, K. (2001) 'Bourdieu and Quotidian Violence', in *Constellations* 8(1) March: 30–56.

Westwood, S. (2000) 'The Politics of Belonging – Imagining America, Remembering Home: Latino/a Cultures in Urban America', in *Trans-nationalism and the Politics of Belonging*, ed. S. Westwood and A. Phizacklea. London: Routledge, pp. 57–69.

Wieviorka, M. (2004) *Violence*. Paris: Balland.

Wodak, R., and T. A. van Dijk (2000) *Racism at the Top: Parliamentary Discourses on Ethnic Issues in Six European Countries*. Klagenfurt: Drava Verlag.

Yar, M. (2002) 'Recognition and the Politics of Human(e) Desire', in *Recognition and Difference: Politics, Identity, Multiculture*, ed. S. Lash and M. Featherstone. London: Sage, pp. 57–76.

# 12 Voices of Migrants: Solidarity and Resistance

## Lena Sawyer (with Paul Jones)

[The] binary division between resistance and non-resistance is an unreal one. The existence of those who seem not to rebel is a warren of minute, individual, autonomous tactics and strategies which counter and inflect the visible facts of overall domination, and whose purposes and calculations, desires and choices resist any simple division into the political and the apolitical. The schema of a strategy of resistance as a vanguard of politicization needs to be subjected to re-examination, and account must be taken of resistances whose strategy is one of evasion or defence.

Colin Gordon on Michel Foucault, cited in Scott 1985: ii

Individuals resist the imposition of illegitimate powers in a wide variety of ways. Sometimes this resistance is framed collectively – drawing heavily on notions of solidarity – while at other times it takes on a much more individualized character. After briefly outlining the relationship between resistance and solidarity we suggest that how migrants define resistance is an empirically significant question whose answer should not be taken for granted, as the actual strategies employed by those in positions others seek to impose vary greatly with context. We seek to contextualize this claim by using migrants' discourses to illustrate how strategies for resisting discrimination are played out in various ways. Our aim in doing this is to draw attention to the 'everyday' nature that much resistance to oppression takes; a major contention in this chapter is that just as the discrimination faced by migrants is broad, disparate and often elusive, accordingly *challenges* to illegitimate uses of power are also (necessarily) many and varied. In drawing on focus group and interview material this chapter provides a substantive focus for the more theoretical discussions on migration and resistance. While attempting to avoid overly pluralistic accounts of resistance that see resistance everywhere and over-estimate the capacity of agents to transform their conditions of action, we do attempt to draw particular attention to the strategies of contestation that are operative on the level of the 'everyday' as opposed to more institutionalized forms.

## Situating Resistance

In *Understanding Everyday Racism* Philomena Essed suggests that 'everyday opposition against racism is a process that exposes and challenges practices that are often unquestioned by the dominant group but that are unacceptable because of their detrimental implications' (1991: 261). In Essed's important study, resistance entails both exposing the illegitimacy of exclusionary discourses and, while it has been suggested elsewhere that historical context affects the type of anti-racist strategies individuals employ, we believe that it is of vital importance to pay attention to the 'everyday', routinized nature that discrimination and resistance frequently take. Our argument here is that just as illegitimate power is applied in multidimensional ways and discrimination experienced in a multitude of contexts, then so too the resistance to such discrimination is also multifaceted. As we illustrate in the course of our discussion, personal strategies for resistance often entail considerable effort and tactical engagement; strategies employed to deal with oppression are frequently highly contingent on the range of capital that individuals can draw upon; often these strategies for resistance are not based on association with migrant status – indeed research participants sometimes resisted the imposition of this category as a primary definer. These understandings provide contours to the landscape of resistance that define legitimate and non-legitimate reactions to 'breaches' or 'ruptures' in migrants' expectations of existing ways of proceeding (Sewell, cited in Barker 1999: 19).

Much research on resistance has focused upon collective resistance, for example in the form of social movements (for example, see Gamson 1992; Castells 1997; Barker 1999). In this tradition collective identities are commonly seen as the starting point for resistance to injustice, with individuals associating their personal struggle or circumstance with that of a group. Although this relationship involves often very complicated negotiations and translations of personalized identities (see chapter 2 by Jones and Krzyżanowski in this volume) it is useful to think about the potential for a collective resistance in migrant communities. Of course, migrants are far from a homogeneous group, and are divided along at least as many lines as any 'native' national community, and the extent to which the overarching – some may say objectifying – status of 'migrant' provides the basis of an individual's personal identity, or of their allegiance to a collective identity, can be highly contested. While associating with a common struggle can be the basis for the development of a collective identity and its subsequent mobilization, unquestioningly grouping a diverse population of people under the banner 'migrant' is highly problematic, as it can imply that some coherence or 'essence' exists in what is a culturally, ethnically and nationally diverse and disparate group of people. Indeed it is clear from the material below that many tensions exist around this very question, with individuals often demonstrating resistance to the label of 'migrant' or 'immigrant' when applied in a way considered oppressive or stigmatizing by a dominant group.

For example, right-wing discourse often defines groups primarily with reference to what they are not (in this case born in the country of residence) in an attempt to stigmatize, devalue and exclude them. Indeed, numerous studies on the discourse of radical right populist parties have demonstrated that anti-immigration discourses are organized around giving coherence and ascribing fixed characteristics to groups in order to construct them as 'others' (for example see Rydgren 2004). Likewise it is also the tendency of some institutions and individuals 'indigenous' to the 'host' countries to define migrants in opposition to a coherent, often racialized self, which serves to objectify and reify both the in-group and the out-group. Ascribing coherence and a solidity to diverse, heterogeneous groups is thus problematic, as it underpins much racist and anti-immigration rhetoric (Banton 1977; Malik 1996). So, in using the term migrant[1] here we are not suggesting the existence of a unitary group or actor, but rather adopt the term as a descriptive term for people who are resident in a country other than their birth; this minimal conception is developed in relation to the empirical material below.

John Scott's work on power and resistance, following Foucault (1970; 1979), has taken up the theme of multiple resistances and their relationship to spaces and discourses. Scott (1985) suggests that aside from social movements and collective protest, much resistance occurs in the 'micro-manoeuvres' of action, which can be individual acts that entail an acknowledgment of injustice and confrontation, as well as those manoeuvres that acknowledge injustice but adopt a strategy based around an ostensibly submissive position, regardless of the *actual* politics of the situation. In this work – and that of Genovese (1974) – a persuasive argument is given for understanding resistance and power, which suggests that in many contexts

---

1 We believe 'migrant' is preferable to 'immigrant' as it has less strong connotations of insider/outsider and is generally a less normatively loaded term.

outward displays of resistance can bring with them a danger of visibility and associated marginalization for those involved in such behaviour. Explicit challenges to existing power inequalities have, at specific historical periods and contexts, meant significant risk for subordinate individuals, such as exposing them to the threat of symbolic or physical violence from power holders and the institutions and structures that legitimate these actors and their power. Within public spaces 'public transcripts' – hegemonic discourses that support existing asymmetries of power – are dominant. While 'ruptures' do occasionally occur in these spaces, through collective organization and other challenges, much critique of the 'public transcripts' occurs within more private settings (family and community networks). Within public spaces subordinated groups are often required to show deference, with potentially much to lose in explicitly challenging existing power relations. However, while subordinated groups may display deference in public, within alternative settings, such as within community and family, alternative critical perspectives and ideas are developed which constitute 'hidden transcripts' (Scott 1990: 4–5).

For example, studies of slavery stress how everyday strategies of resistance were commonplace sources of solidarity and survival in the face of daily humiliation. While there are a few historical examples of explicit and risk-filled strategies of opposition and resistance taken by slaves in uprisings (also see, for example, James 1989; Higginson and McPherson 1998), according to Scott more common in the antebellum South were those tactics that, hidden behind the face of acquiescence, reminded slaves of their own dignity and moral superiority over slave holders (1985). Multiple strategies of everyday resistances are evidenced in 'foot dragging, false compliance, flight, feigned ignorance, sabotage, theft, and not least, cultural resistance' (Scott 1985: 34). The reworking of language and meanings, for example in the development of ironic, subversive, double meanings sung in slave songs, can also be understood as cultural traditions developed in the African American community to resist subordination and humiliation (see for example Genovese 1974; for more work on language see Smitherman 2000). Hence while collective action and mobilization in the form of social movements and organizations are *one* form of challenge to power relations, much resistance to power occurs in 'everyday' settings: according to Scott '[m]ost of the political life of subordinate groups is to be found neither in overt collective defiance of powerholders nor in complete hegemonic compliance, but in the vast territory between those two polar opposites' (1990: 136). These sites of contestation are important for understanding the multifaceted ways in which people creatively construct, and resist, power. Such an understanding of renegotiations and reconceptualizations of social relations is useful for our discussion of migrants' strategies of resistance; in particular, the notion that people behave, speak and act differently in different spaces and that these differences are evidence of the daily negotiations of power asymmetries based on (among other factors) class, gender, ethnicity and sexuality. Certainly domination is not always overt in nature, and is often expressed through more 'coded' forms, for example through language (Wodak *et al.* 1999) and other forms of symbolic violence (see chapter 11 by Flam and Beauzamy in this volume).

Foucault argued that 'the real political task in a society such as ours is to criticize the working of institutions which appear to be neutral and independent; to criticize them in such a manner that the political violence which has always exercised itself obscurely through them will be unmasked' (Foucault, in Rabinow 1984: 6). The absence of collective solidarity and organization in the form of social movements does not necessarily indicate a lack of resistance, or the existence of a 'false consciousness' among migrants who participated in the focus group research. Instead we believe that varied responses to discriminatory behaviour should lead researchers to consider the wide variety of strategies employed in resisting discrimination. It is vitally important to pay attention to the ways in which 'dominated' groups construct a range of tactics of resistance; understanding these also allows us to understand the forms discrimination is perceived to be taking. As is illustrated below, tactics are sometimes (necessarily) subtle, cryptic and encoded due to the (real or perceived) risks associated with outward shows of defiance. Of course, this is not to deny the material nature of discrimination or to celebrate oppression as creating 'resistance', but rather to draw attention to the process through which challenges to established social meanings and practices underpin the notion of resistance.

Due in part to work in this area, some researchers have started to consider the ways in which resistance can be a part of everyday praxis. For example, sociologists and anthropologists have expanded discussions of resistance to include the ways that struggles over power are manifested in the realm of culture, for example in the form of music, dance, language and literature. Eyerman and Jamison's (1998) work on social movements point to the ways in which musical traditions have been intimately linked to individuals' expressions of collective identity and counter-ideology. Similarly Peter Wade analyses rap music as a way for oppressed individuals to gain a sense of control and subjectivity in a context where they have little access to the loci of power (1999: 455) and – recalling Bourdieu's work (1989) on embodied capital – Barbara Browning (1995) and Deborah Heath (1994) have analysed the body in movement as strategically articulating struggle, defiance and resistance. For example, Senegalese women's performance of *taasu*, a bawdy oral poetry accompanied by dance, in specific settings and among specific audiences is understood by Heath as resistance to (localized) gendered norms relating to age, caste and sexuality.

### The Voices of Migrants: Stories of Resistance

It is an interesting initial note that the majority of the strategies discussed in the focus groups were individualized strategies rather than collective or structural strategies. Certainly the notion of solidarity is strongly linked to that of collectivism insofar as it involves an individual recognizing a shared interest with a wider group of people. However, acts of solidarity cannot be understood from the perspective of rational choice theory as purely instrumental, strategic alliances between groups of politically atomized individuals who seek to further their own cause or pursue their own goal within the context of other such individuals. Solidarity frequently involves an individual holding his/her own interests subordinate to those of the group. It is vital then to keep in mind that solidarity can cut across other collective identities based on ethnicity, class or occupation groups, and is predicated on a collective response to a structural, frequently unequal, context. Solidarity is a political consciousness that leads to the support of a collective action usually directed at bringing about social justice.

Although Scott's theorization is a useful model for understanding the variety of ways in which subordinate groups resist, he can also be criticized for idealizing the spaces in which hidden transcripts are produced. There is also a tendency in his work to homogenize groups, overlooking internal dynamics within subordinate groups. According to Barker we 'need to pay attention to the discourses and arguments going on among the oppressed. Scott, in bending the theoretical stick against theories of the "dominant ideology", risks treating the world of the hidden transcript as marked by simple unity and harmonious amity among the oppressed' (1999: 17). Barker, discussing Paul Bagguley's notion of 'informed fatalism', describes this as one way of understanding actors' seeming submission to oppression. Here, people are aware of the power inequalities and circumstances and are not satisfied with them but they do not resist because they believe them to be impossible to change. In a summary of his broader argument Barker suggests that (1999: 20)

[m]ost of the time, people in a condition of informed fatalism ... focus their

practical concerns not on their own incapacity to challenge existing structures, but on more immediate questions which absorb them: matters of everyday life, family, love, grief, work-task problems, lifestyle, cultural pursuits, hobbies and enthusiasms. Thus apparent 'political passivity' is really active engagement with a host of distinct matters.

Gamson (1992) identifies the usage of injustice frames as a basis for collective action, and such a method allows us to conceptualize how migrants construct injustice. Migrants, as with other groups and individuals, make use of repertoires of discourses and frames that are already in existence to order the external world and their relationship to it. Significant for the development of injustice frames are (i) that people make 'heated' normative judgments – for example expressing anger over an unjust use of power – and (ii) that an 'object' can be identified as responsible for the unjust acts perpetrated. Injustice frames are also useful as they 'offer ways of understanding that imply the need or desirability of some form of action' (Gamson 1992: 7) – in other words they provide a way to mobilize resistance. Such strategies both resist and challenge existing power relations, as well as those which are an acknowledgment of unjust usage of power but do not aim to change things. The latter strategies can be understood as coping strategies, or ways in which to 'get by' and survive in a context of unequal power. Within the focus group discussions this was a recurring theme, which was used to increase the appeal of the strategy taken and linked up to broader cultural and political culture. According to Gamson (1992: 135) cultural resonances (here called themes) increase the appeal of a frame by linking up discourse on a particular issue (strategies to combat discrimination) and the broader political culture of which it is part.

## Discrimination, Resistance and Emotions

Summers-Effler (2002) argues that people make choices about how to respond to discrimination that are based not only on an evaluation of the possible repressive sanctions or risks involved, but also on a consideration of the potential emotional energy 'cost'. While such rational choice theories are very limited in their capacity to explain the non-instrumental nature of much social life, such language did frame much of the focus groups' discussion, with individuals thinking about how much emotional energy particular strategies will 'cost' them:

At first you says damn Germans [*Scheißdeutscher*] and the second time and the third time it's ok you learn to live with it and I do not want to invest too many emotions in things I know for sure will happen anyway you learn to live with it.

Germany, male

Here the suggestion is that how one reacts to the experiences of discrimination is to some extent time-dependent, predicated on the number of occasions one encounters discriminatory behaviour. The response also contains a sense of fatalism; the belief that things will not change informs the strategy of ignoring 'it' and learning to live with 'it'. As will be shown in the discussion of the strategies below, such a view of emotions as based on a kind of investment and return informs the kind of strategy used. In particular the strategy of 'giving up' borrows upon this theme heavily and possible injustice frames – those based on 'hot cognition' and anger (frequently described as self-defeating or demeaning) – are neutralized by the view that this emotion will not pay off. As such this aspect of the theme of emotion management is important to understanding why dominated groups apparently do not resist. Summers-Effler points out that this is an internal process which entails managing a conflict between initial reaction and a longer-term strategy based on assessment of energy cost and gain (2002: 46). This suggestion certainly seems to be illustrated by the excerpt above, in which the participant describes a shift from anger that is directed externally ('damn Germans') to an emotion that is managed internally ('anyway you learn to live with it').

While it should be remembered that controlling emotions, and anger in particular, can be necessary for survival in a context of unequal power relations where the threat of expulsion and violence can be perceived to be a real risk, it is also interesting that managing emotions emerged as central to many of the strategies described for coping with discriminatory encounters. Through using such themes people are participating in disciplining *themselves* to manage just the emotion that Gamson (1992) describes as a key component in the development of an injustice frame that is necessary to action and confrontation. Hence such individual usages of emotional 'cost' in relation to their choice of strategy sometimes work to *diffuse* the 'hot cognition' necessary for action, or at least redirect it into a different, more measured response. Scott suggests that such repression plays a part in the reproduction of power when he states that '[w]hile the aristocrat is trained to move every serious verbal insult to the terrain of mortal combat, the powerless are trained to absorb insults without retaliating physically' (Scott 1990: 137).

Lawrence Levine describes how dominated groups develop forms of socializing their members to specific coping strategies, and the management of anger in particular as necessary for survival. For example the African American tradition of 'doing the dozens', a tradition in which mostly men participate in the exchange of rhymed insult in a kind of verbal duel,[2] is analysed as a form of strategic socialization to emotion management. Here this cultural practice is analysed as socialization to verbal insult and the negotiation and restraining of emotions as 'a mechanism for teaching and sharpening the ability to control emotions and anger; an ability which was often necessary for survival' (Levine, cited in Scott 1990: 137).

The theme of managing emotion emerged in a second way in focus group discussions. Although violence was described over and over again as an illegitimate response to discrimination, the strategies proposed often entail aspects of symbolic violence (for a further discussion see chapter 11 by Flam and Beauzamy in this volume). For example, oppressive power was often described as physically affecting the body, and was characterized/spatialized as a force that attempts to 'push' the body downwards into submission. The following citation exemplifies this:

> Because in Sweden this is the worst you can do is charge someone for racism in this country. There is no racism. Then *you* will be thrown out directly. You asked me about this discrimination bureau: XXX was his name but XXX was a Parliament man and they did not let him into a restaurant and what happened then they have charged the wrong door guard to get it over with. And XXX told me that in the Parliament no one talked to him, he was totally frozen out. So he was very aggressive that there was racism in Sweden then he was [makes a sign with his hand hitting hard and fast downwards] less and less [hand on the floor]. Now he sits at the discrimination bureau competitor to the state.
>
> Sweden, Polish man

The above citation describes how an unjust structural power is perceived to come from 'above', and pushes a person downwards; the strong spatial/embodied element is noteworthy. The following citation shows how resistance to unjust power is also symbolically linked to body comportment; keeping the body and head held upright in the face of experiences that attempt to push a person downwards is linked to the resistance to unjust power. Here a Malian woman in France tells of dignity maintained through presenting herself as hard-working, pious, and moral though regulation of the body:

---

2   This practice is an integral part of contemporary transnational rap culture and the verbal duels that occur between rappers. As in the 'dozens', in the art of rapping, verbal and poetic skill are often used to humiliate one's partner while at the same time expressing emotion control. Rap has increasingly been appropriated by different socially and economically marginalized, though not exclusively racialized as black, individuals around the world (for example in Hawaii, Colombia, and Stockholm) to challenge power relations and construct alternative understandings of self and belonging (see for example Wade 1999).

What I can add, with all that, I came to the point where I will not bow my head before these people. I've always been this way … I've chosen to work hard, even doing this hard work, there are certain things I will not accept to be told, and I will not bow my head … It's hard, it's not easy but it's important for me, it helps me live.

France, Malian woman

The above citations show how some of the participants conceptualized power in a symbolic way as something physical that exerts pressure on the actual body. As we suggested earlier, we are interested in assessing how the participants' cultural repertoires invert these hierarchies to place those who are discriminatory 'below' them in the moral scheme people in focus groups frequently described. A young woman in Sweden states:

And it was she and a new democracy girl and they have a little confrontation with each other and it felt like 'hello!' One gets so upset also because they really say [unread] and she's like I do not know … one just becomes so pissed off that it is not how it should be. One should not sink to their level.

Sweden, woman

Here a sense of superiority is achieved through containing the initial emotional reaction of anger. Invocations of vertical space in relationship to discrimination invoke culturally resonant discourses of hierarchical struggle that privilege (and place 'higher') ideas of civility and rationality over lower expressions such as emotional responses (such as anger or sexuality) that are associated with a 'lack of control'. On the one hand, discrimination is an expression of an illegitimate power that debases those who employ it, while on the other hand certain strategies of resistance are given a moral quality that realigns the hierarchical order that unjust discriminatory power seeks to perpetuate. This sense of morality based on civility was frequently invoked by participants as a way to situate themselves above those who discriminate, with these moral standards providing migrants with alternative definitions of worth and dignity based less around who is powerful and more around one's behaviour towards others.

Discrimination was perceived to be an act of objectification of a person into the stigmatizing category of 'Other', which objectifies a person's individuality, dignity and sense of worth. So on the other hand a hierarchical morality also emerged when discussing the type of strategy taken when encountering discrimination – those who discriminate were described as on a 'low' level of morality and anger is portrayed as being uncivil and on a low level of social development. Finally, in the above citation expression of anger is equated with

250

realigning oneself to the moral level of those who discriminate; there is no distinction between just and unjust anger. Such examples of cultural resonances are not only examples of individual negotiations but also according to Lamont examples of 'cultural structures, that is, institutionalized cultural repertoires or publicly available categorization systems' (2000: 243).

## Talking and Reasoning

Relatedly, the strategy of talking and reasoning was presented as a common response to discrimination and racism. This strategy entailed challenging the ignorance of prejudiced individuals, and was frequently grounded in the humanistic belief that forms of prejudice and racism are due to ignorance and lack of knowledge of the Other. Such challenges seemed to occur more frequently on the individual, face-to-face basis, with challenges to institutional racism commonly taking different forms. In Vienna a youth tells of how discrimination was successfully confronted through the employment of a strategy of education, politeness and patience:

> I was walking with my dad and an old lady passed and she started 'castrate all foreigners', and my dad said – he was really nice – and he asked 'why did you offend us like this?' and he really asked politely and then she said 'ok sorry I'm sorry' and when my dad meets her today they greet each other.
>
> Austria, woman

Strategies such as this allow migrants to expose the ignorance of the prejudiced, a way of dealing with the routinized, everyday discrimination described by the vast majority of the migrants who participated in the research. Attempts to educate, or at least to challenge the views of, a prejudiced individual allow migrants not only the potential for resistance but also the opportunity to show 'moral superiority' and maintain a sense of personal dignity. Central to this strategy or theme was the counter theme of the illegitimacy of violence. One such approach is described in the following, a citation from a 33-year-old Ghanaian male studying in Manchester, who gave the following as an illustrative example of how he chooses to tackle prejudice in most situations:

> To me I try [to respond to discrimination] always but it depends how you are. One time I had been doing some door [security] work and this guy came and was saying some 'funny' things about Africa and he said 'You are black' so I looked at him and said [points to skin] 'Is that black?' and he say 'Yeah that *is* black' so I say 'Who told you that is black?' then he say

'No but that [points at skin] *is* black' I say 'that is not *black*. Look at it. Have you got eyes?' So I confused him a bit and I said 'the word black was created by somebody so if the people who lived before us had called it blue you would have called it blue' he say 'I don't understand so there's no colour to anything?' so I say 'yes it depends what you call it' what I'm bringing out here is that if you can be a bit patient you get the opportunity to educate somebody about your worth or your value as an individual. But it is also difficult … because it's painful. Personally if it will bring a fight I will walk away but if it will bring a debate and an opportunity to talk I will go for it to the extreme.

UK, Ghanaian man

Strategies of resistance, and in particular the hegemonic strategy of talking and reasoning, were often described as being in opposition to violence, seen above in the statement 'if it will bring a fight I walk away'. However, when we look closely at some of the descriptions of the strategy of talking and reasoning it is apparent that on the symbolic level violence is still very much a part of how discrimination and resistance are conceptualized. In the following example from Germany:

It always depends on the situation … if it was something verbal then I refute it or or … I refute the person verbally … I talk him into the floor I don't get violent or anything I talk him into the ground until he tells me yes you are right because I want to have my rights and I know I know the laws in Germany I know I know the culture I know eh the social things that's why no one can fool me.

Germany, male

Verbally refuting a discriminatory remark is here characterized as being in opposition to *being violent* but also on the symbolic level it *reproduces violence*, as words are shown as having the power to force a person 'into the floor' and 'into the ground'. This shows that, while violence is seen as an illegitimate strategy, on a symbolic level at least it can still be very much a part of how people experience and retaliate against unjust power. The above excerpt also shows a clear attempt to impose one's will on the other – 'until he tells me yes you are right' – and therefore gain power through a socially legitimated, discursive process. Such a strategy would seem to fit our conceptualization of resistance, as it is directed towards a change in the structure of power relations, albeit on an individualized, face-to-face level.

Finally it is necessary to point out that the strategy of talking and reasoning was described as having emotional costs – in the following citation an injustice frame propels the person to 'fight' verbally at his workplace. A Kurdish man in Sweden describes:

I become really angry with those who discriminate or have prejudices and I have I have conflicts with my colleagues in fact many times and I am close to be called eh a fighter who always protests for example they say 'yes it is a gypsy women and her child' and say 'you know how the gypsies are' eh 'a Lebanon women with five children' and so on. Then I become FURIOUS with my colleagues especially one of them who has eh such eh attitude to immigrants and refugees then I immediately go in a fight [*gå i strid*].

Sweden, Kurdish male

While he describes himself as a fighter, his statement also reminds us that resisting and confronting discrimination takes energy and can have negative physiological repercussions. After such confrontations he 'feels bad', has a migraine and withdraws socially.

Below is another example of how approaches to violence can vary across generations. A Pakistani woman in a Manchester focus group suggests:

Very white areas where they let you know if you've got a different colour skin even if you've got a heavy *tan* you're not welcome [laughs]. There are certain areas you will not go unless you are looking for trouble, because the youngsters of this day and age they don't care and they want to confront the trouble. It's like 'Well who are you to tell us? This is our country as well' so the youngsters of today really go head on and confront it, but it's the parents they say 'look right leave them it'll sort itself out they have a problem we don't' but the youngsters don't listen anymore and say 'no'.

UK, Pakistani woman, 45 years old

Here there is a clearly distinguished 'they' – people in 'white' areas who are hostile to the racialized 'other', who are described in terms of a 'we' or an 'us'. Interestingly the violence the participant intimates with the phrases 'going head on' and 'confront it' is predicated on a sense of belonging, because the children of migrants feel 'this is our country as well'. Different senses of belonging – based in this case on birthplace – seem to be significant in informing the kind of injustice frame called upon; the passive strategies she describes are suggested as indicative of an older generation who employed coping strategies rather than actively seeking change through direct confrontation with racists.

Another strategy, of joking and using irony, was also frequently employed as part of a broader injustice frame. Instead of directly confronting and reasoning with a person, the strategy of joking is also a kind of confrontation but an oblique form, masked in the multiple meanings of 'a joke'. Jokes operate at the level of challenging meanings, and can force reflection on broader power relations; they are also strategies that are more careful about disrupting relations between the actors involved. Here confrontation is given a more masked form, since even if the joke is subversive or makes a perceptive comment about unequal power relations, possible conflict can be avoided with the disclaimer that it is 'just a joke'. Yet we believe it is significant that the strategy of joking and irony very often employs an injustice frame, and accordingly this was evident in many of the transcripts of the focus group discussions. For example, the following example from Berlin, where an Italian man stresses how talking and irony can be used to challenge mistreatment:

> Yes it always like I said depends on the situation when it's possible then I think I have to talk about it it's my personal strategy in the case of discrimination irony … because I don't let myself be discriminated by a German nor an Italian. If something very bad happens in the store or something then I'm not the great hero who steps in or does something but of course, well I don't let myself well be mistreated. I react verbally with words not with weapons, and with irony. Do you all know how superiors act with customers? What do you say? [laughs].
>
> Germany, Italian man

Significant once again is the opposition between talking and violence, seen in his statement that he reacts verbally and 'not with weapons'. It is also significant that these strategies often also require the management or at least repression of the emotion of anger, as joking requires the emotion of joviality and laughter. Potential damage of relations and possible risks involved in more direct verbal confrontation are obscured or 'softened' through the multiple meanings and joviality involved in joking. However, like the strategy of talking and reasoning, in the above citation there is the hope of educating and enlightening, which might result in an apology. After his joke he looks for a response and both makes a statement and poses a question, saying 'what do you say?'

Instrumental strategies were also presented as one way to negotiate discrimination. However, as can be seen in the following exchange, this was also a contested strategy:

> Participant 1: Try to accept that you are strange. That you can try to change yourself.
>
> Participant 2: I think that a strategy can also be to BECOME Swedish

change your name and refuse to speak your mother language with [laugh].

Participant 3: No, that will never be.

Participant 1: Yes yes.

Participant 2: then there will

Participant 1: There are SO MANY (↑) who do that.

Participant 3: And I would say that they FAIL (↑) they are not accepted in the long run.

Participant 4: THOUGH (↑) you never know. You have these girls on Swedish TV who have a Swedish first name and last name, and they look really black that is also a strategy.

Stockholm, Sweden

The above citation and the joking and laughing of the first speaker suggest the acknowledgment of the lack of respectability of an instrumental strategy among some of the migrant participants in this discussion. Participant 1 and Participant 3 both point out that these are strategies that will not bring the desired results, in this case employment. However, in other contexts instrumental strategies were not challenged because they were seen to give the desired results, as the following citations from two different focus group discussions in Germany illustrate:

Participant: But you can feel the foreignness like when you apply for something in order to be allowed to stay here ya or to have a degree recognized ya or at a big factory where you would think that it's fairly impersonal but still you notice ya that they also in politics (unread 4.0) there you can see it more easily that you are foreign in this country

Researcher: And what do you do then?

Participant: What do I do I wait until I get my paper and then I get out of there [laughs].

Researcher: I haven't had any experience at all with other people I don't look like a foreigner if I say two sentences then no one notices and I only have in institutions then I have to put up with it there I can't do anything about it because I need that residence visa I have to lower myself it's can't be different I have to stand in line outside for 5 hours.

Berlin, Germany

In these excerpts discrimination is encountered within institutions, described as a 'big factory', 'in politics' and in 'institutions'. However, within these particular institutional spaces there is evidence that a kind of injustice frame is employed in that there is recognition of unjust and discriminatory behaviour, however, there is a weak emotional reaction, or 'hot cognition', as well as a vaguer identification of the object responsible for unjust action. These can be seen as informing the choice of strategy taken, but equally important, as the speakers describe, is an evaluation of the stakes at hand. The speakers in these institutional spaces perceive themselves to be in an unequal and dependent situation – they hope to get something from their contact with these institutions. They are there applying for work, to get their degree recognized, or to get their residence visa. Although they recognize discrimination, given what is at stake, an instrumental strategy of giving the outward appearance of submission is employed within these institutional contexts. In need of a residence visa, a migrant woman in Germany describes how she 'lowers herself' to get what she wants, an expression that once again portrays negotiations of power as both spatial, hierarchical and embodied.

If emotion management is a strategy that turns conflict 'inside' to the individual, solidarity shifts conflict to the 'outside' and places blame on the environment (Summers-Effler 2002: 51). Collective identity or solidarity is a means by which previously 'managed' emotions can be experienced, for example the experience of anger, which is central to developing a sense of injustice (Gamson 1992). Manuel Castells identifies 'resistance identity' as a significant basis for collective resistance in a globalized context. He suggests that resistance identities are 'generated by those actors that are in positions/conditions devalued and/or stigmatized by the logic of domination, thus building trenches of resistance and survival on the basis of principles different from, or opposed to, those permeating the institutions of society' (1997: 8). It is in this way that Castells attempts to understand how domination is resisted, with reference to communities as providing a form of 'collective resistance' to a dominating power that he also calls '*the exclusion of the excluders by the excluded*' (Castells 1997: 8 – original emphasis). Setting up new value systems, redefining boundaries between groups, inscribing oneself into a diasporic community (Sawyer 2002), and general challenges to existing social injustice all fall within this broad strategy. Of course Castells' notion of a resistance identity is based on a resistance to certain processes associated with globalization, but we believe that this framework has some potential to support our analysis here. Much of the solidarity we encountered came from resistance to a power seen to be contained by a (reified) host country, as was often expressed in responses about 'the Germans', 'the French', 'the Polish' or more generally 'them'.

Only one participant was particularly vocal on the need for solidarity between different groups for successful mobilization against racism and discrimination. Initially she suggested that solidarity between black migrants and the British black population was important:

Here if we don't wake up as black people to our own black people to show them 'this is not the way, you can do it, you can achieve it' then we are always going to be underdogs.

UK, Senegalese woman, 55 years old

This excerpt is significant as the participant is drawing on the same collective identity, that of 'black people', but switching between a use of 'we' and 'them'. It seems that the 'we' in this statement are a politicized group of individuals who have recognized the need for solidarity across other social boundaries. Significant is that this resistance is based on invoking a shared racialized identity. The final 'we' is used in a way that brings together, through awareness of shared oppression and disadvantage, two previously separate typologies. The same participant also mentioned the need for solidarity between migrant groups and the British working-class population, suggesting that solidarity between migrants and the British working class was imperative because they faced similar oppression:

There are two categories of people suffering, but because we don't talk to each other. The lower class British are suffering the same as we are, but they don't see it because of the media.

UK, Senegalese woman, 55 years old

We would like to suggest that such attitudes clearly draw on notions of solidarity, and express an attempt to identify a common oppressor, in this case the state, while drawing on a 'we', in this case including asylum-seekers and other migrants. However, there was also a general feeling in the groups that the hostile climate that exists towards asylum-seekers has had an effect on how migrants are perceived in the host society. The racist strategy of conflating disparate groups of people together was a recurring concern in the focus groups, and the boundaries of solidarity came up in the focus group discussions in a variety of manners, including for example the following questioning of the category 'immigrant':

So that this here that you were in on a while ago about generalization and so everyone is in the immigrant box independent of what country one comes from then you are an immigrant yes all immigrants so what do I have in common with a who comes from an African country more than that we have come to Sweden but we do not have much cultural or traditional commonality. So it is that what it is that what one has to ah work against it is this with not generalizing.

Because we are like we are individuals OK we have a part we who come from a country we have a part of things in common but even within

257

the same country one does not have almost exactly the same traditions like one has in [southern region of Sweden] you do not have up there in [northern region of Sweden].

Sweden, Kurdish woman

Here a discourse culture, tradition, as well as differences within national cultures (between northern and southern Swedes) are used to stress the differences between individual migrants. Comparing her own traditions and culture with those of 'Africans', she reproduces potent European historical meanings that ascribed difference to Africa and Africans (Gilroy 1993). This history is mirrored in some of the focus group descriptions of humiliation and racism as some participants tell of attempts to humiliate them by being named and called 'Negro' and 'Black'.

Joking was an important strategy for coping with prejudice and disempowerment, offering a way in which participants could (collectively) make fun of and subvert the negative meanings associated with, for example, the term 'immigrant'. As such, jokes could also be understood as the creation and enactment of solidarity; jokes both referenced shared positionality (and struggle), for example objectification in Swedish society, and rearticulated negative meanings with more positive ones (Gilroy 1987). Similar to the migration stories some participants described, where migration to the United States, Canada or England (in the case of Swedish participants) brought successful return on previous education, jokes can be understood as collective strategies used by migrants to *remind themselves and each other* that educational recognition, qualified employment and equal treatment are possible, and attainable, goals.

### Conclusion

We believe that the material discussed here is illustrative of the diversity of strategies employed by 'migrants' not only to rationalize the discrimination and prejudice they encounter, but, more than this, ultimately to challenge the existing (unequal) power relations. We would like to support Gamson's suggestion that it is frequently difficult for individuals to identify the structural origins of discrimination and inequality, and that prejudiced individuals offer a clearer opponent to struggle against than, for example, seemingly abstract social structures and processes. Resisting racist and prejudiced behaviour on an individualized level is what Gamson refers to as a personalization of responsibility (1992: 34), and such a strategy was very often in evidence in the focus group discussions. Of course, we are not suggesting that strategies operative at an individualized, face-to-face level do not draw on notions of collective identity and collective action; as is illustrated by the material above sometimes even the most seemingly individualized response to discrimination draws on notions of solidarity. The discursive construction of a group's boundaries, for example between an 'us' and a 'them', was frequently evoked by the participants in the research, suggesting that (imagined) group boundaries were powerful ways of framing resistance.

Developing this notion we have also argued that the participants' reification of 'them' – for example 'the host country', or 'the state' – can be understood because the diffuse and elusive nature of discrimination can mean that those subject to discriminatory pressures can feel it is difficult to identify an agent responsible for their oppression. This argument also explains why we feel that many of the migrants' stories focused on interpersonal encounters, as they allow the identification of a clearly demarcated other. It is also apparent that many of the migrants who participated in the research project felt that there was a definite element of personal risk involved in outward shows of resistance. Following Scott (1985, 1990) we believe that this (real or perceived) risk partly explains why the strategies of resistance described by participants often took on a very symbolic, 'hidden' character. Developing this idea we suggest that the language of symbolic violence is an important part of how power and resistance are described *and* resisted. While people stress they are not violent, the strategies they use sometimes involve themes of physical retaliation – 'I talk him into the floor'. Also significant here is the fact that confrontation as a strategy of resistance is tied to an injustice frame which links emotions such as anger to individual, rather than institutional, objects of unjust acts. Examples of institutional discrimination often had aspects of 'hot emotion' and a sense of unjust use of power, but sometimes lacked a clear object of this perpetuation of unjust power. Instead the research found that injustice frames, and in particular the emotion of anger, are an important part of how individuals chose to react to experiences of discrimination. In short, we would like to suggest that just as racism, and indeed other forms of discriminatory behaviour based on prejudice, is experienced by migrants in a wide range of ways, then so it is resisted in multiple ways. Many racisms and many resistances are played out in a wide range of 'everyday' encounters.

## References

Banton, M. (1977) *The Idea of Race*. London: Tavistock.
Barker, C. (1999) 'Empowerment and Resistance: "Collective Effervescence" and Other

Accounts', in *Transforming Politics: Power and Resistance*, ed. P. Bagguley and J. Hearn. London: Macmillan.

Bourdieu, P. (1989) *Distinction: A Social Critique of the Judgement of Taste*. London: Routledge.

Browning, B. (1995) *Samba: Resistance in Motion*. Bloomington: Indiana University Press

Castells, M. (1997) *The Power of Identity*. Oxford: Blackwell.

Essed, P. (1991) *Understanding Everyday Racism: An Interdisciplinary Theory*. Newbury Park, CA, London, New Delhi: Sage.

Eyerman, R., and A. Jamison (1998) *Music and Social Movements: Mobilizing Traditions in the Twentieth Century*. New York: Cambridge University Press.

Foucault, M. (1970) *The Order of Things: An Archaeology of the Human Sciences*. London: Routledge.

— (1979) *Discipline and Punish*. London: Penguin.

Gamson, W. A. (1992) *Talking Politics*. Cambridge: Cambridge University Press.

Genovese, E. D. (1974) *Roll, Jordan, Roll: The World the Slaves Made*. New York: Pantheon.

Gilroy, P. (1987) *There Ain't No Black in the Union Jack*. London and New York: Routledge.

— (1993) *The Black Atlantic: Modernity and Double Consciousness*. Cambridge, MA: Harvard University Press.

Heath, D. (1994) 'The Politics of Appropriateness and Appropriation: Recontextualizing Women's Dance in Urban Senegal', *American Ethnologist* 21(1): 88–103.

Higginson, T. W., and J. M. McPherson (1998) *Black Rebellion: Five Slave Revolts*. Cambridge and New York: DaCapo Press.

James, C. L. R. (1989) *The Black Jacobins: Toussaint L'Ouverture and the San Domingo Revolution*, second edition. New York: Vintage Press.

Lamont, M. (2000) *The Dignity of Working Men: Morality and the Boundaries of Race, Class, and Immigration*. Cambridge, MA, and New York: Harvard University Press.

Malik, K. (1996) *The Meaning of Race*. Basingstoke: Macmillan.

Rabinow, P. (ed.) *The Foucault Reader*. London: Pantheon.

Rydgren, J. (2004) 'Explaining the Emergence of Radical Right-Wing Populist Parties: The Case of Denmark', *West European Politics* 27(3): 474–502.

Sawyer, L. (2002) 'Routings: "Race", African Diasporas and Swedish Belonging', *Transforming Anthropology* 11(1): 13–35.

Scott, J. (1985) *Weapons of the Weak: Everyday Forms of Peasant Resistance*. New Haven, CT, and London: Yale University Press.

— (1990) *Domination and the Arts of Resistance: Hidden Transcripts*. New Haven, CT, and London: Yale University Press.

Smitherman, G. (2000) *Talkin' That Talk: Language, Culture, and Education in African America*. London: Routledge.

Summers-Effler, E. (2002) 'The Micro Potential for Social Change: Emotion, Consciousness, and Social Movement Formation', *Sociological Theory* 20(1), March: 41–60.

Wade, P. (1999) 'Working Culture: Making Cultural Identities in Cali, Columbia', *Current Anthropology* 40(4), August–October: 449–72.

Wodak, R., R. De Cillia, M. Reisigl and K. Liebhart (1999) *The Discursive Construction of National Identity*. Edinburgh: Edinburgh University Press.

# 13 Transformations of 'Dutchness': From Happy Multiculturalism to the Crisis of Dutch Liberalism

## Marc de Leeuw and Sonja van Wichelen

Just after the installation of the newly elected cabinet members in March 2007, the Netherlands witnessed the beginning of the so-called double passport debate. It followed the vote of no confidence by Geert Wilders, the leader of the right-wing Party for Freedom (PVV), with respect to two of the elected cabinet members: Ahmed Aboutaleb, the Moroccan-Dutch Assistant Secretary for Social Affairs and Employment, and Nebahat Albayrak, the Turkish-Dutch Assistant Secretary for Justice – both members of the Dutch labour party (PvdA). Wilders' vote of no confidence concerned the fact that the two members carried double passports, which he regarded as conflicting with their political loyalty to the Netherlands. Besides the legal debate on multiple nationalities, it prompted intense public discussions on loyalty, integration and Dutch citizenship.

Taking its cues from this debate, our chapter articulates two things. First, it maps out Dutch political and public transformations of the past decade with respect to cultural diversity. As we will illustrate, the Netherlands has been transformed from a multicultural welfare state in the 1990s to a country with an identity crisis whose citizens have increasingly started to support extreme right parties. We attempt to illustrate this transformation through an investigation of different, but interlocking, explanatory levels, namely, the events of two political murders and the emotive interplay of local, national and global fears of the Muslim Other. We argue that these political and public developments have engendered a national mood of *ressentiment* against a 'politics from above'.

Our second aim in this chapter is to assess how these transformations correspond to processes and dynamics of Europeanization. With respect to immigration, naturalization and integration policies, the Netherlands has managed to become one of the strictest countries in Europe. Coupled with populist fears of uncontrollable European expansion (especially with respect to Turkey), costly bureaucracy, and the influx of immigrant workers, this has led the Netherlands, from being one of the founding members of Europe, to vote against the European constitution. Hence, instead of working towards a united Europe, new borders of national belonging are drawn which point towards the reconfiguration of symbolic space and a re-negotiation of the citizen-subject. What does this mean for the project of Europe? How do new definitions of Dutchness relate to new definitions of Europeanness?

Our preliminary contention is that the idea of Europe confronts the Netherlands with the ways in which it has specifically related to cultural Others. The Dutch discourse of liberalism and tolerance has prevented the Netherlands from truly addressing its history – in which Dutchness is also associated with complacency and complicity. The project of Europe, however, coupled with its local and global transformations of the past decade, has forced the country to articulate its distinct historical and cultural baggage with respect to cultural Others. But instead of working through these confrontations, it is moving toward a provincialization of national identity manifested in the strength and proliferation of New Right parties. More importantly, this paradigm shift to the Right is increasingly normalized by a strong discourse of a conservative Dutch liberalism, which reinforces not only the myth of Dutch tolerance but also recent discourses of 'Enlightenment-fundamentalism' inherent to Western liberal civilization paradigms.

### Murder, Politics and Drama Democracy

The Party of Freedom can be regarded as representing the New Right in the Netherlands.[1] From having no seats in parliament the party managed to obtain nine out of 150 seats in the November 2006 elections, a remarkable number for a new group. Its leader, Geert Wilders, is a controversial figure. Coming originally from the liberal right party (VVD), he left the party to start his own, arguing that the liberal right neglected the actual dangers of Islam. He is known for his notorious statements, such as 'the Netherlands is witnessing a tsunami of Islamization', and promoted his party in the election campaigns with the slogan 'less crime, fewer taxes and less Islam'. A decade ago these

---

1   We further assert that people who have voted specifically for Rita Verdonk can also be regarded as belonging to the New Right. Rita Verdonk represents the rightist voice within the liberal right party VVD. Adding her votes to Wilder's votes, we can speak of roughly one million people who have voted for a populist right.

kinds of statements would have been inconceivable. They would have been regarded as racist, xenophobic and utterly 'un-Dutch'. Nevertheless, more and more statements of this kind are appearing in the political and public sphere.

The debate over the loyalty of two newly elected politicians who carry two passports is a recent manifestation of such xenophobic tendencies. This is not to say that the debate on multiple nationalities is xenophobic as such. The topic can be discussed within a less politicized framework, for instance when raised in a general assembly addressing all politicians with multiple passports. This would have been a more legal debate around how issues of nationality are to be shaped in the Netherlands, and could have explored questions such as: what are the legal conditions of national citizenship? What are the practical consequences of having dual or triple nationalities? And what ideas of citizenship underlie Dutch conceptions of nationality? However, Wilders did not raise the issue of multiple nationalities in a legal or practical sense. He raised the issue with respect to two members who 'happen to be' the first Muslim cabinet members in Dutch history. Couched in the new rhetoric of 'loyalty', the resulting discussions illustrate how the Dutch desire new ways of defining Dutch citizenship. The question of loyalty therefore, is framed within mechanisms of inclusion and exclusion, and delineates those who are regarded as adequately 'loyal' against those who are still expected to prove their loyalty to the Netherlands. But what does being loyal to the Netherlands mean?

The recent debate on multiple nationalities in the Netherlands mirrors a larger discussion on Dutch identity that has been ongoing for the past decade. The 1990s witnessed new conservative voices in the political and public domain warning Dutch democracy of the failure or 'drama of multi-culturalism'.[2] However, these voices were largely mediated on the level of intellectual public debate and did not at that time represent common voices in everyday life. Instead, following the end of the Cold War, the 1990s were predominantly characterized by a distinct Dutch consensus model (or so-called *poldermodel*) in which the labour party (PvdA) and the liberal right (VVD) formed a pragmatic non-ideological coalition. In such a way, it seemed to be managing a form of 'Holland, Inc.' without eschewing the concept of a multicultural society for pragmatic and instrumental reasons. This model depoliticized politics and contributed towards the idea that politics operated on the level of the elite whose decisions resemble a form of ivory-tower 'administrative engineering' (Holmes 2000).[3]

2  We refer here to public opinions by the prominent rightist liberal and former EU commissioner Frits Bolkestein, and the academic and social commentator Paul Scheffer.
3  The idea of 'ivory-tower' politics (*achterkamertjes politiek*) was heavily critiqued by Pim Fortuyn and found tremendous support among people who lost touch with politics.

Global events such as the terrorist attacks on the World Trade Center in New York in 2001, the 2004 Madrid bombings, and the 2005 London bombings, have contributed to a general fear of radical Islam and have led to changes in views on multiculturalism in society.[4] But it was not until the occurrence of two local political murders that the views on cultural diversity within broader layers of Dutch society significantly altered.

The year 2002 witnessed the rise of populist leader Pim Fortuyn. The dandy, white, gay man represented for many people the voice that spoke the inevitable truth, namely that the Netherlands had been blinded to the back-lashes of multiculturalism and that it had to take stringent measures in order to control the damage. According to this view, the Dutch had been 'too tolerant' with respect to immigrants in the past and this tolerant attitude had turned out to be detrimental to the country. This rhetoric was supported by references to a range of social situations, such as immigrant criminality, run-down neigh-bourhoods, and so-called 'black schools' with poor performances, but most of all – and this was new – the threat of Islam represented by the one million Muslims in the country.[5] Fortuyn attended to these feelings of unhappiness and advocated a new form of doing politics which went against the politically correct and elite consensus politics. He received tremendous support and with his newly created party, List Pim Fortuyn (LPF), he was working towards the firm consolidation of his political ideas into formal politics.[6]

Shortly before the 2002 elections, however, Fortuyn was shot dead by the radical animal-rights activist Volkert van der Graaf. This political murder caused enormous upheaval in Dutch society. The mourning of the masses for the death of Pim Fortuyn resembled the way in which the British mourned the death of Diana, Princess of Wales. But people were also angry. The Left was blamed for the murder, connected to the ways in which mainstream political figures had demonized Fortuyn. He obtained the status of a hero, and only nine days after the murder, the national elections were held, and people voted *en masse* for the List Pim Fortuyn.[7] The party of the murdered

---

4   It is noteworthy that the bombings in Bali and Mumbai have not had the same impact on the Western imagination. The examples referred to in public discussion have all drawn on terror in the West and have not included terror in the non-West.

5   Before this time, the immigrant population in the Netherlands was rarely referred to as a Muslim population. Rather they were 'allochthonous' (*allochtoon*), which means that they were non-natives. See Shadid 2006 and Essed and Nikamo 2006 for a discussion on the emergence of the term 'allochthonous' in the Dutch realm. By the late 1990s, however, 'allochthonous' was increasingly being replaced by 'Muslim'. This term also marked a certain group of immigrants, namely Moroccans and Turks.

6   For more on Pim Fortuyn and the Fortuyn effect on the Netherlands see Pels 2003.

7   Akin to the events in Spain following the Madrid bombings, the proximity of the murder to the national elections turned the event into a fierce revolt of non-confidence in the former government.

Fortuyn obtained 27 seats in parliament out of a total of 150. Never in Dutch history had a newly formed party obtained so many seats. The consensus model sponsored by the former cabinet had been replaced by a conservative and populist cabinet. The following years marked the beginning of strict immigration policies and increasing debates on Islam in the Netherlands.

This tendency intensified with another political murder. In November 2004, the 'radical Islamic' Mohammed Bouyeri murdered the Dutch social critic and well-known filmmaker Theo van Gogh. The content of a letter that was stabbed into the chest of the director's body made it clear that the murder was intended to frighten the politician Ayaan Hirsi Ali, who was a new member of the liberal-right party and who had become a strong critic of Islam in the Netherlands. Two months before Van Gogh was murdered, Hirsi Ali and Van Gogh screened on national television the film *Submission Part One* which they had made together. This eleven-minute film, which was meant as an indictment of Islam and its relation to violence against women, caused much commotion among the Muslim community in the Netherlands, who found the film to be discrediting Islam.[8] The murder caused a wave of anti-Islamic resentment, polarization and social unrest within Dutch society.

## Aversion to the Muslim Other

Following the Van Gogh murder, global and national discourses often intervened in local situations and events – and vice versa. Civil commotions or disturbances involving Muslims in Amsterdam, for instance, often received national coverage in the media and reports were couched in frameworks of integration, failure of multiculturalism, clash of cultures and terrorism. The intervention of national media and politics in local multicultural contexts has led to the making of symbolic spaces. Hence, plans to build a mosque or the problems of a 'black school' are conflated with national and global issues – turning them into pawns in global debates on 'civilizations' or 'the war on terror'.

A widely mediatized event reflecting this sudden obsession with Muslim problems in particular, and the state of 'drama-democracy' (Elchardus 2004) in general, was the so-called 'handshake' incident. In 2004, the Minister for Integration and Immigration, and prominent representative of the liberal right, Rita Verdonk, organized a meeting in Soesterberg with several imams and as she approached one of them, she stuck out her hand to shake the hand of Imam Ahmad Salam. To this gesture he replied, 'With all due respect but

8   For an analysis of the film and the politics of Ayaan Hirsi Ali, see De Leeuw and Van Wichelen 2005.

I cannot give you my hand.' The minister acted half-shocked and immediately retorted in a harsh tone, 'So, then we have a lot to talk about.' Although all the other imams did shake hands with the minister, this one moment was turned into a public spectacle and became a potent symbol to illustrate that 'Muslim culture' could not be compatible with Dutch culture. Considering 'their' refusal to shake 'our' hands, Muslims, apparently, were not willing to adapt to the Dutch culture in which 'we' shake hands with each other. This symbolic politics, which divides 'our' cultural habits from Muslim habits, acts *as though* a handshake were a clear attribute of being Dutch.

Local, national and global discourses have fuelled feelings of insecurity and have spurred racist sentiments. These racist sentiments have long been there, but overt racism was eschewed in mainstream Dutch society. As many Dutch historians have pointed out, Holland was known for its culture of tolerance.[9] The construction of tolerance as a typical characteristic of Dutch national identity prevented some of the overt racism in society. Hence, it was generally inappropriate to openly complain about Moroccans or Turks. This does not mean that racism was non-existent. On the contrary, structural 'everyday racism' (Essed 1984) was ubiquitously present. It was present across all social strata of Dutch society and institutionalized in various ways. In such a way, tolerance seemed like a meagre replacement for recognition. Following Asad (2003), however, we would further argue that even recognition could not fully account for the representation of cultural others in the imagination of the Netherlands: 'It is also a matter of embodied memories and practices that are articulated by traditions, and of political institutions through which these traditions can be fully represented' (Asad 2003: 178).[10] An acknowledgment of everyday racism could contribute to this. Nonetheless, because her work challenged the Dutch idea of tolerance by asserting that racism was a structural feature in Dutch history and society, Essed's work on everyday racism caused commotion within academic circles working on multiculturalism in the Netherlands (Prins 2004). This illustrates the pervasiveness and dominant discourse of tolerance in the Netherlands.

With the conflation of global discourses of terrorism with Islam, immigrants suddenly became Muslims and the 'Muslim danger' permitted the open manifestation of anti-immigrant sentiments.[11] Highly diverse groups were

9  See for instance Berkvens-Stevelinck and Israel (1997) and also Huizinga (1935).
10 At a later stage in writing this chapter we came across an article by Peter van der Veer who articulates a similar argument. See Van der Veer 2006.
11 According to Shadid (2006), immigrants were already being referred to as Muslims in the 1990s. However, we argue that this was solely within intellectual discourse. It was not until the rise of Fortuyn and the global and national violence that ordinary people started to talk about Muslims as a problematic group in the Netherlands.

monolithically redefined as 'Muslims' and the end of the 'consensus model' was celebrated as the end of multiculturalism and the revival of Dutch norms and values. Through anti-Muslim statements by public figures such as Pim Fortuyn, Theo van Gogh and Rita Verdonk, people had found legitimate grounds for their xenophobic sentiments. These developments also reflected dynamics between the elite and the wider population. Earlier critiques by intellectuals such as the liberal rightist Frits Bolkestein or the sociologist Paul Scheffer did not have widespread appeal. The simple rhetoric provided by Fortuyn, Van Gogh and Verdonk enabled people to articulate their feelings of insecurity towards immigrants – packaged in an anti-Islamic idiom. In such a way, they could (finally) ventilate their fears of cultural Others without being afraid of others calling them racist, intolerant or indecent.

The turn from covert racism to the proliferation of overt anti-Islamic sentiments created a backlash in the idea of Dutch tolerance with respect to multiculturalism. The social critic Sjoerd de Jong (2005) refers in this respect to the manifestation of something which he called a 'regret-revenge' discourse (*spijtwraak*). With this term he aims to explain how the Dutch are regretting their tolerant attitudes towards immigrants in the past and are taking revenge on their earlier positions. We could define the 'regret-revenge' attitude as representing a discourse of *ressentiment* (Brown 1995). In overcoming feelings of powerlessness, alienation or fragmentation, *ressentiment* refers to the production of rage or righteousness, the production of a culprit, and the production of a site of revenge. In the new climate of *ressentiment*, socio-economic and political clarifications with respect to migration, colonialism and racism were declared politically incorrect and any reference to these explanatory factors became taboo in the public sphere.

This also relates to modes of Dutch self-victimization as articulated by the sociologists Essed and Nikamo (2006). In their well-researched article on scholarship and public policy about immigrants and minorities in the Netherlands, Essed and Nikamo point to the deplorable state of critical research in relation to race, ethnic and migration studies in the country. They argue that throughout the 1980s minority research in the Netherlands mostly problematized ethnic minorities while structurally silencing influences of racism, colonial history, and Dutch cultural superiority (Essed and Nikamo 2006: 285). They observe within the academic field strong backlashes against discourses of anti-racism, leading some of the researchers to stop using the term 'racism' in their work. In such a way, researchers act like 'prisoners of tolerance' who are pleading 'guilt' (Essed and Nikamo 2006: 303). This attitude has fostered a climate of scrutiny and aggression against anti-racist work and advocacy. As the emergence of the 'regret-revenge' paradigm in contemporary politics and public discourse suggests, this mood of self-victimization not only emerges in scholarly discourse, but also appears in popular public discourse and is linked to an 'anti-political correctness' attitude. These old but newly defined sentiments bring new meanings to the ways in which Dutch identity and Dutch citizenship are imagined and desired.

In turn, *ressentiment* also exists on the part of immigrants. A recent qualitative study by the political scientists Buijs, Demant and Hamdi (2006) has revealed that immigrants, especially from the younger generation – who have assimilated well in Dutch society, are well educated and have invested greatly in their future – feel excluded and more vulnerable when confronted with discrimination or when they realize that, compared to Dutch peers, they still lag behind. This is what Buijs, Demant and Hamdi refer to as the 'integration-paradox' (2006: 202). Feelings of powerlessness are replaced by *ressentiment* and channelled in two possible directions, one of defeat and pessimism and one of 'revenge', for instance through religious radicalism.

## The Netherlands in Europe

On 1 June 2005, six days after the French voted against the European constitution, the Netherlands also voted in the negative, by two-thirds to one-third.[12] The Dutch 'no' represented a widely shared distrust towards European politics. The French vote was important in facilitating the idea for the Netherlands that they were not alone in their scepticism towards Europe.[13] It was through the French 'no' that the Dutch could defy the idea that only 'nationalists' opposed the constitution. Communicated in both leftist and rightist factions in Dutch public, the 'no' represented a clear public move against the formation of a European democracy as formulated by the constitution. More accurately, it reflected Dutch moods projected onto the European project.

Much of the argument from the Left concerned people's dissatisfaction with the euro, the bureaucracy produced by 'Brussels' and the threat that EU policies could undermine the Dutch social-welfare structure and labour laws. On the Right, central issues included the belief that supporting Europe will lead to more immigration, that Europe – in particular the possible inclusion of Turkey – threatens Dutch liberal values, and, more generally, that the Netherlands will lose sovereignty and national identity when integrated within

12 The precise percentages were 61.6% for the Netherlands and 54.7% for France.
13 It was also through the French 'no' that the Dutch could defy the idea that only 'nationalists' opposed the constitution. Centrists and left-wingers could vote against it without finding themselves in company they would normally avoid.

a larger idea of Europe. The rejection of establishment politics, in which elites in 'Brussels' intervene in national issues, and the perception that the EU suffers from a democratic deficit are what the Far Left and Far Right shared in rejecting the constitution. Mainstream politicians were aware of this and that is why for the first time in Dutch history a national referendum was held.[14] This shared *ressentiment* against elite politics bore reference to Pim Fortuyn's anti-establishment legacy, the idea that Europe is a conceptualization of the European elite and that ordinary people are not included in the decision-making process.

The aversion of Fortuyn's followers to consensus politics, elitist decision-making power, and increasing bureaucracy in the Netherlands was in this way successfully projected onto the idea of Europe. Although the occurrence of the referendum reflected the willingness of the Dutch political elite to succumb to pressures for direct democracy of the general population, it could not convince this same public of the virtues in shaping the idea of Europe through the acceptance of the constitution.

Underlying the anti-establishment attitude is the belief that 'ordinary people' feel that they are not taken seriously by the political elite – both in the Netherlands and in Europe. These feelings have often been supported by the so-called 'displacement' narratives of 'autochthonous' or native Dutch. In this account, people feel they have the right to complain when their neighbourhoods are changing through the arrival of immigrants. Nonetheless, instead of setting these narratives against the background of socio-economic contexts, they are framed in terms of clashes of culture and in this way reinforce the idea that the arrival of immigrants and in particular Muslim immigrants will only lead to the marginalization of Dutch culture. By Fortuynists and followers of the New Right, these discourses of displacement were conveniently conflated with fear of Islamization.

Although anti-establishment rhetoric also intervened in the debates on the inclusion of Turkey in the European Union, the prevailing arguments against the inclusion were based on underlying assumptions that Islam or a Muslim country does not belong in Europe and that Turkey's politics do not reflect the freedom of speech inherent in principles of liberalism and European enlightenment.

Christian-democratic and liberal discourses in the Netherlands argue that the history of Europe does not include histories of Islam. Rather, as the Prime

14 It is important to note that the referendum as a political tool did not exist in the Dutch political system. Apart from local referenda, Dutch political elites have always shunned popular sovereignty in national politics. In their attempts to fill the gap between the political elite and the 'common people' they allowed a direct application of the popular vote.

Minister of the Netherlands, Jan-Peter Balkenende, repeatedly advocated, the European constitution should make reference to its Judaeo-Christian traditions. Balkenende, however, did not receive much support in parliament and the proposal was rejected. The rejection reflected a strong secularist stance in Dutch politics embedded in Dutch liberalism. This secularist discourse, however, should not be understood as entirely without Christian foundations. As Talal Asad argued, 'in the contemporary European suspicion of Turkey, Christian history, enshrined in the tradition of international law is being reinvoked in secular language as the foundation of an ancient identity' (2003: 164). Rather, the rejection by parliament should be understood in light of the Enlightenment tradition which, in retrospect, is taken as quasi-ideological anti-religion.

The rejection of Turkey and the rejection of the European constitution derive from a broader sentiment that we are 'losing our grip' on our country. This is coupled with an anxiety about Islamism, a political threat that has become real since the murder of Van Gogh. EU enlargement further reinforces these anxieties, which are not based only on economic, political or bureaucratic losses of national sovereignty but especially concern losses of symbolic territories of one's own 'society' or 'community'. As such, the idea of a supranation in the guise of the EU fosters a desire to regain control. This control is projected onto the wish to recuperate a clear, singular idea of one's national identity. This Dutchness is then what immigrants, refugees and, in particular, Muslims are expected to assimilate to.

The idea that cultural Others need to become like us is reflected on the European level: 'we' – the Western and Northern European countries (the Scandinavian model in Delanty's terms) – expect new countries from middle and Eastern Europe to become 'like us'. First they are expected to implement existing European rules, laws and treaties. Then 'we' decide whether they can join 'us'. In relation to Turkey this attitude pre-determines the debate: is Turkey 'like us' or 'enough like us' in order for it to be 'tolerable' in Europe? Or will this never happen?[15] While with respect to Eastern Europe, the dividing line was mainly formulated in terms of corruption, the juridical system, or economic equality (for example the fear of the 'Polish plumber'), in the case of Turkey, the dividing line was cast in terms of the 'clash of civilizations'. The wish to exclude Turkey because Muslims cannot be part of Europe conveys the message to Turks and other migrants with an Islamic background that they can never really belong to a Dutch 'us'.

15 Here, local and European perspectives collide: the perspective on Turkey in Western Europe is shaped by 'our' perceptions of Turkish migrants who came twenty years ago from Anatolia.

This also became clear in the suspicion vented towards Turkey's unwillingness to acknowledge the 'Armenian genocide'. Arguments against the participation of Turkey in Europe on these grounds are based on the idea that Turkey threatens the principles of our liberal democracy. The New Right discourse adds to this that they will never be ready because their religious culture is incommensurable with our European culture. The unwillingness of Turkey to acknowledge the 'Armenian genocide' is also played out in internal politics in which Turkish-Dutch politicians (primarily from the Labour party) were forced to voice their position with regard to this sensitive issue. As such, politicians who did not acknowledge the genocide were morally forced to resign from their party. Irrespective of the actual Armenian question, which is a serious concern, the way in which certain Dutch politicians demanded clarification from their 'own' Turks betrays double standards in relation to the credentials of politicians. As such, Muslim politicians are scrutinized in a way that Dutch politicians are not. While Dutch politicians are de-essentialized from their national soil and do not necessarily have to account for their political opinions through Dutchness, Turkish-Dutch politicians will always be connected with and essentialized to their Turkish origins. This also illustrates to what extent the Dutch are merely 'tolerating' the participation of Turks in politics and do not see or acknowledge Turkish participation as part of *Dutch* politics. Turkish politicians, like any other immigrant or Muslim Other, are tolerated on the basis that they play by Dutch liberal rules. That is as much Dutch as one can become. Breaking these rules puts an end to Dutch tolerance.

### Liberalism, Tolerance, Civilization

To understand the recent transformations of Dutchness it is crucial to look at Dutch liberalism.[16] The 1960s witnessed a profound change in the socio-political make-up of the country. It marked the beginning of the de-pillarization process, replacing separate socio-religious systems with systems of welfare and consumption. Not much later, this process was accompanied by the defining liberalist period of the 1970s in which the Dutch freed themselves from the oppression of religion, in which emancipation movements freed women from patriarchal oppression, the gay movement

16 We are aware that 'Dutchness', with respect to tolerance and liberalism, needs an extensive historical analysis which we are unable to provide within the context of this short chapter. However, for excellent historical studies on these matters see Galema, Henkes and Te Velde (1993), Huizinga (1935), Berkvens-Stevelinck and Israel (1994), and the edited volumes by Groenveld and Wintle (1994) and Gijswijk-Hofstra (1989).

freed homosexuals, and the younger generation freed themselves from parental and state control. Political and activist moods characterized the struggle for 'liberal Holland'.

The paradigm of liberalism in the Dutch context, however, is paradoxical. On the one hand, it refers to a socio-cultural liberalism of the 'liberated' youth of the 1960s, namely leftist political activism, sexual freedom, struggle for abortion, and acceptance of homosexuality. On the other hand, it refers to an economic liberalism of the liberal right, embodied in the liberal right party VVD, whose main interest revolves around tax reduction, small governance, and support for the business community and the military. What the two perspectives have in common is a strong emphasis on individual rights and autonomy. In contemporary Dutch politics, these two discourses seemed to have merged. The liberal left paradigm of anti-racism and multiculturalism, which was seen as 'politically correct', is being replaced by a new political correctness, namely, the so-called freedom-of-speech discourse. This freedom of speech, however, did not necessarily refer to intellectual freedom or the right to critique the state, which were the terms on which this right was based on. Instead, in the politicized climate following the murder of Van Gogh, this freedom of speech was extended to include the 'right to insult'.[17] In such a way this new mode of 'freedom' allowed for mocking, ridiculing, insulting and offending – mostly with respect to Muslims who, according to some prominent public figures, were too sensitive and were not able to accept critique.

Besides this paradigmatic shift of political correctness, new populist liberalism discovered feminism, gay culture and secularism as the ultimate signs of an enlightened western civilization. Hence, 'Dutchness', or a successful integration into Dutch society, was measured in terms of whether immigrants (read: Muslims) accepted 'our' women's emancipation, 'our' homosexuals, and 'our' critical ways of approaching religion. In such a way, feminism, homosexuality and secularism were embraced as symbols of Dutch tolerance that – apparently – divided 'us' from 'them'. These new recognitions or incorporations met with support from specific feminist and gay groups as well as from atheist intellectuals. Hence, these groups and individuals were also found to be complicit in conveying civilizational rhetoric. This is illustrated for instance by the dominant discourse of mainstream feminism to 'save' Muslim women from Islamic oppression and the strong discourse in the Dutch gay community of being threatened by Islamic youth groups who

---

17 This is inextricably linked to the figure of Van Gogh, who was notorious for insulting Muslims and Jews, for instance.

are purportedly resorting to homophobic violence.

In sum, the former Left and socio-cultural liberalism, represented by artists, writers, columnists, academics and activists, merged with a rightist economic liberalism represented by people working in business, marketing and property. They both rejected the social-democratic politics of multiculturalism which had given minorities group rights and, thus, supported the supposedly culturally backward and anti-individualist tradition of these groups. In particular, they critiqued the ways in which women, sexuality and freedom of speech were suppressed in these cultures. Especially in the past decade, these different groups have found each other in their anti-Islamic attitudes. Their permanent presence in the media made it easy for broader parts of the population to legitimize the by now 'normalized' anti-Islamic and racist statements. For the liberal right party (VVD) 'Islam' symbolized failed integration, lack of social participation, lack of language skills and anti-individualism. Instead of looking separately at these problems in their situatedness, the problems were framed in a culturalist and civilizational discourse: Islam was fundamentally anti-modernistic, backward, and not compatible with universal values of the Enlightenment philosophy and tradition in the Netherlands.

This new civilizational project conflates the 'clash of civilizations' with a so-called 'realist' approach to the problems of multiculturalism. Leftist and rightist forms of liberalism merged into a 'new realism' (Prins 2004). This new realism represented the new paradigm in the Netherlands with respect to multiculturalism, namely that it had failed and that Islam was a serious threat to Dutch society. This discourse of 'new realism' in society generated debates about 'Dutchness' or the Dutch *Leitkultur*.

The most illustrative example of the confirmation of Dutchness is the film *Naar Nederland*, made by the Department of Justice under the supervision of the liberal right minister Rita Verdonk. The film is part of the civic integration course (*inburgeringscursus*) meant to introduce 'newcomers' to Dutch history and culture. Since January 2007 it is compulsory that immigrants pass the exam accompanying this course *before* coming to the Netherlands. Note, however, that the exam is only obligatory for people from particular countries, primarily from the non-West. People from Western countries such as the EU countries or from Australia, Canada, or the US are exempted. So too are countries such as Japan which are perceived by the department of Immigration and Integration as westernized. In this film, Dutchness is defined in ways that not only exclude cultural Others but that demands of its 'newcomers' a total loyalty to Dutch culture through cultural assimilation. With this exam, the liberal Right has been able to push the greater part of the political majority towards endorsing forms of integration codes in the direction demanded by the extreme right.

Symbolic politics (such as the handshake incident), symbolic spaces (such as the place and height of minarets), and symbolic loyalties (such as the multiple nationalities of cabinet members) represent anxieties about Dutch identity. Insecurity about identity is projected onto these symbolic levels which mark boundaries between us and them. They illustrate that rather than accepting difference, 'the Dutch' expect cultural Others to assimilate to 'our' cultural practices, thus, shake hands with us, build minarets that stay under the height of 'our' churches and – please – only one passport! Only then can immigrants 'successfully' integrate in Dutch society.

Delanty's concept of Europe as a 'regulative idea' (2003) closely resembles the way in which 'Dutchness' is imagined: to define oneself one needs to clarify what the Other is. Although the Dutch were formerly proud to have a 'weak' national identity (Pels 2005), the current reinvention of Dutch norms and values, initiated by the Christian-democratic Prime Minister Balkenende, and turned into a civilization-discourse by the liberal right, marks a return to a desire for a 'strong' or 'thick' national identity. Hence, it was *ressentiment* or the 'regret-revenge' discourse (*spijtwraak*) that turned the 'weak' or 'soft' nationalism, manifested by carnivalesque celebrations of national 'events' such as Queensday or soccer, to a stronger, more bitter, nationalism based on civilizational discourse. As mentioned earlier, the question *what is Dutch?* has – in a awkward manner – turned the upholding of gay rights, the act of insulting minorities, abhorrence of female genital mutilation and honour killings, and in particular the celebration of Dutch women's emancipation into a liberalist civilizational discourse. As such, the 'freedom of speech', homosexuality, and sexually liberated women have suddenly become quasi-universal symbols of the free, liberal world that the 'Dutch' are defending.

The rejection of the European constitution was not 'just' a vote against the implementation of a juridical treaty but should be seen as a symptomatic gesture symbolizing anxiety about a future loss of sovereignty. The wish to reaffirm Dutchness and the demand that migrants show a greater effort to adapt to Dutch norms and values creates a paradox when – at the same time – the prime minister declares that we should be proud of being Europeans. As such, the current Dutch project seems to oppose the current European project. The call for more intervention in immigration and the integration of these migrant communities and the overall wish to strengthen 'Dutch' dominant culture is hampered when 'Brussels' – simultaneously – starts intervening in our national politics. Hence, the geopolitical extensions of the enlarged 'Europe' do not only confront the Netherlands with a loss of international influence but also with a supra-national power that may or may not overrule political decisions on the level of the nation-state. Whereas in economic or financial matters, the Netherlands is not necessarily opposed to further collaboration, the question of immigration, illegal workers and asylum-seekers produces a strong desire to keep national sovereignty on these matters intact. This means that a European overruling in this field is particularly painful, for instance, when Europe asks the Netherlands to adjust and conform to European agreements.[18]

The historian James Kennedy (2005) aptly summarized the Dutch as having developed a kind of overly self-satisfied collective identity which combined a moral arrogance with actual progressive processes of the social-welfare state. In such a way, the Netherlands has not yet actively dealt with its past. As the sociologist Ron Eyerman so eloquently illustrates in his new work on Dutchness and cultural trauma (2008), the Dutch still do not acknowledge their complicity in their shared colonial past, in the deportation of Jews during the Second World War, and the drama by the Dutch battalion of the United Nations (Dutchbat) in Srebrenica where hundreds of Muslim men were killed under their supervision. Instead, the myth of tolerance, Anne Frank and political neutrality remained strongly present.[19]

This complacency in deploying tolerance discourse to legitimize neutrality or innocence corresponds to observations by the political scientist Wendy Brown, who argued that liberal tolerance discourse, comparable to the Dutch discourse outlined above, runs the risk of sneaking liberalism into a civilizational discourse (2006: 8). In such a way, tolerance becomes a form of governmentality that 'regulates the presence of Other both inside and outside the liberal democratic nation-state, and often it forms a circuit between them that legitimates the most illiberal actions of the state by means of a term consummately associated with liberalism' (Brown 2006: 8). The Dutch are not ready to see themselves as perpetrators. The greatest humiliation to a community that sees itself in complacent rather than complicit ways is the charge of being co-responsible for a genocide (as apparent in the Srebrenica drama), a war crime considered utterly immoral by the West. Rather than confronting ourselves with this humiliation, moral arrogance is projected onto cultural Others and turned into civilizational discourse.

---

18 This is clearly illustrated by the European Court's ruling in January 2007 that the Netherlands should change its asylum procedure on the basis of the so-called 'Salah Sheekh arrest'. The court condemned the Netherlands for violating the prohibition on torture and inhumane punishments. In May 2007, the court refused a rehearing requested by the Dutch.
19 See also Buruma 2006.

As argued by several scholars (Asad 2003; Balibar 2003), Europe's identity crisis lies within Europe and not with the conflict that it has with migrant Others. We need the migrant Other to distract us from our own crisis. This is also what is happening to the Netherlands on the level of the nation-state. In prevailing over feelings of powerlessness, alienation or fragmentation, *ressentiment* of the Dutch subject in this context refers to a rage at the way liberalism is being threatened by Islam and also at the manner in which our own tolerance has been guilty of generating this threat. While the production of a culprit relates to immigrants in general and Muslims in particular, the production of a site of revenge includes for instance the new ultra-strict immigration policies. By attending to this *ressentiment*, and insisting that the problem lies with 'them' not with 'us', the Dutch do not have to confront themselves with their own identity problems that concern the ways in which they relate to their pasts and their future. This prevents us from focusing on the ways in which we can imagine Europe in more constructive ways that allow for 'multiple ways of life' to proliferate (Asad 2003: 180). With respect to the Dutch nation-state, it also prevents us from turning a national *ressentiment* into a mode of working through of Dutch complacencies, complicities and sufferings.

## Concluding Remarks

The 2006 elections in the Netherlands seemed to denote a break with conservative and Islamophobic tendencies of the past decade. Although not winning the majority of the votes, the Labour party succeeded in recovering their position in the government. Together with the Christian-democrats (who lost considerably but still came out as the biggest party) and a small, more conservative Christian party, they changed the political course significantly. Muslim members joined the cabinet, a law was passed that enabled the legalization of illegal immigrants, and the new Minister of Integration announced that she would not ban the burqa from the public sphere. The call for assimilation practices was more or less replaced by socio-economic measures to uplift and improve impoverished neighbourhoods and schools. The new cabinet conveys stability and does not necessarily have particular interests in antagonizing or polarizing public matters. Denouncing assimilationist demands from the previous cabinet, and especially the previous Integration Minister Rita Verdonk, these changes seemed a positive and optimistic beginning.

However, as this chapter has attempted to illustrate, many structures underlying Dutch anxieties and Islamophobia will not be resolved by a change of government. Deeper structures are at stake that concern Dutch liberalism and its idea of tolerance, which in contemporary times has been turned into a civilizational discourse. Dutch liberalism is in crisis. As represented in national debates on religious freedom or double nationalities, but also in European debates such as the Dutch rejection of the European constitution and the negative stance towards Turkey joining the EU, the Dutch feel stuck between liberalism's promises of equality and promises of freedom. While happy multiculturalism attended to the commitment to freedom, namely the freedom of culture and religion to proliferate side by side in a liberal framework, the new discourse of assimilation shifts the commitment to freedom towards a commitment to equality, thereby demanding that cultural Others adjust to the same (universal) standards and norms of Dutchness or Europeanness.

However, the debate on multiple loyalties, posed at the start of this chapter, illustrates that an immigrant or Muslim's assimilation, adaptation and hard work is apparently not enough. The vote of no confidence against the two newly elected cabinet members, and the public debate following this occurrence, exemplify the fact that in the current climate immigrants, and especially Muslims, cannot claim Dutchness. In such a way, migrant voices and their quest for full citizenship are still stuck between the idiom of Dutch toleration and a new idiom in which the Netherlands questions migrants' loyalty and integrity. Although the New Right is the visible force that is initiating these new trends of inclusion and exclusion, it is equally crucial to acknowledge the invisible but more pervasive force within Dutch liberalism that is supportive of similar restrictive measures.

## References

Asad, T. (2003) *Formations of the Secular: Christianity, Islam, Modernity*. Stanford, CA: Stanford University Press.

Balibar, E. (2003) 'Europe, An "Unimagined" Frontier of Democracy', *Diacritics* 33(3–4): 36–44.

Berkvens-Stevelinck, C., and J. Israel (eds) (1997) *The Emergence of Tolerance in the Dutch Republic*. Leiden: Brill.

Brown, W. (1995) *States of Injury: Power and Freedom in Late Modernity*. Princeton, NJ: Princeton University Press.

— (2006) *Regulating Aversion: Tolerance in the Age of Identity and Empire*. Princeton, NJ: Princeton University Press.

Buijs, F., F. Demant and A. Hamdi (2006) *Strijders van eigen bodem. Radicale en democratische moslims in Nederland*. Amsterdam: Amsterdam University Press.

Buruma, I. (2006) *Dood van een Gezonde Roker*. Amsterdam: Atlas.

De Jong, S. (2005) *De Spijtwraak. Hoe Nederland afrekent met zichzelf*. Amsterdam:

Prometheus/NRC.

Delanty, G. (2003) 'The Making of a Post-Western Europe: A Civilizational Analysis', *Thesis Eleven* 72(8): 8–25.

De Leeuw, M., and S. van Wichelen (2005) '"Please, Go Wake Up": Submission, Hirsi Ali, and the "War on Terror" in the Netherlands', *Feminist Media Studies* 5(3): 325–40.

Elchardus, M. (2004) *De Dramademocratie*. Tielt: Lannoo.

Essed, P. (1984) *Alledaags racisme*. Amsterdam: Feministische Uitgeverij Sara.

—, and K. Nikamo (2006) 'Designs and (Co)Incidents: Cultures of Scholarship and Public Policy on Immigrants/Minorities in the Netherlands', *International Journal of Comparative Sociology* 47(3–4): 281–312.

Eyerman, R. (2008) *The Assassination of Theo van Gogh: From Social Drama to Cultural Trauma*. Durham, NC: Duke University Press.

Galema, A., B. Henkes, and H. Te Velde (1993) *Images of the Nation: Different Meanings of Dutchness 1870–1940*. Amsterdam: Rodopi.

Gijswijt-Hofstra, M. (ed.) (1989) *Een schijn van verdraagzaamheid. Afwijking en tolerantie in Nederland van de zestiende eeuw tot heden*. Hilversum: Verloren.

Groenveld, S., and M. Wintle (eds) (1994) *Under the Sign of Liberalism: Varieties of Liberalism in Past and Present*. Zutphen: Walburg Pers.

Holmes, D. R. (2000) *Integral Europe: Fastcapitalism, Multiculturalism, Neofascism*. Princeton, NJ: Princeton University Press.

Huizinga, J. (1935) *Nederlands Geestesmerk*. Leiden: Sijthof.

Kennedy, J. (2005) *De deugden van een gidsland: Bburgerschap en democratie in Nederland*. Amsterdam: Bakker.

Koopmans, R. (2007) 'Sta iedereen dubbele nationaliteit toe, maar wijs op de nadelen en let op conflicten', *NRC Handelsblad*, 10 March.

Pels, D. (2003) *De geest van Pim: het gedachtegoed van een politieke dandy*. Amsterdam: Anthos.

— (2005) *Een zwak voor Nederland. Ideeën voor een nieuwe politiek*. Amsterdam: Anthos.

Phillips, A. (1993) *Democracy and Difference*. Cambridge: Polity Press.

Prins, B. (2004) *Voorbij de Onschuld: Het debat over integratie in Nederland*. Van Gennep: Amsterdam.

Shadid, W. A. (2006) 'Public Debates over Islam and the Awareness of Muslim Identity in the Netherlands', *European Education* 38(2): 10–22.

Van der Veer, P. (2006) 'Pim Fortuyn, Theo van Gogh, and the Politics of Tolerance in the Netherlands', *Public Culture* 18(1): 111–24.

# 14   Competent vs. Incompetent Students: Polarization and Social Closure in Madrid Schools

## Luisa Martín Rojo

However, the so-called marginalized, who are none other than the oppressed, were never *outside*. They were always *inside*. Inside the structure that turns them into 'beings for others'. Their solution, then, does not lie in 'integrating' them, 'incorporating' them into this structure that oppresses them, but rather in transforming it so that they can become 'beings for themselves'.

Freire 1970: 80

## An Ethnographic Perspective

In the last fifteen years, the Autonomous Region of Madrid, previously a traditional destination for immigration from other Spanish communities, has become one of the preferred destinations for workers coming from other countries, principally (and in this order) from Ecuador, Colombia, Romania, Peru, Morocco, Bolivia, China and the Dominican Republic. According to data from the City Council ('Ayuntamiento') of Madrid, students from migrant backgrounds represent about 15% of the total school population, a figure that in the city centre reaches 34% (see the Plan Madrid de Convivencia Social e Intercultural [Madrid Plan for Social and Intercultural Co-existence] 2005).

The analysis of ideologies presented in this article is supported by data collected during two research studies carried out in schools of the Autonomous Region of Madrid ('Comunidad de Madrid'),[1] which observed

---

1   These studies are: 'Cultural and Linguistic Diversity: A Proposal of Strategies and Resources for Education' (ref. no. 06/0122/2000), financed by the Council of Education and Science of the Community of Madrid: Humanities and Social Sciences Projects, and *Socio-pragmatic Analysis of*

how ideologies affect classroom management and the processes of teaching and learning. An answer to how to address diversity in the classroom appears to be related to correlative questions, in particular, what is considered to be legitimate knowledge, who is considered to be a 'normal' student and a 'good' or 'competent' student, and what is the legitimate language of exchange. Thus, for example, if the only language considered to be legitimate is the local variety, measures will be put in place to ensure and extend its usage, while other languages and dialects will not be integrated into academic life. And the same thing happens with cultural diversity (norms, values and contents included in the curricula).

The method chosen for both investigations was sociolinguistic ethnography, seeking to find out what use the academic community makes of linguistic and cultural resources, what meanings these have for students and teachers (whether they are considered keys or drawbacks to academic success; whether they are emblems in the construction of identities; whether they are seen as characteristics of membership, an asset or deficit). Likewise, the research project tried to examine how these uses impact on the processes of teaching and learning, relations of inclusion and exclusion, and the negotiation of status in terms of 'good' and 'bad' students. In reflecting on the observed interactions, we analysed how in each and every one of them a social, cultural and linguistic order is reproduced and constructed. Such ethnography – reinforced by a critical analysis of discourse in the study of social representations in interactions and in interviews – added a more nuanced and critical perspective. Critical studies of discourse seek to capture the relation between discursive practices and the social and institutional order.

## Knowledge and Ideology

I was led to explore the underlying ideologies in classrooms by the abundant body of knowledge that has been produced and put into play concerning school, immigration, learning, competence, knowledge, curriculum and the objectives of teaching, all of which seem to be connected and even justify the way diversity is treated. In the study of this production of knowledge, I realized that ideologies are precisely the element that seems to link this constellation of knowledge. Ideologies also explain the interrelation among this body of knowledge and a particular social order in which the different social sectors occupy a particular position.

*Intercultural Communication in Educational Practices: Toward Integration in the Classroom* (BFF 2003-04830), within the National Plan of I+D+1 (2000–2003) of the Ministry of Science and Technology of Spain.

By the term 'ideology' I refer to a system of social representations, related to class/gender/social and national groups and their interests, which plays a role in the legitimation/delegitimation (and production) of the social order. In understanding that this is about a system of representations I incorporate the view of Van Dijk that ideologies make up 'an axiomatic base of social representations shared by a group' (Van Dijk 1998). In addition, in linking these representations to the interests of specific groups and classes, the ideologies remain tied to the social order from which they derive – and which they in turn shape – and to the conflicts and inequalities that penetrate it. Thus, my use of the concept incorporates the Marxist view that links ideologies with the constitution, reinforcement and legitimation of certain interests and of a social order, and of the defence of certain positions within it. This does not mean that I shall consider ideologies as deceptive distortions or mystifications that confuse some for the benefit of others. But they will remain tied to the social order (to power relations) and to their legitimation.

In approaching this legitimation, I incorporate a Foucauldian view, by which power and knowledge are mutually needed and implicated, embodying their relations, which are always productive, in speech. Ideologies could not be legitimated if they did not set into motion 'games of truth and falsehood'[2] that contribute to establishing what is counted as truth (Foucault 1994: 670): thus, for example, in schools, frequently, beliefs which make it possible to identify students' character traits in terms of their place of origin are counted as truths ('Moroccan students are rebellious'). It counts also as truth the idea that students from an immigrant background are poorly educated; or, they will take longer to learn the language of instruction; or, their language is less complicated; or, they need to be separated from the rest of the students to get up to speed. As we see in these examples, the games of truth go beyond ideologies and have a reifying power: they constitute power relations and they constitute practices that derive from them (Foucault 1994; Martín Rojo and Gabilondo 2001).[3] Thus, these images of incompetence could be invoked in assessments by teachers, or could even be internalized by students. As we will

---

2   The form of these games is varied; we can see them in ideologies, for example, but also in moral reflection, in policy analysis or in the production of scientific knowledge.
3   'According to Foucault, discourse produces power, reinforces it, but also exposes it, makes it fragile and permits its localization and detention (Foucault 1976: 123). Indeed, "the relations of power are, above all, productive" (Foucault 1975: 2–5). Instead of locating power in state apparatuses, Foucault sees a multiplicity of "relations of force"; instead of its subordination to the economic order, he proposes its integration into the mode of production; and instead of a power that gives place only to ideological knowledge, he charts a power that produces the real. That favors, or encourages, certain practices' (Martín Rojo and Gabilondo 2001).

see in the following sections, the study of ideologies related to culture and languages permits a better understanding of educational policies and practices, and of the discourse–knowledge–power relationship.

### Cultural Ideologies: Educational Policies and Double Discourses

If we take as a reference point the legislation of the Autonomous Region of Madrid[4] and, specifically, the Regional Plans, we will see that they enumerate a series of guiding principles in immigration policies, consistent with those presented by other autonomous communities in Spain. These principles are: normalization (which assumes that the migrants will be integrated into the general service systems, such as sanitation and education); equality; integrality and transversality (policies will focus on various spheres of community life); globalism, in which actions should be aimed both at the host population (increasing awareness, for example) and at the immigrant population (reinforcement, representation in society); and interculturality (mutual enrichment).

These principles are articulated by ideologies and integrative policies that make compatible the maintenance of diversity and the promotion of inter-group relations, and foster the construction of a plural and diverse society, in which unity is not threatened by social, cultural and linguistic diversity (for the systematization of these ideologies, see Martín Rojo 2003). This ideology would not view the incorporation of a new language and culture and the maintenance of linguistic and cultural features of the community of origin as contradictory: 'the interrelation between languages, cultures and ways of being of peoples has been one of the principal causes of development and progress'. Thus, the circulation of these discourses and ideologies entails the production of a knowledge in which diversity is understood as an asset. In it, the recognition and valorization of other languages, as well as other cultural forms and other values, involves – or, at least, intentionally seeks – the modification of power relations between majorities and minorities, since it seeks mutual knowledge and enrichment. From this position, cultural and linguistic homogeneity does not appear a necessary condition for the configuration and life of a community.

---

4  Plan Regional para la Inmigración de la Comunidad de Madrid (Regional Plan for Immigration of the Community of Madrid) 2001–2003; Plan Regional de Compensación Educativa de la Comunidad de Madrid (Regional Plan for Educational Compensation of the Community of Madrid), 2000; Order 2316/1999, of 15 October, of the Minister of Education, by which the working of the acts of educational compensation are regulated; instructions; definitions of connecting classrooms, 16 July 2003; new regulation of 8 March 2004.

However, when we observe how these principles translate into concrete measures and regulations in the educational field, the contradictions become apparent. The measures adopted include, in the first place, the programme of remedial or compensatory classrooms.

*Example 1*

the programmes for educational compensation will be developed in schools that teach ethnic and cultural minorities, in situations of socio-educational disadvantage, as well as other underprivileged groups, who are lagging behind in education ... or who have difficulties of insertion into the educational system or are in need of support because of late incorporation into the educational system, irregular schooling, or, in the case of the immigrant and refugee student body, lack knowledge of the language of instruction in the teaching process.

Order of 7/22/1999

Thus, the Plan brought together all students who exhibit some 'deficiency' or 'deficit', including those who are culturally or linguistically different. Instead of enrichment, difference is seen as a 'disadvantage' or 'deficit' that needs to be compensated for. The students are separated in order to receive the compensatory 'injection' that will bring them up to speed. Normalization, then, continues to be questioned. Something similar happens with the second procedure put into place, the Welcoming Programme, which teaches Spanish as a second language. In the Community of Madrid, the students take the course in a different school to the one they will eventually attend. For this reason, the programme does not serve to familiarize them with the school or other students.

The form in which both programmes are applied can further exacerbate this separation. In both programmes (compensatory education and linguistic submersion) the students have a referring group in the mainstream classes, in which they follow certain subjects. However, there is not always co-ordination between the teachers in these 'special classes' and those in the 'referring classroom'. If this co-ordination fails, the students in these 'special' programmes are seen as difficult, lost or even incompetent participants in the referring groups. The latter, by contrast, ought to occupy a central place in their schooling and in the establishment of ties and relations. The view has been promoted that taking care of these students and educating them is the task of teachers who are also 'special'. These groups, frequently, seem to be veritable islands in the schools, with 'other' participants, 'other' contents and 'other' forms of teaching, without creating bridges with other classrooms or spaces for interaction, as a consequence of which the students who enter them encounter difficulties later on being incorporated into the mainstream (see Martín Rojo 2003; Pérez Milans 2005).

Both the remedial or compensatory programme and the linguistic immersion are given mainly to students from an immigrant background and not to the student community as a whole, so they depart from the principle of globalism. Indeed, they cause separation and make exchange more difficult, and, consequently, both the principle of interculturality and the vision of integration as mutual adaptation are compromised: students of immigrant origin are taught in the language, knowledge and values of the majority, but the incorporation of their possible contributions to the host population is not fostered. Furthermore, there is barely any consideration of other educational policies aimed at transforming and adapting the organization of the schools, the teaching materials, the curriculum, or the strategies of teaching and learning. The initiatives that we found in practice are frequently the result of volunteerism on the part of some teachers and school principals. And in cases where the number of immigrant children is not high, schools opt for *laissez-faire*, that is, the immersion of these students in 'normal' classes.

The unidirectionality of these procedures, and the understanding of differences as deficits on which they are based, derives from an assimilationist ideology, which does not facilitate maintaining social, linguistic and cultural differences, and which only fosters inter-group relations within the framework of the dominant culture. Frequently, policies consistent with these ideologies are justified with the argument that they seek to avoid making difference a resource for exclusion (what we have called 'the discourse of equality at the expense of difference', Martín Rojo 2003). The perception that society is homogeneous is found to be so naturalized that it is taken for granted that the only ones who can 'be integrated' or progress are those who do not differ from the rest. What is not considered is the possibility that this perception itself evidences a principle of inequality: those who belong to the social groups and sectors whose ways are considered to be the norm would start from a point of advantage. In fact, the achievement of equality can only be accomplished if the rules of the game are modified, that is, if both the norms and contents which are required, and the assessment tools used with them, are changed. Finally, besides these programmes, in the Community of Madrid, students who are newcomers from other countries are not redistributed among the public schools, or among the latter and the partially subsidized schools, with the goal of balancing their numbers. The administration states that such distribution of students would threaten parents' freedom of choice of a school. As a result, in some schools there is an artificial concentration of male and female 'immigrant' students, at times reaching a proportion of 80 and even 90%. Some public schools in the inner city are configured as veritable ghettos. In these cases, nearly all the principles included in the Regional Plans, normalization, equality, globalism and interculturality, are undermined.

Taken together, these measures appear to have a marginalizing effect, since they separate and restrict the paths to co-existence and integration, and, in fact, even though presented as temporary, are likely to be permanent. The rest of the procedures outlined in the Plan are relegated to the background and only move forward very slowly. It is true that gradually they appear to be introducing measures that now incorporate a multicultural orientation, seeking to combat ethnocentrism and pointing out the existence of cultural and linguistic differences. Thus, the regional administration has introduced orientation measures aimed at a diverse population, such as the translation of documents and forms, and an interpreter service to ensure communication with parents. Frequently, though, it is the schools or the teachers themselves who take the initiative in this direction, celebrating activities and multicultural holidays in the schools or presenting linguistic differences and traditions in publications or reading sessions. These activities can destroy the impression of the classroom or school as a homogeneous reality, but, at the same time, they can, by underscoring cultural differences, have an ethnicizing effect, which imposes on the male and female students a feeling of belonging to their parents' country of origin (being 'Moroccans' or 'Chinese', rather than 'from Madrid') (see Alcalá Recuerda 2003 and Mijares 2005). Thus, the school and the classroom can be configured as an international forum, with students who 'represent' other nationalities or cultures, with which they may, in fact, be more or less familiar, and which are not seen in a positive light (frequently, they are seen as 'less developed'). Therefore, rather than contributing to the creation of a cohesive 'us', albeit plural and diverse, the effect can be one of separation (see Rasskin 2007 and Patiño Santos 2007).

Thus far, all we have seen shows the contradiction that exists between the declarations of intent included in the regional plans and their application in concrete policies, at least in the educational world (see also Alcalá Recuerda 2001). This contradiction is not only evident in the autonomous region of Madrid: it is not unknown in other autonomous communities in Spain, where they apply, although with some differences, measures such as compensatory programmes, reinforcement within the classroom, and programmes of linguistic immersion.

Even the European Union presents the same contradictions. Only at the end of the 1990s was an intercultural model of education proposed, one which understands that in order to ensure the integration of students of immigrant origin, it is necessary to combat racism and xenophobia in the population as a whole, change programmes and train faculty (the financing of projects for the design of activities and teaching materials in keeping with this model is carried out through the Comenius Programme; see EURYDICE 2004).[5] Despite that, the European Union itself recognizes that intercultural education is not an extended practice of the EU (EURYDICE 2004: 71). Indeed, in the EU documents, the differential objectives of this model of education are not clearly defined, while teaching the language of instruction is maintained as the key and essential element in integration measures. When presenting programmes, results and directives, they keep talking about the 'immigrant student body', a category that frequently brings together newcomers and second-generation immigrants. That indicates that, just like their parents, second-generation immigrant students continue to be seen as long- or short-term 'residents', rather than as real citizens and an integral part of Europe.

In connection with the production of knowledge, in previous studies I have reflected on these contradictions and the problems they reveal between the declarations of intent and actual practice (educational programmes that have been put in place) (Martín Rojo 2005). I showed, then, how in the Regional Plans new discourses, which present a new, inclusive concept of citizenship and of democratic principles, have found a place (Habermas 1987). In the production of these discourses a new understanding of (linguistic) cultural differences occupies a pre-eminent place, as symbolic capital that is assumed to enrich the community. However, as some authors are showing, this valorization is accompanied by a mercantilization of culture (language), which is understood as merchandise, connected to authenticity which is consumed ('that which sells'), and which, as a consequence, has been assigned an exchange value in the market (Heller 2000, 2002; Cameron 2000). However, these discourses do not appear to have permeated society or managed to displace other firmly rooted precedents. They co-exist, therefore, with discourses and, above all, with practices that are based on previous knowledges, tied to other ways of life and other (less global) kinds of markets. These practices entail other ways of understanding diversity, based on a conception of national society as culturally and linguistically homogeneous, in which what is different appears as something exceptional or deficient.

The result is that assimilationist ideologies are prevalent, ideologies that end up drifting into marginalizing policies, since, with the goal of applying an

---

5 The teaching of the language of origin, now seen as a bridge between cultures and an essential part of intercultural education, does not have any financing programme (Bekemans and Ortiz de Urbina 1997).

(assimilationist) 'reinforcement' they opt for a temporary separation, which, in fact, often seems to become permanent (there are no official statistics that evaluate the success or failure of the programmes imposed by the Autonomous Region of Madrid; we rely on data from our follow-up in different schools, which shows that once the time allowed in the connecting classrooms has run out, the rate of entry into regular education is low). In addition, multicultural procedures have been initiated that take difference into account, but, unfortunately, they do not often, from that point, go on to construct an inclusive 'us', but rather an 'us' and a 'them'.

If we return to the question of the legitimation and linking of ideologies with the interests of social classes and groups, it is fitting to ask what social order this understanding of cultural differences and these policies contribute to maintaining. It is evident that if the content included in the curricula, the assessment of learning, the yardstick on which this assessment is done, and their trajectory are not modified, the integration and success of these students will not be made easy.[6] If this greater rate of academic failure at young ages is confirmed, it would be cutting off the possibility of moving on to higher education that enables access to more specialized and better-paid jobs. In this way, school would be shaped as a potential obstacle to social mobility, rather than as a tool of integration.

## Linguistic Ideologies

In Spain, as happens in the rest of the European Union, linguistic diversity has been compartmentalized, so that different linguistic policies have been designed, aimed at the acquisition and use of official (state) languages, regional ones (in the case of Spain, of the autonomous bilingual communities), both of which are considered to be part of the cultural patrimony, and languages of immigration.[7] This separation reveals the different values attributed to them socially, and, in turn, has contributed to reinforcing an unequal treatment of languages.

The situation of Spain is emblematic, because, although the incorporation of the official languages of each autonomous community has been achieved in the curriculum (of course, to different degrees in the different regions), the

6 Comparative results of the rates of academic performance and absenteeism among native and non-native students can be found on www.eurydice.org; these seem to suggest a greater rate of academic failure in this sector of the student body; even though it is true that a greater tendency and motivation to study has also been documented – as the Report of 2004 of the Defender of the People in Spain shows.

7 The EU distinguishes and observes, in addition, stateless languages (Romany, Yiddish) and sign languages.

languages of immigration have not been integrated into the curriculum, and they are barely visible in the schools.[8]

European policies show, in fact, how the view persists that immigrant languages are the patrimony of the countries of origin and not a European patrimony, which explains why in many cases, the organization of these programmes of ELCO depends on the countries of origin, or, at most, is shared as a result of bilateral agreements.[9] So, just as the speakers of these languages are seen as short- or long-term residents and not as European citizens, their languages are seen as 'resident languages', and not patrimonial. In addition, in the majority of cases, these classes are considered to be extracurricular activities and are not integrated into the curriculum, nor are they accessible to all students (regardless of their origin). This is due to the fact that the motivations for their acquisition and use are linked preferentially to reasons of identity (that even open the path of return to the country of origin), and are not understood as a resource for a multilingual and multicultural society (for example, a resource for increasing commercial relations and exchanges of all kinds).

Only in 2003, the European Commission seems to have incorporated a more global and positive vision of linguistic diversity, by designing a plan for promoting the learning of languages that brings together all the languages spoken in the Union, whether official, regional, minority, of immigrant communities, or sign languages (see the document, and, for a study, the work of the VALEUR research team, in McPake *et al.* 2006). At the present time the EU promotes the acquisition and use of 1+2 languages (the first language and two more languages, which may be foreign or community ones, regional, not territorial or immigrant; see Beacco and Byram 2003). However, in the case of immigrant languages, steps to make this objective possible have barely begun to be taken.

Just as with the policies that have been implemented in Europe, in Spain the varieties and languages of immigration, rather than being considered an asset, seem to be considered an obstacle to integration. This is demonstrated by the fact that educational action and resources are directed preferentially to ensure the teaching of the language of instruction. Likewise, there has not

---

8 For an assessment of the situation of the so-called regional languages in the Spanish state, see the monographic volume 18 of the journal *Textos*, 1998; the Programmes for the Teaching of Language and Culture of Origin (ELCO); Mijares 2005; Bekemans and Ortiz de Urbina 1997; and Broeder and Extra 1998, among others.

9 Something similar has happened with non-territorial languages, such as Romany and Yiddish, where hardly any mechanisms and instruments for their incorporation into the school system have been created; see Bakker 2001.

been an attempt to remedy the clear failure in the application of the European directives for the teaching of the language of origin, nor has any bilingual programme been introduced with languages of immigration (such as, for example, Arabic), which, for the number of speakers and because they are deeply rooted, occupy a relevant position in the sociolinguistic order of EU countries (according to data collected in EURYDICE, 2004: 45, these programmes only exist in northern countries, Finland, Sweden, Norway, Estonia and other countries such as Cyprus).

The procedures in the Autonomous Community of Madrid are in tune with this focus, emphasizing, in addition, as I have already pointed out, how 'unintegrated measures' are chosen for the teaching of the language of instruction, by which students who have another language and do not know the language of instruction are grouped together and separated from the rest (integrated measures would be, for example, support within the classroom: comparative data can be found about the different procedures utilized in different countries of Europe, in EURYDICE 2004: 42–3). This separation is one more element in the monolingual sociolinguistic order that is established in schools and classes, and that means the almost complete dominance of Spanish and the practical invisibility of other languages, except in specific circumstances or moments: for example, multicultural celebrations, some posters or decorative elements.

The dominant sociolinguistic order organizes school as a hierarchized discursive space (Bourdieu 1982), in which one can distinguish more or less valued languages; dialects and usages that can be utilized in certain domains, but that are excluded from others; forms of learning and teaching considered effective and participatory – such as the communicative method – and others considered repetitive or memoristic (see Pérez Milans 2005 for a study of the methods of teaching languages utilized in a connecting classroom and in the Colegio Chino of Madrid and its evaluation). This hierarchization concerns both the use of varieties, and their evaluation ('suitable', 'educated', 'appropriate' varieties, languages that are a hindrance to the learning of others). Finally, this hierarchization reflects on the social order: the speakers who possess capital in the valued varieties and uses will be considered 'competent speakers', and those who don't will be considered 'incompetent'. So, independently of the knowledge of other languages, the linguistic capital of students from immigrant backgrounds will be measured by this standard, and they may be seen as deficient, even though they may be multilingual. In the academic world these differences in valorization are manifested in the labelling of these students as 'normal'/'good'/'competent', or, on the contrary, as 'special'/'bad'/'incompetent'.

This unequal social distribution of valued linguistic resources has consequences for social mobility, since it can facilitate access to different social spaces, or, on the contrary, make this possibility difficult, creating social closure. The linguistic norm embodies and confirms the unequal distribution and value of linguistic resources. It is the linguistic norm that is invoked to demand, in specific social domains, the use of resources that only certain sectors of the population possess, and in order to exclude other voices and other languages, which, in this view, 'should not' be used, or, when they are, are valued negatively. This is what happens, for example, in classrooms where non-peninsular varieties of Spanish are present. Frequently speakers of these varieties are corrected, with the argument that if they suppress these traces of different pronunciation or lexis, they will integrate better. Thus, these norms contribute to reinforcing the belief that in order to be integrated one cannot be different or speak differently. The assumption that a language or an element such as pronunciation can be a drawback occurs only when the language in question is not valued (if the pronunciation shows signs of an English accent, for example, perhaps such a claim would not be made). There are many indications that such a negative evaluation has an impact on the academic path.

*Example 2*[10]

> Teacher: So have you already changed apartments?
> Adela: huh?
> Tr: Have you changed apartments already?
> Ad: my father's going to look for an apartment
> Tr: he's looking for an apartment?
> Ad: yes
> Tr: but are you still with that man?
> Victor: huh?
> Tr: still? // that man (very softly – unintelligible)
> Ad: he's very bad
> Tr: yes / he doesn't let / does he let you watch television now or not?
> Ad: no
> Tr: no?

10 Compensatory Education (second and third grade elementary – seven and nine years of age), March 2001. Length: 57 minutes; participants: Tr: teacher in second A (teacher for Victor's class); Ad: Adela (student of Dominican origin); Vt: Victor (student of Dominican origin, Adela's brother). The teacher of Victor's reference group walks past near the compensatory class where he and his sister Adela meet and walks in to talk with them a few minutes.

Ad: [they discon-]
Tr: [Victor] you're not telling me anything/**boy**/you
Ad: he dis- he di- discon it- /he disconnects it and says that it broke.
Tr: did the television break?
Ad: he disconnects it and says that it broke [and then he blames us]
Tr: [I don't understand this about he disconnects] / I don't understand it /
    let's see if we can manage [to understand each other]
Vt: [he unplugs it]
Ad: aha
Tr: he unplugs the television every time [you watch it?]
Ad: [uh huh] uh huh / and then he says that it got hurt [*se dañó*]
Tr: that it broke [*se estropeó*]
Ad: uh huh
Tr: here we say that it broke [*se estropeó*]
Ad: uh huh
Tr: eh? right // so, then, well! / what a surprise / are you good at home?
*Ad and Vt nod their heads*
Tr: yes?

The sequence of speaking turns in this example shows that the interactional pattern is the following:

- Teacher's question.
- Student's answer.
- Correction: imposition of the linguistic norm, on the part of the teacher.
- Reformulation, if possible, on the part of the student: substituting the term selected for another one in accordance with the local norm.
- If the reformulation is not possible, a new correction is given by the teacher.

Thus, with this pattern a linguistic norm is established: the use of a peninsular variety of Spanish is required and the varieties of other students are not incorporated. The objective sought appears to be the substitution of one form for another, which seems to involve a negative evaluation of the non-normative forms; the correction technique itself used by the teacher is a significant indicator. So is the fact that, in response, the Latin American students decrease their level of participation in class. Indeed, in the interviews, they tell how they perceive that their way of talking is rejected. The previous example shows, in addition, how the teacher doesn't appear to keep in mind that differences exist in communicative behaviour between Latin America and the peninsula and that, as a consequence, the forms that he uses to show that he is cordial and close (in particular, the direct questions reiterated, using the familiar 'tú' form, and expressions such as 'macho', 'boy') can seem out of place for Latin American students and, also, feel quite overbearing to them in an asymmetrical situation like this.

Linguistic differences reveal themselves, thus, as differences in capital, which establish a principle of asymmetry among the students that is perceived by all of them and has repercussions for their relations with one another (we have recorded in the interactions between students examples in which the norm is invoked: 'say it right'; 'in Spanish, so it's understood', to ensure a dominant position).

However, in the educational practices of some teachers we find examples of how linguistic differences could be treated in another way and be integrated into educational practice and enrich the student body as a whole (some teaching materials are already being designed along these lines).

*Example 3*[11]

> Teacher: or when there's a fixed expression / typical of here / specific to Spain / I ask them for their corresponding expressions / I don't know / remembering now, for example, 'salado' (witty) / there was a time in a text that there was a very 'salado' boy / and the Ecuadoreans / at least the majority of them had understood it to mean-/
> Researcher: that he was unlucky.

From a substantial number of examples such as this, we can infer that the sociolinguistic order has still not been modified, either by integrating other uses and other languages or changing their valuation. With regard to Latin American varieties, the sociolinguistic order is depicted as a hierarchized universe in which the local variety of Spanish is presented as the legitimate one and any variation is understood as a deviation.

Teachers in interviews related this normative behaviour to their particular way of understanding school, attributing to it the role of providing male and female students with the capital they need to integrate and progress. So, in Example 2, the phrase 'let's see if we can manage' shows that, for the teacher, the teaching of the norm is an educational goal. In the interviews we see reflected the conviction that the replacement of non-standard forms will increase the possibilities of academic success.

However, the fact that the teaching strategy should be correction in the

11 Interview with the language teacher at IES Evangelista, 2004.

classroom shows that the forms that stray from the local norm are treated as errors, revealing the different value that is assigned to them (some forms are valorized and considered essential; others, eradicable). With regard to the work of enrichment of the students' linguistic repertoire that some teachers take on, in this as in other cases that have been studied, sociolinguistics has shown that, rather than increasing the capital of the students, it generates competition among forms and even resistance to incorporating new forms if they have to replace the forms used by the social and familial context. It is evident that the objective of correction is not to change the linguistic order, opening it up to other forms of saying and doing, or altering its value. We observe, then, the same contradiction that I pointed out in relation to cultural differences: if the plurality of languages and different linguistic forms were considered an asset, one would be committed to its preservation and not to the substitution of languages. Substitution always appears tied to the devaluation of languages and to the consideration of difference as a 'deficit'.

Thus, the present sociolinguistic order in schools generates competition between language varieties, obliges people to choose, and reproduces normative and homogenizing linguistic practices and ideologies. The tie with the social order is evident, since it is the students who, because of their social and regional origin, possess a particular lingustic capital (the knowledge of the language of instruction) that are considered 'normal', but also 'competent', and legitimate participants in that social space.

The same thing happens with the varieties of Spanish of the students' communities of origin. Their presence is expelled from classes, even in the Welcome Programme, where they play a clear instrumental role, aiding in comprehension and orienting the teaching of the second language, highlighting those aspects in which, bearing in mind their grammar, it would be useful to offer the students some reinforcement (some useful teaching materials already exist).

*Example 4*[12]

Teacher: let's see // let's see if we can come// Halyna / place yourself by Xiao / together (ruckus)

Tr: and you too / all together

*He addresses Liwei and Mateo.*

Tr: Liwei / not Chinese / eh! / with Xiao // Spanish only // let's see // let's see / today we're going to see something new.

12 Connecting classroom, 2004. Researcher: Miguel Pérez Milans. IES Violetas.

The same tendency towards substitution that we observed in relation to the varieties of Spanish also appears in relation to the languages of the community of origin. And, in fact, studies show that in time these students stop using the languages of their community of origin (Broeder and Mijares 2004).

It is interesting to observe the production of knowledge and the games of truth and falsehood on which these educational policies and practices are based and justified. What stands out in this regard is how bilingualism is understood. The belief that learning two languages generates confusion in individuals appears to be firmly rooted (for which reason some teachers recommend forgetting or losing one language in order to learn the other; and never learning more than one at a time). As in the case of the corrections by the professor in Example 2, this belief implies a system of values. If learning two languages is confusing, it is necessary to abandon the one that is dispensable, the one that has less value. It is obvious that if an English-speaker wants to learn Spanish, it would not be recommended for them to forget or avoid the first of these languages (on the contrary, perhaps they will be told that it is not worth it to learn the second one). This presupposes that bilingualism is understood as a period of transition/loss, in which the language of the community of origin is going to be replaced by the language of the host community, in order to guarantee integration. We observe that a problematic proposal of linguistic use is being made: either you speak the language of origin or you speak Spanish, but bringing the two together does not seem possible.

Thus, the perceptions of the different varieties of Spanish and of the languages of immigration converge: they share in common not being valued and having their disappearance considered a necessary condition for integration. This assimilationist pressure for loss is linked to the persistence both of difference as a negative and of society as homogeneous, but also to a hierarchized logic of languages, by which a different value is attributed to them. In this way, in the Autonomous Region of Madrid, Spanish is the language that is required to replace the languages of the communities of origin, while in the United States it is the minority language, in the face of which the same dichotomous vision of bilingualism is mobilized (see García 2006).

This particular understanding of bilingualism explains some decisions that have been made in schools, not only in traditionally monolingual zones like the Autonomous Community of Madrid, that have presupposed the elimination of a third language from the curriculum of these students (a practice contradictory to the 1+2 model of the EU): in some schools, to facilitate the acquisition of Spanish for these students, they have removed the students who are descendants of immigrants from the teaching of French or English, subjects in which, on the other hand, they could have stood out as successful, since, due to the European colonization of their countries, they are familiar with these languages to some degree (for example, French for the Moroccan or Algerian population; English for people coming from India or Pakistan).

> Because, of course, in the end, these kids that come to you from away, have a mixture that they can't sort out. Between their own (language), the one from here, plus another third language that we impose on them... that in the end, to my mind, well, they don't know any of them.[13]

Underlying the 'impossibility' of bilingualism is a vision of linguistic competence as a compartmentalized knowledge, if not a monolingual one, where some kinds of knowledge are supplanted by others during the learning process. Molina and Maruny show how, from a normative and ethnocentric perspective, people cannot value linguistic and communicative competence among speakers who know several languages and know how to take good advantage of their communicative strategies (Molina and Maruny 2003). This view of competence impedes the understanding of a good number of practices that speakers engage in, such as distinguishing between languages in terms of contexts, or, on the contrary, alternating their use, or even mixing them, using them interchangeably, or using them in a creative way to increase expressivity or create complicity. They are probably seen as exceptions or oddities. Languages continue to be understood as abstract entities, repertoires of very fixed and delimited unities, that the speakers know or don't know, that they speak or don't speak, rather than as practices whose use is flexible and whose limits are unclear.

Such an understanding of competence as a monolingual kind of knowledge and one that, in the case of bilingual people, would organize itself into watertight compartments, in tension with one another, if not independent, involves a particular vision of the learning process that frequently reveals itself in some of the welcoming classrooms we have studied. This happens especially when the teachers in charge of immersion do not have training in the teaching of Spanish as a second language (until now the teaching of Spanish was traditionally oriented in the peninsula to Spanish as a foreign language; but also, the teachers of these programmes in the Community of Madrid do not necessarily have specific training in language instruction).[14]

The system of social representations of languages and linguistic realities in which these 'truths' become crystallized appears, as in the case of ideologies

---

13 Interview with a teacher at the Public School Los Santos, 2001. Researcher: Esther Alcalá.
14 In the Basque Country, the teachers of Model A are those with the least preparation in the teaching of languages, while the teachers in Model B and D have more tools and preparation.

pertaining to culture, tied to social and national groups and their interests, and plays a role in the legitimation/delegitimation (and production) of the social order. The social order that they prefigure does not facilitate the maintenance of social, linguistic and cultural differences, nor is it oriented to modifying the sociolinguistic order: despite the changes in the school population there are no changes in the varieties and languages that are required, in the valuation that is made of them, or in the role that is assigned to them in the learning process. This reinforces the social position of the groups that possess the treasure of the language of instruction and poses a disadvantage for those who, in view of the teaching methods being applied, find themselves compelled to learn a language without recourse to the knowledge and learning instruments they possess. Furthermore, these students may see themselves arbitrarily deprived of the capital implied in learning a third language (whether the official language of the community, or one of the languages of the European Union), which hinders both their integration and their future professional development. Thus, the imbalance between competent and incompetent speakers is reproduced and reinforced.

The unidirectionality of the educational models and methods (programmes of immersion) and the isolation that they often entail show how inter-group relations are fostered, above all, in the framework of the majority language.

In the discourses produced by teachers, perhaps less restrained than those of the administration, the students with an immigrant background end up being held responsible for the results of this sociolinguistic order and these linguistic policies. Thus, for students who have been separated from the language(s) of instruction of the host community (by being schooled in a monolingual model, or having imposed on them programmes of linguistic immersion that isolate them socially and are oriented towards substitution), the learning that they acquire from the language(s) of instruction is interpreted as an indicator of attitudes towards integration:

*Example 5*

> right / but I have four kids / he says / they are / Moroccan / he says / and and / they're prison meat next ye – tomorrow / they don't want to have any part of anything // so / why don't they learn / because they don't feel like it / because they're not motivated / because it doesn't appeal to them / to speak Spanish // but you have to look at everything / of course // a kid who makes an effort to speak Spanish is not the same as another who won't have anything to do / with Spanish // so / he's going to be more difficult to educate // logically.

So, knowledge and use of the standard variety of Spanish functions as a criterion of belonging to the community. And the same could be happening with the official languages of the bilingual autonomous communities (Basque Country, Catalonia). Language is, in principle, an element that can facilitate integration: if one does not know a language it can be learned – its presence or absence can be modified, unlike physical features or one's birthplace. Nevertheless, on introducing the local norm as an exclusive criterion (you speak or you don't speak) and by imposing educational models that promote monolingualism, language comes to be treated as a defining feature that immediately separates, unless it turns into the only language and manages to erase any trace of difference. We again find the dominance of homogeneity in the face of diversity. What is more, diversity is seen as a threat to the language of the community, whether because it 'corrupts' or 'dismembers' (with vulgar and incomprehensible variations), or because it is considered to limit the success of the processes of language recovery.

All of this confirms the belief that these students 'have come' and 'are useful for work'[15] and the resulting social order, whereby extracommunity migrants occupy the niche in the labour market left by emigrants from the south and centre of the peninsula, and are seen as an unspecialized manual labour force for the future. For the legitimation of this social order, another ethnicizing and essentialist knowledge is produced, which is the object of our current research and entails putting into circulation old and new stereotypes ('Moroccan children are rebellious', 'the Chinese are strange').

## Conclusions

The study of cultural and linguistic ideologies in the educational policies and practices introduced by the Autonomous Region of Madrid reveals the existence of multiple contradictions between discourses and practices, and the assumption of incompatible ideologies. However, despite these contradictions, the predominance of assimilationist ideologies is confirmed both in relation to culture and to languages. These contradictions, frequent

---

15 Following the last elections in the Community of Madrid, the contradictions between declarations of intent and practices have diminished. The discourse of the Administration in the Community of Madrid echoes the image that you cannot expect good academic, much less integrating, results from the children of immigrants and other minorities. An example of this is the declaration of the Undersecretary of Education, Carmen González, who has stated that 'anyone who has come over in a raft hasn't come to study the third level of ESO (Compulsory Secondary Education)'. Likewise, according to González on the subject of gypsies, 'What the child wants is to go with his father with the truck to sell fruit in the market' (*El País* 28 May 2004).

in moments of social change, appear also in the discourses and educational policies of the European Union.

The case that we have examined reveals the rootedness and naturalization of the view of difference as a deficit and of linguistic communities as homogeneous. Assimilationist pressure is very strong, and we see barely any movement of adaptation towards a now more diverse reality on the part of the educational system, with the goal of integrating citizens who do not necessarily share the language or other cultural features. This implies that 'remedial' programmes predominate and that the personal, educational and linguistic experiences of students are not incorporated into the curriculum, which works to the detriment of their academic performance and hinders anchoring their new knowledges on those that have already been acquired.

The orientation towards substitution means that the language whose acquisition, in principle, would ease integration, will become a defining feature, by introducing the norm as an exclusionary criterion. By reproducing this system of values, school reproduces the process of categorization and assignation of a subordinate social position to students of immigrant origin. Whether or not they respond to these characteristics, the expectation that these are not competent students and that they do not want to learn the language will increase the probability that this is what will happen. As happens with the Pygmalion effect, it is possible that they will end up seeing themselves as the others say they are or expect them to be.

If school does not guarantee the integration of these students, but rather places obstacles in their path or hinders their access to higher levels of education, it will be contributing to an ethnicizing dualization of society in which young people from an immigrant background are treated as a labour force, for which social mobility is neither expected nor favoured.

## References

Alcalá Recuerda, E. (2001) 'How to Normalize and Respect Differences? Legislative Speech on Compensatory Education', Madrid. Paper presented at the Jornades d'Anàlisi Crítica del Discurs (ACD), Barcelona, 23 and 24 November 2001.
— (2003) 'Colegio Público 2', in Martín Rojo *et al*. 2003.
Bakker, P. (2001) 'Romani in Europe', in *The Other Language of Europe: Demographic, Sociolinguistic, and Educational Perspectives*, ed. G. Extra and D. Gorter. Clevedon: Multilingual Matters.
Beacco, J.-C., and M. Byram (2003) *Guide for the Development of Language Education Policies in Europe: From Linguistic Diversity to Plurilingual Education*. Strasbourg: Language Policy Division, European Council.
Bekemans, L., and Y. Ortiz de Urbina (1997) *The Teaching of Immigrants in the European Union*. Luxembourg: European Parliament.

Bourdieu, P. (1982) *Ce que parler veut dire: L'économie des échanges linguistiques*. Paris, Fayard.

Broeder, P., and G. Extra (1998) *Language, Ethnicity and Education: Case Studies on Immigrant Minority Groups and Immigrant Minority Languages*. Clevedon: Multilingual Matters.

Broeder, P., and L. Mijares (2004) *Multilingual Madrid: Languages at Home and at School*. Amsterdam: European Cultural Fundation.

Cameron, D. (2000) *Good to Talk? Living and Working in a Communication Culture*. London: Sage.

EURYDICE (2004) 'The Academic Integration of the Immigrant Student Body in Europe', Brussels: EURYDICE (European Commission), http://eurydice.org, last accessed 9 September 2007.

Foucault, M. (1975) 'Pouvoir-corps', *Quel Corps* 2: 2–5.

— (1976) *La Volonté de savoir: Histoire de la sexualité*, vol. 1. Paris: Gallimard.

— (1994) 'Le Souci de la verité', in *Dits et écrits*, ed. D. Defert and F. Ewald. Paris: Gallimard, vol. 4, pp. 668–78.

Freire, P. (1970) *Pedagogy of the Oppressed*. New York: Continuum.

García, O. (2006) 'Lenguas e identidades en el mundo hispanohablante. Desde una posición plurilingüe y minoritaria', in *Lingüística Aplicada del español*, ed. M. Lacorte. Madrid: Arco Libros.

Habermas, J. (1987) *Geschichtsbewusstsein und posttraditionale Identität*. Frankfurt am Main: Suhrkamp Verlag.

Heller, M. (2000) 'Bilingualism and Identity in the Post-modern World', *Vigo: Estudios de Sociolingüística* 1(2): 9–24.

— (2002) 'Globalization and the Commodification of Bilingualism in Canada', in *Language Learning and Teaching in the Age of Globalization*, ed. D. Block and D. Cameron. London: Routledge, pp. 47–63.

McPake, J., W. Martyniuk, R. Aarts, P. Broeder, S. Latomaa, L. Mijares and T. Tinsley (2006) 'Community Languages in Europe: Challenges and Opportunities', unpublished manuscript.

Martín Rojo, L. (2003) 'Escuela y diversidad lingüística', in L. Martín Rojo *et al.* 2003. Madrid: CIDE.

— (2005) 'Dilemas Ideológicos', in L. Martín Rojo, L. Nussbaum and V. Unamuno, *Escuela e Inmigración: Estudios de Sociolingüística* 5(2): 191–2005.

Martín Rojo, L., and A. Gabilondo (2001) 'Michel Foucault', in *The Handbook of Pragmatics*, ed. J. Verschueren, J.-O. Östman, J. Blommaert and C. Bulcaen. Amsterdam: John Benjamins, vol. 4, pp. 1–21.

Martín Rojo, L., and L. Mijares (eds) (2007) *Voces del aula*. Madrid: CREADE.

Martín Rojo, L., E. Alcalá, L. Gari, and A. Rodríguez (2003) *¿Asimilar o integrar? Dilemas de las políticas educativas ante los procesos migratorios*. Madrid: CIDE no. 154.

Mijares, L. (2005) 'El programa de ELCO marroquí', in *Multiculturalidad y educación: Marco conceptual, ámbitos y programas*, ed. T. Fernández García and J. García Molina. Madrid: Alianza.

Molina, M., and L. L. Maruny (2003) 'Motivacions, funcionalitat i usos lingüístics en l'adquisició de competència plurilingüe', in *L'educació lingüística en situacions multiculturals i multilingües*, ed. J. Perera, L. Nussbaum and M. Milian. Barcelona: Institut de ciènces de l'Educació, pp. 235–46.

Patiño Santos, A. (2007) 'Somos mayoría: extraños en las aulas', in Martín Rojo and Mijares (eds) 2007.
Pérez Milans, M. (2005) 'Spanish Education and Chinese Immigrants in a New Multicultural Context: Cross-cultural and Interactive Perspectives in the Study of Language Teaching Methods', *Journal of Multicultural Discourse. Multilingual Matters* 1.
Rasskin, I. (2007) 'Identidades en proceso de construcción: ¿Y tú cómo me ves?', in Martín Rojo and Mijares (eds) 2007.
Van Dijk, T. (1998) *Ideology: A Multidisciplinary Approach*. London: Sage.

## Documents

European Commission (2003) Promoting Language Learning and Linguistic Diversity: AN Action Plan 2004–2006. Brussels: European Commission.
Instrucciones: definiciones aulas de enlace 16 de julio de 2003; nueva regulación de 8 de marzo 2004, nueva regulación de 24 de junio de 2005.
Orden 2316/1999, de 15 de octubre, del Consejero de Educación, por la que se regula el funcionamiento de las actuaciones de compensación educativa. BOCM no. 253, lunes 25 octubre 1999.
Orden de 22 de julio de 1999 por la que se regulan las actuaciones de compensación educativa en los centros docentes sostenidos con fondos públicos. BOE no. 179, miércoles 28 julio 1999.
Plan Regional para la Inmigración de la Comunidad de Madrid 2001–2003. Consejería de Servicios Sociales de la Comunidad de Madrid, 2001.
Plan Regional de Compensación Educativa. Dirección General de Promoción Educativa, Consejería de Educación de la Comunidad de Madrid, 2000.
Recomendación no. R (84) 9 del Comité de Ministros a los Estados miembros sobre los inmigrantes de segunda generación.
Recomendación no. R (84) 18 del Comité de Ministros a los Estados miembros sobre el componente intercultural en la Formación del Profesorado.
Recomendación 1093 (1989) del Comité de Ministros a los Estados miembros sobre la educación de los hijos de inmigrantes.
Resolución adoptada por la Conferencia Permanente de Ministro de Educación Europeos (10–12 mayo 1983).
Resolution on the languages and cultures of regional and ethnic minorities in the European Community. Strasbourg: European Parliament, 1987. http://www.ciemen.org/mercator/UE21-GB.HTM, last accessed 9 September 2007.
Resolution on linguistic minorities in the European Community. Strasbourg: European Parliament, 1994. http://www.ciemen.org/mercator/UE23-GB.HTM, last accessed 9 September 2007.

# Conclusion: Discrimination as a Modern European Legacy

## Masoud Kamali

The classical work of Gunnar Myrdal, *An American Dilemma* (1944), was used in the USA to frame racist discrimination against blacks. According to Myrdal, prior to the civil rights movement there existed a huge discrepancy between the American creed of equal values and rights for all and the reality of racism and apartheid against blacks in American society. Myrdal pleaded for a way out of the 'dilemma', namely through the abolition of 'race-laws' and apartheid in the USA. At the time the 'American dilemma' was seen as an exception, with European racism and discrimination not receiving as much attention. However, Europe is also haunted by a dilemma. The fact is that racism and discrimination have been inseparable parts of European history and modernity. Jesse Taylor's (1999) typology identifies three interrelated properties – otherism, racism and narcissism – and suggests that European modernity needed 'inferior others' to legitimize its colonial wars, occupations, slavery and genocide. This resulted in racisms and discrimination towards 'the others' during the long history of the establishment and expansion of European civilization. Such an inferiorization of 'others' as inferior cultures also had the effect of developing a sense of narcissism among European nation-states and colonial powers.

Paradoxically, ideas of equal rights, universalism, humanism, and democracy were also a part of modern European history; but the fact remains that these Enlightenment ideals were not extended to the 'others'. The contemporary European dilemma is based mainly on the contradictory nature of an 'imagined creed' of universalism, equal treatment and humanism, whose selective application is based upon imagined 'races' and 'cultures' that divide humanity in a hierarchy ordered around a superior 'us' and an inferior 'them'. Europe's colonial past, its history of slavery and genocide, provides stark evidence of the shortcomings of the Enlightenment's 'equality claim',[1] but this

---

1  For more discussion see Eze (1997) and Goldberg (1993), among others.

history is not just in the past; it is an inseparable part of the everyday life and the institutional arrangements of many European countries today.

A short overview of relevant research on discrimination in Europe shows how widespread racism and discrimination against 'the others', namely non-Western groups living in Europe, has been.[2] The discrimination that is a part of the normal reproduction of many European institutions needs to be understood in terms of social relations, structures of domination, and rules and procedures in the settings of social institutions. However, it is not enough to address the existence of discrimination. We also have to study the *mechanisms* behind the reproduction of discrimination and racism to help us understand why racism and discrimination are still major problems in Europe, even if the EU and its member states have issued many declarations and policies against racism, xenophobia and anti-Semitism (see http://www.eumc.eu and http://www.fra.europa.eu).

## The History of Xeno-Otherism: States Constructing 'Others'

Human history is dominated by descriptions of wars and confrontations. The existence and the threat of 'them', i.e. 'our' enemies, has been an inseparable and constitutive part of the social construction of 'us'. The family, the clan, the group, the empire and the nation to which we developed a sense of belonging and identification contributed to the construction of different levels of the sociopolitical 'us'. However, the intensity of the levels of identity formation and conceptualizations of 'us' has varied through historical socioeconomic and political formations. There is little doubt that it has been intensified in modernity when other forms of political organization – cities and empires – became allied to the nation-state. Nation-building programmes or the 'nationalization of the nation' laid the ground for the development of national sentiments which gradually became institutionalized within political borders.

One of the major tasks of states concerns the nationalization of the nation as a homogeneous group distinct from other nations. As Étienne Balibar (2002: 220) puts it: 'a social formation only reproduces itself as a nation to the extent that, through a network of apparatus and daily practices, the individual is instituted as *homo nationalis* from cradle to grave'. There has been a tendency in the social sciences to consider belonging to a nation as a primordial property of individuals, as well as a solid ground for collective

---

2　However, exclusion and discrimination also affects 'traditionally European' groups, such as the Roma and Sinti (in Eastern Europe, but not exclusively) and Jews (most explicitly in the EU enlargement countries, such as Poland and Hungary).

identity (also see the critique in chapter 2 by Jones and Krzyżanowski in this book).[3] Despite the fact that nationalism is a relatively new phenomenon in human history, many social scientists – in collaboration with the politically powerful – have sought to present it as a common denominator for all human communities, as the very basis of the collective identity generated in the process of the creation of a homogenous nation. A good example of this position is found in the work of Anthony Smith (1991), who argues that nationalism is a political ideology that has a cultural doctrine at its centre with a great potential for the political mobilization of a population. Although making a distinction between territorial nationalism and ethnic nationalism, for scholars such as Smith the very basis of nationalism remains the same; he considers territorial nationalism as 'open' and based on legal rights, with ethnic nationalism based on a common origin in time and space. Furthermore, he presents territorial nationalism as civic and rational and ethnic nationalism as 'natural'.

The history of the twentieth century suggests that distinctions between these two kinds of nationalisms are questionable. The history of countries such as Sweden, France, Italy and even Germany demonstrates the interchangeability of the 'rational' and the 'natural' as a basis for the nation. The projects of political parties and groups have influenced the basis of collective and national identities. The metaphor of 'family', which is one of the most important properties of ethnic nationalist mobilization, is not exclusive to ethnic nations, but was also used by others, such as in Sweden, where the social democratic project for the homogenization of the nation, begun in the early 1930s, was legitimized by the notion of *Folkhemmet* (the people's home); 'The People' was presented as a family constituted by Swedes with a common origin 'in time and space' (of course this concept of *Volk* was mobilized to very different ends than was the version mobilized by the Nazis).

However, this national exclusiveness was not only a specific characteristic of modern nation-states and political parties, but also an integral part of the creation of a nation against the 'others'. The national project of all countries, either territorial or ethnic nationalism, has entailed a process of self-construction against the 'others'. In other words, the construction of 'we-ness' of the nation goes hand in hand with the construction of the 'others', both as

---

3 Among the 'classics', Max Weber makes the clearest distinction between the nation and the state, with the nation concerned with the realm of *Kultur*, while the state is concerned with the realm of power (see Beetham 1985: 128). The nation was therefore considered as a natural entity that has *a* culture and *a* history. Other social scientists claimed that the nations are 'natural entities ordained by God', and that state formations which contain more than one nation run the risk of losing identity and are doomed to decay (Kedourie 1993: 52).

other nations and as internal minorities (for example see Wodak *et al.* 1999; Busch and Krzyżanowski 2007; Persson and Stråth 2007). This modern otherism that has been part and parcel of the nationalization of a community can accordingly be divided into three categories: (i) ethnic/religious/racist otherism; (ii) nationalist otherism; and (iii) xeno-otherism. These are parallel processes by which a group, often a majority, by controlling the sites and means of power categorizes and inferiorizes other groups based on their ethnicity, religion, constructed 'race', nationality and/or immigrant status.

One of the most lasting and problematic otherisms is ethnic otherism, where a self-defined ethnic group, often a majority group, dominates the powerful institutions of a country. Ethno-national categorization is a powerful mechanism that does not leave any real possibility for the inclusion of the others in the mainstream category of 'us' (the ethno-nationalism of Germany and Turkey are just two cases in this respect). The process of ethno-nationalism is sometimes reinforced by some otherized ethnic groups who, as a reaction to the mainstream ethno-nationalism, develop their own ethno-political nationalist projects. Some Kurdish or Assyrian ethno-political groups, who construct a belief in a primordial ethnicity and act accordingly, belong to this category.

Nationalist otherism is mainly based on situating the creation of a nation – a major organizing principle of identification and categorization of 'us' – within certain geographical boundaries. Language, history, 'race' and religion have been the most powerful denominators used for belonging. In the case of nation-state formation, Balibar (2002: 221) comments on a kind of national belonging, which makes a people a 'people', a community which recognizes itself in advance to the institution of the state (see also Anderson 1990; Billig 1995). No modern nation possesses a given 'ethnic' basis, and that is why it is imperative that the state 'make people' who are invested in seeing themselves as nationals, as a part of a national community. The process of nationalization entails the otherization of 'other nations'. This otherism is one of the main political forces behind the wars and conflicts between various nation states which formed the modern history of the 'Dark Continent'.[4]

Meanwhile, while nationalist otherism is normally, but not exclusively, a process of external exclusion of the 'other nations', xeno-otherism should be considered mainly as a process of internal exclusion. However, this process is not entirely internal and is a kind of 'spillover' exclusion and inferiorization of 'the others' that has resulted from colonial and imperialist wars and

---

4 Mark Mazower (1998) in his book, *The Dark Continent*, explores the role of nation-states in the wars which formed the history of Europe during the twentieth century.

expansions and is now increasingly taking place *within* the national boundaries of such countries. Inward migration, on the one hand, and the success of xenophobic populist parties in many European countries, on the other, have recently exacerbated xeno-otherism and created a situation in which internal barriers and borders are increasingly more important than external ones (see Rydgren 2005). Xeno-otherism has become a part of many otherized groups' everyday life. Although the process of otherization makes use of 'differences', real or imaginary, between 'us', the categorizing groups, and 'them', the categorized 'others', for construction and reconstruction of exclusionary and discriminatory attitudes and practices against 'the others', it does not make a convincing ground for a definition of racism and xeno-otherism. Oppression and aggression against 'the others' for a 'particular end', which Memmi (1999: 102) considers necessary elements for the definition of racism, are equally valid for xeno-otherism. Furthermore, the process of otherization entails unequal power relations between the otherizing and the otherized groups which enable the oppression and aggression against 'the others' to take both symbolic and physical forms. The categorization and otherization of a group of people is not necessarily based on intentional actions and practices of another group; it can also be an unintended consequence of the actions of a majority society in producing itself as 'us', implying forms of everyday racism as described for example by Essed (1992) (see also chapter 3 by Wodak in this volume).

Otherism also has several dimensions, such as racism, sexism, homophobia and so on (for present purposes the form of otherism related to racist and exclusionary practices against migrants and minority groups is of central importance). One of these features is the homogenization of the nation as a political *and* cultural entity. Such modern sociopolitical and cultural projects created what some researchers, such as Philip Lawrence (1997), have called 'modern culture' whose very foundation was otherism, racism and narcissism (while Lawrence's point does not reveal anything new it does connect seemingly different parts of the same process). Thus we can say that the definition and constitution of the nation is always related to the creation of 'others'. This may be one of the first findings of social sciences dealing with the evolution of modern institutions and modern changes.

The concept of 'xeno-otherism' may be a useful one with which to frame this question (see also the Introduction in this volume). Xeno-otherism seeks to avoid the dualism between 'institutional' and 'individual' racism. To maintain a sense that structural and/or institutional racism can be truly unintentional, and need not involve individual attitudes, undermines the conception of racism as an ideological construction and makes it synonymous with the statistical inequality and apparent social inefficiency of any group with a sense of racial or ethnic identity, whatever the actual causes of its situation might be (Fredrickson 2000: 80). The concept of xeno-otherism takes us behind the duality of intended/unintended or conscious/unconscious discriminatory action. As Fredrickson (2000: 82) suggests: 'We must be careful to avoid giving credence to the view that racism is an essential or primordial human response to diversity, something that inevitably takes place when groups that we would define as racially different come into contact.' He argues that negative stereotyping of 'that there' or 'alien groups' may be an inescapable component of identity and boundary maintenance for a group. But who the outsiders are and how much or in what ways they are despised and mistreated are the product of history, not basic human instincts.

Xeno-otherism must be understood in terms of attempts to investigate the stereotypes and prejudices concerning migrants and minorities through socio-cognitive structures (classification schemes, stereotypes, prejudices, beliefs), institutional arrangements, power structures and interaction processes in which inequalities between groups are related to biological and cultural factors attributed to those who are defined as belonging to a different 'ethnicity', 'culture', 'race' or nation (see Essed 1992: 43–4). The socio-cognitive dimension refers to the shared social cognitions of groups, and involves the opinions, attitudes, ideologies, norms and values that constitute racist stereotypes and prejudices, and that underlie racist social practices, including discourses (Van Dijk 1998: 21). A socio-cognitive approach to understanding racism and xenophobia must not be reduced to the sources of stereotypes and prejudices but should be put in a broader context of social institutions and the structural properties of a society in a given time. Socio-cognitive structures are not static but dynamic factors that both influence the institutional arrangements of a society and are themselves influenced and reproduced by them. In other words, the normal daily actions of influential individuals in various institutions and organizations, such as schools, courts, police and business, coupled with established norms, patterns, rules and laws, reproduce the *otherness* of 'the other'.

Xeno-otherism must thus be considered in relation to the power structures and institutional arrangements of a society. The fact that dominant groups have access to, or control over, scarce resources (such as residence, nationality, jobs, housing, education, knowledge, health and capital) must be considered (Van Dijk 1998: 20; Flam in this volume). Xeno-otherism is therefore an inseparable part of the social structure based on a system of inequality that perpetuates the domination of the dominant majority society (typically white Europeans) over others – in particular non-Europeans and especially those from economically poorer countries. In the European countries schools produce and reproduce dichotomies of a superior 'us' against an inferior 'them'.[5] This inferiorization of the 'others' goes hand in hand with a sense of narcissism on the part of majority society. This is evident when Europe's modern history is purified, purged of its 'down side' and made an ideal type of progress and humanism.[6] European history starts with the title 'The Birth of Europe', framed by the Renaissance, revolutions and democracy. Devastating wars, colonialism, and genocide are essentially absent. This is a selective historiography that suits the overall purpose of being a part of Europe, 'a good nation' with a common good heritage which makes the basis of belonging to the fair and progressive 'us' against the inferior others. The inferiorization of the 'others' and the superiorization of 'us' is a complex and often hidden process that is not easy simply to observe. It is often understood by many members of the majority society as 'normal' and 'objective'.

Indeed, one of the most effective ways of reproducing the status quo of the European societies through which many influential and powerful groups reproduce their dominance in society is a strategy of *denial* of racism and discrimination (Van Dijk 1998; Billig 1995; see also Chapter 3 by Wodak in this volume). As Miles (1993) puts it, what is novel about contemporary forms of racism is not the proliferation of racist social movements, but an intensification of ideological and political struggle around the expression of a racism that often claims not to be racism.[7] The strategy of denial is well established among the gatekeepers of many institutions of the majority society, such as the educational system, the political system and the judicial system. It is also reinforced by 'cultural-competent' individuals and groups with immigrant backgrounds. As mentioned earlier, it is fruitless to discuss these

---

5  For instance, within the seemingly secular and 'objective' Swedish schools educational materials, such as history books and books used for educating pupils about religion, are highly selective, nation-centric and Christian. History books discussing European history, for instance, ignore 600 years of the Ottoman Empire's European history and reduce it to half a page under the title 'Turks', who are simultaneously presented as 'the others'. In schoolbooks on religion Christianity is purified and considered the religion of 'us' and Islam and Judaism as the religions of the 'others'. Christianity is presented as 'a good religion' and the only religion with an 'ethical' code of conduct. Besides the 'Christian ethic' there is no discussion of, for instance, an Islamic or a Jewish ethic. Others, such as Batelaan and van Hoof (1996), Cohen and Lotan (1997), Runfors (2003) discuss the categorizing principles that students from majority society both learn in school and take with them to school and apply to students from the non-majority society. Many students in schools are subjected to the same status-hierarchy that exists in the larger society (McLaren 1993; Willis 1991).

6  Compare with Philip Lawrence's (1997) discussion on the narcissism of modern culture in his book *Modernity and War*.

7  See also Miles 1989.

groups' intentions concerning reinforcing discrimination and racism in society. Ellison (1966: xiv) studied decades ago how 'the slaves often took the essence of the aristocratic ideal (as they took Christianity) with far more seriousness than their masters'. This is very common today in Europe and other places in the world where some otherized individuals and groups, by defending the status quo of the power relations in a society, reinforce the established discriminatory order of society.

In order to explore the complex institutional patterns of racism and discrimination, we must, as Hall (2002: 64) argues, avoid two problems of inquiry in the sociological field: firstly a reductionism which must deny almost everything in order to explain something, and secondly a pluralism which is so mesmerized by 'everything' that it cannot explain anything. Racism and discrimination is one of the most lasting properties of European societies and must be taken seriously in a time when camouflaged racism is increasing. Deeper knowledge of the institutionalized mechanisms of discrimination and racism, knowledge that is possible only through systematic study, is necessary in order to combat racism and discrimination and monitor social cohesion.

## References

Anderson, E. (1990) *Streetwise: Race, Class, and Change in an Urban Community*. Chicago, IL: University of Chicago Press.

Balibar, E. (2002) *Politics and the Other Scene*. New York: Verso.

Batelaan, P., and C. van Hoof (1996) 'Cooperative Learning in Intercultural Education', in *European Journal of Intercultural Studies* 7(3): 5–16.

Beetham, D. (1985) *Max Weber and the Theory of Modern Politics*. Oxford: Polity Press.

Billig, M. (1995) *Banal Nationalism*. London: Sage.

Busch, B., and M. Krzyżanowski (2007) 'Inside/Outside the European Union: Enlargement, Migration Policies and the Search for Europe's Identity', in J. Anderson and W. Armstrong (eds), *Geopolitics of European Union Enlargement*. London: Routledge.

Cohen, E. G., and R. A. Lotan (eds) (1997) *Working for Equity in Heterogeneous Classrooms: Sociological Theory in Practice*. New York: Teachers College Press.

Ellison, R. (1966) *Shadow and Act*. New York: New American Library.

Essed, P. (1992) *Understanding Everyday Racism: An Interdisciplinary Theory*. London: Sage.

Eze, E. C. (1997) *Race and the Enlightenment: A Reader*. Malden, MA: Blackwell.

Fredrickson, G. M. (2000) *The Comparative Imagination: On the History of Racism, Nationalism, and Social Movements*. Berkeley, CA: University of California Press.

Goldberg, D. T. (1993) *Racist Culture: Philosophy and the Politics of Meaning*. Oxford: Blackwell.

Hall, S. (2002) 'Race, Articulation, and Societies Structured in Dominance', in *Race Critical Theories*, ed. P. Essed and D. T. Goldberg. Oxford: Blackwell.

Kedourie, E. (1993) *Nationalism*. Oxford: Blackwell.

Lawrence, P. K. (1997) *Modernity and War: The Creed of Absolute Violence*. New York: Macmillan.

Mazower, M. (1998) *Dark Continent: Europe's Twentieth Century.* London: Vintage.

McLaren, P. (1993) *Schooling as Ritual Performance: Towards a Political Economy of Educational Symbols and Gestures.* London: Routledge.

Memmi, A. (1999) *Racism.* Minneapolis, MN: University of Minnesota Press.

Miles, R. (1989) *Racism.* London: Routledge.

— (1993) 'The Articulation of Racism and Nationalism: Reflections on European History', in *Racism and Migration in Western Europe*, ed. J. Wrench and J. Solomos. Oxford: Berg.

Myrdal, G. (1944) *An American Dilemma: The Negro Problem and Modern Democracy.* New York: Harper.

Persson, H.-A., and B. Stråth (eds) (2007) *Reflections on Europe: Defining a Political Order in Time and Space.* Brussels: Peter Lang.

Runfors, A. (2003) *Mångfald, motsägelser och marginalisering: En studie av hur invandrarskap formas i skolan.* Stockholm: Prisma.

Rydgren, J. (2005) 'Is Extreme Right-Wing Populism Contagious? Explaining the Emergence of a New Party Family', *European Journal of Political Research* 44: 1–25.

Taylor, J. (1999) 'Philosophy, Law and the Black Experience', *APA* 98(2).

Van Dijk, T. A. (1998) *Ideology: A Multidisciplinary Approach.* London: Sage.

Willis, P. (1991) *Fostran till lönearbete.* Gothenburg: Röda bokförlaget.

Wilson, William J. (1987) *The Truly Disadvantaged: The Inner City, the Underclass and Public Policy.* Chicago, IL: Chicago University Press.

Wodak, R., R. de Cilla, M. Reisigl, K. Leibhart, K. Hofstätter and M. Kargl (1999) *The Discursive Construction of National Identity.* Edinburgh: Edinburgh University Press.

## Reports

The National Consultative Committee on Human Rights (Commission nationale consultative des droits de l'homme, CNCDH) (1998).

Human Rights Documentation Center (2001) *Racial Discrimination: The Record of France*, http://www.hrdc.net, last accessed 9 September 2007.

# Index